THE ILLUSTRATED
FOODS OF INDIA

The Oxford India Collection is a series that brings together
writings of enduring value published by OUP.

Other titles include

The Oxford India Illustrated Corbett
The Second Oxford India Illustrated Corbett
The Oxford India Illustrated Children's Tagore
The Illustrated Premchand: Selected Short Stories
The Illustrated Sálim Ali: The Fall of a Sparrow
The Illustrated Tigers of India
The Illustrated Cultural History of India
Theatres of India: A Concise Companion

THE ILLUSTRATED
FOODS OF INDIA
A–Z

K.T. Achaya

OXFORD
UNIVERSITY PRESS

OXFORD
UNIVERSITY PRESS

YMCA Library Building, Jai Singh Road, New Delhi 110 001

Oxford University Press is a department of the University of Oxford.
It furthers the University's objective of excellence in research,
scholarship, and education by publishing worldwide in

Oxford New York
Auckland Cape Town Dar es Salaam Hong Kong Karachi
Kuala Lumpur Madrid Melbourne Mexico City Nairobi
New Delhi Shanghai Taipei Toronto

With offices in
Argentina Austria Brazil Chile Czech Republic France Greece
Guatemala Hungary Italy Japan Poland Portugal Singapore
South Korea Switzerland Thailand Turkey Ukraine Vietnam

Oxford is a registered trademark of Oxford University Press
in the UK and in certain other countries

Published in India by Oxford University Press, New Delhi

ISBN-13: 978-019-569844-2
ISBN-10: 019-569844-4
Illustrations by Amit John

Typeset in AGaramond Pro 11/14 by Jojy Philip
Printed and bound in India at Repro India Ltd., Mumbai
New Delhi 110 020
Published by Oxford University Press
YMCA Library Building, Jai Singh Road, New Delhi 110 001

Contents

vii

Publisher's Note

viii

List of Headwords

1–299

THE A–Z OF INDIAN FOOD

Publisher's Note

Drawing from two OUP classics—
Indian Food: A Historical Companion
(OUP 1994) and *A Historical
Dictionary of Indian Food* (OUP
1998)—and with an appealing new
format, *The Illustrated Foods of India*
showcases the wide range and richness
of Indian cuisine. More than a decade
earlier K.T. Achaya successfully
presented to the world, Indian food in
all its diversity. This illustrated edition
uses the timeless appeal of his work to
reach out to a wider audience.

The book looks at food from a
wider perspective: the principles,
the ingredients, the regional
influences, therapeutic diets as
prescribed in the ayurvedic system
of medicine, colonial eating habits,
Indian diaspora food as reflecting
the cultural and regional origins of
the immigrants. And through it all
it does not to forget the religious

influences—for example, how the
complicated mass of rituals dictate
Hindu domestic cooking practices,
and how seviyan are an integral part
of Id celebration.

Combining startling insights into
the complex world of food with
practical considerations of availability
of food materials and climatic
suitability, this interesting book
situates Indian food in time and place.
Including information on a host of
historical factors that influenced the
regional cuisines of India, particularly
the migration of food plants from
the New World to India, and the
interesting transfer of words across
languages, for example, from Tamil
and Malayalam (often by way of
Portuguese or Spanish) into English,
this latest addition to the Oxford
India Collection should appeal to
all our readers.

List of Headwords

achar	1	ash gourd	12
adai	1	ashvamedha	12
adhrak	1	aval	12
agriculture in India	1	aviyal	12
ahara	3	ayurveda	12
ahimsa	3		
ajamedha	3	badam	14
almond	3	baghar	14
alms as food	3	bajra	14
amaranths	4	baking	14
amla	4	balanced meal	15
amphorae	5	bamboo	15
aniseed	5	banana	16
annaprasanna	5	banyan	18
antelope	5	barks	18
appam	5	barley	18
apple	6	basil	19
apricot	7	bath	20
apupa	7	beans	20
areca nut	7	beaten rice	20
arhar	10	beef	20
arishta	10	beer	21
aroids	10	bellows	21
arrack	11	Bengal gram	21
asafoetida	11	Bengali food	22
asava	11	Bengali sweets	24

ber	26	cassia	42
besan	26	cattle	42
betel leaf	26	cauldrons	42
beverages	26	cauliflower	43
beverages, alcoholic	28	chakki	43
bhang	31	chana	43
birinj	31	chapathi	43
biriyani	31	*Charaka Samhita*	43
biscuit	31	chaval	44
bittergourd	32	cheese	44
black gram	32	cherry	44
boar	32	chhana	45
bottlegourd	32	chicken	45
Bower manuscript	32	chickpea	46
brandy	32	chidva	46
bread	33	chikki	46
breadfruit	33	chilgoza	46
brinjal	33	chilli	46
broad bean	34	China, foods from	47
Buddhist food and literature	34	chini	48
buffalo	36	chironji	48
butchers	37	chocolate	48
butter	37	chowka(i)	48
buttermilk	38	chulah	49
buryron	38	chunam	49
Byculla soufflé	38	churning	49
		chutney	49
cabbage	39	cigar	50
cakes	39	cinnamon	50
calamondin	39	citrus fruits	50
camphor	39	claret	52
caper	40	clove	52
capsicum	40	cluster bean	52
caraway	40	coconut	52
cardamom	40	coconut products	55
carrot	41	coffee	55
cashew	41	'cold' food	56
cassava	42	colocasia	57

Colonial repast	57	ekadashi	73
colostrum	59	elephant	73
conjee	60	elephant foot yam	73
cooking principles	60	elk	73
cooking practices	60	etiquette of dining	73
cooking and related utensils	61		
cooks	62	falooda	75
copra	62	fasts	75
coriander	62	fats in cooking	76
cottonseed oil	63	feni	77
cow	63	fenugreek	77
cowpea	63	fermentation	77
cream	63	festival and temple foods	77
crocodile	64	fig	79
cucumber	64	fire	80
cumin	64	fish	80
curd	64	foot pounder	82
curry	66	fowlers	82
curry leaves	66	French bean	82
		French cuisine	82
dahi	67	fruit	83
dahi-vada	67	fruit drinks	85
dalia	67	frying	85
date	67	fumigation	85
deer	68		
dhal	68	game, wild	86
dhenki	69	Ganges water	87
dhokla	69	gardens, floating	88
diet	70	garlic	88
dietetics	70	gayal	89
distillation	70	ghani	89
dosa(i)	70	ghee	91
dosha	70	ginger	92
drumstick	71	ginger grass	94
duck	71	gluten	94
dumpukht, dumpoke	71	Goa, foods from	94
		goat	96
eggs	72	gonkuru	96

goose	96	ice-cream	117
gourds	97	idi-appam	118
grafting	99	idli	118
gram	99	Iguana	119
granary	99	Indrajau	119
grape	100	Indus Valley civilization	119
grapefruit	102	irrigation	121
Greek contacts	102	Islam and food	121
green gram	104	Italian millet	122
green leafy vegetables	105	Italy, trade with	122
griddle	106		
grilling	106	jackal	123
grinding devices	107	jackbean	123
groundnut	108	jackfruit	123
guar	108	jaggery	125
guava	108	Jain food ambience	126
guest and host	108	jambu	128
Gujarat, food in	109	jamoon	128
gulab-jamun	111	jeera	128
gur	111	Jewish food	128
		jilebi	129
halal	112	Job's tears	130
haldi	112	jowar	130
haleem, harees(a)	112		
halwa	112	kabab	131
handa, handva	112	kaccha food	131
health and food	112	kadamba	131
hearth, domestic	112	kadubu	132
hemp	112	kahwah	133
hen	112	kanji	133
honey	112	kapha	133
horse	114	karela	133
horsegram	115	Karnataka, food of	133
host	115	Kashmir, food of	137
hotels	115	kattha	139
'hot' food	115	kedgeree	139
		Kerala, food of	139
ice	116	kesar	143

kesari-bath	143	lotus	151
kesari dhal	143		
khadi	144	mace	152
khaman	144	madhu	152
khand	144	madhuparka	152
khandsari	144	madhya	152
khaskhas	144	maharaja	153
kheel	145	mahashali	153
kheema	145	mahua	153
kheer	145	maida	154
khichdi, khichiri	145	maireya	154
khoa	145	maize	154
kidney bean	146	makki	154
kitchens	146	malabathrum	154
kneading pan	146	mandarin orange	154
knives	146	mango	154
Kodagu, food of	146	masha	157
kodhra	147	masoor	157
kosher meat	147	mat, moth bean	158
kulfi	147	mattar	158
		meal, order of	158
laddu	149	meat consumption	160
ladles and spoons	148	meat dishes	162
lady's finger	149	meen	166
leaf plates and cups	149	melogara	166
leather vessels	149	melons	166
lehya(m)	150	methi	167
lemon	150	Mexico, food materials from	167
lemon grass	150	mice	167
lentils	150	milk	168
lima beans	150	millet	170
lime	150	milling	171
lime paste	150	mint	172
linseed	150	mirchi	172
liquor	151	mishti-doi	172
litchi	151	modak	173
lobia	151	Mughal period, food of	173
loquat	151	moley, moile	177

morabba, murabba	177	ovens	188
mosambi	177	oxen	188
moth bean	177		
motichur	177	paan	189
mulberry	177	pak	189
mulligatawny	177	pak, pakku	189
Munda	178	pakoda, pakauri	189
mung	178	palak	189
murmura, muri	179	palao	189
murukku	179	palms	190
Muslims, food of	179	palmyra	190
mustard leaves	179	panchagavya	191
mustard oil	179	panchamritha	191
mustard seeds	180	panchphoron	191
mutton	182	paneer	191
Mysore pak	182	panicum grains	191
		pao	192
naan	183	papad	192
Nalapaka	183	papaya	192
navy bean	183	papdi	192
neem	183	paramanna	192
neera	184	parata, paranta	192
nigella seeds	184	parboiling	193
niger	184	parching	193
nigger fowl	184	Parsis, food of	194
nutcrackers	184	partridge	195
nutmeg	184	parwal	195
nutrition	184	passion fruit	196
nuts	185	payasa(m), payesh	196
		peach	196
oats	186	peacock	197
oils, oilseeds	186	pear	197
oil pressing	186	pearl millet	197
olive	186	peas	197
onion	187	pepper, long	198
opium	188	pepper, round	198
orange	188	Persian words	200
oregano	188	pestle	201

pewter	201	puri	216
phala	201	puttu	216
phalsa	201		
pheasants	201	quail	217
pheni	201	querns	217
phulka	202		
pickle	202	rabbit	218
pig	203	radish	218
pigeon	204	ragi	219
pigeon pea	204	rainwater	220
pineapple	204	raisins	220
pishta	205	raitha	220
pistachio	205	rajasic	220
pitta	205	Rajasthan, food of	221
plantain	205	rajmah	222
plates, leaf	205	rajmasha	223
plum	206	rape-mustard	223
poli(ka)	206	rasa	223
pomegranate	206	rasa, rasam	223
pomelo	207	rasogolla, rasmalai	224
pongal	207	rava	224
poppy	207	relishes	224
porcupine	208	rice	224
pork	208	ridge gourd	229
Portuguese impact	208	roasting	229
pot herbs	210	rock salt	229
potato	210	Rome, contacts with	231
pots	211	roselle	233
poultry	211	roti	233
pounding	211		
prasad(am)	211	sacrifice	237
prathaman	211	safflower	238
preserves	211	saffron	238
pucca food	211	sag	238
puffed grains	211	sago	238
pulses	212	salt	239
pumpkins	216	sambhar	240
punch	216	samosa	241

samovar	241	South America, foods from	255
sandal	241	south India	255
sandesh	242	soybean	255
Sangam literature	242	spikenard	256
sann-hemp	242	spinach	256
Sanskrit sources	242	spit	256
Sanskrit words	244	spoons	256
sapota	245	squash	256
sarson	246	stale food	257
sattu	246	star fruit	257
sattvik	247	steaming	257
saunf	247	Stone Age paintings	257
seafood	247	sugarcane	258
seasons and months	247	sugarcane products	259
sem	248	Sultanate, food of	261
sesame	248	sura	262
sev	250	suran	263
seviyan	250	Sushrutha Samhita	263
Seville orange	250	Sutras	263
shaka	250	sweet lime	263
shali	251	sweet potato	263
sheep	251	sword bean	263
shellfish	251		
shraddha	251	tamarind	264
shrikhand	251	tamasic	265
shukto	252	Tamil literature	265
shula	252	tandoor	266
sigdi	252	tangerines	266
Sikhs, ceremonial food of	252	tapioca	266
singhada	252	tastes	267
sitaphal	253	tea	267
snails	254	tejpat	269
snake gourd	254	temple foods	269
soma	254	tempura	270
sooty fowl	255	thali	270
sorghum	255	thava	271
sorrel	255	therapeutic diets	271
soups	255	thuvar	271

tiffin	272	wadi	288
tobacco	272	walnut	288
toddy	273	water	288
tomato	273	watercress	290
tools, prehistoric	273	waterpots	290
toothpicks	274	weights, measures, and lengths	290
tortoise, turtle	275	wheat	292
tubers	275	wheat dishes	293
turkey	275	whey	295
turmeric	275	wine	295
		winged bean	295
Unani medicine	277	winnowing basket and tray	295
urad	278	woodapple	295
utensils	279	words for food, in English	296
vada	280	Xuan Zang, and other	297
varagu	281	Chinese pilgrims	
vata	281		
Vedas	281	yams	298
vegetables	281	yavana	298
vegetarianism	284		
venison	285	zakat	299
vinegar	285		
visitors to India	285		

achar Word for pickle in Urdu and Hindi, commonly thought to have a Persian or Arabic origin, but stated by Rumphius in AD 1750 to derive from terms like axi or achi used for the chilli (*see also* pickles, chilli).

adai Shallow-fried circlet of the Tamil country. The thick ground batter consists of almost equal parts of rice and as many as four pulses. It is described in the Tamil Sangam literature between the third and sixth centuries AD as a snack served by vendors on the seashore.

adhrak Hindi for green ginger, from the Sanskrit ardraka, which in the *Atharvaveda* is adara. Dried ginger has its own Sanskrit name, srngavera or injivera, of Tamil origin: ver is root, and inji is a word still used in south India. The Hindi term is sunthi. Though the ginger is almost certainly native to South-East Asia, long cultivation has obscured the sites of original domestication. Several species are grown in Malaysia, and wild forms are still found in India (*see also* ginger).

agriculture in India Even the Indus Valley civilization of 2500–1500 BC shows evidence of advanced agriculture. At Kalibangan in Rajasthan, on the sand-dunes of the river Ghaggar, believed to be the ancient river Saraswathi, was excavated a field that had been ploughed about 2800 BC and then abandoned, for some reason now unknown. The north–south furrows were spaced widely apart, and those running east–west more closely. Even today in Rajasthan, horsegram is grown on similar wide furrows so as not to cast shadows on the shorter mustard plants grown at right angles to them. Beautiful toy clay models of wooden ploughs have been found. Annual flood inundation along natural channels, a feature in the area, probably served for irrigation, and bullocks for ploughing were readily available. It is surmised that the pottery jars with deep grooves in the middle, which have been found in large numbers in Mohenjodaro, were tied to wheels for raising water from rivers.

The Aryan civilization that followed from about 1500 BC set the patterns of agriculture that are still largely followed, such as ploughing using two oxen and a light wooden plough, raising water from rivers and deflecting them into man-made channels for irrigation, transplanting rice, weeding, reaping, and threshing. The common fertilizer was cowdung, and later also oilcakes. Silaging of fodder crops, termed sujavas in the *Rigveda*, was known. Pest control included the use of mantras, charms, and amulets. By AD 500 elaborate seed dressings had developed.

Land fallowing, seasonal sowing, and crop rotation were all practised from very early times. Three clear crop seasons (q.v.), and the produce to be grown in each, are firmly set out in the *Arthashastra* (*c.* 300 BC). Grain was threshed on the ground in the field itself or near the village, winnowed, sun-dried, and measured by volume. Grain was stored for year-long family use in clay pots (later called kothis), in woven rope containers plastered with mud, or in underground pits.

Supplementary foods were raised on the outskirts of villages. Pumpkins and gourds were grown on river banks, while lands that were frequently flooded were rated best for long pepper, grapes, and sugarcane. Vegetables and root crops thrived in the vicinity of wells, and leafy crops on low grounds like the moist bed of lakes. Marginal furrows between rows of other crop plants were recommended for fragrant herbs and other medicinal plants.

Foreign visitors refer admiringly to Indian agriculture. Nearchos of Crete, who accompanied Alexander to India in 325 BC, noted that crops were grown both in summer and winter, and attributed this 'great facility of the soil' not only to the rains, but to the silt which the rivers brought down in great quantities from the mountains. Megasthenes, the Greek ambassador a few years later at the court of Chandragupta Maurya in Pataliputra, remarked that agriculturists constituted the bulk of the population; they 'were exempted from military service, and pursue their labours free from all alarm. Indeed it often happens that at the same time, and in the same part of the country, the army is engaged in fighting the enemy, while the husbandsmen are sowing and ploughing in the utmost security. The entire land is the property of the king, to whom they pay one-fourth of the produce as revenue.'

Later visitors like Ibn Haukal (AD 950), Al-Idrisi (AD 1080), Ma Huan (c. AD 1460), Domingo Paes (c. AD 1520), and Francois Bernier (AD 1659–66) all wrote extensively of the fertility of the Indian soil and the variety and abundance of produce in various parts of India like Sindh, Bengal, Vijayanagar, and Kashmir.

ahara Sanskrit term meaning food and nourishment. Thus phalahar would signify the use of only edible fruits and vegetables, which is one variety of fasting in the science of dietetics, itself called aharatattva. Under aharayogi, the food permitted to ascetics, Charaka lists the oils of sesame, mustard, and the like.

ahimsa Concept of non-injury to life, enjoined by the Buddha in the Mahayana *Sutras*, in particular the *Lankavatara*. Emperor Ashoka, a devout Buddhist, emphasized ahimsa in his edicts, and Mahatma Gandhi adopted it in modern times as a means of passive, non-violent political protest (*see also* meat consumption; vegetarianism).

ajamedha The Vedic goat sacrifice enshrined in the *Sutras* in which a male goat is seized, his feet carefully washed, the joints neatly cut up, and cooked using cauldrons and utensils made to rigid specifications. The

sacrificed animal was simultaneously bidden to go to the third heaven, where the righteous dwell, and the sacrificial meat was considered sanctified for consumption.

almond In Hindi badam, from the Sanskrit vatama (the sweet variety) and vatavairi (the bitter variety), both derived from the old Persian term vadam, and first used by Charaka and Sushrutha. The almond, *Prunus amygdalus*, is of Central European/West Asian origin, along with other related *Prunus* species like the cherry, plum, peach, and apricot. In fact in Mughal times, almond trees were used to graft apricots. Though fairly plentiful by the time of Akbar, they were always expensive. Ralph Fitch notes in 1583 that in Cooch-Bihar almonds were used as small money. They find extensive use in Indian epicurean cuisine, ground with honey or sugar and fashioned into confections (badam burfi, badam-ki-jali); beaten, after grinding, into sweetened milk (badam kheer); as a flavourant for tea, or a stuffing in samosas, for dressing pulaos and halvas, and the like.

alms as food Begging for food from citizens residing in the area was considered part of the discipline of humility expected of older students living as apprentices with their teachers. Of Buddhist student-monks (bhikshus), Xuan Zang wrote that 'though their family be in affluent

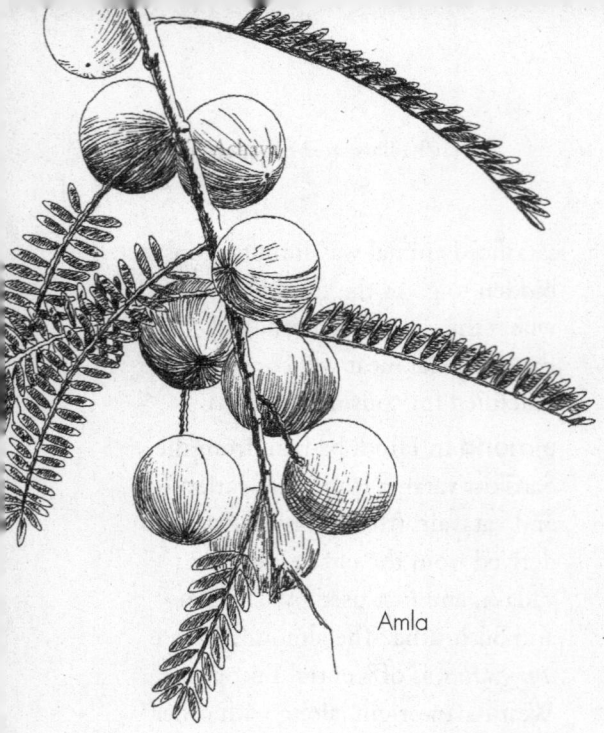
Amla

circumstances, such men make up their mind (after their studies) to be like vagrants and get their food by begging as they go about. With them there is honour in knowing truth and there is no disgrace in being destitute'. A begging bowl (patra) and a water-strainer (parishravana) were among the eight prescribed personal items. Anything given as alms by the householder, even if this was meat or fish, was expected to be eaten; it was the responsibility of the giver to ensure that the food was 'blameless' in that the killing had not been seen, heard, or suspected by the begging bhikshu.

amaranths A genus of very ancient South American origin, of which three species have become fairly widespread in India. *Amaranthus hybridus* subsp. *hybridus*, called ramadhana, chua, bathua, and pungikeerai, is the commonest,

with an impressive yellow or purple inflorescence. The grains are dehusked by popping on hot sand, and the kernels ground into flour or fashioned with jaggery into a chikki. *A. hybridus* subsp. *cruentus* has green or purple leaves, which are eaten as chaulai, methi-bhaji, or pungikeerai, while the grain is called rajgeera. The third is *A. caudatus*, a wholly ornamental plant with heart-shaped, showy, red-veined leaves, commonly called love-lies-bleeding.

Certain other amaranth pot herbs have either Indian or New World progenitors. *A. spinosus* has green or purple leaves, eaten as kantha-chaulai or mullukeerai. *A. tricolor*, with leaves of many hues, is called araikeerai or tandukeerai. *A. viridis* (kuppakeerai, sinnakeerai) has both edible leaves and an edible tuber which resembles asparagus.

amla The Indian gooseberry, *Emblica officinalis*, is an ancient fruit now recognized as one of the richest natural sources of vitamin C. Carbonized remains have been excavated at Navdatoli (1600 BC), but it is first mentioned only about 500 years later in the *Jaiminiya Upanishad Brahmana*. The amla was used to make a refreshing beverage (genetically termed panaka), or pickled in oil, or preserved as a murabba (q.v.) in sugar syrup. It was one of the items recommended by Sushrutha for universal everyday consumption that transcended restrictions of body type and season. The amla was one of three myrobalans, the others being the chebulic myrobalan and the belleric myrobalan, *Terminalia chebula* and *T. bellirica*, which in equal proportions make up the important medicine triphala, recommended for debility. It is also the base of other restoratives like chyavanapras.

amphorae Two-handled Roman wine jars found in large numbers at an excavated warehouse in Arikamedu, near Pondicherry. Marks of schools of Roman potters like VIBII, CAMURI, and ITTA are clear evidence of trade between Rome and south India in the first and second centuries AD.

aniseed Saunf, *Pimpinella anisum* is native to the Mediterranean region, but is now cultivated in northern and eastern India, perhaps since Muslim times. The slender green aromatic seeds are often served after a meal as a mouth-freshener and digestive, and are a component of panchphoron (q.v.), the five-spice mixture of Bengal. The French traveller Francois Bernier (*c.* AD 1665) mentions carrying sweet biscuits flavoured with aniseed during his travels in India.

annaprasanna Ceremony at which a child about six months old is first given solid food on an auspicious day. This food took the form of a paramanna (q.v.) of boiled rice, milk, sugar, and honey, a little of which was gently placed in the child's mouth. In early Vedic times some flesh was also included, and the *Grhya Sutras* were of the opinion that the kind of meat given would influence the child's nature. Ram's meat would confer physical strength, partridge meat saintliness, fish a gentle disposition, and rice and ghee glory.

antelope Antelopes are shown in Stone Age paintings at Bhimbetka; their bones show up in excavations; and in Sanskrit there are a number of terms for them (krishnasar, harini, etc.). Antelope meat is listed among others in the *Vishnu Purana* (third to fourth century AD) as very meritorious for use in the ancestral shraddha ceremony. Emperor Jahangir found the milk of the female antelope 'palatable' and remarks that it was said to be 'of great use in asthma'. Thomas Coryat (1612–17), an early English visitor, saw antelopes for the first time in the Mughal court, and notes that 'Robert Sherley and his lady' took back to England with them two elephants and eight antelopes. Later British colonialists considered antelope meat dry and lean, needing constant basting during roasting.

appam A circular pancake of a toddy-fermented batter of rice, baked on a well-seasoned clay dish to yield a product with a thick spongy centre and lacy browned edges. It is a breakfast food in Tamil Nadu, served with sweetened milk or coconut milk, and in Kerala is eaten by Syrian Christians with a meat stew accompaniment, and by Nairs and Nampoothiris with aviyal (q.v.). Tamil Sangam literature of about the fifth century AD describes it as being eaten with a milk accompaniment, and as an item served by kaazhiyar and kuuviyar, vendors of snack foods, on the seashore. The name appam may derive from the Vedic fried dainty, the apupa. The British corruption of appam, hoppers, is widely used in Sri Lanka.

There are many variations of the appam in Kerala. Heating on a stone or metal plate held over boiling water yields kal-appam. Yele (or leaf)-appam describes a mix of rice batter, grated coconut, jackfruit pulp, and jaggery steamed in a banana leaf

Appam

packet. Kuzhal-appam is a crisp, tube-like fried product, and nai-appam (the athirasam of Tamil Nadu) is a dark, chewy, deep-fried doughnut fashioned from a toddy-fermented rice and jaggery mixture. A crisp rose-cookie is the acch-appam, in which a metal frame (accha) is dipped in batter and then immersed in hot oil, which fries the cookie and frees it from the frame.

Another food mentioned in Sangam literature is the idi-appam (called nu-puttu in Kodagu and string hoppers in Sri Lanka), which is a pat of noodles shaped from a mash of boiled rice. It is eaten in Kerala and Tamil Nadu with sweetened coconut milk or milk, and in Kodagu with a meat or chicken curry.

apple The apple originated in the mountainous belt running across Asia Minor through Himalayan India and perhaps into China. As recently as in 1908 Sir Francis Younghusband described wild apple trees laden with fruit in Kashmir, and wild apple forms like the patol (*Malus baccata*) are still used as a vegetable in the north-western Himalayas. Amri and tarehli (*M. pumila*) are believed to be indigenous Kashmir varieties. Charaka mentions the sinchitikaphala, which could have been an apple of Chinese origin, and also the paravata, which as palevat still grows in Assam. In about AD 1100 Dalhana describes 'a ber as

Apple

big as a fist and very sweet' grown in the northern regions of Kashmir, which does suggest an apple. Amir Khusrau mentions apples in India in about AD 1300. They were given attention by the Mughals in their efforts to grow temperate fruits of high quality in suitable locations in India.

apricot *Prunus armeniaca* has been allotted Chinese ancestry but a wild form called zardalu still grows in India. Though Xuan Zang records in about AD 650 that apricots brought from Kashmir were 'grown on every side', a thousand years later Jahangir states that 'the sweet cherry, pear and apricot, so far imported' were being raised in Kashmir. Grafting of the apricot was carried out on almond trees, which are of the same genus. Like many sweet fruits, dried apricots are classed as 'cold' foods in ayurvedic terms, and have an alkaline reaction in the body.

apupa A Vedic fried sweet item of barley or rice flour sweetened with honey, and later with sugarcane juice and sugar. The apupa was an item permitted for use at annual ancestral shraddha ceremonies. Made in Buddhist times with broken rice, it was termed kanapuvam. Later fig-like shapes, and stuffing with fried wheat flour are described, though the sweet connotation survives throughout. A Sanskrit variation of the name is pupa, which is reflected in the pua and malpua of modern Bengal. Even the term appam (q.v.) in south India could have been derived from apupa.

areca nut The nut of *Areca catechu,* a tall slender palm, is always associated in India with the betel leaf (*Piper betle*), a climbing vine, which are chewed together at the end of a meal as a stimulant, digestive, and mouth-freshener. Both plants are of South-East Asian origin. They may have entered India as a pair, and can conveniently be considered together. It is likely that the betel leaf was introduced into south India to begin with.

Though the nut is called arec in the Talinga dialect of the Sunda Islands, the word areca that is now used in English, is believed to be a Portuguese adaptation of the Malayalam word adakka, itself formed by combining adai (a close cluster) with kai (fruit or nut). Tamil has another word, puga, for the areca nut; Hindi has supari, and scented areca grits are sometimes chewed by themselves without the leaf.

Areca nut palm

The term betel for the leaf is again a Portuguese derivation from the Malayalam/Tamil vetrilai or vettile, meaning truly-a-leaf. The Hindi term paan for the quid is also derived from a word for leaf, the Sanskrit parna. A common colloquial term for the quid in south India is paak, a word which Garcia da Orta notes as early as in AD 1560. The Sankrit words thambula for the leaf (and later for the quid itself) and guvaka for the nut, and indeed the 'vetr' stem of the Tamil word vetrilai, are believed to be structurally related to such words as blu, balu, and mlu that were used for the betel leaf in the Munda dialects of some aboriginal Indian peoples, and later absorbed into early Tamil and Sanskrit usage. Another Sanskrit term for the quid, vida, is the beeda of common current usage.

Northern literature mentions these items as late as in *c.* 400 BC, both in the Buddhist *Jataka* tales in Pali, and in the Sanskrit *Dharmasutra*s. Kalidasa in his *Raghuvamsa* and Shudraka in his *Mrcchakatika* recognize the practice of chewing the quid as a custom of south India. References in the famous Mandasor inscription (*c.* AD 473) of the silk-weaver's guild in Indore, in Varahamihira's *Brhat Samhita* of *c.* AD 530, and in the ancient medical texts, all serve to indicate that it had by then become common practice everywhere. In the Tamil classic *Silappadikaram*, the heroine Kannagi offers her husband Kovalan betel leaves and areca nuts to chew at the end of his last meal with her, before he departs for Madurai on his fatal mission of selling her anklet.

There can be other components in the quid. The use of a dab of slaked lime (chunam) on the leaves, which releases the alkaloid and is responsible for the red colour that develops on chewing, is probably very old, since skulls dated 3000 BC with characteristic red-stained teeth have been found in the Philippines. Another frequent practice in India is to smear the leaves with kattha, the astringent, chocolate-brown, thickened extract of the heartwood of *Areca catechu*, a habit noted by Charaka, Sushrutha, and Vaghbhata. The use of camphor by grandees in Kerala is mentioned by Garcia da Orta (*c*. AD 1560), and in a Kannada work of AD 1594. The addition of aphrodisiacs yields a quid with the appellation palangtod (bed-breaking)! The *Manasollasa* (AD 1130) written by King Someshwara of Kalyana in Central India describes pancha-sugandha as a thambula with five aromatic ingredients, namely the cardamom, clove, nutmeg, mace, and camphor, a truly kingly concoction.

Apart from its significance in stimulating saliva and gastric flow after a meal, paan is also regarded as an auspicious symbol of hospitality, and was offered as a moral and even legal commitment when an agreement was drawn up. The goddess Lakshmi was believed to reside in the fore part of the betel leaf, Jyestha at the back, the lord of speech on the right, Parvati on the left, Vishnu inside, the Moon outside, Shiva in all the edges, and Manmatha (Cupid) everywhere; Yama, the lord of death, resided in the stalk, which is therefore always pinched away and discarded before the leaf is used. The *Shivatattvaratnakara* written in *c*. AD 1700 by Basavaraja, king of the Keladi kingdom, which stretched from Goa to Kannoor, carefully noted the locations of the best betel leaves and the best areca nuts in his domain. Such information for the same period is also available for the Maharashtra area. The quid kulapavida was made up of 10–12 leaves, and must have been very large; in addition to the usual filling of betel nuts, slaked lime, and kattha, it also carried cardamom, nutmeg, almond, pista, and coconut shreds.

Muslims, when they came to India, quickly took to chewing paan. In about AD 1350 Ibn Battuta describes how it was served in the Delhi Sultanate at the end of elaborate palace meals. At pavilions set up in Delhi by Muhammad bin Tughlak, any citizen, whether a native or a stranger, could help himself without cost to sherbet, betel leaves, and areca nuts. European visitors all refer to the ubiquitous chewing habit, and Niccolao Manucci in 1654 described his first experience as a young man of chewing the betel quid: '... my head swam to such an extent that I feared I was dying. It caused me to fall down; I lost my colour, and endured agonies; but (an English acquaintance) poured into my mouth a little salt and brought me to my senses. It happens with the eaters of betel, as to those accustomed to tobacco, that they are unable to refrain from taking it many times a day.'

arhar *Cajanus cajan*, the pigeon pea, called thuvar in south India, arhar in the north, adhaki in early Buddhist literature (*c.* 400 BC), and thuvarika by Charaka. The progenitor is some species of *Atylosia*; even today wild forms grow in the Western Ghats of south India, which cross easily with thuvar. Arhar is a tall shrub bearing yellow

Arhar dhal

flowers streaked with purple and long maroon pods with four or five seeds. The southern thuvar is a short plant with exclusively yellow flowers and short green pods carrying three seeds. Thuvar is the common edible dhal of south India, used in making rasam and sambhar (*see also* thuvar).

arishta Generic term for medicated alcoholic concoctions, the name itself meaning absence of injury in Sanskrit (*see also* beverages, alcoholic).

aroids Edible tubers of three families distributed all over the southern hemisphere. The *Alocasia* family originated in India/Sri Lanka, and includes two species. *A. indica* is the giant taro (Sanskrit manaka, Hindi manakanda, Bengali mankachu), a tall plant, and *A. macrorrhiza* is the boromankachu of Assam, a giant plant with a high content of bitter calcium oxalate in the tuber which has to be leached out before cooking.

The genus *Colocasia* also originated in India. It includes *C. esculenta*, the well-known arvi, seppam-kizhangu or shamagadde, whose tubers, of myriad shapes and sizes, are coloured white, yellow, purple, and red. There is a suggestion that the ancient terraces now used to grow rice in Kashmir may have originally been set up to raise colocasia tubers.

Also of indigenous origin is the huge elephant foot yam (suran, senaikizhangu), the *Amorpophallus campanulatus*. It has two Sanskrit names, surana (Charaka) and arasagna, meaning destroyer of piles; dried slices were till recently sold in bazaars under the name of madanamast for the treatment of piles and dyspepsia.

arrack Originally an Arabic word, arak, for the exudate of date palm sap but later in India and elsewhere it became a term for distilled liquor, especially that from toddy (q.v.), the fermented sap of the palmyra palm. Pedro Texeira (AD 1587) states that 'araca' is very strong, but improves with age, and that raisins were thrown into it to take off its roughness and sweeten it. Edward Terry (c. AD 1615), chaplain to Sir Thomas Roe, was of the opinion that arrack is very wholesome if taken in moderation. An arrack-based drink was offered by Emperor Jahangir to Sir Thomas which was very strong and made him sneeze; this was a clear spirit made by keeping arrack with sugar in barrels containing the dregs of other wines. The drink punch (q.v.) (from the Sanskrit pancha) was created by the British in India by mixing five components, namely arrack, sugar, spices, lime juice, and water, and was first noted as palepuntz by Albert de Mendelslo in 1638. Toddy was widely distilled in India; the British administration noted in 1870–90 that in the Bengal Presidency alone, there were 8000 arrack shops, besides 30,000 for toddy, and stills in almost

every village; an attempt was made to bring both the manufacture and storage of liquor under control by instituting a still-head duty which had to be paid before any liquor was issued from the stores.

asafoetida Resinous exudate from incisions made in roots of the shrub *Ferulla alliacea*, the aromatic components of which resemble those in onion and garlic. The exudate is separated into the white, water-soluble hing(u) with a high proportion of gum, and the black, oil-soluble and highly aromatic hingra, rich in oil. Kandahari hing is the commercially prized product, followed by Irani hing, and Pathani hing. The word hingu occurs in the early Buddhist *Mahavagga*, while meat dishes flavoured with the spice are mentioned in the Mahabharata. Only a trace of asafoetida is used in certain current savoury dishes of India. In AD 1518 Christoforas Accra described the characteristics of various kinds of asafoetida imported into India, while the difference between hingu and hingra was noted in *c.* 1680 by John Fryer.

asava Generic name for a distilled liquor afterwards flavoured and sweetened. A prefix is used to indicate its source, such as pushpa- (flower), phala- (fruit), madhvika- (mahua), sharkara- (sugar), sura-(grain), and narikela- (coconut). Some have a medical connotation.

ash gourd Botanically *Benicasa hispida*, the Sanskrit kushmanda, Hindi petha, Tamil pushinikayi, and English ash gourd, is perhaps native to Malaysia, though long known in India. It is cooked as a vegetable, made into halwa, and candied in hot sugar solution to give the fibrous and jujube-like petha.

Ash gourd

ashvamedha The Vedic horse sacrifice, described in great detail in the 162nd hymn of the *Rigveda*. The animal was sacrificed, roasted whole, the oozing fat collected, and the body carved to rigid specifications. Each portion had a specific recipient: thus the right thigh went to the brahmin who had chanted the mantras, and the two jawbones and tongue to the prastota priest. In later times, a king would set free a spirited horse to roam freely, accompanied by an army, and battle was given to anyone who challenged the animal, which symbolized the king's authority. On its return the animal was honoured and sacrificed ritually.

aval Tamil for flattened or beaten rice, the Hindi poha. Then as now, rice grains were soaked, roasted on hot sand till ready to puff, and then beaten flat in a pounder. Aval is mentioned in the Tamil Sangam literature of between the third and sixth centuries AD as eaten after being soaked in milk.

aviyal Vegetable dish of Kerala that uses green bananas, drumsticks, various soft beans, and fresh coconut gratings. These are first cooked in coconut milk and then tossed with some aromatic coconut oil and spiced sour curd. The product, served as prasadam in the Padmanabhaswami temple in Thiruvananthapuram, does not contain the inauspicious mustard seeds.

ayurveda Literally the science of life as it was developed in India, being a holistic view of the body, mind, and spirit viewed in relation to the cosmic moral cycle, in which a well-adjusted diet had an important role to play. Concepts and practices that developed over centuries were codified in the *Charaka Samhita* and the *Sushrutha Samhita* (each of which include accretions till as late as AD 400), and in Vaghbhata's *Ashtangahrdyasamhita* (mid-seventh century AD). All material things were believed to be composed of five elements (earth, air, fire, water, and space) in various combinations. In the body these combinations take three forms, vata, pitta, and kapha (loosely translated as wind, bile, and water, but with a far more dynamic connotation; *see* individual entries) which, when in balance, result in good health. Anna (diet) is the main agency by which this is brought about, the two others being the use of medicinal herbs and drugs (aushada), and various exercises (vihara). The choice of food must take into consideration the person's physical constitution and natural temperament (whether sattvik or serene, rajasic or excitable, and tamasic or courageous; *see* individual entries), the nature of the malady, the season of the year, and the habitat.

All foods are characterized by their rasa (taste) and guna (property). There are six basic tastes, and ten pairs of contrasting gunas, such as light/heavy, dry/unctuous, and compact/mobile. Deranged vata is calmed by food products that are salty, sour, or sweet in taste, and hot, oily, or heavy in nature. A pitta-type malady needs food that is bitter, astringent, or sweet, and also hot, heavy, compact, and slimy. The third dosha, kapha, is countered by pungent, bitter, and astringent products that are keen, hot, and dry.

Two other concepts are virya, the potency of the food, and vipaka, its aftertaste, which could differ from its rasa or taste.

The class of foods termed sweet include cereals, pulses, milk and its products, most legumes, flesh foods, sugarcane products, coconut products, and nuts. Acid foods include the mango, pomegranate, tamarind, grape, citrus fruits, and amla. All types of salt (sea, rock, mineral) constitute salty foods, while pungent foods include most spices (ginger, mustard, pepper) and the betel leaf. The bittergourd, products of the neem tree, the jamoon fruit, and fenugreek seeds are examples of bitter foods. Astringent foods comprise mainly the barks of trees, and the kattha that is smeared on betel (q.v.) leaves.

Most cereals are sweet and also heavy, and hence build up tissues and provide energy. Honey, though sweet, is predominantly astringent in its aftertaste, and hence weight-reducing. Amla is sour, and being also cold and soft, is exceptionally effective in restoring balance.

Ailments like dyspepsia, rheumatism, tuberculosis, diabetes, and jaundice are explained on the same principle of dosha or imbalance, and treated by administering corrective foods. Thus antidotes for diabetes include the bitter foods earlier listed.

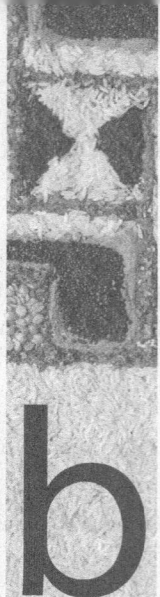

b

badam *See* almond.

baghar Derived from the Sanskrit bagharna, this cooking operation connotes the initial shallow frying in fat of spices or flavourants, not usually together, but one after the other (for example, mustard seed, then onions) before the vegetable or meat to be cooked is introduced. Sometimes the baghar is performed separately, and poured hot over the finished dish, say, of dhal.

bajra Hindi word for *Pennisetum americanum*, which despite its name originated in the Sahel zone of western Africa, where many wild forms still exist. Bajra must have entered the western seaboard of India around 2000 BC. It has been found (somewhat doubtfully) at Hallur (Karnataka) in 1600 BC, and more certainly about five hundred years later in Ahar (Rajasthan) and in Saurashtra sites. Indeed bajra, jowar, and ragi, all of west African origin, show tip at about the same time in archaeological excavations in India. They are all current staple dietary items of the common folk in the west-lying areas of the country, made into baked rotis called bhakri (from bajra and jowar), or a porridge termed hittu, or a ball called muddhe (from ragi).

baking Though baking enjoys a Sanskrit term, putapaka, it is not a common style of Indian cooking. Ovens have been excavated at Mohenjodaro and other Indus Valley cities, but many of them are large kilns that were used to fire pottery and calcine metal ores. Baking in a tandoor, where the oven is open and intensely hot, has a somewhat different connotation and is perhaps more akin to grilling. Even the Vedic sacrifices enjoined such operations, using either a broken potsherd called kapala, or, for the purodasha offering, a clay plate called the garhyapatya with a number of hollows of different shapes and sizes that yielded cakes of varying kinds. In the Karnataka area, a hot tile called kenchu was once employed in domestic cooking.

balanced meal Drawing, without doubt, on ayurvedic practice, Kautilya in his *Arthashastra* recommends that 'a gentleman's meal' should consist of one prastha (an uncertain quantity, but perhaps around 500 grams) of pure unbroken rice, one-fourth this quantity of pulses, one-sixth of a prastha of ghee or oil, and one-sixty-fourth of a prastha of salt. For everyday consumption, Sushrutha recommended the shali (winter) rice, shastika, barley, mung, venison, butter, amla, rock salt, honey, and rainwater; these foods were considered least likely to upset the equilibrium of the body doshas. In general, quantities were not specified in ayurveda, but left to the capacity of each individual, with a warning to avoid overeating. The total quantity of food was termed sarvagraha.

bamboo An extract of green bamboo stems was one of the beverages permitted to Jain monks. The Ramayana lists tender bamboo leaves as among the edible items available to exiles in forest areas.

Bamboo shoots and bamboo rice, as the grains are called, are both edible delicacies. The *Shivatattvaratnakara* (c. AD 1700) of King Basavaraja of Keladi describes how bamboo shoots are steeped in salt water to remove astringency before shallow-frying, a procedure still used in the Kodagu district of Karnataka to make the dish called baimblay. Basavaraja also refers to bamboo rice as rajannaakki, or rice fit for a king. In Tamil it is called mungilarisi, a product, in the

Bajra field

Bamboo

and new shoots appear quickly. Seeds produced in such abundance are naturally an important famine food for the poor in those areas. The seeds resemble small grains of paddy, and are husked by pounding; the starchy grain is either cooked like rice, or ground and baked into a roti.

banana Both the Sanskrit terms for the banana, mocha and kadali (from whence the Hindi kela), are believed to be of Munda origin. Mocha was adopted into the Latin botanical nomenclature for the banana, which is *Musa paradisiaca*, the fruit of paradise. The Tamil term vazhai is of indeterminate origin.

The banana is a rare example of a fruit in which three genes from one of its wild parents, *M. acuminata*, confer the ability to produce fruit without the need for seeds.

The word banana is of African origin, from banana, a single finger or toe, or its plural banan. The word was carried by African slaves to the Americas, where it became established. In British India the term plantain was in common use. Later it developed the connotation of a cooking, as opposed to an eating variety—an untenable distinction since many varieties are both. The word plantain is itself an anglicization of the Spanish plantano, still in use in the Philippines, and derived perhaps from the Latin planta, for a spreading leaf.

Foreign visitors to India noted the

Sangam period, of mountainous kurinji areas. As venuyava, the bamboo grain is first mentioned by Apasthamba (*c.* 400 BC) as an uncultivated foodgrain which is a permitted food for ascetics who have renounced the world. Bamboo rice is an unusual commodity. A Kodava verse states that once in sixty years bamboos decay, and once in seventy years famine holds sway. A whole thicket of bamboos will flower, set grain profusely, and die; the seeds fall abundance and variety of bananas. Ludovico di Varthema, who was mainly in the Vijayanagar region in AD 1505, described three varieties—one long, one short and sweet, and one bitter.

Among the several fruit juices, panaka, permitted to Buddhist monks was that from the banana, and green bananas were permitted at an ancestral shraddha ceremony. In ayurvedic parlance, the banana is classed as a cold food, which suppresses pitta.

Ripe bananas are an ingredient of southern confections. The unni-appam of the Ganesha temple in Kerala takes the form of spongy fried pieces of a mixture of rice powder, banana, jackfruit, and jaggery. Thin banana slices are deep-fried in coconut oil to crisp yellow chips, and trucker wedges are dipped in jaggery paste ground with ginger, before deep-frying. The koaleputtu of Kodagu is a mash of ripe bananas, roasted rice powder, and wedges of coconut, steamed in a banana leaf packet, and eaten hot or cold with fresh butter.

Green bananas are cooked in the south and east as a vegetable. The Kerala aviyal (q.v.) uses it. The core of the banana stem, called thod, is also a delicacy, and features in a meal served to the mystic Chaitanya (AD 1480–1533) by his admirer Sarvabhauma.

Banana leaves are large and waterproof, tailor-made for use as disposable plates that avoid cross-pollution. Concepts of ritual purity also dictate that while bananas, and other fruits with enveloping skins, can be bought in the marketplace

Banana tree

even after being handled by all and sundry; when brought into the kitchen area and peeled, they become restricted kaccha foods to be used only by members of the family.

banyan With its aerial roots descending into the earth, and the huge canopies that it creates, the banyan tree, *Ficus benghalensis*, was an object of astonishment to visitors to India. Its small, insipid fruit was described as a fig by Pliny the Elder (AD 23–79) in his encyclopaedic *The Natural History*, and it is mentioned in the earliest Sanskrit text, the *Rigveda* (*c.* 1500 BC). Though at best an emergency human food, banyan figs are relished by birds. Banyan figs, and those from related trees, are shunned by Jains (q.v.). Banyan leaves are stitched together using bamboo slivers to yield waterproof and disposable cups and plates, which keep well on drying, even if they are somewhat brittle.

barks The astringent barks of trees like the kapittha (*Limonia acidissima*), mesashringi (*Gymnema sylvestre*), and kadamba (*Anthocephalus cadamba*) were employed historically to flavour wines and distilled liquors. Cinnamon (q.v.) and cassia barks constitute condiments.

barley One of the oldest staple foods, which originated in the Fertile Crescent area of the Middle East. The wild forms are only 2-rowed, but after about 6000 BC, cultivated forms that are both 2-rowed and 6-rowed appear. The finds of barley at Mehrgarh in Afghanistan after 5000 BC, and in neolithic Chirand (*c.* 3500 BC) in

Barley field

Bihar, are all cultivated 6-rowed forms, but of two types, naked and hulled. Today naked forms are preferred for growing in hilly areas, and hulled forms in the plains.

In the Indus Valley, barley accompanied wheat as a staple in Mohenjodaro, but in Chanhudaro, where the alkaline soil is less suited to wheat, barley appears to have been the main staple. Later sites in western India like Inamgaon (1600–700 BC) near Pune, and Jorwe (750 BC) have yielded barley. In Vaghbhata's time around the seventh century AD, barley was a distant second to rice as a staple, though it was ahead of wheat. Today it is only a minor cereal crop.

Barley in Sanskrit is yava, the only cereal mentioned in the *Rigveda*. It was eaten thereafter in many ways: as saktu (sattu) or coarse flour; in fried form; as apupa or cakes of barley flour, which were then boiled or fried and dipped in honey; after parching to dhanah and eaten as a gruel, vatya; and ground and mixed with jaggery to yield abhyusa. It was a staple recommended to Buddhist monks for daily use. Barley was prescribed by Sushrutha for loss of appetite, debility, and thirst.

Visitors to India noted the use of barley as a food of the poor in about AD 1200 in Kashmir. It was the base of a sweet drink called fuqqa in the Delhi Sultanate court

c. AD 1340. Its use as a food for horses about the same time is remarked on by Ibn Battuta, and about two centuries later in Vijayanagar by Domingo Paes.

basil *Ocimum sanctum* is an ancient aromatic herb with a Sanskrit name, thulasi, that may even be of aboriginal origin. The small shrub with ash-green leaves is sacred to Vishnu, and is grown on a square brick pedestal-urn in almost every Hindu courtyard, and worshipped daily. Decoctions of the leaves are used against common colds and skin complaints.

Basil (tulsi)

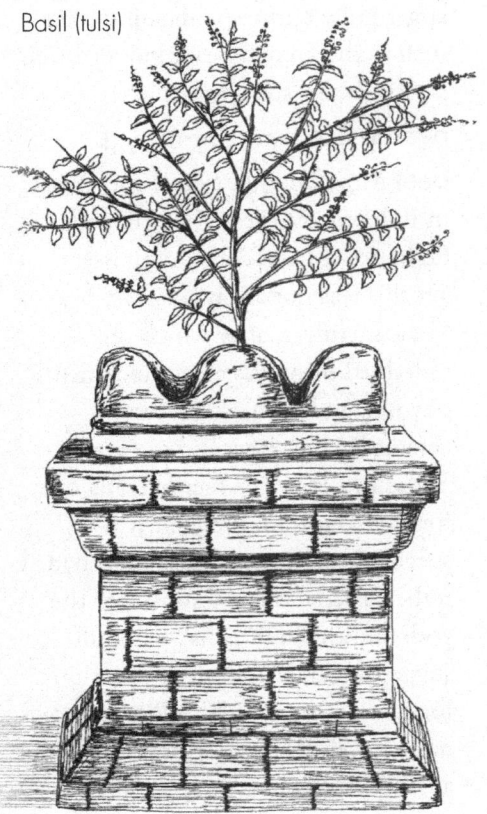

bath Derived from the Sanskrit bhatka, the term bath (more correctly bhath) means a pottage, generally made of rice or wheat. It is perhaps of more frequent use in south India. Thus kesari-bath is a sweet thick concoction of fried wheat grits flavoured with saffron stamens (kesar) which impart a golden colour and a fragrant aroma. Vangi-bath is a Tamil dish of brinjals and rice with tamarind spicing.

beans Term often loosely used for any legume, and especially for masha (urad or black gram), when translating Sanskrit texts into English. It is more appropriately applied to larger pulse entities with shiny coats such as the French bean, kidney bean, haricot bean, and soybean.

beaten rice *See* aval; parching.

beef Most Hindus, Sikhs, and Parsis in India today, even when they eat flesh, desist from consuming beef. Yet this was not always so. The Vedic sacrifices, after which the sanctified meat was eaten, included bovines, and even at a funeral ceremony, the *Ashvalayana Grhya Sutra*s prescribe the sacrifice of a cow for consumption. Frequently it is specified that the sacrificed cow had to be a barren one, 'destined for the gods and the brahmans', or a bull, suggesting an economic motivation for sparing the cow. The *Rigveda* itself has two verses in praise of the cow as Aditi, the sinless one, yet in the

Shatapatha Brahmana, the imposing Vedic sage Yagnavalkya, after listening to all the arguments against eating beef, declares: 'That may well be; but I shall eat of it nevertheless if the flesh be tender (amshala).' In their *Dharmasutra*s, Vasishta, Gautama, and Apasthamba prohibit eating the flesh of both cows and draught oxen, while Baudhyayana exacts penances for killing a cow, and stricter ones for a milch animal or draught ox. Starting with prohibitions on cow slaughter for ritual brahminical sacrifice, revulsion spread to the eating of all types of beef derived in such sacrifices, and eventually to all slaughter for food.

The observant visitor Al-Biruni in the mid-eleventh century AD gives his reasons why cow-eating 'though prevalent earlier, was not allowed later'. 'Other Hindus told one that the Brahmans used to suffer from the eating of cow's meat ... as it is essentially thick and cold ... the power of the digestion is so weak that they must strengthen it by eating the leaves of the betel after dinner, and by chewing the betel nut.... As for the economic reason, we must keep in mind that the cow was the animal which serves man in travelling by carrying his load, in agriculture in the works of ploughing and sowing, and in the household by the milk and the products made from it. Further man makes use of its dung, and even of its breath. Therefore it was forbidden to eat cow's meat.' Perhaps surprisingly, even Emperor Humayun in the late sixteenth century AD decided, after much reflection, that 'beef was not a food fit for the devout'.

Beef continued to be eaten by non-brahmins. Sushrutha even described beef as being a pavitra or pure food. Today even Hindus who eat meat avoid beef. The Syrian Christians of Kerala relish beef; eracchi-olathiyathu is a fried beef dish served at their weddings, eracchi-thoran is a dry cubed beef dish, and kappa-kari is beef cooked with pieces of tapioca. Bohri Muslims have a malai-tikka kabab of beef, and most, but not all, Muslims partake of beef.

In India buffalo (q.v.) meat is also termed beef. The Ramayana reflects the mores of kshatriya nobility, and for a feast given by King Dasharatha, the father of Rama, 'buffalo calves (were) roasted on spits with ghee dripping on them'. Buffalo meat, in the view of Edward Terry (c. AD 1600), was not as 'wholesome' as English beef.

The people of south India, before the advent of the Aryans, relished beef, as reflected in the literature of the Sangam age (q.v.), and old Tamil even had four names for it. The *Perumpanuru* describes a fat bull being slaughtered in the open, and even the meat of the buffalo was eaten.

beer Beer was imported by the British from almost the start of their

stay in India. Beer manufactured on European brewing principles was first produced in the country in AD 1825 in Shimla. By the Second World War some 3 million gallons were being produced annually.

bellows Made of leather and fitted with an outlet tube, the bellows for fanning embers to a blaze was termed dhmatr in Sanskrit.

Bengal gram So called because it was first encountered by the British in Bengal, the Bengal gram is chanaka in Sanskrit, chana in Hindi, kadalai in Tamil, chickpea in English, and botanically *Cicer arietnum*. The khalva of the *Yajurveda* (c. 1000 BC) may refer to it, while chanaka occurs in early Buddhist writings (c. 400 BC). It has been found in 2500 BC layers in the Indus Valley site of Kalibangan, and slightly later in Atranjikhera. The postulated centre of origin of the chickpea is the Caucasus or Asia Minor, and it shows up as early as in 5400 BC in Hacilar in Turkey.

In the event, two seed types evolved: in India a small, wrinkled, dark-coloured seed, and in the Mediterranean a larger, smooth, light-coloured one. The very large kabuli chana (which is made into the spicy relish chole) is a very recent introduction into India, perhaps in the eighteenth century from the Mediterranean by an overland route. South India may have received the chickpea only as late as around 500–300 BC, probably from overseas, since the Tamil word kadalai (meaning seashore) bears no resemblance to the Sanskrit. Tamil Sangam literature (q.v.) refers to 'the bean that grows on stout creepers' which is 'fried in sweet-smelling oil'. This could well refer to the spiced sundal snack of the present.

Bengal gram is the major pulse of India. The whole pulse is cooked in a gravy or to dryness, or is cooked with gourd in Bengal. It can be cooked in Karnataka (q.v.) with greens to give a melogara, or in sweetened milk to yield a payasam. The chickpea is an auspicious item, the use of which is banned in a house of mourning.

Puffing the gram in hot sand causes the skin to loosen and the grain to swell to a crunchy, shining, yellow product. This can be cooked in water as a dhal dish, or fashioned into laddus using jaggery or sugar syrup, or shaped into vadas and deep-fried. Grinding puffed Bengal gram yields the versatile yellow flour besan (q.v.).

Bengali food Bengal has always had an abundance and variety of food. A medieval text, the *Shunya Purana*, notes that fifty kinds of rice were then grown in Bengal. European visitors later exclaimed in wonder at its bounty: 'The country abounds in grain of every kind, sugar, ginger, the best place in the world to live in' (Varthema, *c.* AD 1505). And from Bernier (*c.* AD 1660): 'Bengal abounds in every necessity of life ... rice ... wheat ... three or four sorts

An assortment of Bengali food

of vegetables ... geese and ducks ... goats and sheep ... pigs ... fish of every species, whether fresh or salt, in the same profusion ... this is a fertile kingdom.'

Bengal has long been the home of the sugarcane. From the Pundra area emanated the famed paundra variety of superior sugarcane, which Charaka contrasts with the inferior vainsaka variety. Even the Sanskrit word guda for jaggery is stated by Charaka (though others demur) to be derived from the old name for Bengal, Gauda. Apart from the sugarcane, another source of jaggery in Bengal was the sweet juice that flowed from incisions in the trunk of the palmyra palm, which was collected in clay pots smeared with lime to prevent fermentation. This was then boiled down in cauldrons and stirred with wooden ladles till the 'strike' occurred, when the hot mass was transferred to smaller vessels to set. Palm jaggery gives a distinctive flavour and sweetness when used in Bengali sandesh and sweet curd (mishti-doi).

Panicum grains were grown even a century ago in Bengal, and termed chinakaon. Bananas abound: a small, sweet variety, chapal, was served to Chaitanya in about AD 1530, and sonkel and bankel are current varieties. Certain exotic fruits first took root in Bengal. Pineapples are one; the litchi fruit from China is another, and so is the large citrus, the pomelo. Being the seat of the British empire in India for a century and a half, a Royal Botanic Garden was set up in Sibpur in AD 1787 which served as the conduit and nursery of many exotic food plants brought into India. These include tea, coffee, maize, tapioca, potato, arrowroot, several European vegetables, cocoa, vanilla, and new varieties of ginger and cardamom.

The range of food materials in moist and fertile Bengal is exceptionally wide. A variety of harmonious combinations is employed: pumpkin and shrimps, pumpkins and stems of puin (the climbing spinach), urad dhal with spices like saunf, ginger, and asafoetida, whole chana with gourd, and sponge gourd with posto (poppy seeds). Green bananas and ginger are considered an incompatible combination. Flowers of the pumpkin and banana are eaten, so is the pith of the banana, called thod. Tender drumsticks, water reeds, raw jackfruit, and the peels of the potato and pumpkin are utilized. A spice mixture of five seed components unique to Bengal is panchphoron, consisting of equal quantities of onion seed, celery seed (radhuni, which can be substituted with mustard seeds), aniseed, fenugreek, and cumin (jeera).

The style of cooking in West Bengal differs from that in East Bengal (now Bangladesh). The staple in both is of course rice, but the latter hardly employs dhal and is strong on fish. West Bengalis prefer fish bred in tanks and estuaries, like mangor and tapsee, and East Bengalis fish from big rivers, but the river fish hilsa is rated highly everywhere. Both cuisines employ mustard seeds in several ways: fried in oil, carefully crushed to yield a pungent paste, and as a source of oil used as a cooking medium. The choice of spices is different, with a liberal use of poppy seeds (posto) in West Bengal. The latter cuisine is strong on fried stuffed snacks like kachuri and singhada, and in a variety of milk-based sweets.

The procession of tastes at a Bengali meal runs from a bitter start to a sweet finish. Lunch will start with a bitter item shukto (this is usually omitted at dinner) made from neem or other bitter leaves, the bittergourd, brinjal, potato, radish, and green bananas, with spice pastes that use turmeric, ginger, mustard, and celery seed. Rice is first savoured with hot ghee, salt, and green chillies; then comes dhal accompanied by fried vegetables (bhaja) or boiled vegetables (bhata), followed by spiced vegetable items like dalna and ghonto. Then come fish items, first lightly spiced ones like maccher-jhol, and then those more heavily spiced, followed by a sweet-sour ambal or tauk (chutney), and fried papads. A dessert of mishti-doi (accompanied by dry sweets), or payesh (accompanied by fruits like the mango) ends the meal, with paan (a betel quid) as a terminal digestive. Meals were traditionally served on a large circular bell-metal thala and in bhatis (bowls), except for the sour items. The night meal might include fried wheat lucchis, a palao, and a dalna of delicately spiced vegetables. Bengali palao is of a sweetish kind, with raisins, dried fruits and nuts, coloured and flavoured with saffron. Bengal perhaps has the lowest proportion of vegetarians of any state in India. The brahmins of Bengal have from early times defended the eating of fish. After quoting the views of earlier arbiters like Yagnavalkya, Manu, and Vyasa, the brahmin politician and scholar Bhatta Bhavadeva (eleventh century AD) says: 'All this prohibition is meant for the prohibited days like chaturdasi and others ... so it is understood that there is no crime (dosha) in eating fish and meat.' The reformer Srinathacharya also allowed Bengali brahmins the use of meat and fish except on some parvan days. Even the great Bengali spiritual leaders of recent times ate fish. In AD 1822 Ramakrishna Paramahamsa stated: 'I love to eat fish in any form', and it is on record that Swami Vivekananda enjoyed a nee meal that included a shukto of fish, maccher-jhol (a liquid fish curry), a sour fish preparation, sweet curd, and sandesh.

Even the Gowda Saraswath brahmins of Karnataka eat fish, probably a carry-over from their original home in Bengal (Gauda). The strict vegetarians of Bengal are the Vaishnavites centred in Navadvip (the home of Chaitanya) who consume neither meat nor fish, nor even 'hot' foods like onions and masoor dhal.

Bengali sweets The Bengali has always had a sweet tooth. Even in AD 1406, the Chinese admiral Ma Huan visiting Bengal notes the prevalence of 'white sugar, granulated sugar, candied or preserved fruit'. The *Chandimangala* (AD 1589) mentions kheer, rabdi (thickened and sweetened milk), manda, kandu, and nadu, and the *Chandidas Padavali* of the same period mentions various sweets (bibidha-mishta and sakar-mittai) which were distributed by his father Nanda when Sri Krishna was born, while the baby itself received from the cowherds anna, curds, mishta, mittai, chini (sugar), and small bananas (chapakola). Other works of the sixteenth century mention chhanabora, khaja, jilebi, pishtak, modak, malpo, sitamisri, and sandesh.

A new thrust to sweet-making in Bengal occurred when the Portuguese gathered there; by AD 1650 they numbered 20,000, being settled mostly near Hughli. They were skilled in the art of preparing sweet fruit preserves, and were fond of cottage cheese, which Bengali sweetmeat makers began to first furnish and then utilize in imaginative ways. Simple sweetened chhana is kanchagolla, but soon sandesh began to be cast in various moulds (to resemble flowers, fruits, and shells), given various colours, sweetened with palm jaggery, sugarcane jaggery, and sugar, sugar-coated to yield manohari and flavoured with jackfruit, orange peel, and rose essence. Sandesh (the name traditionally derived from the term given to the bringer of good news) has of course long been known, and may even have been a khoa-based product till the efflorescence of sweets

An assortment of Bengali sweets

based on chhana came about.

In 1868, 22-year-old Nobin Chandra Das created from chhana the spongy rasogolla cooked in sugar syrup. Some fifty years later his son Krishna Chandra Das created the rasmalai, flattened chhana patties floating in thickened sweet milk, which he went on to manufacture commercially through his firm, K.C. Das and Co. Many new products were developed by enterprising moiras; khir-mohan and cham-cham, mouchak (shaped like a beehive), sitabhog, resembling rice grains, gulab-jamun, lal-mohan and totapuri, fried products in sugar syrup, and the raisin-stuffed ledikeni, a corruption of Lady Canning, the Vicereine of India in whose honour it was created. Pantua and chitrakoot are again chhana-based, and in Bengal even the jilebi is termed chhanar-jilipi and employs chhana to create whorls that are deep-fried before placing in syrup. So numerous are professional sweet-meat makers, and so varied and excellent are their products, that households prefer to buy them, making at home only the simpler payesh and pithe desserts that derive from milk and thickened milk, rice, rava, coconut, and sugar or palm jaggery.

ber Fruits of the *Zizyphus* species are termed ber, and at least six varieties now grow in India. It is a very ancient fruit. A clay representation was found in Harappa, and carbonized remains in Navdatoli (*c.* 1600 BC). Sanskrit literature, starting with the *Yajurveda* and the *Brahmaads*, describes several varieties of ber fruit: the large badara or vadari (which Xuan Zang calls bhadra), the medium-sized kuvale or kharkhandu, the sauvira variety, and a wild type, orange in colour. Dalhana (*c.* AD 1100) of Kashmir talks of a 'ber as big as a fist, and very sweet'. Tamil Sangam literature also mentions the fruit.

In ritual eating terms, it was classed as a food that had to be chewed (like the grape and pomegranate), and was served at a meal before fruits like the orange, mango, date, and pieces of sugarcane that could be sucked. Ber fruit was permitted to Jain monks and was one source of the class of sweet fruit beverages termed panaka. Like certain other sweet fruits, the ber was also fermented to obtain alcohol. Dried ber fruits lose their sliminess and develop a slight sourness, like dried apple rings, that makes for pleasant eating.

besan Puffing the Bengal gram (q.v.) on hot sand also causes its brown covering to disengage, releasing a shiny yellow kernel. This is ground in stone mills (chakkis) to yield besan flour, or kadalai-mau in Tamil. It is the batter usually chosen to make deep-fried snacks. The batter by itself is deep-fried to yield a variety of crisp snacks, like pellets of boondi, strings of sev, and the Gujarathi snack forms nasto and ganthia. Boondi pellets, coarse or fine, are moulded with jaggery or sugar syrup into laddus, an ancient confection. The dhokla of Gujarat is curd-fermented besan steamed in a thick layer to a spongy yellow product, while the khandvi is a thin, rolled-up pancake of besan. Various materials may be dipped in besan batter and deep-fried: arvi-na-patra (colocasia leaves), bhaji or bhajji (onion rings, green chillies, and slices of potato, tomato, and brinjal), bonda (mashed potato), pakoda (perhaps cashews or groundnuts), and certain types of vadas. Fried lumps of fermented besan yield the wadi or warrian.

Baking besan together with grated coconut and sugar yields the sweet Goan concoction Dos de Grao, with a thick, firm crust, and a chewy centre. Mysore pak, with a delicious granular texture, is essentially besan cooked thick with ghee and sugar.

betel leaf *See* areca nut.

beverages In the past diverse materials furnished beverages. Panaka connoted the juices of sweet fruits like the mango, pomegranate, citrus, grape, date, ber (q.v.), banana (q.v.), apricot, and jackfruit. Three such fruit juices with honey and water constituted panchamrutha, while a panaka thickened by boiling down was yusa. Raga denoted the juice from sour fruits like the phalsa, tamarind, lime, and jamoon, sweetened with sugarcandy and spiced with black mustard seeds, while sadhava were sour fruit juices thickened over a fire. In south India, beverages were made from two sour materials, tamarind and nellikai (amla). The water of the tender coconut was an ancient southern thirst-quencher, and a mixture of this with sugarcane juice and the sweet sap of the palmyra palm yielded munnir, a popular drink with women in the *Purananuru*. A popular morning beverage all over south India was the water from boiled rice, soured overnight by fermentation to kanji or kanjika, and usually drunk salted and spiced.

Milk of course was itself a beverage of high prestige, but even more common was buttermilk, which was of two kinds. One was lassi, made by whisking curd with water, salt, and some spices (lemon, ginger, curry leaves). The other was chhas, the liquid left after curd has been churned and butter removed. Buttermilk was drunk to accompany a meal or as a refresher in summer; it was popular all over India, and has five names in old Tamil.

The natural sweet beverage of India was sugarcane juice, often drunk spiced with ginger. The Muslim advent in the second millennium AD brought in new types of sweet sherbets, often coloured and flavoured with essences like rose, kevda (screwpine), and herbs. The sweet falooda (q.v.) was a blend of milk or cream with the strainings (gluten) of boiled wheat, gelatinous seed granules (for which a later substitute was sago), and sometimes fruit juices. A drink called fuqqa, served at the court of the Delhi Sultanate in the thirteenth and fourteenth centuries, was based on barley.

Some beverages had medicinal qualities. The juice of the radish, parwal, and neem fruit was specified for fever by Sushrutha, and barley water (yavodaka) was prescribed for thirst, fever, and debility. Milk was indicated in dysentery and sugarcane juice for biliousness.

Two composite beverages had ritual significance. Panchagavya was the supreme purificatory material, mostly sipped ritually or even rubbed on the body. It was a mixture of five products derived from the cow—its milk, curd, ghee, urine, and dung, so sacred that no one other than a brahmin could use it! Madhuparka was an auspicious ritual beverage consisting of ghee, curd, milk, honey, and sugar. It was offered when welcoming a guest to one's home, given to women after five months of pregnancy, placed at birth on the lips of the firstborn son, and offered to a student when he left home for a long apprenticeship with his guru. A suitor received it on arrival at a girl's home, and again when he arrived as a bridegroom for the wedding ceremony.

beverages, alcoholic As early as *c.* 2000 BC, the Indus Valley civilization seems to have practised not only alcoholic fermentation, but even distillation. From clay items found in excavation sites, a complete distillation outfit has been assembled. The distilled product may well have been the intoxicating liquid called sura (q.v.), derived from fermented rice and barley, which is condemned in the *Rigveda*.

Later Vedic literature mentions a sweetened drink made from fermented cereals called kilala, a filtered rice gruel liquor, masara, and a fermented product from certain flowers and grasses called parisruta. Subsequently, numerous liquors find literary mention. The Ramayana has four, Kautilya mentions twelve, and Charaka lists no less than eighty-four.

A variety of starchy or sweet materials was used for fermentation. These were grains (rice, barley), honey, sugarcane products, sap drawn from the coconut and palmyra tree, numerous sweet fruits (grape, mango, date, ber), and flowers (mahua, kadamba).

Among the grain-derived products were masara, kilala, kashaya, prasanna, and svetasura. With sugar as a base, madhira of a high quality was brewed, as well as the distilled liquor shidhu which was red in colour from the dhataki flowers that were added as a flavourant. Asava was a generic term to which was prefixed

Palmyra sap being extracted

the source, like pushpa- (flower), phala- (fruit), madhvika- (mahua), sharkara- (sugar), and narikela- (coconut). Asava is sometimes classed as simply an extract, but in other contexts it was a distilled drink with fruit and flower additives. From fruits as raw material come sanakarasura and mahasara (both probably from the mango), khajurasara (date), kadambari (the kadamba fruit), kaula (ber), and madhu and mrdvika (grapes). The alcoholic drinks that were flower-derived were parisruta, varuni (mahua), and jathi (jasmine). The distilled drinks were sura, madhya, and shidhu. The favourite drink of royalty was maireya, which was offered, for example, to Sita by Rama in the Ramayana; since kshatriyas were not permitted grain-based liquors, maireya must have been based on sugar or fruit, almost certainly distilled, and spiced, flavoured and often sweetened with expensive honey, with cheaper guda, or with even cheaper molasses. The sweet exudates from the spathes of the palmyra or coconut palm were fermented to yield thalakka (thari, toddy). From Afghanistan were imported kapisayani and harihuraka, derived from white and black grapes respectively.

At the height of its trade with Rome in the early Christian era, south India also imported wine in containers called amphorae (q.v.) for use by the nobility. But the common liquor was toddy derived from palmyra and neera saps. The *Purananuru* tells us that 'toddy flows like water in the port town of Muziris'. The best toddy was claimed to be made in Kuttanad, now in Kerala. From this toddy was distilled arrack, a favourite with sailors. Rice grains were also fermented 'in strong-mouthed jars', to yield 'in two days and two nights a high-flavoured wine'. A home-brewed product was called thoppi, and the wealthier people could add fragrant dhataki flowers during brewing. The flavour of wine was enhanced by filling it in the hollows of stout bamboo stems which were buried underground. Wine brewed from honey in mountainous regions was also matured underground. Mandai was the term used for the liquor drinking bowl.

Brewing was practised all over the country, as indicated by stray references. Extensive drinking was noted around AD 600 both in Kashmir and in Assam, where tribes brewed a rice beer called laopani. Xuan Zang in the seventh century noted that kshatriyas drank liquor brewed from the grape and sugarcane, vaishyas preferred strong distilled liquor, and brahmins drank only fruit juices.

The Quran prohibits the use of alcohol and of games of chance since 'in both there is great sin and harm'. Elsewhere wine is referred to indirectly as khamar, which means to cover up, because it clouds the brain. Despite this, the Muslim nobility in India did generally imbibe liquor right from the Sultanate period in Delhi. The first Mughal emperor, Babar, had periodic bouts of abstinence, when he would break up his flagons and goblets of gold and silver and give away the pieces, only to resume drinking and the use of bhang, with the explanation: 'The new year, the spring, the wine and the beloved are pleasing; enjoy them, Babar, for the world is not to be had a second time.' Akbar, according to Father Monserrate, rarely drank wine and preferred bhang. He enforced prohibition in court, but relaxed the law for European visitors. Jahangir, by the end of his reign, would imbibe twenty cups of double-distilled liquor in a day. Shahjahan drank in moderation, and Aurangzeb was a strict teetotaller who issued severe prohibitory orders on all his subjects, Hindu and Muslim alike. In contrast, his unmarried sister Jahanara Begum was extremely fond of wine.

From the beginning, drinking was frowned upon in the *Rigveda,* and subsequently always interdicted for brahmins and students. Yet the *Sutra*s enjoin that strong liquor be served to guests as they enter a new house, or when a bride first enters her husband's home. Kshatriyas and vaishyas could take liquor brewed from honey, mahua flowers, or jaggery, but not spirits distilled from fermented grain flours. Thus Sita promises the river Ganga a thousand jars of wine should the party return safe from exile. And when they do so, the atmosphere of Ayodhya reeks with wine as its citizens celebrate. The *Arthashastra* refers to public taverns in almost every village, well furnished with seats and couches.

The classic Indian medical authorities took a balanced view of drinking. Moderation was counselled, since alcohol increases the mental principle pitta, while diminishing both the physical and vitality principles, kapha and vata. A light wine mixed with mango juice could be enjoyed 'together with friends'. Wine was to be particularly avoided in summer and the rainy season, when the digestive fire was at its lowest ebb, but could be consumed in winter and spring.

In colonial times, Portuguese monks in Goa developed a distilled liquor with a distinctive flavour from the cashew 'fruit', called feni. The British administration noted the widespread production of toddy and arrack all over India. Being excisable items, some measure of control was attempted, especially in the Bengal Presidency. Rice wine was also made and distilled, as was that from mahua flowers; the latter was organized by Parsi distillers, working under British control, in the island of Uran off Bombay. The first distillery set up in India was in 1805 near Kanpur, and thirty years later another unit (still in production today) was installed in Rosa near Kanpur. By 1901 there were fourteen registered distillers, and at Independence in 1947 about forty, producing annually 10,000 LP gallons of potable spirit.

bhang It is doubtful whether the bhanga of the *Atharvaveda* is indeed *Cannabis saliva*, or refers to the Indian sunn-hemp, the plants of which look alike. The narcotic properties of bhang seem to have been realized only as late as in the tenth century, and in time three forms of use developed. Bhang refers to the dried leaves and flowering shoot, ganja to the dried flowering tops of female plants, and charas to the resinous exudate or an extract. Visitors to India have remarked on its widespread use. Linschoten (*c.* AD 1580) noted that the poor chewed bhang with nutmeg and mace (which disorder the mind), and the rich with cloves, camphor, amber, musk, and even opium.

birinj Persian for rice, from which is derived the name of the rice-meat dish biriyani. Birinj itself comes from the old Persian term virinzi for rice, which also gave rise to the vrihi of Sanskrit. The rice-milk sweet concoction was called kheer-birinj by the early Muslim Indian nobility.

biriyani A spicy dish of meat cooked with rice, referred to by this term in the thirteenth century. Numerous variations occur all over India. One is the kacchi-biriyani of Hyderabad, with the meat very soft and almost disintegrating into the rice, and irregular patches of yellow saffron colouring. A palao (q.v.) is very similar, and the word itself is of older usage in India. Recipes in the *Ain-i-Akbari* (AD 1590) show little distinction between a biriyani and a palao.

Biriyani

biscuit This is not a traditional Indian food item, though even in *c.* AD 1660 Francois Bemier does mention 'sweet biscuits flavoured with anise'. Biscuits were first imported into India from Britain in about 1847, and imports touched a peak figure of about 2200 tonnes annually before the Second World War. Manufacture in India started in *c.* AD 1885, and by Independence about 10,000 tonnes of several varieties were being produced.

Bittergourd (Karela)

The traditional nankhatai of western India resembles the biscuit.

bittergourd This is first mentioned as karivrnta, and later as karavella (Hindi kartla) in early Jain literature (*c.* 400 BC). Kannada literature of the sixteenth century refers to the practice of debittering the bitter-gourd by steeping it in salt water and washing it. Where a bitter-tasting food item is needed, as in the shukto of Bengal, bittergourd serves admirably. Rings of it deep-fried yield a crunchy relish, especially if first steeped in salt and dried. The vegetable can be cleaned out, stuffed with vegetables or minced meat, tied with string, and fried.

black gram *See* urad.

boar A fierce, tusked denizen of India's forests, hunting of the wild boar using dogs and nets is described in the Tamil Sangam literature of between the third and sixth centuries AD. It is valued as a strong meat. In an early work from Assam of between the sixth and eighth centuries AD, boar meat is specially recommended. A wild boar was sent by Jahangir to Sir Thomas Roe with a polite request that the tusks be returned. The Syrians of Kerala and the Kodavas of Coorg cook it with heavy spices to mask the strong flavour, or pickle it in oil, or smoke-dry it for later currying or roasting. The British considered wild boar fine eating, but were chary of the domestic pig unless farm- or home-raised.

bottlegourd A climbing plant that originated in Africa, but has been in India for so long that it is described (as alabu) even in the *Rigveda*. Now called lauki, *Lagenaria siceraria* is widely used as a soft vegetable. The hard-dried shells find use as water bottles, blowing horns, and musical wind instruments, for example those used by snake charmers.

Bower manuscript Discovered early in the twentieth century in a monastery, the text of the so-called Bower manuscript (after its discoverer) is essentially a copy of the *Charaka Samhita* (q.v.), with some extraneous material. It was probably compiled by four Buddhist monks from Kashmir who had migrated to Kuchar. A major topic in the work relates to the medicinal value of lasuna (garlic).

brandy Not an indigenous liquor, but extensively imported all throughout the colonial period for either direct use or blending, for example in a punch (q.v.). By 1900 it was being distilled in Shimla and Amritsar, and flavoured with imported essences, although an excellent Indian cherry brandy is also mentioned. By Independence, Indian production of brandy was 300,000 LP gallons, with imports alongside of 227,000 LP gallons.

bread Indigenous bread implies products like the roti, chapathi, parata, naan, tandoori, and so on (*see* roti). Western-style loaf bread, raised using yeast, was baked in the home almost all through the colonial period, and it was only around the 1920s that bread was made commercially; this was by hand, and in very unhygienic surroundings. In 1937 the Bengal Presidency counted 470 very small bakeries, while the United Provinces had 134 bakeries, 'mostly of the teashop variety', in twenty large towns. In 1937 machine-made bread loaves were noted in 'one or two concerns in Calcutta and Bombay'; large hygienic bakeries were set up only after Independence.

breadfruit *Artocarpus atilis*, native to the South Pacific islands, was introduced into India perhaps

in colonial times, and is used as a vegetable. It is far less popular than the ancient related jackfruit (q.v.), *A. heterophyllus*.

brinjal The Sanskrit words vrntaka and vartaka may be of earlier Munda origin, and the brinjal (Hindi baingan, Portuguese bringella, English eggplant or aubergine) may have originated from a wild ancestor in India by human selection for reduced spininess and bitterness, bigger fruit size, and annual habit. The brinjal comes in a variety of shapes and sizes (small and globular, large and long) and colours (purple, green, yellowish, white, striped), and is found abundantly all over India. The many ways in which it can be cooked are well illustrated in the historical literature of Kannada. Thus the brinjal could be seasoned with ghee, salt, methi, urad, and cream before boiling; or coated with ghee, roasted on live coals, and mashed to a baji (bartha); or cut into small pieces and cooked with jaggery.

Boar

Yet again, the brinjal could be fried along with rice grits and chopped onions, wrapped in a turmeric leaf, and steamed to give a pude, a generic dish. An uncooked dish consisted of a brinjal mash with coconut shreds and curry leaves, flavoured with asafoetida and cardamom. In Bengal, wedges of brinjal are spiced and lightly fried, and it can form part of a bitter shukto dish. Brinjals stuffed with their own mashed and spiced contents, or with spiced minced meat (a dish called purabhattaka in the *Manasollasa* of AD 1130) and then shallow-fried, are delicacies everywhere. Tamarind-spiced rice cooked with brinjal is termed vangi-bath in the Tamil country.

broad bean *Vicia faba* is probably of Mediterranean origin, with a 6250 BC find in Jericho. It seems to have first been cultivated and acclimatized on the Himalayan heights before it was introduced in the plains for use as a vegetable that has the Hindi name bakla.

Buddhist food and literature

Canonical Buddhist literature consists essentially of three *Pitaka*s written in a dialect of Sanskrit, Pali, and are termed *Vinaya, Sutta,* and *Abhidamma.* Also relevant are the *Dhammapada,* 400 verses expounding Buddhist ethics, and the 500-odd *Jataka* tales relating to the Buddha's previous incarnations as a man, animal, and tree. A rough nodal date

for these works is 400 BC.

Frequently, food materials find mention for the first time in writing in these works. Examples by way of pulses are the chanaka (chickpea, Bengal gram), the small marbled green pea kalaya, and the cowpea or lobia, nishpava. The *Mahavagga* of the *Vinaya Pitaka* (along with the roughly contemporary Sanskrit *Dharmasutra*s) refer to hingu (asafoetida), and the use of the black mustard seed as a condiment. Several common fruits first find mention in Buddhist literature, like the coconut, banana, jackfruit, palm, tinduka (*Diospyros melanoxylon*), grapes, phalsa, karamoda, and several citrus species. In the Buddhist *Jataka* tales there occurs the first reference to sugarcane crushing in a yantra (machine).

The Buddha's own views on food are stated to be recorded in the *Lankavatara Sutra:* 'I enjoin the taking of food made out of rice, barley, wheat, mudga, masha, masura and other grains, ghee, oil of sesamum, honey, molasses, sugar, fish, eggs and others, which are full of soul qualities but devoid of faults; they were consumed by the Aryas and rishis of yore.' On many occasions he counselled moderation in order to guard 'the doors of the organs of sensation', meaning lack of self-control, or enjoyment of the pleasures of the table. Monks were advised to eat solid foods only between sunrise and noon, and nothing between noon and sunrise; this would subdue passions and lead to spiritual strength. Anything that was offered, whether coarse food or no food, should be accepted without cavil. Among the eight essential items permitted to a Buddhist monk were a begging bowl and a water-strainer.

The desire not to distress the giver of food, and to avoid the extreme austerities of orthodox brahmins, led the Buddha to turn down suggestions that meat and fish consumption be prohibited for Buddhist monks. However the flesh eaten had to be 'blameless' in three ways: the killing should not have been seen or heard, or suspected by the monk (adrastam, asrutam, aparivirtakam), it being the responsibility of the person giving the food as alms to ensure this. The *Mahayana Sutras*, in particular the *Lankavatara*, stress total ahimsa (q.v.). In the third century AD, the Buddhist Emperor Ashoka practised and preached non-killing. Indian Buddhists, though few in number, are vegetarians, but the Hinayana monks of China and South-East Asia, and the Tantric Buddhists of Tibet, have generally consumed flesh foods. Even with regard to liquor, wine was permitted to Buddhist monks when they were ill.

Eight drinks were permitted to Buddhists: the juices of the ripe mango, jamoon, banana, grape,

phalsa, coconut, edible water-lily, and diluted honey. These could be consumed after the last (noon) meal of the day. For drinking, pure rainwater was recommended. Water meant for drinking had to be 'clear, cool, shining like silver, health-giving and with the fragrance of the lotus'. Food was viewed as of two types. Panchabhojanyas were soft and wet foods, such as rice, boiled barley, peas, and baked cakes, that could be swallowed, while panchakhadinyas were hard and solid foods that needed chewing, like roots, stalks, leaves, and fruit.

Two Buddhist Chinese pilgrims who visited India about fifty years apart left accounts of the meals served to them at the great Nalanda monastery. Shaman Hwui Lui, the disciple of Xuan Zang (AD 629–645) I, records:

Every day he received 120 jambhiras (*Citrus jambhiri* fruits), 20 areca nuts, 20 nutmegs, a tael (*c.* 30 grams) of camphor, and a shang measure (perhaps about 6 kg) of mahashali rice. This rice is as large as the black bean (urad), and when cooked is aromatic and shining, like no other rice at all. It grows only in Magadha, and nowhere else. It is offered only to the king, or to religious persons of great distinction, hence its name mahashali, or in Chinese kung-ja-tin-mai (rice offered to the great householder). He was also supplied every month with three tou (3 kg?) of oil, and as regards milk and butter he took as much every day as he needed. I Ching (AD 671–695) says that on arrival guests were offered one of the eight syrups prescribed by the Buddha. At a meal, monks were first served with two pieces of ginger with some salt, and then boiled rice, on which was poured a thin extract of beans, and hot ghee; these were mixed with the fingers, after which cakes, fruit, ghee, and sugar were served. Toothpicks were provided after the meal, and pure water for rinsing the mouth, and sometimes a perfumed paste with which to clean the hands. The beverages that accompanied the meal were cold or warm water, whey, buttermilk, or fermented sour rice gruel (kanjika). Betel leaves with fragrant spices were served at the end to help digestion, remove phlegm, and make the mouth fragrant.

In contrast to the prohibitions on monks, the food of ordinary Indian Buddhists resembled that of their brahmin contemporaries. Indeed Buddhist doctors followed ayurvedic principles, as did Jivaka, who was the Buddha's personal physician. A later Buddhist doctor of the seventh century AD, Vaghbhata, wrote a standard ayurvedic compendium, the *Ashtangahrdaya Samhita*, which deals extensively with the choice of food in relation to the season. The *Rasaratnakara* of Nagarjuna, a Buddhist doctor-monk of south India

of about the same period, enlarged classical ayurvedic concepts with his own pioneering contributions on the use of metals, like black sulphide of mercury, for rejuvenation.

buffalo Referred to as buff, buffe, and buffle by the early Europeans in India, the Indian buffalo (from the Portuguese bufalo) was wrongly also called the water buffalo, presumably from its penchant for wallowing to escape the heat. *Bos bubalus* is derived from a wild species of east Bengali origin. It is known to have played an important part in the cultivation of the swampy Gangetic plain by the early Aryans. While only a beast of burden in South-East Asia, in India it has also been a source of both milk and, less so, of meat (q.v. beef).

Buffalo milk is far richer in fat than that of the Indian cow (8 and 4.5 per cent respectively). In south India especially it has long served admirably for preparing domestic curd and butter, and more recently to give body to the strong coffee brew. In the barter system of early south India, a herdsman's wife, in exchange for ghee, 'accepts, not a piece of fine gold, but instead a she-buffalo, a cow, or a black heifer, worth its value'. The *Nilamata Purana* (sixth century AD) mentions its use in Kashmir, and Ibn Battuta in the fourteenth century AD relished a porridge of dehusked shama grains mixed with buffalo milk. Even today the Todas of the

Nilgiri hills in south India breed buffaloes ritually, centred around dairy temples.

Buffalo meat was declared edible in the *Brhat Samhita* and must have been a food in regular use. As late as in the eleventh century AD Al-Biruni observed that the killing of the buffalo by brahmins was allowed. Another fourteenth-century traveller noted that in certain dry tracts adjacent to the Sindh desert, fish and buffalo meat were plentifully available. In about AD 1600, Edward Terry commented that buffalo flesh 'was like beef, but not so wholesome'.

butchers From early Vedic days, the marketplace had separate stalls for the vending of the meat of various animals, such as gogataka for cattle, arabika for sheep, shukarika for swine, nagarika for deer, shakuntika for fowl, and giddabuddaka for alligator and tortoise. The abattoir for beef was called garaghatanam and for swine shukarasam. With the advent of the Muslims, it became necessary to ensure that the prescribed ritual procedure of halal was followed. In this an animal is slaughtered by cutting its jugular vein, or by piercing the hollow of the throat, using a sharpened knife, and allowing the blood to flow, while uttering the name of Allah. Most butchers in India today are Muslim.

butter Being a perishable commodity, butter is much less used in India than is its clarified product ghee, which has always been the cooking and table medium of choice. A pat of fresh butter sometimes accompanies certain items at the table, like sarson-ka-saag, or a masala-dosa, or the steamed jackfruit relish of Kodagu, koale-puttu. The ancient Vedic sacrifices had a special vessel, sapirdhana, to hold butter, and it was one of the five cow-based components of panchagavya (q.v.), the supreme purificatory concoction. Freshly churned butter in Sanskrit is navaneetha; this was a favourite with the god Krishna, who as a child annoyed his mother by stealing it right out of her churning pot.

Various devices were in use all over the country to churn diluted curds into butter. A common device, sculpted in the thirteenth-century Khajuraho temples, consists of a long stick, with a corrugated device fixed at the bottom which was pulled to and fro by women using a rope

Bread

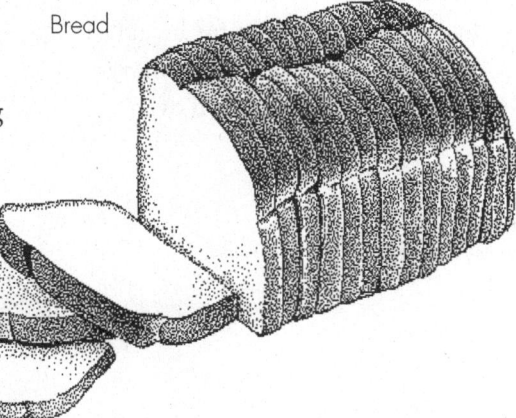

wound round the stick. The Sangam Tamil literature (q.v.) of south India, between the third and sixth centuries AD, vividly describes the making and vending of vennai (butter). The sound of the churning is poetically compared to the 'growl of a tiger'. After churning, the cowherd's wife sets off to sell butter, 'placing the pot, with its speckled mouth on her head, supported by a circlet of flowers'.

Vegetables in south India are described as being cooked in fresh cow's butter. However, references to cooking in butter by foreign visitors to India are suspect; more likely this was in ghee, a commodity unfamiliar to strangers.

Early colonialists made butter at home from cream, often separated from the milk of their own cows, by placing it 'in very large open-mouthed bottles, which were closely stoppered and then thumped up and down on the ground'. Fresh butter is an item mentioned at an afternoon meal in Calcutta in 1780 by Mrs Eliza Fay, and about a century later Edward Lear (of limerick fame) had bread and butter for breakfast. By 1905, there were 48 Military Dairy Farms scattered all over India, and their surplus production of butter and other western-style dairy products could be bought by civilians. In 1947, major Military Dairy Farms were operating in Quetta, Rawalpindi, Pune, Pimpri, Kirkee, Jabalpur, and Secunderabad. The first distribution on a national scale was by the Polson Model Dairy in Anand, Gujarat, which packed salted butter in tins or waxed paper cartons. In 1947 some 8000 tonnes of this kind of butter was produced.

buttermilk *See* beverages.

buryron Term used by contemporary Italian writers for the ghee exported in leather skin bags from south India to Rome in the first two centuries of the Christian era.

Byculla soufflé This concoction of the Byculla Club in Bombay is said to embody 'the epicurean standards of the Raj at its best'. Four liqueurs (kummel, green chartreuse, orange curacao, and benedictine) were stirred into a warm gelatine solution. This was folded gently into thick, beaten-up double cream, along with some eggs whisked with a little sugar, and the whole was served in bowls topped with macaroon crumbs.

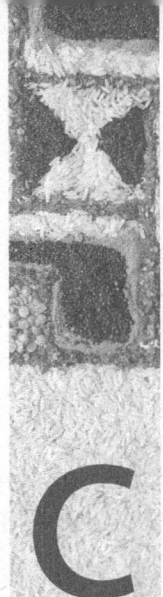

C

cabbage *See* cauliflower.

cakes Western baked sweet confections in India date only from colonial times, but the term is rather loosely applied in translations of historical literature into English, to roasted, rather than baked, items. Thus the Vedic sacrifice employed two items, the ashtaka and the purodasha, that were roasted on potsherds and are referred to as cakes. Even the steamed idli would be described loosely as a rice cake.

calamondin The fruit of *Citrus madurensis,* called hazara, a local, unclassified Indian citrus variety. Others are the Rangpur lime (*C. limoni*) and the Guntur sour orange, *C. maderasapatna.* Not all authorities give these citrus varieties even a species ranking.

camphor The karpura of Sanskrit may be an indigenous term, or a derivation from the Javanese kapur, or vice versa. In AD 1585 Ralph Fitch accurately noted that though camphor was much used in India, it came from China, while the best type was from the great island of Borneo. This seems to have always been so, since the Indian tree *Cinnamomum camphorum,* from the exudate of which camphor is steam-distilled or sublimed, is a far poorer source than the *Dryobalanops aromatica* of Indonesia. Yet the use of camphor in India, not only in religious rituals, but also in food items, is fairly old. The Indian medical authorities knew of both types of camphor, the pakva type involving heating and therefore probably indigenous, and the apakva type, natural and perhaps imported. The export of camphor from south India in the early Christian era is mentioned, but these could have been re-export.

With regard to food, the use of camphor to flavour pickles in the Karnataka area is noted in AD 1130, and in a curd-rice dish in Gujarat in AD 1520. Wealthy people used it as an ingredient in a betel quid; it was used with four other expensive spices by the royalty as a panchasugandha; by the gentry of Kerala in AD 1563 (Garcia da Orta); and in the *Lingapurana* in Kannada in AD 1594. In AD 1598 Linschoten noted that the wealthy chewed bhang (opium) along with aromatic spices that included camphor. Camphor was an item served daily in the seventh century AD to Xuan Zang while resident in the Nalanda Buddhist monastery, perhaps to flavour his betel quid or drinking water, or for use as incense.

caper The sour bud and fruit of *Capparis decidua*, mentioned in the *Rigveda* as karira, is eaten pickled, both in green and ripe form. Caper sauce is a popular accompaniment to baked fish in the West, a practice which continued in colonial India.

capsicum The comparatively 'sweet' bell-pepper or capsicum is one of many types of the chilli (q.v.) family, *Capsicum annuum*, that came to India from Mexico following the opening up of sea-routes from Europe to America and India. It is cooked as a vegetable.

caraway The shajira (*Carum carvi*) is not a traditional Indian product, being native to the Middle East and mostly imported. Two Indian seeds resemble it somewhat. These are *Trachyspermum ammi* (ajwain, omum, whose main constituent is thymol rather than the carvone of caraway) and *T. roxburghianum* (ajmud, radhuni or celery seed, which is one component of the Bengali spice mixture panchphoron).

cardamom This spice is of southern origin, with cognizance as elain in the *Arthashastra* (*c.* 350 BC). A substitute for *Elettaria cardamomum* is the large Bengal cardamom, badi-elaichi, or daruharidra in Sanskrit, from *Ammomum aromaticum*, which is raised in Bengal and Assam. The distinction is made even in the *Manusmriti*, and clearly spelled out with correct Sanskrit and Sri Lankan names by Garcia da Orta in AD 1563.

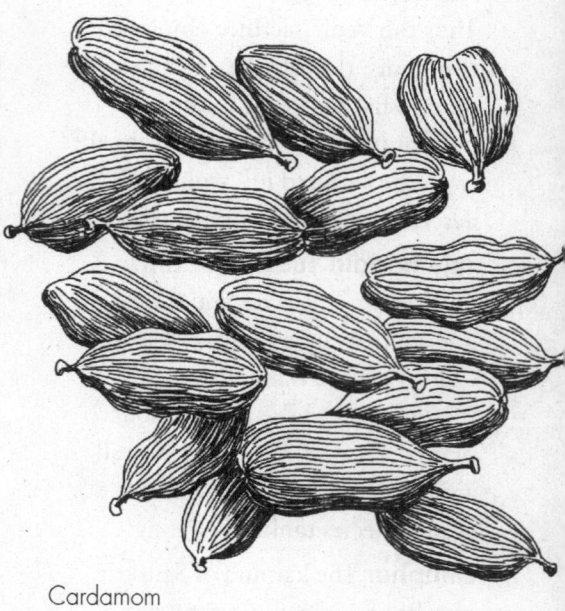

Cardamom

Apart from the large Bengal cardamom, three cardamom types are at present recognized in the trade: the inferior Sri Lankan, the palegreen and more delicate Mysore, and the larger and more robust Alleppey green (now grown in Kerala, but originally derived from Mysore).

Cardamom flavouring is popular in a wide range of dishes. It is used in the samyava of Charaka, a confection of wheat flour, milk, ghee, and sugar, and the kasara of the *Manasollasa*, which employs the same ingredients. A curd-rice flavoured with several spices including the cardamom features in a work of the eighteenth century AD from Maharashtra, and an unfried brinjal baji in early Karnataka was flavoured with camphor and cardamom. Fruit juice beverages, panaka, and some using whey and sugar, are mentioned as being cardamom-flavoured in the *Manasollasa*. Kashmiri tea brewed in samovars is frequently flavoured with it. As is to be expected, there is mention of the cardamom in early south Indian literature. As a component of rather fancy betel quids, the cardamom finds a place in the panchasugandha-thambula of the *Manasollasa* and in the kulapivida, made with 12–15 betel leaves, in eighteenth-century Maharashtra.

carrot This is a very old vegetable in India, called in Sanskrit garjara (Hindi gajar) and shikamula. These constitute the *desi* carrots of today, globular in shape and greenish in colour (due to the presence of anthocyanins). George Watt remarks that the carrot 'seems to have been eaten, in India when in Europe it was scarcely more than a wild plant', and in the seventeenth century AD John Fryer remarks on the 'good carrots of the Deccan'. The primary centre of domestication is probably Afghanistan, and when the globular type moved westwards around the tenth century AD, it was transformed by breeding into the long, orange type, notably the horn carrots developed in Holland in the eighteenth century. European carrots were first acclimatized in Shimla; both types are now raised in India, the desi being preferred for making traditional carrot halwa. An underground tuber, the carrot is not a food item permitted to Jain monks.

cashew A native of southeast Brazil, the cashew must have been an early transfer, since even in AD 1578 Acosta describes the 'caiu ... found in the gardens at the city of Santa Cruz in the kingdom of Cochin'. The so-called cashew 'fruit' is really the swollen stalk or peduncle, from which Jesuit priests in Goa developed the strong distilled drink feni, with a distinctive flavour. The kidney shaped nut hangs below this 'fruit', as is aptly denoted by the Tamil word mundiri for it. In Kerala the nut is called parangi-mav or -andi (meaning foreign stone), and the fruit is called gomanga, perhaps because it came to Kerala from Goa. The name caju, which the Portuguese brought to India and which is still used in Indian languages, derives from the term acaju of the Tepi tribe of Brazil, which was later anglicized to cashew.

cassava *See* tapioca.

cassia *See* tejpat.

cattle In Baluchistan, where cattle were first domesticated in *c.* 5000 BC from the primitive form *Bos primigenus,* excavations show only the hump-backed form, *Bos indicus,* now called the zebu or Brahminy bull (perhaps from its association with Lord Shiva). The term zebu is of uncertain origin. Indus Valley seals clearly depict both the humped zebu and the urus with forward-pointing horns. The buffalo (q.v.) appears to have been domesticated in India, while the domestication of the goat and sheep preceded that of cattle in the same area. All these were well-known species in the Indus Valley. That cattle were beasts of burden then is certain from early cave paintings (q.v.), and from numerous clay representations of bullock carts and draught animals. In later Aryan times cattle came to be objects of near-veneration (*see* beef), and even the occupation of tending them was considered highly honourable. Fine Indian breeds were sent back to Greece by Alexander.

In colonial times, herds of some Indian dairy breeds were maintained in dairy farms. Pure Red Sindhis were maintained at the Allahabad Agriculture Institute, the Government Cattle Farm, Hosur, and the Imperial Dairy Research Institute, Bangalore, and pure Sahiwals in Lyallpur, Ferozepur, and Pusa. Other fine breeds are the Deoni, Gir, Hariana, Kankrej (this is the dewlapped animal that figures on an Indus Valley seal), Malvi, Sahiwal, Ongole, and Tharparkar. High-yielding buffaloes are the Nili, Surti, Nagpuri, Jaffarbadi, Mehsana, and Murrah (which was kept in many dairy farms). High-yielding goat breeds are the Jamna Pan and Bar Bari. The White Revolution ushered in during the 1950s brought about quick yield improvement by crossing Indian animals with very high-yielding foreign breeds like the Jersey, Holstein, and Frieisian, mostly using artificial insemination techniques.

cauldrons Even though the potter's wheel was known, very large cauldrons for ritual Vedic sacrifices were fashioned each time from clay by hand to very rigid specifications, and baked afresh (*see* ashvamedha). Among such huge cooking vessels were the general-purpose shrapana; the ukha, a square pot for cooking flesh; the wide-mouthed mahavira for heating milk and ghee; the gharma for boiling milk; and the kumbha for boiling rice.

The last-mentioned later became a standard measure of volume.

cauliflower The phool-gobhi (cauliflower), like the gobhi (cabbage) and ganth-gobhi (knol-khol), all varieties of *Brassica oleracea*, were introductions into India after *c.* AD 1850 for use by colonials, but are now extensively cultivated for general use as vegetables, with an anti-diabetic reputation.

chakki The term chakki for grinding stones is derived from the Sanskrit chakra (wheel, to turn) by way of the dialectical chakka. The chakki takes the form of circular stones held slightly apart, either vertically or horizontally, for dehusking or grinding wheat, rice, and pulses. Animal and water power used for centuries was later replaced by oil engines and electricity. A stout circular stone with a central hole found both at Mohenjodaro and Lothal was initially identified as part of a chakki, but is more likely to be either a pulley placed atop a well, or an edge-runner working in a trough for mixing or grinding. The double chakki in common domestic use, with an upright peg on the periphery, appears only around 200 BC in association with Roman artefacts like amphorae (q.v), and is perhaps not of indigenous origin (*see also* utensils).

chana *See* Bengal gram.

chapathi A thin 20-cm circlet of wheat dough, rolled out after

Chapathi

thorough kneading and some resting, and then dry-roasted on a slightly concave iron griddle, the thava. It can then be puffed out by brief contact with live coals to yield a phulka. Both are major ways in which wheat is consumed in India. Cave paintings (q.v.) do show balls of dough being made, and in Harappan sites, flat metal and clay plates that could be thavas have been found in plenty, so the chapathi could go back a long way (*see also* roti; wheat dishes).

Charaka Samhita A compendium of the principles and practice of the Indian medical science of life or ayurveda (q.v.), which may well represent a redaction of knowledge as it existed around the fifth century AD. The common noun charaka has a connotation of roving, and Charaka may have been one person, or several persons who adopted a descriptive name, or even a school or tradition, all building over centuries on an ancient existing text. The *Charaka Samhita* consists of eight major sections, made up of 120 chapters. The fundamentals (*Sutrasthana*) are covered in 30 chapters, and therapeutic treatments (*Chikitsa*) occupy another 30 chapters. The former section describes basic concepts, physiological processes, and food and drink groups, while the latter is a systematic approach to how a doctor should diagnose an ailment and prescribe integrated remedies, of which diet is foremost. Drugs are divided accordingly into their pharmacological action into 50 groups, and their action on the body is interpreted on a rational basis based on actual observation. There are details of 341 medicinal plants and their products, 177 drugs of animal origin, and 64 drugs of mineral origin. The science of dietetics is aharatattva, and the effects of food on bodily health are viewed in relation to temperament, physiological effect, cooking, and season. The *Charaka Samhita* represents a 'momentous step forward from magico-religious therapeutics to rational therapeutics with perceptible results'.

All food items are divided into six vargas or types, and in each class the most and least beneficial items are noted. There are lists of compatible combinations, as well as of foods considered particularly unwholesome in particular seasons. Thus ghee for cooking is recommended only in autumn, in spring animal fats are preferable, and in the rainy season vegetable oils. Meat is regarded as a nourishing food, prescribed for use by the weak, the convalescent, those engaged in hard physical work, and those addicted to debilitating pleasures; deer meat (jangalavasa) and its sauce are considered particularly nourishing. Eight varieties of honey are commented upon as food, and five types of salt. A scientific synopsis of the *Charaka Samhita* has been made (*see also* ayurveda).

chaval Hindi for rice, and a word believed to have arisen from chomla, itself derived from the Monda term chom, meaning to eat.

cheese Even early Vedic literature contains a reference to dadhanwat, which simply means an abundance of curds. This is stated to be of two types—with and without pores—which may simply denote undrained and drained curd (paneer, q.v.), rather than cheese, as has been suggested. The latter has never become a popular product in India, though a few cheeses from buffalo milk were known locally. These are termed Dacca, Bandal, and Surd, the first two being smoked products and the last a salted one. Cheeses were imported throughout the colonial period, and perhaps this, rather than any local product, is the 'very good cheese' that was served at a meal in Calcutta in AD 1780.

cherry Wild cherries, called paddam or phaya, are still found along the length of the Himalayas. They are not eaten, but the stones are made into

Cherry

necklaces and rosaries, and the fruit makes an excellent cherry brandy. The sweet cherry is of Chinese origin; it was imported into India until its cultivation in Kashmir, and its improvement by grafting, were taken in hand by the Mughals.

chhana Acidification of milk, either deliberately or through spoilage, yields chhana as a precipitate. However, an Aryan taboo on the deliberate 'breaking' of milk meant that this was not a favoured food item. When the Portuguese who had settled in Calcutta in the early nineteenth century needed cottage cheese, which is similarly made, Bengali sweetmeat makers found themselves with a new raw material, chhana, on which they could lavish their creative energies, to produce a profusion of sweets

(*see* Bengali sweets). Mild precipitation of milk using whey from a previous run yielded a soft but perishable chhana, while the use of lime juice yielded a gritty one that set to a hard, grainy, long-lasting chhana. Even the fried jilebi in Bengal can be made from a chhana-khoa mix, and is called chhanar-jilipi.

chicken The Indian jungle fowl, *Callus gallus,* is the acknowledged progenitor of domestic fowls the world over. It is native to a wide region all the way from Kashmir to Cambodia, with perhaps the centre of origin in the Malaysian land mass. The bird may have been domesticated not as a source of meat, but for purposes of divination which entailed an examination of the entrails or the perforations in the thigh bones (practices that still prevail in parts of South-East Asia), besides of course that of cock-fighting between birds of spirit. Moreover, the fowl is a scavenger, and perhaps for this reason, the domestic fowl frequently finds a place in lists of foods prohibited for brahmins. In the list of Akbar's permitted meats in the *Ain-i-Akbari*, which includes the goose, duck, heron, and bustard, the fowl is conspicuously missing.

However, chicken kabab, palao with murg-masallam, and roasted fowl (dojaj) all figure in meals served at the Delhi Sultanate court. In Vijayanagar, Domingo Paes remarks on 'poultry fowls, remarkably cheap', and in AD 1780 Mrs Eliza Fay serves 'roast fowl' for lunch in Calcutta. Since good beef was scarce or unavailable, the domestic fowl was indeed the great colonial standby, whether at home or when travelling.

The people of pre-Aryan south India, whose lifestyles are reflected in Sangam literature, had no reservations about eating the karugu or kozhi.

Few pure breeds of chicken were developed in India. The aseel, with valiant fighting qualities, has a scantily feathered back. The golden Chittagong has very scarce plumage at the breast bone. The Ghagus comes in many colours and has a typical baggy neck. In AD 1668, Bernier described 'a small hen, delicate and tender, which I call Ethiopian, the skin being quite black'; other writers have called these birds Sooty or Nigger fowls. Though this breed seems largely to have vanished, a recent news item describes such a kalimasi in the Jhabua district of Madhya Pradesh, which was renamed kadaknath by a local official.

chickpea *See* Bengal gram.

chidva One of the names in Sanskrit for parched and beaten rice is chipita, and chidva (also pronounced chivda, chevda) are spicy, crunchy snack items based on it. These may also carry roasted groundnuts, raisins, coconut shreds, and the like.

chikki A sweet confection eaten as a snack, in which crunchy materials like roasted groundnuts, sesame, seeds, cashewnuts, puffed rice, and the like are kneaded with a hot, viscous solution of jaggery or sometimes sugar, into balls or slabs that set hard.

chilgoza *See* nuts.

chilli There is no mention whatsoever of the chilli in Indian literature before the sixteenth century AD. In AD 1563, the meticulous book of Garcia da Orta, the doctor-botanist, does not record it, and in AD 1590, not a single recipe of the fifty or more given in the *Ain-i-Akbari* uses anything other than pepper to achieve pungency. Indeed it is apparent that in many Indian languages, the word for the green chilli is simply an extension of the word for pepper. Thus Hindi has kali-mirch and harimirch, Tamil milagu and milagai (milagu-kayi), and Kannada harimenasu and menasinkayi.

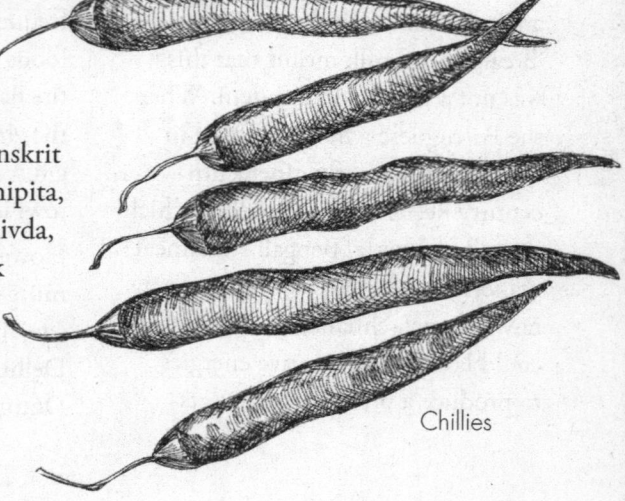

Chillies

In course of time, when pepper reached the New World, the compliment was reversed. In 1604, Acosta quotes Grimston on Indian pepper: 'In the language of Cuzco it is called Vchu, and in that of Mexico Chili', and in 1631 Bontius refers to the pepper as Piper e Chile. The name axi (x is pronounced h in South America) for the chilli is mentioned even in AD 1494 by Chanca, the physician who accompanied Columbus on his second voyage. In AD 1750 Rumphius notes that it is written 'axi or achi, hence comes the Indian name achar for pickles'. This must be a coincidence, since achar (q.v.) is usually granted a Persian or Arabic origin.

The chilli must have entered India soon after the voyages of Columbus and Vasco da Gama. The great south Indian composer Purandaradasa (AD 1480–1564) sang of the chilli: 'I saw you green, then turning redder as you ripened, nice to look at and tasty in a dish, but too hot if an excess is used. Saviour of the poor, enhancer of good food, even to think of (the deity) Panduranga Vittala is difficult.' A Sanskrit work written in AD 1650 in Maharashtra, the *Bhojana-Kutuhala* of Raghunatha, refers to the chilli as mirasana. All forms of the chilli, which had been fully developed in the New World, eventually found their way into India. They belong to four or five varieties of *Capsicum*, each

domesticated in different regions of Mexico and South America. The main form, *Capsicum annuum*, was domesticated in Mexico, where wild forms go back to 5000 BC. Other forms appear in Peru (2000 BC) and slightly later on the coast. Even the mild, globular capsicum types like bor were known early, but have become popular as vegetables only in recent times. Other types are the tiny and very pungent bird chilli (birds play a large part in its dispersal), the common bright red, thin-walled form, Guntur (which is dried in the sun, either spread on the ground or on rooftops, and ground to a powder), the green chilli, the red pimento, and the very pungent Irish chilli, used to make Tabasco sauce. The most pungent Indian chilli is the purplish birdseye or tejaswin; others go by such names as sannam, mundu, Coimbatore, and Bombay chilli. An intensely coloured but non-pungent variety of chilli is grown in Kashmir, and also in north Karnataka and Goa, where it is known as the bedige or bydagai.

China, foods from Sanskrit terms for several food products indicate their Chinese origin. These are chinani for the peach, chinarajaputra for the cultivated pear, and cnlnasalit for lettuce. Charaka mentions a sinchitikaphala, which could refer to an apple of Chinese origin. The cinnamon in Sanskrit and Hindi is dalchini, meaning Chinese bark, an item known to have once been imported from China. A common current Hindi word for sugar is chini. Granulated white sugar was imported into south India in the early Christian era, and perhaps into western India, which may account for the name. On the other hand there is evidence that a Chinese delegation visited Emperor Harsha in the seventh century AD to learn Indian techniques of sugar processing, while in AD 1406, the Chinese admiral Ma Huan visited Bengal and noted both white sugar and granulated sugar (*see also* sugarcane products).

Apart from the fruits earlier listed, the white mulberry, *Mortis alba*, was brought to India from China, as also the blackberry, and in more recent times, the litchi. Of Chinese origin also are both the sweet cherry and the peach, which later became popular throughout the world. Camphor has all along been imported into India from China, and is even called chinakarpura. China developed the leafy variety of the *Brassica juncea* (rai), which in India is used as a vegetable.

Two accretions from China are of more recent origin. The small, thick-leaved tea (q.v.) plant grown from varieties found in Assam when the first tea plantations were raised there around AD 1835, were later extensively crossed with Chinese varieties, and

some from Myanmar, to yield the tea types now grown. The Chinese words cha and teh for tea have entered every language in the world. The soybean (q.v.) originated as early as in 1200 BC in China, and was called shu or sou by Confucius. In 1908, soybean from China was noted growing in eastern India, but the crop made little headway till the introduction in the 1970s of American-type soybean varieties, which, after acculturation, exploded in India (*see* soybean).

chini *See* China, food from.

chironji See nuts.

chocolate A factory to make chocolate set up during the First World War in Bilimoria, Bombay Presidency, by a person called Sardesai soon closed down, as did two others put up about 1936. Sathe Biscuit and Chocolate Co. Ltd. was established in Pune during the Second World War, and before the War ended, more factories had come up in Bombay, Agra, and Madras. By Independence, about 550 tonnes of cocoa powder and chocolate were manufactured in India, with imports of these products well below this figure.

chowka(i) Squares of cloth, often beautifully worked, on which food was served to diners sitting around them. Later, a chowki dinner was served by nobility, for example in Hyderabad, on low square tables, around which sat four or eight cross-legged diners.

Food being cooked on a mud chulah

chulah A mud fireplace, common even today, usually some 15–20 cm high, with an inlet for inserting logs of firewood or twigs, and knobs on the rim to support the cooking vessel. The device is very old. The Vedic sacrifices prescribe the use of a chulli and excavations at Nageshwar (2500–2000 BC, an Indus Valley settlement) have revealed a U-shaped chulah with a front opening and three round knobs. Remnants of chulahs have been found dated between 1500 and 1000 BC in Ahar, Navdatoli, and Jorwe in Maharashtra, those at Ahar being so designed that several pots could be cooked simultaneously. Chulahs found at Atranjikhera (600 BC) had no knobs. The Ajanta paintings (seventh century AD) depict a kitchen with knobbed chulahs.

chunam Hindi for slaked lime, probably from the Sanskrit churna, a powder. A dab of it is frequently smeared on the betel leaf (q.v.) before mastication, where it serves to release the alkaloid.

churning Even the *Rigveda* (*c.* 1500 BC) has several references to the churning of diluted curds with a corrugated stick, the mixture after the operation being called prasadjya. The Lakshmana temple in Khajuraho shows a woman rotating, with a length of stout rope, a stick in a pot; this would certainly have carried at its end a corrugated wooden block to achieve concussion, as is still common today throughout rural India. An unusual churning unit in parts of Karnataka is a long bamboo pole fitted at the end with a concave piece of coconut shell bearing three holes; this is worked up and down to achieve churning in a tall, narrow cylinder of tinned copper. Standard commercial butter churns entered India soon after the turn of the twentieth century, and a very large one was installed in 1930 at the Polson Model Dairy in Anand, Gujarat.

chutney Anglicization of the Hindi word chatni, meaning a freshly ground relish consisting of ingredients such as the coconut, sesame, groundnuts, puffed Bengal gram, several dhals, raw mangoes, tomato, mint leaves, and the like. In colonial times it was used to denote a preserve, usually of mango slices, slightly spiced and placed in sugar syrup. These were manufactured in

India for export mostly to England, and brand-name recipes developed, like Colonel Skinner's, Major Grey's, and Bengal Club chutney.

cigar An unusual cigar with which to end a meal is described by Sushrutha. A reed was smeared with sandalwood paste containing ground spices like nutmeg and cinnamon. This was allowed to dry and the reed withdrawn to leave a fragrant cigar with which to perfume the breath.

Narangi, a common citrus fruit

cinnamon This is the coca of Kautilya's *Arthashastra*, also mentioned as tvak by Vaghbhata. It is the delicately flavoured bark of *Cinnammomum zeylanicum*, which grows wild in south India. An inferior cinnamon is the bark of *Cassia tamala*, which grows in the Himalayas and the eastern Khasi Hills; this tree also yields the tejpat (q.v.) leaves used as an aromatic flavouring. The best cinnamon has always been imported from Sri Lanka, and the Sanskrit/ Hindi word dalchini for the product means Chinese bark, probably once imported from China.

Historical writings reflect these facts. Ktesias (416–398 bc) mentions karpion as a product of India, and Calicut, according to Nicolo dei Conti (*c.* AD 1500), 'abounded in cinnamon'. One of the cargoes in a ship of the *Carriera da India*, set up for exports to Portugal, included nine tonnes of cinnamon. Marco Polo noted that cinnamon grew 'in the

Pandya country' and Thomas Stevens (who arrived in India in AD 1579, stayed for forty years, and was perhaps the first Englishman in India) accurately recorded that 'coarse cinnamon grows here but the best cinnamon comes from Ceylon where it is pilled from young trees'.

Curd in ancient south India was sometimes flavoured with pepper, ginger, and cinnamon. In AD 1623 Delle Valle, while in Surat, 'drank a hot wine, boiled with cloves, cinnamon and other spices which the English call burnt wine ... drinking it frequently in the morning to comfort the stomach ... particularly in the winter to warm themselves'.

citrus fruits A family of enormous variety found all over the world, the original home of citrus fruits is now accepted as being northern India. No wild ancestors are known, and no dates can be assigned. New hybrids and sports constantly arise, earlier by chance in South-East Asia, and more recently by the hand of man. Because of uncertainty in the criteria necessary for the classification of any variety as a species, the citrus family has variously been assigned 14, 36, 145, and 157 species.

A simple classification comprises four main groups, and one miscellaneous group that could itself include a dozen types. The acid group includes several species native to India. The large citron is *Citrus medica*, whose Sanskrit names are matulunga and bijapuraka. The lemon is *C. limon*, native to India which includes in its fold varieties like the galgal of Punjab, the patnimbu of Assam, the bara-masia of western Uttar Pradesh and the genoa of Cuddapah. The rough lemon *C. jambhiri* is the sour jambhir of antiquity, and the karnakatta is *C. karna*, with an orange skin and an orange flesh. The meeta-nimbu or sweet lime, of Indo-Iranian origin, is *C. limettoides*, exemplified in India by the rather insipid chikna of Saharanpur. The familiar yellow nimbu and kagzhinimbu (*C. aurantifolia*) are probably native to Malaysia, despite their Sanskrit names (nimbuka, numbaka, of probably Munda origin), the sobriquet Indian lime, and an undoubtedly long history in India. The orange group of citrus plants includes two of likely Indian origin. The narangi (Sanskrit nagaranga

and airavata), *C. aurantium*, could be native to north-east India, but its association with the Nagas could suggest a south Indian identity. The mosambi, sathkudi, or sweet orange (*C. sinensis*), could be of Assamese or Chinese origin. The third group, mandarin-tangerine, includes the loose-jacketed citrus fruits of Nagpur and Kodagu. The fourth includes only two varieties, the pummelo or pomelo of Malaysian origin, which is called chakotra in India, and the grapefruit (q.v.) that was developed from the pummelo in the West Indies. Under the fifth or miscellaneous group would fall such India-generated citrus fruits as the gajanimmu (*C. pennivesiculata*), the Guntur sour orange kichili or valpudi (*C. maderasapatana*), and the cala-mondin or hazara (*C. madurensis*). Of course many recently imported varieties also grow in India: the chikna (*C. limetta*), several tangerines with deep orange to red skin colours, and the kinna or kinnow, an orange-tangerine cross with abundant acidic juice developed in California and brought to India in the 1960s.

Though first mentioned only around 400 BC in the Buddhist-Jain canonical literature (they are fruits permitted for adherents), many citrus fruits go back much longer. Babar listed eight citrus fruits that he encountered in India: the orange, lime, citron, santhra, galgal, jambhiri, amritphal (perhaps the mandarin orange), and amal-bid. Bernier in AD 1616 noted the preparation in Bengal of sugar preserves from large citrons.

claret Now a term applied to the dark red wines of Bordeaux, claret once simply denoted wines of a light red colour. Claret was the favourite drink of Britishers in India, as Delle Valle reported in AD 1623. Later in Calcutta, a gentleman drank three bottles of claret after dinner. It was never manufactured in India, but could have been among the 'red wines, white wines and brandies' for which Maharaja Ranbir Singh of Kashmir won a gold medal for 'purity and excellence' at the Calcutta International Exhibition of 1884.

clove *Syzygium aromaticum* is originally from the Moluccas, also called the Spice Islands, in eastern Indonesia. The Sanskrit lavanga derives from the Malay term bungalavanga, and occurs in writing in the Buddhist-Jain literature, the Ramayana and the *Charaka Samhita*, suggesting the presence of the clove in India a few centuries before the start of the Christian era. The English word clove is from the Latin clavus, a nail, which the dried flower head strongly resembles.

Tamil Sangam literature of between the third and sixth centuries AD contains references to the clove. It was used as a meat spice, in sweet pickles, mixed with bhang for chewing by the wealthy, and to fasten a betel quid for the nobility, a practice common even today among the wealthy. A shipload carried back by the Portuguese *Camera da India* included nine tonnes of cloves. In making the 'burnt wine' of early colonial times, cloves were used as a component, besides cinnamon (q.v.).

cluster bean *Cyamopsis tetragonoloba* is the guar (Hindi), which may have originated in Africa and been brought by Arab traders to southern or western India. It is mentioned as valor in a book written in Gujarat in AD 1520. The pods are eaten, and the leaves and stems constitute an excellent nitrogen-rich cattle fodder and manure. In recent years, the pods have found a non-food use as the source of a valuable galactomannan gum.

coconut Indian mythology credits the creation of the tall coconut palm with its crown of leafy fronds to the sage Vishwamitra, to prop up his friend King Trishanku when the latter had literally been thrown out of heaven by Indra for his misdeeds. Botanists place the origin of the coconut palm in the Papua New Guinea area, in some very distant past. The plant evolved as far back as 20 million years ago, long before man appeared on earth, to judge from fossil remains, including one from Rajasthan. Coconuts can float in the

sea for very long periods, and then sprout when they beach on a shore. Man was thus not required to spread coconut in the lands of the southern seas. The Sanskrit term narikela (Hindi narial) for the coconut is itself believed to be an aboriginal word, derived from two words of South-East Asian origin, niyor for oil and kolai for nut. The coast line of the Deccan must have been familiar with the coconut and its oil long before the northern mainland was (despite a clay representation found in Harappa and thought to be that of a coconut). Indeed the Tamil word nai for a semi-solid or greasy fat appears to come from words like ngai and niu used for coconut oil in Polynesia and the Nicobar Islands.

Literary evidence seems to bear this out. The Tamil word for coconut, thengai, means either a sweet fruit (which seems unlikely) or, more plausibly, a fruit from a southerly direction. Tamil literature only goes back to about 100 BC, but the coconut is constantly mentioned. In Sanskrit the narikela only surfaces after *c.* 300 BC in the Ramayana, Mahabharata, and *Vishnu Purana*. Megasthenes, who lived in Pataliputra (Patna) about 300 BC, is believed (from a later reference to his writings by Aelian) to have mentioned coconuts in Trapobane (Sri Lanka). The late adoption of the coconut into Aryan rituals also argues for late familiarity with the nut in north India.

The people of south India, as expected, were familiar with the coconut from antiquity, and early Tamil literature has numerous references to it. Thus in the *Patthupattu*, we read that 'women, bright-wangled and garlanded, drink the juice of the coconut, which grows in "the sand"'. The diverse uses of the coconut are best exemplified in the cuisine of Kerala. Aviyal is a dish of soft vegetables like green bananas, drumsticks, various beans, and even green cashewnuts cooked in coconut milk, and then tossed in with some fresh coconut oil in sour curd. Kalan is the same preparation that uses only green bananas, while olan uses white pumpkin and dried beans. Pulisseri refers to a dish of small pieces of ash gourd or raw mangoes cooked with coconut, curds, and chilli. Prathaman is a generic term for a popular sweet confection; in one version, mung dhal is boiled in coconut milk and flavoured with palm jaggery, cardamom, and ginger powder, and sprinkled with fried cashewnuts, raisins, and coconut chips. Most flesh foods and fish, though spiced, employ a generous quantity of coconut milk (*see* coconut products) which tempers the spice. The morning appam or idi-appam is accompanied with sweetened coconut milk, or a mutton stew cooked in coconut milk, or fish

in coconut sauce with tiny pieces of raw mango. Shreds of dried coconut (*see* copra) set in a mould of thickened jaggery or sugar, kopri-mittai, is a popular confection all over India. Common to all of south India as an accompaniment to many snack foods, like the dosai, adai, pesarattu and vadai, is a chutney of ground coconut with some green chilli. Shreds of coconut or copra frequently find a place in a betel quid. Freshly grated coconut is frequently sprinkled over a dish of cooked beans or other vegetables.

Two unique confections of Goa use the coconut. Bibinca is a dessert of egg yolk, flour, and coconut milk which is built up in layers that are baked successively, and then turned upside down to cool. Besan (q.v.), ground coconut, and sugar, when baked together yield Dos de Grao, with a thick firm crust and a chewy centre. The moley (q.v.) of the British in Madras uses plenty of coconut in making a thick wet curry, the name being a corruption of the word Malay, from where the dish originated.

The coconut is called sriphala, the blessed fruit, and to cut down the palm is regarded as a definite sin. The dehusked coconut is an auspicious symbol in Indian rituals. It is offered to guests, used in marriage ceremonies, and, placed on a brass pitcher along with mango leaves, is used in consecrating a house or installing a deity. A coconut, split open and dabbed with vermilion, later replaced the animal head of early Vedic sacrifices. The fisher community of Maharashtra have a festival, Nariyal Purnima, when the sea is propitiated by offering coconuts before the fishermen resume voyaging in their boats.

coconut products *Coconut water*: The abundant liquid product in fresh tender coconuts is a delicious natural drink all along the coast, particularly in south India. As the nut matures, the volume of liquid is reduced considerably, and the taste turns brackish. In ancient Tamil country, a drink called munnir, relished by women, was made up equally of green coconut water, sugarcane juice, and fresh neera (q.v.). In the Indian medical system, coconut water is specific to cure a derangement of pitta (biliousness).

Coconut milk is a hand extract of fresh coconut gratings with hot water, the first extract giving a thick milk and the second a thin one. It is used in preparing many vegetable and meat dishes, to which it imparts a distinct flavour, and as an accompaniment to rice items like the appam and idi-appam (*see* appam).

Coconut honey is described by Ibn Battuta in the thirteenth century AD as the product obtained by boiling down the sweet extract of several palms (neera, q.v.): 'The merchants

of India, Yemen and China buy it and take it to their own countries where they make sweetmeats of it.' Perhaps what is meant is the boiled-down juice prior to the point when jaggery crystallizes.

Coconut oil: Long obtained domestically in south India by boiling with water either the shreds of fresh coconut (to release venthenna or avel, with a delicate perfume) or of copra (to release muthel, of coarser flavour). The ghani (q.v.), called chekku in the south, was also employed for the large-scale extraction of oil from copra. Coconut is extensively used in Kerala as a hair and body oil, for burning in wickered oil lamps, and as a lubricant. It is also used in medication, for example for eczema, with garlic segments crushed in the oil, or for anointing bums, with hariali grass (*Cyanodon dactylon*) infused in it. It is of course the prime culinary fat of Kerala (q.v.).

Coconut flowers are edible; they are mixed with curds for consumption by diabetics, and are given to newly weds as an aphrodisiac.

coffee Edward Terry makes the first reference in writing to coffee in India in AD 1618 using an anglicization of an Arabic word: 'Many of the people who are strict about their religion use no wine at all. They use a liquor more healthful than pleasant (which) they call cohha: a black seed boiled in water, which little alters the taste of

Coffee beans

the water. Notwithstanding, it is very good to help digestion, to quicken the spirits and to cleanse the blood.' Sixty years later, Jean de Thevenot remarked that in Sindh the brahmins drank nothing but 'water wherein they put coffee and tea'.

Coffee plants originated in Ethiopia, where the leaves were chewed as a stimulant. From there it went to Yemen in Saudi Arabia, which is credited with raising the first coffee plantation in the fourteenth or fifteenth century. Coffee seeds were brought to India by Arab traders from middle-eastern ports for use by the gentry. By the seventeenth century both seeds and plants had been carried from Saudi Arabia to southern Asia and South America. Arabs introduced coffee planting in Sri Lanka even before the Dutch invasion in AD 1665, and the same year a plantation (nothing is known of its fate) is noted in south India. Around AD 1720 a Muslim divine, Baba Budan, returned from a pilgrimage to Mecca with seven coffee seeds,

which he grew outside his cave in the Chikmaglur hills in Karnataka.

From about AD 1830, British pioneers embarked on a rapid development of coffee estates, and by 1895 a peak of 100,000 hectares had been reached. Two types were raised: *Coffea arabica* at higher altitudes, and the sturdier *Coffea robusta* in the lower reaches. The berries are plucked when ripe and red, and the outer pulp removed by wet or dry methods to yield a variety of beans (Cherry, Plantation, Parchment, etc.), from which the silvery inner skin is removed mechanically (curing) before the beans are roasted and ground. As much as 49 per cent of roasted chicory root may be added, which lends a dark colour, some aroma, and a certain bitter taste which is frequently relished.

'cold' food In the science of ayurveda (q.v.), the effect of any food on body equilibrium is by reason of its taste (rasa) and property (guna). Of the ten pairs of contrasting gunas, an important one is 'hot/cold' (ushna/shita), not in the sense of temperature, but of physiological action. This medical theory in its time travelled round the world to the Middle East, Greece, Spain, South America, and the Philippines, and directly from India to the Far East, where this food theory likewise held sway.

While common perceptions of which foods are 'cold' do differ, in general they embrace most pulses, some vegetables, most green leafy vegetables, many juice fruits, sugarcane juice, honey, and dairy products. 'Hot' foods include many whole grains, most forms of meat, fish and seafoods, nuts, many spices (and especially mustard seeds), jaggery, and fruits like the mango, papaya, and jackfruit. In practice, 'hot' mangoes and papayas should be eaten accompanied by milk, 'hot' pepper, ginger, and turmeric will counteract a head cold, and 'cold' buttermilk will quench the fires of diarrhoea. In terms of season, 'cold' and 'heavy' foods are avoided, and pungent foods preferred in spring, whereas in the summer months, the choice is of 'cold' and 'sweet' foods, and in the monsoon season of 'hot' foods. Winter 'hot' foods would be items like meat and fish, sweet confections of sesame seeds, copra, almond, and sweet laddus rich in fat.

In a modern scientific experiment, human volunteers given a diet of only 'cold' foods (in contrast to others giving a composite diet of only 'hot' foods) showed a desirable alkaline body reaction, a much lower excretion of sulphur, and a lower retention of nitrogen. Thus 'hot' foods conduced to an acid balance in the body (*see also* ayurveda).

colocasia *See* aroids.

Colonial repast Early European officials in India laid lavish tables. Mandelslo in 1638 noted '15 or 16 dishes of meat, besides the dessert' in the home of the president of the English merchants at Surat who all lived together. Even in 1780 in Calcutta, Mrs. Eliza Fay, a lawyer's wife and herself a dressmaker, wrote: 'We dine at 2 o'clock in the very heat of the day ... A soup, a roast fowl, curry and rice, a mutton pie, forequarter of lamb, a rice pudding, tarts, very good cheese, fresh churned butter, excellent Madeira (that is very expensive, but eatables are very cheap).' To prepare and serve these meals a whole array of servants and kedmutgars was in attendance. In 1809 in mofussil Mymensingh, the wine was always claret; 'you buy and fatten your own deer, oxen, sheep, calves, kids, ducks, geese, rabbits, etc.' Bread was made at home; so was butter, from the milk of one's own cows, made by pouring cream into 'very large open-mouthed bottles, which are closely stoppered and gently thumped up and down on the ground'. Edward Lear, known to posterity for his limericks, had a breakfast while in India in 1874 of boiled prawns, prawn curry, cold mutton, bread and butter, and plantains'. A painting of an English family at breakfast shows fried fish, rice, oranges, and a baked casserole of some sort.

By the turn of the twentieth century, eating patterns had altered. In the eighteenth century the main meal, exemplified by the huge spread described by Mrs Fay, was in the middle of the day, followed by a siesta, evening visits, and a light dinner at night. A century later this midday meal had become lighter, and a highly rated book on British cuisine in India, *Wyvern's Indian Cookery Book* by Colonel Kenney-Herbert, exults in this change from quantity to quality. About 1910, a suggested lunch consisted of pea soup, roast chicken and tongue, bread sauce potatoes, cheese macaroni, and lemon pudding. The main meal had moved to seven or in the evening, and in 1909 the writer Maud Divers declares that 'India is the land of dinners, as England is the land of five-o'clock teas ... all India is in a chronic state of giving and receiving (this) form of hospitality.'

The kind of food served had also clearly changed. The early British travellers had been fascinated with Indian food, and Sir Thomas Roe had both an Indian and an English cook. With the arrival of the memsahibs, the accent had shifted to English-style soups, roasts, baked pies and puddings. Of course the Indian ambience could not be avoided. A number of hybrid dishes conjured up between the English lady of the house and her Indian cook appeared, like Windsor soup, Patna rice, a broth of doll (dhal), Burdwan stew, cabobs, fish moley, curry chutney, and the renowned Byculla soufflé.

Sir John Malcolm, who succeeded Montstuart Elphinstone as Governor of Bombay in 1827, wrote that 'the only difference between Monstuart and me is that I have mulligatawny at tiffin (lunch), which comes of my experiences at Madras,' whereas the latter lunched on 'a few sandwiches and figs and a glass of water'.

The early Europeans saw virtues in toddy brewed from palm juice, and the arrack distilled from it. Then changes set in. Punch was a blend of arrack with spices, sugar, lime-juice and water; it was first noted in 1638 by Mandelslo as palepuntz, and became a popular drink in all the British colonies.

Once western-style liquors became available, there was a fair amount of drinking. It was usual for a gentleman to have three bottles of claret after dinner each day, besides the Madeira wine that he consumed with his meal; a lady frequently went through a bottle of wine a day. The favourite drink was claret, but one reads also of burnt wine, burnt champagne, brandy, and beer. Delia Valle (1623) describes 'drinking a little hot wine, boiled with cloves, cinnamon and other spices which the English call burnt wine ... drinking it frequently in the morning to comfort the stomach, sipping it by little and little for fear of scalding ... particularly in the winter to warm themselves'.

Apart from the food items we have noted, some unique Anglo-Indian terms arose in the area of food. Punch was from panch, and denoted the five components used in making the drink. Toddy came from the Hindi tari for the fermented sap of the tala or palmyra palm, first called by the Portuguese palmeira or the excellent palm. The peg as a measure of liquor got its name, according to British humourists, because each one was a peg in one's coffin. Rice congee, an invalid beverage, was the Tamil kanji, a translucent liquid which was also used by the dhobi as an accessible source of starch for stiffening cotton clothes! Kedgeree for breakfast was the Hindi khichri, which visitors like Ibn Battuta in 1340, and Abdur Razzak in 1443, describe as a dish of rice cooked with dhal, usually that of mung. Rice cakes, appa or appam in Tamil, appeared at an English breakfast as hoppers; this was a word particularly in use in Sri Lanka. Pepper water (rasam) was literally rendered into English as mulligatawny, a fiery soup. The baking of meat in a seal of dough, dumpukht, meaning air-cooled in Persian, and mentioned along with a recipe in the *Ain-i-Akbari*, became dumpoke, frequently applied to a dish of boned and stuffed duck.

The most widely used Indian term was curry. This was originally used for any spiced relish, employed by south Indians to accompany rice, and is noted as early as 1502 by Correa as caril. Later the word curry was very much enlarged in Anglo-Indian usage to mean a liquid broth, a thicker stew, or even a dry dish, all of which of course appear in a south Indian meal as successive courses, each with various names. The moley was a corruption of the word Malay perhaps indicative of its origin, and is a wet dish of Tamil Nadu with plenty of coconut, which the British adopted. And what of the ubiquitous tiffin, the present late-afternoon snack meal of south India? Originally the word stood for the Anglo-Indian luncheon, and surprisingly its origin is not Indian at all. The word derives from both the slang English noun tiffing, for eating or drinking out of meal times, and from the verb to tiff, which was to eat the mid-day meal. When dinner became a heavy evening meal, only a light snack lunch was customary, which explains why the word tiffin appears only as late as 1807 in Anglo-Indian writings.

colostrum The thick secretion of a dairy animal soon after birth of the calf, which in a few days progresses to normal milk. It is rich in nutritive elements for the newborn, but was considered unclean and interdicted as a human food for ten days in Vedic times.

Plate excavated from Indus Valley site

conjee Anglicization of kanji (q.v.), the residual water from boiled rice used as a beverage for invalids in colonial times (*see also* mulliga-tawny).

cooking principles Four elements provide the key to the taxonomy Indian cooking: fire, ghee, cultivated grains (anna), and non-cultivated food materials for which the plough is not employed (phala)! Two main categories of cooking can be discerned: Cooking without fire, the first category, can be performed with water or manual techniques (washing, soaking, peeling of fruits and vegetables); or with milk products (sweetened or flavoured milk, a raw vegetable raitha); and with the air and sun (pickling, dehydration). The second category is cooking on fire, either with or without the use of ghee, food items like cultivated grains, fruits and vegetables, or other milk products. An important concept is that milk and ghee are considered to be already fully cooked and ritually pure, and so confer purity on foods cooked in them.

Cooked food falls into two main ritual classes. Kaccha foods are those freshly cooked using water (like rice, roti, dhal, khichdi) within the kitchen area following ritual rules (described later), to be served to the family dining within that area. Pucca foods are those cooked using ghee, which can be taken out of the kitchen for consumption, and shared with people outside the family. Concepts of pollution underlie these practices. The domestic hearth in a Hindu home was an area of high purity, even of sanctity, frequently next to the area of worship. It had to be located far from water disposal areas, and well demarcated from sitting, sleeping, and visitor-receiving areas. Before entering the cooking area, the cook was obliged to take a bath and wear fresh, unstitched garments, frequently removing any upper garment while cooking. After a death in the family, the hearth would frequently be demolished and built afresh.

cooking practices Classic Sanskrit literature lists these as thalanam (drying), kvathanam (parboiling), pachanam (cooking in water), svedanam or svinnabhakshya (steaming), apakva (frying), bharjanam (dry roasting), thanduram (say grilling), and putapaka (baking).

Devices and practices for each of these also developed: chulahs (q.v.) and ovens, spits (shula), the thava, grills, rolling pins, steaming devices, and cooking in a seal of dough (dumpukht, kenchu).

Modern cooking practices use several specific Hindi terms. Thus bhunao is the initial surface browning of vegetables or meat by slow dry roasting or pan frying with frequent turning, before boiling down to a wet or dry curry. Baghar is the initial frying of spices in the pan in a little oil before adding the vegetables, dhal or meat; sometimes the spices after baghar may be used to put the finishing touch on, say, a thick cooked dhal. Deep-frying in a kadhai is talna, and tandoor-grilling is bhunana. An Indian technique for rendering a dish fragrant with the aroma of, say, ghee or cloves is quite old: the latter are placed in a small katori of hot embers, or even a cup of onion skin, and the dish covered to fumigate its contents.

cooking and related utensils

A variety of utensils in clay, bone, copper, and bronze have been found even in Indus Valley excavations, like pans, plates, frying pans, large copper vessels, spouted vessels, and spoons and knives of flaked chert. The Vedic sacrifices employed numerous utensils made to rigid specifications, which can be classified as containers, large earthen cooking pots, ovens, skewers and potsherds for roasting, ladles and spoons, offering vessels, stirrers and scrapers, cutting implements, trays, fire-pokers, strainers, pounders and grinders, and leaf plates and cups. Many of these are still in domestic use, like the chulli (chulah, q.v), the flat grinding stone drshad, the spit shula, grinding stones both upright and horizontal, and numerous vessels. Some vessels mentioned in later literature are iron pans (aluhi), a boiler (pitara), frying vessels, a roasting plate, bhrasta (perhaps the modern thava), a molasses pot (phanitasthali), and leather bottles to hold water and oil.

Tamil literature of between the third and sixth centuries AD is a rich source of information on daily life. Among the vessels mentioned are the mortar and pestle for pounding, stone millers for wet grinding, pots of many shapes and sizes for specific uses, spoons and

Pot excavated from Indus Valley site

ladles, fire-raisers and censers, pokers, winnowing pans, sieves, and bamboo coops to cover foodstuffs. Kitchens were constructed with storage lofts; they had mats to sit on, and plates and cups made of leaves (lotus, banyan, teak, and above all banana) to eat from.

Many Indian utensils reflect the shapes of natural objects. Gourds were the inspiration for lotas and chombus, and fluted pumpkins for numerous rounded, base-heavy water and cooking pots. The shapes of the coconut, mango, lotus flower, and banana leaf were transferred to vessels made of clay, stone, leather, and metal.

cooks Among Sanskrit terms for cooks were supakara, bhojanadatr, alarika, odanaka, and sudas. The specialists in frying and baking were the apupika and kandavika respectively, and the avalika was the expert in spicing. The sumptuous food served at a picnic meal described in the Mahabharata was prepared by 'clean cooks, under the supervison of diligent stewards'. The *Arthashastra* gives details of the spices that a cook would need to dress 20 palas (*c.* 700 grams) of fresh meat—one kaduba (175 grams) of oil, two-thirds of a kaduba (120 grams) of curds, one pala (35 grams) of salt, and one-fifth of a pala (7 grams) of pungent spices (*see also* cooking).

copra Copra is the kernel of the coconut. Drying hemispheres of the

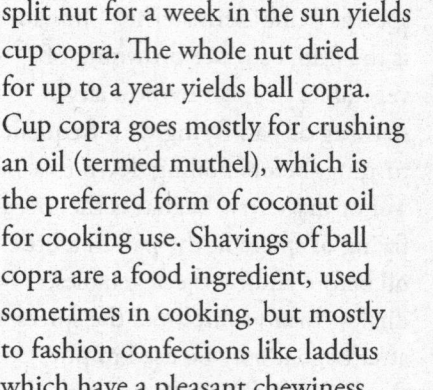

Coriander leaves

split nut for a week in the sun yields cup copra. The whole nut dried for up to a year yields ball copra. Cup copra goes mostly for crushing an oil (termed muthel), which is the preferred form of coconut oil for cooking use. Shavings of ball copra are a food ingredient, used sometimes in cooking, but mostly to fashion confections like laddus which have a pleasant chewiness. Copra is an anglicization of the Malayalam word koppara, which may have a connection with the Sanskrit kharpara, a skull.

coriander The two Sanskrit words for the seed, dhanyaka (from whence the Hindi dhaniya) and kusthumbira, first occur in Sanskrit in Panini's grammar (*c.* 600 BC) and the *Arthashastra* (*c.* 300 BC). The latter word is thought to be of Dravidian origin, and resembles the word kothamalli used in the south for green coriander leaves (the Hindi term is kothmir). The seed in powder form is used to flavour curries and confectionery, and the leaves serve as a topping for raitha, dahi-vada, kosumalli, khandvi, and the like. *Coriandrum sativum* is native to the Mediterranean.

cottonseed oil The cotton plant, its seed and fibre have been known in India since 4500 BC. The oil when expressed is black in colour; it contains undesirable compounds, and was earlier not considered edible. The means of removing these compounds were developed mostly in America about a century ago, and refined edible cottonseed oil was first made in India in Punjab in the early 1930s, and more widely after the 1960s.

cow Cattle were an integral part of Vedic life, and Sanskrit literature before 800 BC is full of references to the cow, itself called vara or blessing, and its milk. In the *Rigveda* alone there are 700 references to the cow (as many as to Indra himself) as a symbol of endless bounty in numerous contexts. Dairy products were highly venerated; the urine of the cow was sipped; and the dung was the usual disinfectant smeared on the hearth and the courtyard. The supreme purificatory material, panchagavya, was a mixture of five products of the cow, namely milk, curds, ghee, urine, and dung. The interdiction of the meat of the bounteous cow as food (*see* beef) was the first step to total vegetarianism (q.v.), an ethical concept that may have been triggered off by an economic one.

cowpea The cowpea (Sanskrit nishpava, Hindi lobia, and chowli, Tamil karamani) came to India from West Africa, from where also originated ragi, bajra, and jowar. *Vigna unguiculatus vaf. sesquipedalis* has long pods and small edible kidney-shaped seeds, and is first mentioned as nishpava in Buddhist canonical literature (*c.* 400 BC). The Hindi term may derive from the Sanskrit lobhya, meaning alluring, and the word cowpea is an American corruption of the English word cavalance which was then in use.

cream This is not a key product in traditional Indian milk handling, and it is only mentioned incidentally in literature, as satanika in Sanskrit, and edu or perugu in Tamil. Xuan Zang records it in a list of the 'usual foods' served to him in the Nalanda monastery in the seventh century AD, and again as one of the 'pure articles of food' that he was served by the Khan of the Turks at the city of Su-yehi, the others being rice cakes, sugarcandy, honey sticks (?), and raisins.

A traditional Indian delicacy is malai, a form of white clotted cream. A large volume of milk is kept simmering, to allow a layer of fat and some coagulated protein to collect on the surface. This is skimmed off with a flat ladle and allowed to cool, and the process is repeated twice. In the home, it is still a common practice to allow boiled milk to cool undisturbed, and then skim off the cream into a bottle; after this has collected for a few days and soured, it is diluted and churned to butter by shaking the bottle for a while, or thumping it repeatedly on the floor.

A cream separator was first brought into Bombay in 1890, and in the next three decades thousands were in operation all over the country in military and other dairies catering to local European needs. By Independence about 10,000 tonnes of cream was being produced, some for local sale, but mostly for conversion to butter and ghee.

crocodile Among a formidable list of meats declared edible in the *Charaka Samhita* is that of the alligator. In the same work, an aphrodisiac called vrsya-pupalika is mentioned, consisting of a large omlette of crocodile eggs and rice flour cooked in ghee. The fat of the alligator was permitted for cooking by the Buddha when a monk was ill, suggesting perceived medical properties.

cucumber Occurring as early as in the *Rigveda* (*c.* 1500 BC) under the name urvaruka, in the *Arthashastra* as chidbhita, and elsewhere as sukasa, the cucumber, *Cucumis sativus*, or khira in Hindi, is undoubtedly of Indian origin. Indeed bitter wild forms are still found in the Himalayas, and an occasional cultivated fruit will still taste bitter. It grows on the banks of rivers and on their dry beds. The cucumber is often eaten raw with salt, or in a raw green

vegetable mix like the kosumalli, kocchumber, and pacchadi, or diced into a curd-based raitha, or even in a cold soup, like the sarki of the Bohras. Cucumber is grown all over India, and Varthema in AD 1508 noted the 'vast quantities' that he saw in Kannoor on the west coast of south India.

cumin The seed of *Cuminum cyminium*, native to the Mediterranean region, but mentioned in Indian literature after about 300 BC (Charaka, Sushrutha, Kautilya) as ajaji, karavi, and kuchika. Late Sanskrit has jeeraka (Hindi jeera) from the Persian zlra. Jeera seeds or powder are an essential component of curry spicing. They have the reputation of being a good digestive, and are pungent, dry, and heating.

curd For millennia, curd has been prepared in every Indian home by seeding fresh cow or buffalo milk, boiled and cooled to body temperature, with a small quantity of curd from a previous run, and leaving the mass to set undisturbed overnight in a warm place. A sweetly acid, mild flavour is prized in curd, determined chiefly by the organisms present in the starter. These should by modern knowledge be mainly *Lactobacillus acidophilus* and *Streptococcus lactis,* but several others in smaller proportions play a part in the final taste and flavour. Very early Vedic references suggest, in place of a curd starter, materials like the ber fruit (q.v.), the bark of the palash, and the putika creeper. Tamil literature poetically and aptly compares the pat of starter curd used to 'a white mushroom'. Curd of different degrees of acidity was believed to have different effects on the body. To store curd, leather bags were used, though obviously for short periods, since curd that was not immediately used at the table or in cooking was churned without delay to butter (q.v.). A curd seller is termed mathitika in the *Arthashastra*. In Bengal, milk to be curdled was first thickened by boiling down; to this was added caramelized palm jaggery, cane jaggery or sugar, before the curd was set, to yield mishti-doi for consumption as a dessert.

Numerous historical references testify to the wide-ranging use of curd. In Vedic days it was eaten first as an accompaniment to staple barley dishes, and then with cooked rice. A blended curd-rice dish is mentioned even in the *Rigveda* as karambha. This name is still in use in Gujarat, and is mentioned in the *Bimalprabhanda* of Lawanyasamay around AD 1200, and three centuries later in the *Varanaka Samuchaya*. Curd was a versatile base material. The addition of rai (black mustard seeds) yielded the rajika-raddha of the *Manasollasa* (twelfth century AD), and themana was a soup made of curds. In early Tamil literature, thayiru (curd) is spiced

with pepper, cinnamon, and ginger. Green materials like the cucumber, onion, and radish in diluted curds yielded raithas and pacchadis. The palidhya of Karnataka was a dish of spiced vegetables cooked in curds and finished with a dressing (baghar) of spices fried in oil. In a meal served in about AD 1000, a curd dish of this type was served as the seventh course, before the last one of sweet, thickened milk. The moru-kozhambu of the Tamil area is a curd-based vegetable stew. Vadas (q.v.), which are patties of deep-fried pulses, were placed in salted curd to yield dahi-vadas, the Hindi word dahi for curd deriving from the Sanskrit dadhi. A dish termed kadha described in early medical literature (perhaps resembling the yellow khadi of the present) was made by the acidification of dahi with the sour woodapple fruit (kapittha) and the Indian sorre leaf (changed, *Oxalis corniculata*, amrul in Hindi), followed by seasoning with pepper and cumin. Further additions of oil, sesame seed, and urad dhal yielded kambalika. To dewater curd, it was hung in a muslin bag for a few hours; sugar and spices added to the mass yielded shikarini (identical with the modern shrikhand), first noted around 500 BC.

Marinating meat with curd and spices prior to cooking is mentioned in the *Arthashastra* and again in literature on Akbar's kitchen. In a traditional dish eaten by Rajput royalty, strips of roasted pork are first marinated in spiced curd, then baked with ghee in a wrapper, and finally grilled on a skewer.

Diluted salted curd is itself a beverage, called ghola in early medical literature, while asaradadhi was the product from skimmed milk curd, rated as a 'hot' food. Mixing bits of clove and raw pomegranate seeds with curd, with camphor added for fragrance, yielded sattaka. Whisking three parts of curd with one of sugar, and seasoning with dry ginger and rock salt, yielded rasala or marjika. The medical authorities did not favour the use of curd at a night meal, and not at all in three of the six seasons of the year, namely autumn, summer and spring (see seasons and months).

Curd as a product of the cow is one component of panchagavya (q.v.), the supreme purificatory Vedic material. Unlike milk and ghee, which have in Hindu cooking a special connotation of being already fire-cooked and 'pure', with dahi it is not so. Curd carries living micro-flora; the latter are now recognized as regularly replenishing those in the lower intestine, thus being conducive to digestion and warding off infection. Curd more than 24 hours old is forbidden to Jains.

curry From the Tamil word kari, a term for black pepper, derives the Indo-Anglian curry, which has come to symbolize Indian food for the westerner. The term originally denoted any spiced dish that accompanied south Indian food, and was first so referred to, using the term caril, by Correa as early as in AD 1502 and by Garcia da Orta sixty years later. Later the word curry was greatly widened in usage to include a liquid broth, a thicker stewed preparation, or even a spiced dry dish, all of which appear in turn in a south Indian meal, each with its own name. Colonials like Mrs Eliza Fay served 'curry and rice' as a matter of course in AD 1780 in Calcutta, as did thousands of other colonials living everywhere in India.

curry leaves The fresh leaves of *Murraya koenigii,* kari-pak or karve-palli in Tamil, meetaneem and gand-hela in Hindi, are widely used especially in south India to impart a distinctive multi-spice flavour to items like uppuma (q.v.), curd-rice, fried snack mixtures, and dry and liquid curries. Thus early Tamil literature notes the serving of a dish of 'the tender fruit of the pomegranate cooked with butter and fragrant curry leaves'. A few centuries later Kannada literature records 'an untried brinjal baji, which contained coconut shreds, curry leaves and cardamoms, mixed well, and flavoured with citrus juice and a little camphor'.

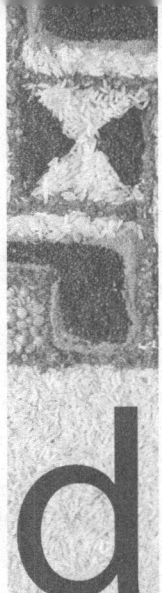

d

dahi *See* curd.

dahi-vada The deep-fried pulse preparation vataka first occurs in the *Sutra* literature *c.* 500 BC. The *Manasollasa* in the twelfth century refers to the soaking of vadas in milk to give kshiravata, and in soured kanjika (rice water) or curd, but these dishes could well be even older (*see also* curd; vada).

dalia A term for broken grain, for example of Bengal gram. This was often a by-product of the milling process (*see* chakki), and was ingeniously put to use in making laddus, idlis, porridges, and gruel. The southern term for broken rice grains was than.

date The original home of dates stretches in a belt across the Middle East and into north-western India. Both the wild date (*Phoenix sytvestrc*) and the cultivated form (*P. dactylifera*) grow sporadically in various parts of India. Wild date palms are an important source of palm jaggery in Bengal, but the cultivated form requires an exacting combination of low humidity, low rainfall, and adequate irrigation. They are not raised in India on any appreciable scale, and the demand for dates has always been met through imports. Faience sealings in the characteristic form of date stones, with a strong longitudinal furrow, have been found at Harappa and the term khajura occurs regularly in Sanskrit literature from the *Yajurveda* and *Brahmana*s onwards. Visitors to Sindh, like Al-Idrisi in AD 1080, speak of the abundance of dates, yet Xuan Zang four hundred years earlier categorically states that dates are unknown in India, which suggests localized usage then, as now. Muslims in India frequently follow the Quranic injunction of breaking their fasts with dates. Dates are fruits permitted to Jains, and are foods for 'sucking' in Hindu perception, being served as a second course in a meal, after a first course of fruits for 'chewing' and before the next course of foods for 'licking'. In health terms, the date is a 'hot' food (*see* 'cold' foods). It was a source of panaka fruit beverages (*see* beverages); the wine khajurasava was made from it, and in Jahangir's court, dates were used to sweeten and flavour a distilled liquor.

deer Venison seems to have had a special place in the Indian perception.

Deer

Charaka extols jangalavasa and its sauce as particularly nourishing, and Sushrutha lists it among the foods recommended for everyday consumption. The *Vishnu Purana* (third/fourth centuries AD) recommends its use at a shraddha ceremony. Xuan Zang lists it among the permitted meats, and about the same time, an Assamese work, *Kamampa Yatra*, notes that it is permitted for the upper classes. A favourite food of Sita in the forest was rice cooked with deer meat and spices, called mamsabhutadana. Elsewhere in the epic we read of large haunches of venison boiled in different ways with spices and mangoes, and sprinkled with condiments. In south India, venison was sufficiently esteemed to be an item of barter, with, say, sugarcane or beaten rice. A dish of venison 'cut in slices' served to Edward Terry in the court of Jahangir was described as 'the most savoury meat I ever tasted'. The British in India rated highly the meat of the spotted deer; that of the antelope was dry and needed basting during cooking.

dhal Most pulses are dicotyledons, and splitting them with simultaneous dehusking in a stone chakki (q.v.) yields two clean halves, called dhal. At least a dozen of the latter, like thuvar, chana, urad, and masoor, are in common use. Charaka lists twelve under the class shamidhanya.

In ayurvedic perception, all dhals reinforce the wind principle vata (q.v.), and most of them have a 'cold' connotation. Mung dhal is recommended for everyday consumption, and is now known to be the least gas-forming of common dhals, with Bengal gram the worst.

Dhals are used in a myriad ways. They can be cooked into thick, medium, and thin preparations, exemplified by the meeta masoor dhal of the north, the spicy thuvar sambhar of the south, and the soup-like rasam based again on thuvar. These are regular accompaniments to roti and rice. Mixed dhals feature in the dhansakh of the Parsis, and the panchbele-usal of Maharashtra. Whole pulses with a binder like besan can be fashioned into deep-fried vadas and wadian, and used to stuff spicy kachauris and sweet products like the holige (poli, q.v.). The flour of certain dhals yields fried snacks; that of urad (q.v.) dhal gives the fried medhu-vada, and the flour of puffed Bengal gram (*see* besan) provides the base of a whole gamut of fried snacks. Items that use cereals and pulses together are important in that they provide protein complementation in Indian vegetarian diets; examples are the holige itself, the idli and dosai, the dhokla of Gujarat, and innumerable others.

dhenki A foot-pounder for dehusking paddy, common in Bengal

Scene from rural Bengal showing the dhenki

and along the Indo-Gangetic plain. It consists of a wooden plank, pivoted in the middle, and worked up and down using a foot at one end; at the other end is fixed a stout wooden peg, which falls heavily on paddy held in a wooden or stone basin. The dhenki is of uncertain historicity, but is probably quite old, being the vahana or vehicle of the ancient sage Narada, and worshipped at a marriage or sacred thread ceremony.

dhokla The dukkia is first mentioned in AD 1068 in Gujarathi Jain literature, and dhokla appears in AD 1520 in the *Varanaka Samuchaya*. A 2:1 mixture of rice flour and besan (q.v.) flour is fermented overnight with curd, and steamed in slabs, which are then cut into pieces and dressed with fresh coriander leaves, fried mustard seeds, and coconut shreds. A coarser version is khaman, and both are popular breakfast and snack foods in Gujarat.

diet Once used for therapeutic food injunctions, as in the phrase 'going on a diet', the word diet has now come to mean the customary daily food of people.

dietetics The *Charaka Samhita* uses aharatattva for the science of dietetics. The science of ayurveda (q.v.) is itself largely occupied with dietetics, being the effect of food materials on bodily health seen in relation to temperament, season, and habitat.

distillation *See* beverages, alcoholic,

dosa(i) A fairly thick batter of rice grits and urad dhal in a ratio of 2:1 is ground together, left to ferment overnight, and steamed as patties to yield idlis (q.v.). Often the same batter is thinned to make shallow

Dosa

pan-fried dosais. The dosais of Tamil Nadu are thick and small; those of Karnataka are thin, large, and crisp, and are frequently folded over to enclose a 'masala' of mashed potatoes, onions, and green chillies. Accompanying both types would be a sambhar (q.v.) or ground coconut (q.v.) chutney. Tamil Sangam literature in the sixth century AD mentions the dosai but not the idli (q.v.), which only appears in Kannada literature four centuries later. The *Manasollasa* written in the twelfth century AD in Sanskrit mentions the dhosaka, for which only pulses, and no rice, were used (*see* idli for a discussion).

dosha A key concept in ayurveda, dosha has been defined as 'one of the three forces governing all biological processes'. A balance of the three doshas is expressed in good health and any imbalance in various symptoms. The three doshas are vata, which is governed by the elements air and ether; pitta by the element fire; and kapha by earth and water. Their relative strength in each individual determines his or her body type and temperament, which in turn defines susceptibility to disease and response to medication. The vata principle is responsible for the sensations and activities of the body; it regulates breathing, animates the psyche, and generates activity. Pitta is related to every reaction in which heat is generated, in particular the metabolism of food in the body. It stimulates intellect and enthusiasm, and encourages singleness of purpose. The principle kapha structures everything in the body, from a cell to the structural frame, lending strength, stability, and suppleness; it builds resistance against disease, and accelerates the healing process (*see also* kapha; pitta; vata).

drumstick *Moringa oleifera* (Sanskrit sigru and shaubhanjan, first mentioned in the *Sutra* period; Hindi sajuna and saonjana; Tamil murungakkai) is native to the sub-Himalayan region. It is grown commonly in villages and kitchen gardens in Bengal, Assam, and south India. The long, whip-like pods with soft inner seeds are cooked when tender, for example as a bhaja in Bengal, in sambhar in the south, and in aviyalin Kerala. The root was used by colonials as a substitute for the pungent horseradish.

duck There is little mention of duck meat in Sanskrit literature, perhaps because, like the chicken (q.v.), it is essentially a scavenging domestic bird. An Assamese work of AD 600–800 recommends duck meat. The *Ain-i-Akbari* (AD 1590) states that ducks for use in the emperor's kitchen were brought from Kashmir, and a dish termed shikar consists of duck cooked with vinegar, garlic, and chillies. The Syrians of Kerala frequently eat for a Christmas meal a roast duck with stuffing called mappas. The British in India enjoyed duck in roast and other forms. A deboned and stuffed bird cooked in a seal of dough was termed dumpoke, from the Persian dumpukht (q.v.).

dumpukht, dumpoke These terms refer to the baking of meat in a seal of dough. The Persian word dumpukht literally means air-cooked (baked), and occurs in the *Ain-i-Akbari* (AD 1590) along with the following recipe: '10 sers meat; 2 sers ghi; 1 ser onions; 11 misqals fresh ginger; 10 misqals pepper; 2 dams cardamoms.' The word was anglicized to dumpoke in colonial India, and frequently denoted a boneless stuffed duck cooked in a seal of dough.

The style of cooking was not confined to the north. Even in AD 1068, the Kannada writer Shantinatha in his *Sukumaracharite* refers to slow cooking under a seal of wheat dough used to hold down the lid, as kanika. Such long, slow, enclosed cooking resulted in the retention and permeation of the flavour of all the ingredients; it could also be used to perfume a dish with any desirable flavour, say that of camphor or clove (*see* cooking; fumigation).

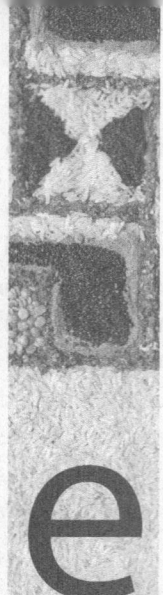

e

eggs Some sort of taboo seems to have prevailed in Hindu India against the eating of eggs. In AD 716, Al-Masudi noted 'the prohibition of all kinds of eggs among the people', and Father Sebastian Manrique, writing of Bengal in the mid-seventeenth century, says that eggs were not eaten. Yet even the Buddha in the *Lankavatara Sutra* permitted his followers eggs, so they must have been in use, perhaps by the kshatriyas.

Some unusual egg preparations may be noted. A dish of minced meat and eggs is termed mussaman in the *Ain-i-Akbari*. A baked dish of minced meat topped with beaten eggs yields the lagania-sheekh of the Bohri Muslims. Hyderabad has the nargisi-kofta, in which full-boiled eggs are coated with a layer of minced meat and fried. When cut into half, the golden yolk surrounded by the white and then the brown suggests the narcissus (nargis) flower, which grows close against the brown earth. Parsis bake eggs on a bed of various greens to give the generic dish akuri. An unusual egg preparation is the muttamala (egg garland) of the Moplahs of Kerala. This is a chain-like string of egg yolks cooked in sugar syrup and then removed; frequently this is served with a snow-white pudding called pinnanthappam, made by whipping

Eggs

the separated egg whites with the residual sugar syrup, allowing it to set, and cutting the mass into diamond shapes.

In the common view, the egg is perceived as a 'hot' food.

ekadashi The eleventh day of the lunar month, when Vishnu redeemed mankind; in gratitude for this, abstention is expected, especially from Vaishnavites. Only one meal is eaten the previous day, without either salt or vegetables, and only one evening meal with rotis and fruit, but no rice, on the ekadashi day itself.

elephant The meat of the elephant could not have been common; which is perhaps why Xuan Zang, in the seventh century AD, lists it as a forbidden food. Ascetics in Buddhist times were noted as living on elephant meat. Tamil Sangam literature observes that the meat of elephants that had either been hunted or killed in battle, was dried and stored for consumption.

elephant foot yam *See* suran.

elk Among items of the chase sent by Emperor Jahangir to Sir Thomas Roe (AD 1615-19) was 'a mighty elk' which he described as 'reasonably rank meat'. Perhaps this was a nilgai or sambar.

etiquette of dining A brahmin householder followed a strict ritual at mealtimes. He would enter the dining-cum-cooking area, where a brahmin cook would have recently prepared a meal having observed ritual rules (*see* cooking). He would have had a bath, changed into freshly washed-and-dried clothes, and would be without footwear or head-gear. Food had to be eaten sitting on the floor, facing east, and never either standing or lying down. He was required to eat alone and keep total silence. His wife would eat afterwards, but it was his duty to ensure that all his dependants were fed. Any guest had a very special place, since feeding a guest was considered as meritorious as worshipping god or performing a sacrifice. Hospitality, even to the basest caste, was one of the five duties of a householder. Some food had to be always set aside for feeding small creatures.

Morsels of food were first cast into the fire as a sacrifice to the fire-god Agni, brief muttered prayers (japa) and oblations of ghee (homa) were offered to the various deities, and oblations of water (tarpana) to ancestors. The leaf on which food was served was sanctified by sprinkling a few drops of water on it. When the food was served, a few drops of ghee were put on it to sanctify the meal. Only the right hand was used for eating, the left being reserved for lifting the tumbler of water, or for other baser functions of life. Food had to be broken up on the plate, never between the teeth, and eaten with the fingers.

Each item of food had its allotted place on the leaf. The six tastes had to be represented at every major meal. Generally, one started with a sweet item, followed by salty and sour items in the middle courses, and ending with items that were pungent, bitter and astringent. Another order, which could also encompass the six tastes, was to begin with foods to be chewed, and follow with foods to be sucked, foods to be licked, and sweets. After these lesser items would come boiled rice, then liquid preparations of vegetables and the like. The sixth course would be curd-based items, followed by milk-based desserts. After thoroughly rinsing the hands and mouth, a betel quid would end the meal. It was enjoined that the food eaten should suit the person's temperament and the season of the year. The amount of food eaten should be just enough to satisfy, and this quantity depended upon the digestive power of individuals.

A guest was expected to praise the food, show his delight in consuming it, and eat in a thoughtful frame of mind. He was never to commence eating before anyone else, or to rise from his meal when others were still eating. Both had to be done by common consent.

Concepts of ritual pollution pervaded the cooking, serving, and eating of food. Saliva was highly polluting, so water had to be poured into the mouth from above using a tumbler. Water used for rinsing the mouth could not be swallowed and had to be spat out. Cross-pollution was guarded against by the use of disposable plates and cups made of plant leaves (see leaf plates and cups). Caste also governed pollution: food could only be exchanged among equals, given to lower castes and taken from higher ones.

Food governed every stage of the life cycle. A student who left home to reside with his teacher was subjected to numerous interdictions on foods that might raise his baser appetites. When slightly older, he was expected to beg for his food from families in the neighbourhood. A woman who had given birth was considered highly polluted, and was therefore not permitted to enter the kitchen for a considerable period. After a death in the family, food was not cooked, and in particular the initial frying of spices in oil (baghar) prior to cooking the main material was forbidden; the family lived on austere food sent by relatives, and many auspicious foods (like milk and turmeric) could not be consumed till the period of mourning was over. Auspicious foods were likewise abjured at the meal served during the annual ancestral shraddha ceremonies.

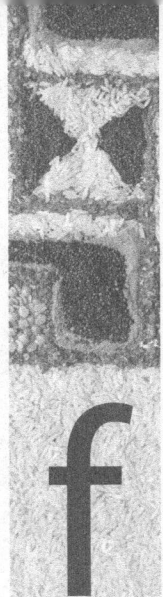

falooda A rich drink, of perhaps Turkish or Persian origin, a favourite of Emperor Jahangir, and described as a jelly made from the strainings of boiled wheat, mixed with fruit juices and cream. A simpler form of falooda, with a body of softboiled sago granules (replacing a type of soft seed that swelled in water), with added cream, fruit, jam, and ice, was once an item served by Irani restaurants in India.

fasts Fasts or vratas rarely involve complete abstention from food. They usually require various degrees of abstentions of several kinds. Sometimes this may even take the form of using only pure ghee to induce pure, sattvik (q.v.) thoughts, or to replace sea salt with rock salt in domestic cooking. In some fasts, plough-grown grains like rice are abjured in favour of wild grains.

In others, only restrictive boiled (kaccha) foods are permitted, and in some others only foods that have been cooked the previous day, which would normally be considered stale and not eaten. A common form of fasting is to eat only fruit, or to eat only before moonrise or only after sunset. Some element of deprivation is clearly the intention in observing fasts. Modern practices, like not eating a meal on a Friday or a Monday, or giving up a particular dish, may be dietetic in intention, but frequently have a ritualistic origin.

The *Bhavishya Purana* (first composed in 500 BC, with later accretions over several centuries) prescribes no less than 139 fasts in a year. The eighth and eleventh days of the bright half of every month are ekadashi or fast days: the eleventh days are all sacred to Indra, the other days to various other deities. Particularly important is Vaikunta Ekadashi which celebrates the redemption of mankind by Vishnu in his incarnation as Krishna; the previous day, a single saltless meal unaccompanied by any vegetables will be eaten, followed by a day-long fast and an evening meal of fruit and rotis, but no rice.

Around AD 1000, five kinds of fasts are noted in north India. Vara fasts are observed on week-days, the adityavaravrata to Surya being an example. The thithivratas are kept on certain days of the lunar month; there are a large number of these, Durgashtami and Krishna-janmashtami being examples. On certain days of the lunar stations the nakshatra fasts are observed. Masavrata fasts are observed in certain months, like Karthika, while samvatara fasts with restrictive eating could even spread from one ekadashi (q.v.) to the next, a whole year later. Day-long fasts commonly observed in orthodox homes, especially by womenfolk, are Ram Navami, Shivaratri, shankranthi and ekadashi.

Al-Biruni, who spent thirteen years in India in the mid-eleventh century and observed matters carefully, noted five kinds of fasts among ordinary people. Ekanatha was non-eating from one noon to another, upavasa from noon to sunset or to the noon of the third day. Kricchra was a certain sequence of fasting: from noon to the following evening, and then on the third day eating only what was received unasked and by chance. Paraka involved eating only once at noon for three days, at sunset for three more days and then fasting uninterruptedly for three whole days. Chandrayana was a fasting sequence of slightly increasing quantities of daily food (starting from nothing) for a fortnight, followed by a diminishing sequence for the next fortnight. Masavasa was interrupted fasting stretched over a whole month.

Jains observe twelve pratimas or fasts, and abstain even from milk, curd, ghee, oil, and sweetmeats.

As everywhere, Muslims in India fast during Ramzan, the ninth month of the Muslim lunar year, which falls around March. A meal, termed fatoor, is eaten before sunrise and another, sahoor or suhoor, after sunset. The latter frequently begins with a few dried dates, indicative of its middle-eastern origin. The French traveller-doctor, Jean-Baptiste Tavernier, refers to the 'great fasts' which Aurangzeb observed, which in his view contributed to his being 'lean and thin'.

fats in cooking Fats are solid, and oils liquid, but the term fat is used genetically to mean both. Ghee in the Aryan view was the supreme (almost the only) cooking fat: it was a product of the sacred cow, 'born of fire' and hence pure, and conferring purity when used. The vegetable oils used by non-Aryans were looked down upon; there were of course a large number of them, notably sesame, mustard, safflower, and coconut. These were derived from their parent materials either by boiling with water, or by expelling under pressure in a ghani (q.v.). Almost certainly vegetable oils were in use in the Indus Valley; besides the fat from milk, and a variety of animal and fish body fats. In later times, both the production and use of vegetable oils tended to become regional: mustard oil was; used all along the long Gangetic plain, coconut oil in the Chera area; of the Tamil country (now Kerala), and safflower oil in northern Karnataka and southern Maharashtra, while sesame was grown and its of used all over the country.

Fats have always had an important place in Indian cuisine. In fact, other than boiled rice and raw ground items like chutneys, raithas, and fruit mixes, it would be difficult to find an Indian cooked item that did not use at least a modicum of fat at some stage.

In ayurvedic terms of rasa, fats are 'sweet' foods, as are cereals and pulses. Fats in general, and ghee in particular, are unique in that they mitigate all the three doshas (q.v.), vata, pitta, and kapha. Charaka recommended the use of ghee in autumn, animal body fats in summer, and vegetable oils in the rainy season; but in general

terms, the use of fatty foods should be minimal in autumn and spring, and reduced in summer. Sushrutha noted that fried foods were difficult to digest, and urged moderation in the use of oil in the kitchen. No less than 60 oil-bearing vegetable materials are listed by Sushrutha, besides numerous animal fats, and the effect of each on the body is meticulously catalogued.

feni Distilled liquor with a distinctive flavour developed in Goa by Catholic monks from the red 'fruit' of the cashew (q.v.) tree. Distilled coconut toddy is also sometimes loosely termed feni.

fenugreek The name *Trigonella foenum-graecum* means triangular hay, a name given by the Romans considering how common the plant was in Greece. Methi is native to a wide region in the Middle East, the Mediterranean, and hilly north-west India. The leaves are first mentioned in *Sutra* literature, and both these and the small, hard, bitter seeds are used in cooking. The seed is a component of the Bengali mixed spice, panchphoron. In the ayurvedic system, the seeds are classified as having the bitter rasa tikta and, like several other bitter substances, are considered to be anti-diabetic.

fermentation *See* beverages, alcoholic.

festival and temple foods Most socio-religious festivals in India have an association with food. The sesame seed, considered highly auspicious, features in several festivals. One is the feast of the six sesamums which is part of ekadashi (q.v.), and another is Naraka Chaturdasi which celebrates the defeat of Yama, the lord of death, by Vishnu. The coconut features in almost any religious or social function in India as an auspicious symbol. It even has a festival named after it, Nariyal Purnima, when coconuts are cast into the sea to propitiate the sea-gods before fishermen resume their forays, once the monsoon is over. Sweets for the festival are all based on the coconut: a sweet-stuffed nariyal karanja, a paak of coconut shreds in

Lord Ganesha holding his favourite sweet, the modaka

thickened sugar solution flavoured with cardamom, and a sweet coconut rice bath.

In Makara Sankranthi in January, sesame laddus are given to family members and friends with the words: 'Eat sweet sesame and speak to me sweetly.' At the joyous Holi festival in March, necklaces of yellow and white sugar medallions are given to children. The exchange of sweets is very much a part of Deepavali (q.v.) in October, with sugar-moulded animals given to children. Fried vadas made of pulses are eaten on Vataka Pournamasi, a practice that was noted even in 200 BC by Patanjali. Pongal is a harvest festival of south India, when a pot of rice is put to boil in milk; cries of 'Pongal, Pongal' are raised when the pot is just about to boil over, the word deriving from the Tamil term for boil. A type of poli (q.v.), the dry obattu, features at the New Year Ugadhi festival in Karnataka.

Each of the gods is supposed to relish a certain food, which is offered to them at their festivals. Lord Ganesha is frequently sculpted holding in his hand modakas, a sweet-stuffed rice envelope, which is his favourite food. In south India, laddus of sesame seeds substitute. Lord Rama, at any rate in south India, is favoured with sweet fruit juices, and an uncooked dhal preparation called kosumalli.

Temples prepare foods that are first offered to the presiding deity; having been sanctified, they are distributed as prasad (q.v.) to the assembled devotees. The Padmanabhaswami temple in Thiruvananthapuram has a special mixed vegetable dish, aviyal (q.v.), in which no mustard seeds are used, and the Ganesha temples of Kerala serve the unniappam, spongy brown fried pieces of a mixture of rice powder, banana, jackfruit, and jaggery. The panchamrita (crystal sugar, honey, ghee, cardamom, and several fruits) of the Muruga temple on the Palani hills is a prasad that keeps fresh for several weeks. A giant spiced idli is the speciality of the great Vishnu temple at Kanchipuram, to the Vishnu temple at Srimushnam is a confection from the sweet korai root (*Cyperus rotundas*) held to be dear to Varana, the boar incarnation of Vishnu. Laddus made of urad dhal are served as prasad at the great Venkateshwara temple on the Thirupati hills, and over 70,000 are made every day. Enormous quantities of nearly a hundred items of food of all kinds are made daily for sanctification, distribution and sate at the great Jagannatha temple at Pun in Orissa.

fig The true fig, *Ficus carica* or anjir, is native to the Mediterranean. It is not mentioned in early medical literature, and there is even a record of Bindusara, son of Chandragupta

Fig (anjir)

Maurya, writing to Antiochus in Greece for figs. However they did eventually come to be grown in India, notably in Pune, where Smyrna white figs are grown. It is thus appropriate that the colonial administrator, Monstuart Elphinstone, had for lunch 'a few sandwiches and figs and a glass of water' while fighting the Peshwas in Pune. Other types now grown are the bronze Brunswick and the purple Partridge. Some travellers have reported having seen figs in India, like Amir Khusrau in Delhi in about AD 1300 and the Rev. Patrick Copland in Surat in the mid-sixteenth century. The Mughals attempted to graft the fig on mulberry trees.

Figs are dried in the sun, pressed flat when still soft, and the discs strung on some strong vegetable fibre for transport and sale. They are popular for breaking the Ramzan fast.

Small, fig-like fruits are borne by at least five *Ficus* species, including the banyan (*F. benghalensis*) and the peepal (*F. glomerata*). Though insipid and dry, these are popular with birds and small animals. The Jain community is expressly forbidden to eat figs, collectively called udumbara.

fire Fire was integral to Aryan concepts of cooking, the two major divisions of which were cooking without and with fire (*see* cooking). The latter was of course the bigger category, and had two sub-divisions, cooking with ghee and without it Ghee, the fire-derived product, was the supreme Aryan cooking material.

Firewood, charcoal and dung cakes were the major sources of heat. Vedic sacrifices involved cooking (q.v.), for which ritual implements of strict shapes and sizes were specified. For raising a fire a spindle called arani, worked with a length of string, was used. A wooden device called upavesana was used to remove embers, a vessel called sata to carry them, a poker, dhrsti, to stir the fire, and tongs called parista to lift vessels from the fire. The Sangam literature of south India mentions friction devices made of wood to raise a fire, censers called tadavu and indalam to hold embers, and pokers (nelikol) to rake the embers afresh. In a home, a perpetual fire was kept going in a pot called kumpatti, with a stick called sulundu, sometimes tipped with sulphur, stuck in it.

The digestive principle, by which food is broken down and then absorbed, was also referred to as fire (agni). There is a major agni, jathara, and twelve other minor ones, and good health depends greatly on a smooth and strongly functioning agni. Agni is strongest in winter, and at a low ebb during summer and the rains. Apart from its relation to food, fire in the Hindu belief is the supreme purificatory force, which is invoked in worship, in sacrifice, and in every ritual, including cremation.

fish The use of fish in India is ancient and well documented. The prehistoric Bhimbetka cave paintings show fish being speared. The Indus Valley sites have yielded fish hooks and bones in abundance, as have the slightly later south Indian excavations. The Greeks noted an enormous amount of fish at the estuary of the river Indus. Arab visitors record that fish was eaten by Jats living near Cambay, and Chinese pilgrims note that fish was eaten fresh, and sometimes salted. In the Tamil Sangam period, the meenavar (meen was a Tamil word for fish that entered Sanskrit) were coastal dwellers, and fish like varal, aral, horned valai, and prawns are mentioned, while salted fish was even exported. In Vijayanagar, Nuniz noted the availability of fish in large quantities. Bernier observed in Bengal 'fish of every species, whether fresh or salt, in profusion'. Babar wrote: 'The flesh of Hindustan fishes is very savoury, they have no odour or tiresomeness.'

Little is said in historical works of ways of cooking fish. The *Naishada Charita*, a late work of about AD 1200, mentions a 'broth of fish', and a twelfth-century work, *Samaraichchakaha*, directs that the skin of rohu fish be peeled off, the fish marinated in asafoetida and salt, and then dipped in turmeric water before being fried.

Current regional cuisines illustrate the approaches in India to cooking fish. Bengali food, and especially that of eastern Bengal, has lightly spiced, liquid preparations called maccher-jhol, and more heavily spiced ones, like steamed maccher-paturi. Fish is obtained from big rivers, estuaries and tanks, with hilsa, rohu, bhekti, mangor, and tapsee as favourites. Even the brahmins of Bengal eat fish (*see* beef), as did the great spiritual leaders of Bengal,

Ramakrishna Paramahamsa and Swami Vivekananda. In Orissa, a morning meal of boiled rice covered with water and kept overnight, is eaten with fish, and in Assam, a favourite curry is an alkaline salty extract of banana roots cooked with fish. Kerala is a fish-eating state, and the Syrians there have a deep red fish curry cooked with the sour kokum fruit (kodampuli), and another sweet-sour dish cooked in coconut milk with tender mango pieces. Oily fish are frequently grilled in their own fat. Goa has the golden caladine curry with turmeric, a green-masala mackerel, and the roe of the kingfish, lightly salted and fried, as a breakfast delicacy. The Kodavas of Karnataka state cook a mass of tiny whitebait fish, called koylay-meen, bones and all, to a dry, spicy dish. Kashmiris cook fish with lotus roots (nedr), while a garlic-flavoured fish dish is

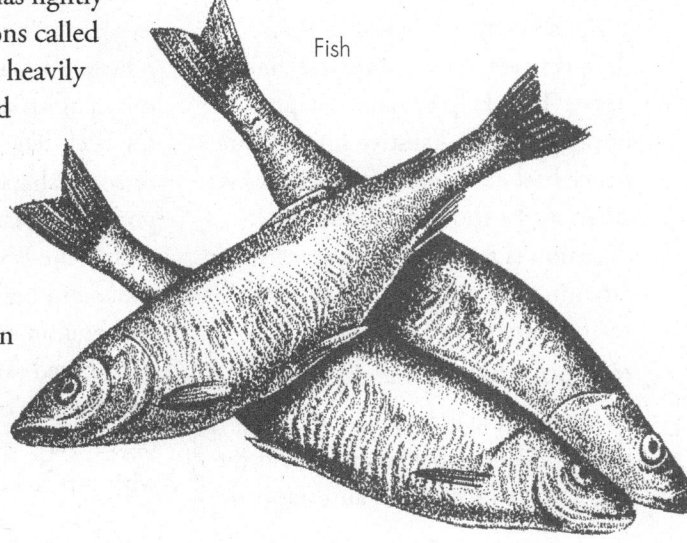

Fish

called gardmuf. Parsi cuisine has two unusual fish preparations. One, called patra, is fish in a thick, strong masala steamed in a banana leaf packet, and the other, patia, is pomfret cooked in a dark vinegar sauce. The poisson capitaine of Pondicherry is a dish of steamed fish served with mayonnaise and garlic paste. Fried fish frequently figured at an English breakfast in India, as did a kedgeree (q.v.) (khichdi) of rice and fish.

Past literature makes occasional mention of both dried and salted fish, with an added tamarind dressing noted in Tamil literature. In colonial times, the salting of fish was extensively carried out on both the east and west coasts, and attempts were made by the government to improve hygiene and quality. At Independence, some 200,000 tonnes of dried and salted fish products were being exported annually from India.

In the Indian medical view, fish are anupana or water dwellers. Their flesh is sweet, fat, carminative, and heavy. They help to reduce kapha, but depress the digestive fire, and are hence best consumed during seasons when, or by those in whom, the digestion is strong. Freshwater fish are fattening and leave no residue, and sea-fish are muscle builders.

foot pounder *See* dhenki.

fowlers Vedic literature describes how punjistha (fowlers) waited at the edges of a lake or pond and trapped wild fowl with nets, or with their feet, using birds calls, decoys, and camouflage headgear to approach and trap their prey. Even in the early seventeenth century, nearly three millennia later, Joannes de Laet writes that Indians 'show great cunning in catching water-birds; for they take a skin of a bird of the same kind as they wish to catch, and stuff it so skilfully that it seems like a real bird; then they immerse themselves in water up to the neck, cover their heads with the sham bird, and then make their way into the flock of wild birds, which they catch by seizing their feet below the water.' Bows and arrows, and falcons, were used to bring down birds in flight. There was always, it would appear, a ready elite clientele for wild fowl and game.

French bean *See* sword bean.

French cuisine An amalgam of French sensibilities and the Indian environment gave rise in Pondicherry to a distinctive cuisine, which however remained localized. Three forms of bread are the crisp pain sec, the stick-like baguette, and the soft, crescent-shaped croissant. A spiced pork liver paste constitutes paté, laced with some Bourbon; jambon is pork cooked in beer and then smoked; and boudin and saucisse are spicy, pork-based sausages. Beef is filleted and roasted, or diced to make a ragout stew with vegetables. Stuffing with minced beef gives a tomato

Bharhut sculpture showing veneration of the white mango tree created by the Buddha

farcie, and boulette consists of fried minced meat balls. Steamed fish smeared with mayonnaise and garlic paste constitutes poisson capitaine, and fish croquettes are fried after being rolled in an egg-breadcrumb mixture. Gateau mocha is a sponge cake with coffee, cream and rum; there is a crème caramel custard, and another custard with grated nutmeg called flanc.

fruit Fruits that are either indigenous to India, or have been here since recorded history, include the her (*Zizyphits* spp.), pomegranate, amla (*Emblica officinalis*), sweet orange, narangi, lemon, lime, mango, sugar-cane, jamun (*Syzygium cumini*), phalsa (*Grewia subinequalis*), and grapes, with the coconut, banana, and jackfruit as essentially southern entities. The minor fruits from ancient times include the bilva or bael (*Aegle marmelos*), figs of the banyan and peepal, tendu (*Diospyros ntelanoxylon*), karaunda (*Carissa carandas*), and kamrakh (*Atropa carambola*). Among the later arrivals were some forms of the apple, the mulberry, peach, pear, plum, and apricot; many of these were not of high quality but were improved by grafting in Mughal times. A wave of immigrant fruits came in after AD 1500 from South and Central America, like the papaya, sapota, guava, pineapple, the sitaphal group (*Annona* spp.) and the avocado (*Persea americana*), while from China came the litchi (*Litchi sinensis*).

In terms of food, fruit falls into the category of items called phala that are not cultivated using the plough, in contrast to foodgrains, and indeed phal is the common spoken term for fruit. It is a commodity that can be bought and sold; but when brought into the kitchen area and peeled or skinned, fruits become ritually pure and therefore restrictive (*see* cooking). In the Jain (q.v.) view, fruits plucked from a tree can be eaten, but not those that have fallen down; also, very small, seeded varieties like the fruit of the fig family could harbour animal life and are forbidden. Fruits in ayurveda are sweet and sour, heavy and cold. They are recommended for dyspepsia, and dried fruits are 'cold' foods with a highly alkaline reaction in the body.

Fresh fruits are of course enjoyed as such for their taste, flavour, and texture, or are converted into juices for use as beverages (q.v.). Historical Kannada literature refers frequently to seekharane, a class of ripe mixed-fruit mixtures. A fruit like the matulunga (*Citrus medico*) could be stewed to remove the acidity, and then boiled in buffalo milk with sugar and cardamom. In current practice ripe mashed bananas are convened into a dessert, koale-puttu, by steam cooking them in Kodagu, and a similar process with jackfruit yields the unni-appam in Kerala.

Fruits could be employed in items served at a meal. Green mangoes sometimes serve as a souring agent in cooking fish. Another common souring agent all along the west coast of India is the kokum fruit (*Garcinia indica*), which goes into Kerala and Goan pork and fish preparations. Cooking both meat and vegetables in the acid juices of fruits was a common practice all over India in the past; the *Manasollasa* describes yams thus cooked as pralehaka. Ripe wild mangoes of a distinctive taste are cooked in buttermilk in Kodagu into both a liquid curry and a thicker relish, mangay-kari and mangay-pajji, respectively.

Fruit was traditionally preserved in India in the form of spicy pickles of, say, the mango, lime, citron, and so on, with sweet-sour flavouring in Gujarat. With the Muslim Unani medical tradition came the murabba (q.v.), in which fruits were preserved in a thick sugar syrup, with spices like ginger and cloves added for flavour. It is probably these which are referred to as preserves by Bernier in Bengal around AD 1660. The British colonial took a liking to these sweet chutneys (q.v.) and murabbas (q.v.), and their manufacture developed into a sizeable industry, with exports, in the year of Independence, of about 3000 tonnes of murabbas, and an equal quantity of chutneys, sweet-spiced Indian and western-style fruit drinks, jams and jellies.

Fruits

Fruits were also preserved by dehydration: grapes give rise to raisins and sultanas, figs to discs, apples to rings, dates to compressed, seedless masses, and mango juice to chewy slabs (called am-papad and amras). These were not however major enterprises, and indeed raisins and dried figs were mostly imported.

In the past, a major use of fruit was to ferment it to obtain alcoholic beverages. Charaka has a long list of fruits used for this purpose, which included the sugarcane (and its products molasses and jaggery), grape, mango, woodapple, date, ber, banana, jackfruit, and pomegranate. Sometimes very sweet dried fruits like raisins and dates were added to soften and sweeten both undistilled brews and distilled liquors (*see* beverages, alcoholic).

fruit drinks *See* beverages.

frying Copper frying pans have been found in Harappan sites, and these were termed pravani in later Sanskrit literature. In the *Rigveda*, there is mention of apupas being deep-fried in ghee (ghrtavantam) and in the *Dharmasutras*, deep-fried vatakas (vadas) are mentioned. Later apakva, based on the word pakva for cooking in general, came to mean frying. The modern Hindi terms, all based on Sanskrit, for the frying of spices is baghar. for shallow meat frying bhunao and for deep-frying in a vessel, talna. Frying is perceived as an auspicious act, and is not allowed in a house of death during the mourning period.

Fried meat occurs repeatedly in old Tamil literature as thallita-kari. Another word for such meat is porikari, where pori signifies fried (*see* cooking; besan).

fumigation An ancient cooking technique, fumigation is utilized, for example, in the *Manasollasa* to perfume a dish with the desired flavour, for example that of ghee, or cloves, or camphor. These ingredients are placed in a small container (a katori, or an onion skin, or a piece of tile), which is then placed in a hot cooked dish, and the dish kept covered or sealed. Fumigation is called dhuanar in Hindi.

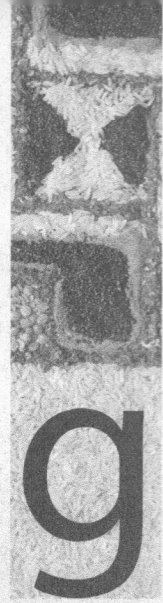

game, wild There is extensive evidence that India was at one time under heavy forest cover.

And these forests abounded in game. In about AD 1660 Niccolao Manucci travelled from Surat to Burhanpur (where Aurangzeb was holding court). 'The road,' he wrote, 'passed between sturdy and pleasant woods, peopled with many varieties of animals of the chase ... without hindrance (I) killed whatever I wanted, there being no scarcity of things to kill.' Mughal paintings frequently depict the emperors on hunts, and Sir Thomas Roe records being sent game by Jahangir, on one occasion 'a mighty elk' (perhaps a nilgai or sambar) and on another a wild boar.

Deer meat was a favourite all over the country. While in exile in the Dandakaranya forest, Sita was frequently brought deer by Rama and Lakshmana, which she cooked along with rice and vegetables to yield mamsabhutadana. Other game mentioned in the Ramayana are the hare, hedgehog, porcupine, tortoise, and iguana. In the Mahabharata too, the Pandava princes, while in the Kaniyaka forest, ate deer of many kinds. Food served at a picnic feast in their happier days included 'large haunches of venison boiled in different ways with spices and mangoes, and sprinkled over with condiments'.

Early Tamil literature of between the third and sixth centuries AD abounds in references to wild game. The wild boar, rabbit, and hare were trapped using dogs and nets. Captive boars were fattened with rice flour and kept away from the female to improve the taste of the flesh. A dish of 'iguana red meat, big with ova resembling chank shell (conch) beads' is noted with a gourmet's eye. Game birds mentioned are the quail, peafowl, and parrot. A king is mentioned as feeding his guests with the 'rich roast flesh of lampreys' and the fat of turtles.

The medical authorities recommend as food innumerable animals of the chase as well as game birds. Jangalavasa (deer meat) and its sauces were considered particularly nourishing and balanced, and were accordingly recommended for consumption every day. Other game meats rated highly were those of the hare, tortoise, parrot, quail, partridge, peacock, and alligator (godha), while the pigeon, porcupine, and jackal also find mention.

Two types of meat were recognized. Jangala regions are hilly and arid; these harbour animals of eight kinds, one example being creatures who live in burrows and caves. The flesh of all jangala animals is lean, sweet, and light (in ayurvedic terms); it stimulates the appetite and regulates all the three body doshas (q.v.), in particular a reduced vata condition. Animals and birds from anupana terrain, which is forested and wet, have flesh that is fatty, sweet, and heavy (in ayurvedic terms). They are recommended only for certain individuals, and during seasons when the digestive power is particularly strong.

Ganges water The sacred river Ganga (Ganges) is believed to flow from Shiva's matted locks, and has for Hindus a special sanctity. Thousands bathe in it every day for purification, and most Hindus try to do so at least once in a lifetime. Many homes keep a vessel of Ganges water to be given to a dying person as the last ministration. Indian rulers with access to the river, like Emperor Harshavardhana at Kannauj, which lies on it, used only Gangajal for ablutions and cooking. Even the Portuguese physician Garcia da Orta, who from AD 1534 spent some thirty-five years in Goa and Bombay, claimed to have proved on himself the medicinal efficacy of Ganges water.

Muslim rulers likewise set great store by it. When Muhammad bin Tughlak shifted his capital from Delhi to Daulatabad around AD 1340, Ganges water was brought to him by runners from some 1500 km away. Akbar termed it the water of immortality, and according to the *Ain-i-Akbari*, 'both at home and on his travels he drinks Ganges water. For the cooking of food, rainwater or water taken from the Jamuna and Chenab is used, mixed with a little Ganges water.' In Agra and Fatehpur Sikri this water came from Sarun, and when in Punjab from Hardwar. Jahangir continued these practices and was very particular about drinking only the water of the Ganges. Even Aurangzeb, according to his physician Francois Bernier, 'keeps in Delhi and

Agra kitchen apparatus, Ganges water and all the other articles necessary for the camp.' His contemporary, Tavernier, muses that 'considerable sums of money are expended to procure Ganges water' and that 'by many it is constantly drunk in view of its reputed medical properties'.

During colonial rule a British physician, C.E. Nelson, noted that the water on ships taken from the river Hughli in Calcutta (as the Ganges is called there) would remain fresh all the way to London, but returning ships were obliged to replenish their English water en route.

Numerous experimental studies have shown that Ganges water drawn above Hardwar, where it enters the plains, has an unusual capacity for self-purification, and is exceptionally lethal to bacteria and cholera germs. Organic pollutants discharged into the river were removed 10 to 25 times faster than in any other river in India. Riverbed samples taken from the Ganges destroyed bacteria in the laboratory within a fortnight.

There appear to be four causes for this activity. One is the presence of bacteriophages which are lethal to many organisms; mosquitoes, for example, will simply not breed in Ganges water. Secondly, the river absorbs oxygen from the air with great efficiency. The next is the presence of heavy metals with known bactericidal properties, like copper, iron, chromium, and nickel. Copper vessels are commonly used in India to store boiled drinking water. The fourth reason for the prolonged keeping quality of Ganges water is believed to be the presence in it of minute quantities of radioactive minerals such as Bismuth-214, one of the decay products of Uranium-238. Sadly, however, recent studies have shown that below Hardwar the water of the great river has now become so highly polluted as to be even unsafe for human consumption.

gardens, floating These are unique to the lakes of Kashmir. They consist of water weeds bonded with lake mud, on which are grown cucumbers, melons, tomatoes, radishes, and mint, which are collected using boats.

garlic *Allium sativum* is a very ancient material, probably native to Afghanistan. Clay models of the

Garlic

bulbs have been found in pre-3000 BC Egyptian tombs, and in mummy stuffings. The high-born Aryan despised the garlic as a food of the natives (mlecchas) and foreigners (yavanas, q.v.), and it was forbidden on ceremonial occasions. In fact it is not even- mentioned in Sanskrit literature till the *Charaka Samhita* (say *c.* 200 BC).

Medical authorities have given the garlic considerable importance. Charaka classes it under harid, along with the onion, radish, and ginger. In the Bower manuscript (q.v.), a major topic is the medicinal value of garlic. It is believed to possess five of the six rasas or tastes of ayurveda; only the sour taste is missing, because of which the garlic earns its Sanskrit name rasona (lasuna). It is thus versatile in aligning humoral imbalances. Because of its aphrodisiac qualities, garlic is not allowed in the food of adolescents, widows, and those under a vow or on fast. Even rajasic (q.v.) types could get overexcited through its use, while sattvik (q.v.) types avoid it. In fact the two Chinese pilgrims, Fa Xian in the fifth century AD and Xuan Zang in the seventh, state flatly that the use of garlic was little known, which would have been true in the Buddhist circles in which they moved. Those addicted to opium, Father Monserrate noted, avoided garlic, onion and oil, and ate only pulses or sweet food before passing into a heavy sleep. Garlic was of course a valuable spice for discriminating users; thus the *Manasollasa* describes its presence in an elaborate dish of sheep mutton, and another of roast pork, meant for royal consumption.

gayal A bovine, *Bos frontalis*, the meat of which is commended in the *Vishnu Purana* (third/fourth century AD) as being very meritorious to serve at an ancestral shraddha ceremony, the others mentioned alongside being the meat of the hare, hog, goat, antelope, deer, and sheep.

ghani A mortar-and-pestle device made of stone or wood that uses a perambulating animal to extract oil under pressure from oil-bearing seeds, or materials like copra. It is mentioned as thaila-peshana-yantra by Panini in about the sixth century BC, and appears to have developed from two crushing devices for extracting soma (q.v.) mentioned in the *Rigveda*. One is the ulukhala-musala (mortar and pestle), and the other is a set of grinding stones, called gravan. Words in several spoken languages, like ghavan in Marathi for a stone mortar, ghatani in Gujarathi for a mill, and ghatanika for a heavy club in the Ramayana, besides inscriptional evidence, all seem to suggest that ghana, later ghani, was a colloquial word for the oilpress. It is also called kolhu, which again is probably derived from ulukhalika, meaning grinding. The Tamil word chekku for the oilpress is from the Sanskrit chakra, meaning revolving, by way of the Pali chakka. The *Manusmriti* and the *Arthashastra* list a number of Indian oilseeds crushed in ghanis.

The word thaila comes from the Sanskrit tila for sesame seed, and originally meant sesame oil; later it became generic for all vegetable oils, with suitable appellations. The oilmiller was a telika (Hindi teli) or chakrin. Among the guilds (shreni, q.v.) of craftsmen were those of oilmillers, which were later demarcated into two: one of lowly artisans, and the other of rich merchants who traded in oilseed products.

In south India, again, the term for sesame oil, ennai, became generic for all liquid oils, while nai was used for a semi-solid fat, such as ghee.

Not many old ghanis have survived. At a park in Dwarka, in Gujarat, a number of stone mortars have been assembled from the surrounding districts. Though labelled as soma-crushing devices, these appear to be old stone ghanis, which one authority dates as from between the first and the second centuries AD. There is a sculptural panel of a stone chakki drawn by bulls in the twelfth

century AD temple at Darasuram near Kumbakonam, in connection with the tale of a Shaivite saint who offered his own blood when oilseeds for crushing were not available. A historic chekku, one that was drawn in Coimbatore jail during the political incarceration of V.O. Chidambaram Pillai, has been transferred to Madras for display as a memorial. As a political prisoner sentenced to hard labour in the cellular jail on the Andaman Islands, V.D. Savarkar was forced to draw a ghani, which is now on display in the museum there.

It was only in 1930, when the All-India Village Industries Association

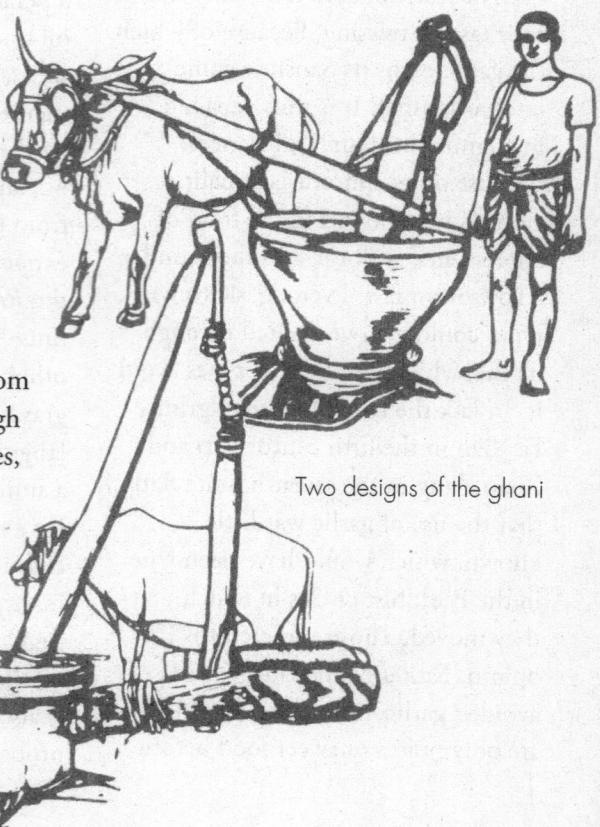

Two designs of the ghani

was formed in Wardha with the backing of Mahatma Gandhi that the ghani received critical attention. The best features of various regional designs were put together and tested by building models, to yield the Maganvadi ghani. This incorporated improvements which, Gandhiji wrote, 'have lessened the labour of both men and animals who work at the ghani and at the same time have improved the output of oil'. Further improvements led to the Wardha ghani of 1943, and improvements in design continued to be made even after Independence.

At the turn of the century, almost the entire oil needs of India were produced on 400,000–500,000 ghanis scattered all over the country. At Independence, this number remained essentially the same, but the outturn of oil from them had halved, because oilseeds were also being absorbed by the mechanized sections of industry.

ghee *See also* cooking; fats in cooking; frying.

Butter (q.v.), itself obtained by the churning of curd (q.v.), is boiled down with constant stirring till all the water has evaporated, and heating is continued till a pleasant cooked flavour emanates. The product is allowed to stand for a while, then decanted or filtered through muslin, to remove sediment. Hot ghee is frequently served at the table. Annaji,

a Kannada poet, refers to 'freshly-made ghee that flashed in (leaf) cups like amber'. On long standing, ghee tends to separate into a mass of grains in a liquid medium. Cow ghee is yellow in colour, and buffalo ghee cream-coloured.

Ghee in India has always been regarded as the supreme cooking fat. The Aryans would countenance no other fat than ghrta (another name was sarpi), though numerous vegetable oils were in use by other strata of the populace. Two highly auspicious ritual beverages had ghee as a component, madhuparka (q.v.) and panchagavya (q.v.). Examples of shallow and deep frying in ghee abound in Sanskrit literature (the apupa is ghrtavantam, ghee-fried, even in the *Rigveda*), in Tamil literature (as nai), and in cuisines all over the country (*see* frying). Both the Sultanate court in Delhi, and the later Mughal kitchens, employed ghee extensively; the *Ain-i-Akbari* (AD 1590) records that ghee for Akbar's kitchen came from Hissar.

Indian cooking distinguishes between restrictive kaccha boiled foods, and fried pucca foods that have wider scope for cultural transactions (*see* cooking). Even the stage of contact of the ghee in the sequence is sometimes critical. Thus to make kshirika (kheer), a pucca fried food, the rice must first come into contact with the ghee, before milk, sugar, and fire enter the picture. If rice is first boiled in milk, and ghee and sugar added later, the resulting dish is doodhbath, a kaccha restrictive boiled food. In fact, cooking with ghee, and cooking without ghee, are major sub-divisions of cooking with fire. Ghee is itself already cooked and ritually pure, and cooking with it is a ritually superior act. Even when sitting down to a meal, a few drops of ghee will first be sprinkled on the rice as a purificatory measure.

In ayurvedic terms, ghee is a 'sweet' food; it is strengthening, aids digestion and tempers the over-activity of all the three bodily doshas (q.v.). It acts quite powerfully on the mind, improving the memory and intellect. It is a pure, sattvik (q.v.) food, which was listed by the Buddha as one among those 'full of soul qualities'. Thus in the Bengali *Chandimangala* (sixteenth century), Lord Vishnu, a sattvik type, is given food cooked in ghee, while Lord Shiva, a choleric tamasic (q.v.) type, gets food cooked in pungent mustard oil. Charaka recommends ghee for cooking in the autumn season. The qualities of ghee made from various animal milks are listed: sheep milk ghee is easily digested, ghee from mare milk stimulates the digestion and pacifies kapha, and ghee from human

milk improves the eyesight and acts as an antidote to poisons. Ghee kept between 10 and 100 years, called kumbhaghrta, and that kept over 100 years, called mahaghrta, are powerful tonics, which reduce fever and have rejuvenating properties.

Ghee seems to have been a regular export item from India. In the first two centuries of the Christian era, it was exported as butyron to Rome for use by the wealthy in cooking and domestic sacrifices. Around AD 1680 Fryer remarks that in Bengal 'butter (almost certainly ghee is meant) is in such plenty that although it be a bulky article to export, yet it is sent by sea to numberless places'. In the decade before the Second World War, 1500–2000 tonnes of ghee were exported annually from India.

ginger This is an ancient material, with names in Sanskrit that are borrowed from even earlier usage (*see* adhrak). Both the green and dry forms of ginger, adhrak and sunthi in Hindi, are still in active use. They are viewed somewhat differently in ayurvedic terms. Dry ginger is simply

Ginger

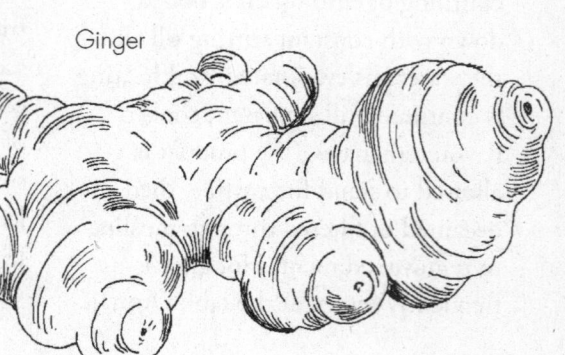

pungent, while the green material is considered both pungent and sweet, though both have a sweet aftertaste. While sunthi or dry ginger is light and oily, adhrak is considered heavy, drying and penetrating. Green ginger boiled with milk and sugared is a household remedy for colds and chills. A piece of fresh ginger, placed with some salt on the dining leaf in south India, starts the meal and stimulates the process of digestion.

Buddhist monks, as noted by I Ching in the fifth century AD and Xuan Zang in the seventh, were served fresh ginger with salt to begin the meal at the great monastery at Nalanda. Edward Terry noted in the Mughal period that the food of the poor was often no more than boiled rice with a bit of ginger. Being an underground product, ginger is not used by Jains.

Almost every visitor to south India remarks on the abundance of pepper and ginger, particularly in the Kerala area. Soon after their arrival there, the Portuguese set up the *Camera da India* to organize exports, and even a single cargoload included, among other spices, no less than 28 tonnes of ginger.

Ginger has always found use in the spicing of beverages. The three medical authorities employ it to spice both classes of fruit beverages: the lighter panaka juices drawn from sweet fruits, and the thickened sadhava products. Spicing curd

products with green ginger is almost the norm. The *Manasollasa*, written in the reign of King Someshwara in the twelfth century, has buttermilk spiced thus, and the practice continues in every home. A pacchadi of ginger paste in curd is used in the Karnataka area; a composite dish of curd blended with rice is also seasoned in this way; and dahi-vada contains small wedges of green ginger.

Today practically every curry of meat, chicken, fish, and seafood in India includes fresh or dried ginger in the spicing, often in the form of a ground garlic-ginger paste. This too has a long history. The Mahabharata features a picnic meal in which meat dishes are simmered with ginger among other spices, and much later the Sultanate court in Delhi relished meat dishes cooked in ghee, with onions and green ginger. Practically every recipe for meat dishes in the *Ain-i-Akbari* (1590) of Akbar's court includes green ginger. Ground meat for stuffing, called vesavara in the *Sushruta Samhita,* is flavoured with molasses, black pepper, and green ginger.

Ginger is also employed to give a certain snap to sweet items. The samyava of Charaka, a sweet concoction of fried wheat flour, is flavoured with cardamom, pepper, and ginger. A preserve of ginger in sugar solution, made by the Portuguese living in Bengal, is noted by Bernier in AD 1665, and such morabbas (q.v.)

were commonly eaten by the Muslims and had a medical connotation. Wedges of banana dipped in thick jaggery batter and deep-fried, a popular snack in Kerala, owe much of their appeal to the liberal use of ground ginger in the sweet coating.

ginger grass A perennial aromatic grass, *Cymbopogon martini*, of which there are two forms. Motia yields by steam distillation the superior rosha, palmarosa or lemon grass oil, and sofia the inferior ginger grass oil. The genus *Cymbopogon* has innumerable species, one of which yields citronella oil. Early Tamil literature refers to export to Rome of spikenard oil brought from the Ganges, and Marco Polo, more than a thousand years later, noted that Bengal produced spikenard, besides ginger and sugar. It was Garcia da Orta who around AD 1560 first identified spikenard with the rosha grass that grew along the banks of the Ganges, yet till even a century ago, George Watt was of the opinion that ginger grass and lemon grass oils were derived from different species. Rosha oil has mostly medicinal uses—as a massage in lumbago and a mosquito repellent, while ginger grass oil is used to perfume soaps, cosmetics, etc.

gluten A protein unique to the bread wheats (*Triticum sphaerococcum*), gluten is what gives wheat dough its sticky, rubbery and elastic quality. This is essential in the making of baked products from wheat, from a chapathi to a loaf of bread, because it forms a radiating network that holds the starch in place. Washing wheat flour in a slow stream of water will leach out the starch and leave behind a rubbery ball of gluten. Isolated gluten can be used to strengthen low-gluten wheat flours, and it is the base of the chewy confection, sohan-halwa. In Mughal times the rich drink falooda (q.v.) seems to have employed isolated wheat gluten as a component, besides fruit juices and cream.

Goa, foods from An exceedingly ancient settlement, the name Goa can be traced in the Gubi of Sumerian tablets (2100 BC), the Gouba of Ptolemy, the later Govapuri and Gopapuri, and even the aboriginal Munda word Goen-Bab, meaning an ear of corn. In 1510 it was captured from the Sultan of Bijapur by Alfonso da Albuquerque; the Estado da India was established, and lasted for about 150 years before it yielded first to the Dutch and then to the English.

Goa was the point of entry of numerous plant species brought in with commercial intent by Portuguese and Spaniards from South and Central America. One of these was the sapota (cheeku), and another the cashew tree; the yellow-red 'fruit' (really the swollen stalk) of the latter is in fact called go-manga in Kerala, perhaps after its Goan source. The Indian mango (q.v.) was skilfully grafted to yield varieties with Portuguese names: Alfonso, Pairi (from Peres) and Malgoa. Around AD 1700, Niccolao Manucci wrote: 'The best mangoes grow in the island of Goa ..., I have eaten many that had the taste of the peaches, plums, pears and apples of Europe.' The doctor, Garcia da Orta, lived in Goa and Bombay for thirty-five years from AD 1534, and the Dutch botanist, John Huygen van Linschoten, for six years around AD 1580.

It was largely the Catholic monks of Goa who developed a cuisine which amalgamated Iberian with local (mainly Saraswath Hindu) sensibilities. Vinegar, an essentially European material (though not unknown in India), was made from; coconut exudate and employed. So were chillies of various kinds. The peripери masala uses the intensely red but mild chilli varieties grown in Kashmir, Goa, and north Karnataka (where they are known as bedige chillies). Green chillies go into the cafreal masala, and a fiery button chilli is used on occasion. Bread in Goa is based not on wheat, but on rice flour; some molasses are added, the mass is leavened with palm toddy, and glazed before baking with egg white, to yield bole. Saanas is a round steamed bread of rice-pulse flour fermented overnight with toddy. From wheat is made a

hard, ring-shaped dinner roll called kankod, and a whorl-like pastry, barki. Pork is variously employed. One form is the distinctive garlic-flavoured Goa sausage, called chourico or chourisam: Sorpotel is a curry of the blood, meat, liver, and fat of pork with both tamarind juice and vinegar, and in vindaloo, a more liquid curry, the souring agent is the dried rind of the kokum fruit Pork assado is marinated in feni. Pork cooked with beans gives feijoada. Pork can be salted, and then pickled. Fish and prawns are abundant, and distinctive dishes have been developed. A curry of salmon is cooked with the sour-sweet kokum fruit; a yellow fish curry that uses turmeric is caladine; and the pomfret is cooked with coconut vinegar after being stuffed with periperi masala of red chillies, pepper, cloves, ginger, and garlic. The roe of the kingfish, lightly salted and fried, is a breakfast delicacy. Mackerel is cooked in a green cafreal masala of green chillies, coriander and spices. Prawn balchao contains vinegar and lots of chopped onions that give it a sweet-sour flavour, and it keeps well enough to be bottled for use as a pickle. Shallow-fried chicken or meat constitutes chacuti.

Quite distinctive are the desserts of Goa. Bibinca is a concoction of egg yolk, flour and thin coconut milk which is built up in layers and baked repeatedly; it is then turned upside-down to cool. Spaniards carried a baked dish of this name to the Philippines and even to Hawaii, though the layered baking appears to be distinctive of Goa. The flour of the Bengal gram, besan (q.v.), is baked with grated coconut and sugar to yield Dos de Grao (this last is the Portuguese word for pulses, which in English became gram), which has a thick, firm crust, and a chewy centre. Baked yams are coated with melted jaggery; mangada is a moist, chewy mango cheese, and perada a brown guava cheese. Pastry is frequently decorated with strips of tender coconut meat dipped in melted sugar, a unique Indo-European combination. Dodol is a soft fudge of jaggery. Monks were responsible, in Goa as in Europe, for developing alcoholic beverages, like the distinctive-tasting feni distilled from cashew 'fruits' and coconut palm toddy, imbibed directly, or as cocktails of many kinds.

goat Goat meat was the major meat commodity consumed in 1947, followed by that of the sheep; one-third of the goat population was slaughtered every year, which meant that it was raised entirely for meat. Prime Indian breeds are the Jamna Pari, Bar Bari, and Jodhpur.

From Vedic times the goat has been a prime animal for sacrifice, and a large goat was the basis of the elaborate ajamedha (q.v.) sacrifice, with special cauldrons (ukha) and utensils. Its flesh was rated highly by medical authorities, and being an animal easy to rear and a diligent forager, the goat went on to become the prime source of meat in many poorer countries, till warning notes were sounded of environmental denudation caused by roving goat herds.

Jahangir recorded his observations on the wild goat thus: 'I found the flesh of the mountain goat more delicious than that of all wild animals, though its skin is exceedingly ill-odoured, so much so that even when tanned the scent is not destroyed.'

In more recent times, Mahatma Gandhi drank only fresh goat's milk, and a milch animal even accompanied him when he went to the Round Table Conference in London in 1931.

gonkuru The tall plant *Hibiscus cannabinus* is also called nalita and ambadi in India, and kenaf and mesta elsewhere. Its fibre is twisted into ropes, and the sour leaves are eaten, notably as a pacchadi in the Andhra region. The plant has long been acclimatized in India, though it is of West African origin.

goose Not a common flesh in India, though it finds a place in the long list of edible meats noted by Charaka. Domingo Paes noted the availability in Vijayanagar of 'lake birds that look like geese' (perhaps the wild form was used all along).

Gourd

In colonial times, geese, along with hens and ducks, were fattened domestically for eating, especially for a Christmas lunch.

gourds Trailing or climbing plants, whose fruits are characterized by a hard skin, soft body, and numerous seeds, and commonly called gourds, melons, pumpkins. Early Vedic literature describes them as being grown on the 'banks of rivers, beaten by foam', and they have always been raised before the onset of the rains on the dry beds of rivers and tanks.

Gourds and pumpkins are largely used as vegetables in India, while the melon group serves both as vegetables and fruit. Charaka describes a generic term asuta for gourds and radishes preserved in vinegar.

Several gourds are of considerable antiquity in India and Africa. The common cucumber, khira in Hindi, chirbhita, urvaruka, and sukasa in Sanskrit, and botanically *Cucumis sativus*, is undoubtedly Indian, with a bitter wild ancestor, *C. hardwickii*, still found in the Himalayan foothills. The *Cucumis* family also includes some melons. Of these *C. melo*, the popular kharbuza or musk melon, probably originated in Africa, but 'exploded in terms of variety when it came from Africa to India' . Three other varieties are also edible: *Var. utilissimis*, the khakri; *var. agrestis*, the meki or tak-mak; and *var. mormodica*, the kachra or phunt. Other melons (q.v.) belong to the *Citrullus* family, the best known being the luscious water-melon or tarbuz, *Citrullus lunatus*, of Indo-African origin. It is an ancient fruit, and its Sanskrit name kalinda is believed to be of prior Munda origin. The delicate vegetable tinda is *C. lunatus var.*

fistulosus. Another long-known species is *C. colocynthis*, the Sanskrit indrayan or mahendravaruni, whose spongy, bitter fruit is sold in a dry form for use as a rather drastic laxative.

The *Cucurbita* species carry such common names in America as pumpkin, squash, marrow, and gourd. All originated in the New World, with progenitors even 10,000 years old, yet some of them have Sanskrit names of considerable antiquity. This may be due to the ability of gourds to float in seawater without losing seed viability when crossing from continent to continent. The red pumpkin, or winter squash of America, is urubaka in Sanskrit, and lal-kumra, kaddhu, and kumbala-kayi in other Indian tongues: round to oval fruits, bluntly ribbed, with yellow to reddish flesh, which are cooked as dry or wet curries. Two other winter squash species, *C. moschata* and *C. maxima*, are known in India as kaddhu, kumra, dudhi, and dumbala: some smooth and oblong, others fluted and either spherical or flattened. Yet another winter squash in America is the cushaw, *C. mixta*, known as the African gourd in India (suggesting a two-stage transfer to India). It is a fruit of large size with a swollen peduncle at the top; it takes a high polish and is frequently employed to make bowls of Indian musical instruments like the thanpura and

vicchitra veena. *Cucurbita pepo*, the summer squash of America, is a green, deeply ridged, pear-shaped vegetable known in India as safed-kaddhu, kumra, and surai-kayi.

The term gourd has increasingly developed a more restricted connotation that embraces four plant families. Under *Benicasa* falls *B. hispida* (petha, pushnikayi, ash gourd, in Sanskrit kushmanda), perhaps native to Malaysia. It is cooked as a vegetable, and soaked in strong sugar solution to yield the brittle confection, petha. The genus *Luffa* has three species with old Sanskrit names, and is therefore probably indigenous. These are *L. acutangula,* the ridged-gourd, *L. acutangula var. amara*, and *L. aegyptiaca*. All of them carry slight variations of the same Sanskrit name koshataki (which is first mentioned in the *Arthashastra* of *c.* 300 BC), the Hindi word thorai, and the Tamil pirkankayi. The last of these is used as a vegetable and also yields on drying the firm, net-like loofah sponge.

Apart from *Luffa*, the two other gourd families are *Trichosanthes* and *Momordica*. *Trichosanthes dioica* is the Sanskrit putulika, Hindi parwal, and Bengali potol, a small, tender vegetable. *T. anguina* is the long snake gourd, chachinda in Sanskrit, and pottalakaya in Telugu, while *T. cucumerina* is the Hindi rambel; the first two are probably of Indian origin, the last perhaps Malaysian. In the *Momordica* group, the best-known is *M. charantia,* the bittergourd or karela, in Sanskrit karavella, which is first mentioned *c.* 400 BC in early Jain literature. A smaller version of the bittergourd is *M. dioica,* kaksa or golkandra in Hindi, and palupakayi or tholpavai in Tamil; an even smaller knobbly kind is *M. tuberosa,* kadavanchi in Hindi and athalaikayi in Tamil, which is pickled, or sun-dried and fried to crisps. The bhat-karela or kakrol of Hindi is *M. cochinchinensis,* also used as a vegetable.

Thus the extended gourd family is important in the diet of the people of India (*see also* melons; squash).

grafting Grafting is listed in the *Kamasutra* of Vatsyayana (fourth century AD) as one of the 64 arts. The *Brhat Samhita* of Varahamihira, dated AD 505, describes grafting very explicitly as 'smearing a branch with cowdung and transplanting it on the branch of another; or it may be done by cutting off the branch of a tree and transplanting it like a wedge on the trunk of another tree'. The trees amenable to grafting are listed as the jackfruit, banana, lemon, citron, pomegranate, grape, jasmine, and some others, but not the mango. The Portuguese in Goa in the sixteenth century used grafting to produce excellent and stable varieties of mango, like the Alfonso (*see* mango). Jahangir rewarded good horticultural

results, including those derived from grafting, obtained at the royal gardens in Kashmir, Punjab, and Agra, and Shahjahan later extended these benefits to non-royal plantations. Grafting was applied to cherries and apricots in Kashmir, and to oranges and mangoes in Bengal. Figs were grafted on mulberry trees, peaches on plum trees, apricots on almond trees, and vines on apple trees.

gram The Portuguese word for grain, grao, was first applied in India to the Bengal gram or chickpea, and later applied generally to all pulses; thus arose the terms red gram, green gram, black gram, horsegram, etc. Its use is unknown outside India.

granary A large structure, generally state-maintained in India, for the storage of grain for extended periods in an edible condition. Small village or home devices for grain storage are considered under agriculture.

Mass storage of foodgrains in the Indus Valley (2500–1500 BC) was on a scale and of a sophistication hardly ever matched later in India's history. The granary in Harappa took the shape of a mud platform, 52 by 42 metres in size and 1.2 metres high, on which stood two identical granary blocks, reach 17 by 6 metres, placed 7 metres apart and with walls 3 metres thick. Each block had 6 chambers, with corridors between them which opened only on to the outside, and were approached by a short flight of steps. Each chamber was divided into four storage spaces by full-length walls. The floor rested on sleepers, and air could circulate in the void below and enter the chamber for aeration through small triangular vents. The granary faced the river, along which the grain possibly arrived. The sheer size of the granary almost certainly implies state authority.

All that remains at Mohenjodaro is a massive brick platform with steep sloping sides, on which stood the bases of some 27 storage blocks arranged crosswise to facilitate air circulation. The granary itself was probably built of wood, and has disappeared. Halfway up the brick platform is an unloading platform with niches, on which carts bringing in grain could well have stood while being unloaded.

At Lothal, the storage unit appears to be more in the nature of a warehouse which overlooked the dock. It took the form of an enormous mud platform, 34 by 45 metres and 3.5 metres high, on which rested twelve square brick pallets, 3.7 metres each way and 1 metre high. A great deal of melted material was found inside, suggesting that the original wooden chambers had burnt down.

A row of circular platforms, each 3 metres across and constructed of bricks placed on edge fanwise in circles, was found near the granaries at Harappa and Mohenjodaro.

Fragments of husk, barley, and burnt wheat were lodged in the crevices, and a central hole indicates where the pounding was carried out using wooden pestles, an operation still in vogue all over India. Perhaps a special class of workers carried out these operations.

In later centuries, only oblique references occur to state granaries for food storage. Writing in about AD 1340, the Moroccan, Ibn Battuta, records that when famine broke out, Muhammad bin Tughlak ordered that every resident in Delhi, rich or poor, free man or slave, should be given a six-month supply of foodgrains from the state granary at the rate of about 675 grams a day. Considerable stocks must have been held for this to be feasible.

grape Grape seeds have been found in extremely ancient tertiary deposits 10–15 million years old. Even in the fourth millennium BC the grape-vine was cultivated in the Middle East. Practically all the 10,000 grape cultivars now known are mere ecovariations, and not different species, of a single wild form, *Vitis vinifera*.

Indian grapes however have certain characteristics that indicate introgression from other species. Besides *V. vinifera* itself, there is *V. indica*, a climber with indifferent fruit, whose root-juice is used as a blood purifier. India also has *V. labrusca* or the fox grape, which is well represented commercially by the long-standing Bangalore Blue, with its thick skin and abundant, slightly acid juice, popular as both a table and a wine grape. At one time the sturdy and very old wild fruits of Kashmir were classed as *V. latifolia*, but these have now been reclassified as *Ampelocissus latifolia*, which is described as a woody, climbing shrub that is highly resistant to pests and other diseases, and bears edible fruit.

Thus the grape must have been known at least in the north of India since very early times. Rather surprisingly it receives only late mention in Sanskrit, as draksha and mrdvika, by Panini and Charaka, in *c.* 500 BC. The Buddhist stupas at both Bharhut and Sanchi, dated about the second century BC, show beautiful carvings of vines and grape bunches. Varahamihira in the *Brhat Samhita* (*c.* AD 500) mentions the grape as one among several fruits that can be grafted.

Grape cultivation in India seems to have moved in cycles. Its use for making wine and spirits may have led to its suppression by puritanical rulers. Xuan Zang notes in the seventh century AD that grapes were brought (presumably to Nalanda in Bihar) from Kashmir. Around AD 1340, Ibn Battuta notes that, except for being grown extensively in Daulatabad, and available in Delhi, grapes were rare. Firuz

Tughlak took steps to grow seven kinds of grapes near Delhi, and with abundant production its price fell to just five times that of the same weight of wheat. Babar encouraged grape production, and by the time of Akbar, grapes had become plentiful. Writing about Agra some thirty years later, Francisco Pelsaert of Holland noted that 'great and wealthy amateurs there plant in their gardens Persian vines which bear seedless grapes, but the fruits do not ripen properly one year out of three'. Bernier in AD 1660 rejoiced in the meadows and vineyards of Kashmir, and Thevenot shortly thereafter remarked on the 'passion for the cultivation of the grape', possibly as a result of Portuguese encouragement. In his memoirs, Jahangir noted that two crops of grapes had been raised in Malwa, and yet by the end of Aurangzeb's long reign of fifty years in AD 1707, grape production in India fell into a decline from which it never really recovered till the remarkable resurgence of the 1960s.

Grape products like the raisin and sultana have always been imported into India under the name kishmish, which is actually the name of the grape grown in Quetta and Kandahar. In India, the production of alcohol by fermentation has generally favoured starchy materials and palm exudates, though a variety of fruit has also been used. Madhira

Grapefruit

appeared to have been a grape-based wine (*see* beverages, alcoholic).

grapefruit One of a very large citrus family (q.v.), *C. parodist* is a cross native to Thailand between the mosambi (*C. sinensis*) and *C. grandis*, the shaddock or pomelo, called in India chakotra and bombelinas. It was taken to the West Indies and called grapefruit, and introduced by the surgeon-general of the Napoleonic army into Florida in the USA. A hemisphere of grapefruit sprinkled with sugar is frequently a starting course at dinner in America.

Greek contacts Indian connections with Greece go back a long way. Even the Old Testament carries some words which indicate an Indian origin. One is the word rice, oryza (also now the botanical genus, Indian rice being *Oryza sativa*), which is believed to have originated in the Tamil arisi. The other is peperi (pepper) from pippali (in both Tamil and Sanskrit), and yet another is karphea or karpion for

cinnamon, from the Tamil karuva or karappapattai. From Greek these terms passed into other European languages.

Two other Greek words for oil, elaion and oleum, also appear to have an Indian connection. This link is by way of the words ell and enn (which were old Tamil names for sesame seed) through the term ennai, which first meant sesame oil, and later all liquid vegetable oils. Yet another connection is seen in the term yavanapriya, 'beloved of the Greek', employed in Sanskrit for pepper.

Direct contact between Greece and India was established with Alexander's incursion in May 327 BC, followed by a stay of eighteen months. Even before this, stray and often inaccurate information on matters Indian was published in Greece. Ktesias (416–398 BC), a court physician and historian, based his *Indika* on talks that he had with Persian officials who had visited India, and with seven Indians, including two women, whom he met at the Persian court at Susa. He recorded that both sesame and coconut oils were in use, and that there were palms in India with huge fruits (coconuts). The hill people dried a sweet fruit called siptakora (perhaps the ber, q.v.) in the manner of raisins, and packed them in hampers to be traded for grain with those living in the plains.

Aristobolus of Kassandrelia, who accompanied Alexander, described rice as a strange plant, which was sown in beds and stood in water. He observed that the food of two brahmin priests cost them nothing, since they simply helped themselves from food stalls to whatever they liked, for example to abundant cakes of sesamum and honey (probably til laddus made with jaggery). Nearchos of Crete was a senior leader who commandeered Alexander's return fleet (largely built in the Punjab area) down the river Hydaspes (Jhelum) to the sea and thence to Iraq. He mentioned 'a reed tree' (the sugar-cane) that 'produced honey without the association of bees' and the abundance in India of medicinal plants and herbs. There was, he noted, both a summer and a winter crop, and this 'great facility of the soil' was attributed correctly not only to the rains, but to the abundant silt which the rivers brought down from the mountains. A grain, a little smaller than wheat, and repeatedly called bismoron by the Greeks, was first threshed and then roasted 'in a common enterprise', following which each took his requirement for the year. Describing the visit by Apollonius of Tyana (born 295 bc) to Takshashila, Philostratus, another of the party, noted that while the king did hunt, this was solely for exercise; he gave away what he killed, and lived on vegetarian food.

Megasthenes was appointed around 330 bc by Seleukos Nikator (who had been defeated by Chandragupta Maurya) as ambassador to the latter's court at Pataliputra. Though only fragments of his *Indika* survive, much more is preserved in numerous quotations by later writers like Diodorus, Strabo, Arrian, and Pliny. He wrote:

Indians live frugally, especially when in camp ... they lead happy lives, being simple in their manners and frugal. They never drink wine except at sacrifices. Their beverage is a liquor composed from rice instead of barley, and their food is principally rice-pottage.

Megasthenes noted that agriculturists formed the bulk of the Indian population. Of them he writes:

They are a most mild and gentle people. They never resort to the cities either to transact business or to take part in public tumults. They are exempted from all military service, and pursue their labours free from alarm. Indeed it often happens that at the same times and in the same part of the country, the army is engaged in fighting the enemy, while the husbandmen are sowing and ploughing in the utmost security ... The entire land is the property of the King, to whom they pay one-fourth of the produce as revenue.

Indian agricultural practices came in for admiration; he expressed surprise that the water-wheel (ashmanchakra), with clay pots attached, could raise water by 20 cubits (about 10 metres) to the river brim, and a further 10 metres to inundate the fields.

Of the upper classes Megasthenes wrote:

When Indians are at supper, a table is placed before each person, this being like a tripod. There is placed upon it a golden bowl, into which they first put rice, boiled as one would boil barley (the Greek dish chondros), and then they add many dainties according to Indian recipes.

The *History of Alexander the Great* written by Quentin Curtius-Rufus (*c.* 30 BC–AD 30) has a description of the emperor Chandragupta Maurya at dinner: 'His food is prepared by women, who also serve him wine, which is much used by all Indians. When the King falls into a drunken sleep, his courtesans carry him away to his bedchamber, invoking the gods of the night in their native hymns.'

Alexander's Indian visit continued to be a subject of fascination in Greece. Strabo relates how from Takshashila he received 3600 oxen and 10,000 sheep, and how in the country of the Ashvakas he captured 20,000 oxen of a fine breed which he sent back to Macedonia. The *Anabasis of Alexander*, written by Arrian (Flavinius Arrianus, *c.* AD 96–160), mentions that Alexander's return fleet going down the Indus, 'came to a large lake formed by the river in widening out ... to give it the appearance of a gulf of the sea ... for salt-water fish were now seen in it of a larger size than anything in our sea'. Another curious bit of information

from Arrian was that elephant wounds were cured in India by the application of roast pork.

The sixth of Pliny the Elder's (AD 23–79) thirty-seven books, called *The Natural History*, is on India, and is based again on the lost writings of Megasthenes. Pliny describes several Indian trees: the fig (banyan) which produced small fruit, the pala tree (?) with wonderful sweet fruit called ariena, favoured as food by sages, and the 'olive' tree (perhaps the ber), the pepper plant, and the grape-vine.

In about AD 40, a Greek sailor, Hippalos, discovered for the West the monsoon winds to and from India, thus briskly fanning the trade that already existed between south India and Rome. Shortly thereafter, a remarkable book, *Periplus Marts Erythraei* (Circumnavigation of the Erythrean Sea) was written posthumously by a Greek sailor posted in Alexandria.

It lists exports as ivory from Dosarena (Orissa), muslins from Maisolia (Macchilipatnam), pearls from Korkai (Colchi) in the Pandyan kingdom, and pepper from Muziris (Cranganore) in the Chera kingdom. The other items exported were spices, perfumes, herbs, and precious stones, in exchange for which was imported gold, silver, tin and lead, glass vessels, horses, coral, wine, and linen cloth.

green gram *See* mung.

green leafy vegetables These must have figured as food items in India from the very dawn of history, but can only be identified when recorded in the earliest Sanskrit literature. The Vedic corpus mentions patha (which could be *Corchorus capsularis*, later called pathua), varuna (*Crataeva nurvala*, Hindi barna), avaka (stated to be a Kashmiri pot herb) and lakshmana, described as a green leaf with red spots. Aquatic herbs also find mention, like the pushkarna (lotus) and the waterlily family (*Nymphaea*); four species of the latter exist in India, called in Sanskrit kumuda, pushkara, andika, and shaluka, of which the seeds, carpels, fruit, and tubers were all consumed. In the subsequent *Sutra* period (800–300 BC) many more leafy vegetables were noticed. The watercress was mandukaparni (Hindi brahmi, *Nasturtium officinale*), and the pigweed was vasthuka (Hindi bathua saag, *Chenopodium alba*). The spinach, palankya in Sanskrit and palak in Hindi, is *Spinacia oleracea*, native to south-west Asia and known in India long before it went to the West. Other leafy vegetables mentioned are methika (Hindi methi, *Trigonella foenumgraecum*, fenugreek [q.v.] in English), and the Sanskrit sigru or shaubhanjana, the drumstick tree (*Moringa oleifera*, Hindi sajuna), whose leaves and long pods are still popular vegetables (*see* drumstick).

The trio of medical authorities, and especially Charaka, list numerous leafy vegetables. Tender leaves of certain trees, like the palm and bilva (*Aegle marmelos*) are edible, and the tender sprouts of the bamboo and the vetragra (Hindi bent or vetasa, *Calamus rotang*, also a cane) were considered delicacies. Leaves of several shrubs find a place: some of these are amaranths, tandulikaya (*A. spinosus*, Hindi kanta-chaulai), and anarisa (perhaps *A. cruentus*, Hindi chaulai); sarshapa (Hindi sarson-ka-saag, *Brassica napus* var. *glauca*); jivaka, stated to be a Himalayan plant, perhaps *Pentapetes phoenicia*; and savarchela, a flowering plant. As is to be expected, many pot herbs noted in this period have a medicinal connotation. Two are of the *Cassia* family (to which also belongs the aromatic tejpat): chakramarda (Hindi chaksu, *Cassia absus*) and susa (Hindi kasaundi, *C. sophera*), while several are related to the popular vasthuka, like kutinjara (jangli-bathua) and javashaka (Hindi khat-papli). A medicinal slant also shows up in the changed (Indian sorrel, Hindi amrul or chaupatia, *Oxalis comiculata*); lonika (the common purslane, *Portulaca oleracea*, Hindi khursa or baralaniya); maruvaka (Hindi marua, *Meyna laxiflora*); javani (Hindi ajwain, omum, *Trachyspermum ammi*; see caraway) and kalashaka (Hindi karipatta, the curry leaf [q.v.], *Murraya koenigii*). An even greater medicinal value is ascribed to the jivanti (which Charaka refers to as a superior pot-herb; it is the Indian sarsaparilla, Hindi magrabu, *Hemidesmus indicus*); satavari (Hindi satavar, *Asparagus racemosus*); chitraka (Hindi chita, *Plumbago zeylanica*); and two members of the hogs weed family, punamava (which is also its Hindi name, *Boerhavia diffusa*) and kathillaka (Hindi visakhapara, red hogsweed).

Tamil literature of between the third and sixth centuries AD mentions several edible leafy vegetables. Leaves of the chembu (the taro, *Colocasia esculenta*), kuppukeerai (*Amaranthus viridis*), munnai (*Meyna laxifolia*), vellai (*Cleome viscosa*), and vallarai (*Centella asiatica*, Asiatic pennywort) are valued mainly for their culinary rather than medicinal qualities.

Green leafy vegetables were best raised on low grounds, like the moist beds of lakes. They had the general connotation of being cold, 'sweet' foods that promote digestion, with specific therapeutic uses. Thus the changeri is active against dyspepsia, piles, and anaemia, astringent and antiseptic; the lonika is beneficial in matters urinary; and punarnava is very effective against dropsy and as a diuretic.

While the Buddha praised the use of leafy vegetables as food, they are interdicted for Jain monks, perhaps through fear of killing the minute insects they could possibly harbour.

Leafy vegetables are particularly popular in moist and fertile Bengal and Assam. Even Sushrutha mentions that in the Suhma country (Bengal), tender leaves were boiled, the excess water squeezed out, jeera and rai seeds added and the mass shaped into a delicacy called sindhaki. A soup called kadha (kadhi?) was made using tender greens. Nalida (*Corchorus* species), the climbing spinach puin, colocasia leaves, amaranthus leaves, and many aquatic plants are items consumed frequently. In the Bengali work *Chandimangala* (AD 1589), which relates food to temperament, Lord Shiva, who is of a choleric temperament, relishes pungent mustard leaves, and a rich merchant's wife, a spoilt woman, is served with a variety of pot herbs. In Punjab, sarson-ka-saag (with butter) is served with makki-ki-roti, made from maize, both 'hot' foods appropriate for consumption in winter.

griddle The Sanskrit kharpava, Hindi thava, and Kannada kavali, a thick, flat or slightly concave iron plate on which Indian rotis are roasted. Gay and metal plates of this kind have been found in Indus Valley excavations, suggesting an ancient lineage for griddle cooking.

grilling Use of a wire network for cooking a dry dish directly over a flame is not common in Indian cooking, except perhaps for the dried meat of game, pork, deer, etc. Tandoor cooking (q.v.) is sometimes referred to as grilling.

grinding devices Neolithic times in India saw the use of simple stone units with a slight inward or outward depression, paired with a grinding stone (muller), which progressed from a simple, naturally rounded pebble to dressed convex or concave stones. Two types of querns show up in the Indus Valley. One is more or less flat, and with it goes a cylindrical muller rolled with both hands. The other has a small circular depression, in which grains can be crushed with a rounded stone held in one hand. A flat, four-legged quern of the latter kind is depicted in a Sanchi sculpture of about 250 BC. A later type consisted of a cylindrical stone base on which revolved a heavy-domed stone, worked by two women with a stout pole that passed through two holes opposite each other. Later, in about the early Christian era, the upper domed stone was replaced by a heavy circular stone with a central opening, which revolved on a firmly fitted central peg on the lower stone, and also had a short upright wooden peg on the periphery for movement. This is the familiar domestic device for grinding grain.

Sanskrit literature provides further insights. The *Rigveda* (*c.* 1500 BC) describes two devices, both meant to crush soma juice (q.v.) for sacrifices. One consisted of a set (perhaps a pair) of grinding stones, and the noise of grinding was compared to the exertions of bulls and horses.

The second crushing device was the mortar-pestle, ulukhala-musala, which was presumably of shallow design. In course of time the stones came to be termed peshani or gharatta; the flat lower portion was the drshad, the upper the drshadputra or upala. Both devices are used in homes to this day. One is the flat grinding stone with a long, thick cylindrical muller, worked horizontally for grinding materials either dry, or with a sprinkling of water, and the other is the pot-like stone unit with a short, stout, upright stone that works in a circular motion for wet grinding (of an idli batter, for example).

The more capacious upright mortar, worked in a standing position using a long, stout, wooden pestle, is used mostly for dehusking or pounding grain rather than for grinding (*see* pounding).

In south India also similar grain crushers, milling stones, mortars, and pestles have been found in neolithic sites of the second millennium BC. Sangam literature in Tamil of between the third and sixth centuries AD employs the terms ammi, thiruvai, attukal, and kulavi for the flat grinding stone, which was often

Groundnuts

later in Gujarat, and thereafter in many regions. The large Brazilian groundnut may have entered the country via Africa, and the small Peruvian type from Manila or China, independently of each other.

guar *See* cluster bean.

guava The botanical name *Psidium guajava* reflects the Spanish name of the fruit, guajava. It originated in Peru in South America, as is evident from remains dating to 800 BC, which have been excavated. Blochmann's English translation of the *Ain-i-Akbari* (AD 1590) has a suggestion that guavas were served at Akbar's table, but this could arise from an error in translating the word amrud used by Abul Fazl, which even today stands both for the guava and the much older pear. Though as early as in AD 1550 Benzoni correctly describes the fruit in the east of India, the first unambiguous mention is by Fryer in 1673. Two other *Psidium* species that grow in India yield small edible fruit: the Guinea guava (*P. guinense*) and the strawberry guava (*P. cattleyanum*).

guest and host Guests had an honoured place in Vedic society, ranking below only the father, mother, and guru. On arrival, a guest was ceremoniously received, given water to wash his hands and feet, and offered the ambrosial beverage

made in animal shapes, like that of the tortoise. The stone mullers that accompanied them were called puttil and vatigai.

groundnut This popular nut, eaten directly and also used in cooking, is of surprisingly recent provenance in India. In 1850 there were just a thousand hectares devoted to the groundnut, but by 1895 this had gone up 70-fold. Production of nuts, which was 2.5 lakh tonnes in 1910, went up 6-fold in the next two decades, and at Independence stood at about 35 lakh tonnes. Most of it was crushed for oil, and groundnut oil had the major share in the total Indian production of vegetable oil. About a tenth of the produce is consumed as nuts.

Even ancient Peruvian tombs of 3000–2000 BC carry *Arachis hypogea*, of which two sub-species eventually arose, one an erect plant and the other a trailer. In India, four major kinds were soon recognized in the trade: Virginia, Valencia, Peruvian Runner, and Spanish, respectively, all cultivated first in south India, madhuparka (q.v.). In early Vedic times, if the guest was an honoured brahmin or a member of the royalty, a large bull or goat would be sacrificed in his honour, even if the guest was himself a vegetarian. Later this ritual became symbolic, and the guest was given a knife in token of the sacrifice, which he returned after a prayer. During the meal, the host had to be solicitous, either eating later, or finishing his own meal quickly, so as to rise early and look after his guests.

In the *Manava Dharmashastra* (*Manusmriti*), a host is exhorted in these terms:

Let him, being pure and attentive, place on the ground the seasoning for the rice, such as broth and pot herbs, sweet and sour honey, as well as various kinds of hard foods that require mastication, and soft foods, roots, fruits and savoury and fragrant drinks.

All these he shall present, and being pure and attentive, successively invite them partake of each, proclaiming its qualities: cause them to partake gradually and slowly of each and repeatedly urge them to eat by offering the food and extolling its qualities.

All the food shall be very hot, and the guests shall eat in silence. Having addressed them with the question: 'Have you dined well?' let him give them water to sip, and bid farewell to them with the words, 'Now rest'.

Gujarat, food in Till fairly recently, in geological terms, Gujarat was connected by land with Africa. Stone Age cleavers and hand axes that go back 50,000 years and more, have been found there in comparative abundance. Much later Gujarat formed part of the enormous Indus Valley civilization (2500-1500 BC, q.v.). Lothal and Rangpur were important settlements, in the excavations of which rice spikelets have been found.

Many centuries later, Emperor Ashoka chose to set up one of his rock edicts at Girnar in Gujarat, which opens with the lines: 'No living being may be slaughtered for sacrifice; no festive gatherings (for the purpose) may be held. Formerly slaughter in the King's kitchen (that is, his own) was great, now it has almost been stopped.' This seems uncannily appropriate, since Gujarat state now has the highest proportion, 69 per cent, of vegetarians of any state in India. Two major

An assortment of Gujarati food

influences were at work: Jainism and Vaishnavism both of which had powerful presence in Gujarat.

The *Bimalprabhanda* (*c.* AD 1200) of Lawanyasamay, though written in Sanskrit, mentions such typical Gujarathi dishes as kur (boiled rice) and karambho (curd-rice), papads and vadi, and a number of sweets like vedhami, khaja, laddu, sukhadi (from rava), kheer, and talwat (fried molasses). Jain literature from the seventh to the fourteenth centuries AD has frequent references to numerous food items, like dukkia (dhokla, first mentioned in AD 1066), veshtika (vedhami), ghari, chopada, vati, kacchra (kacholi), kosamri, pralehaka (chatni), kshiraprakara (chhana), shikharini (shrikhand), sarkara (dudhpeda), and shaskuli (sankli). Rice items were karambho and sakthu (sathvo), and wheat items mande, pahalika (khaja, pheni), phenaka (sutar-pheni), murmura (mumra), udumbara (puranpoli), suhali, and ghrtapura (the juicy ghebar or ghevara of Surat, with its porous honeycomb texture, that is eaten soaked in sugar syrup).

These works are in Sanskrit, but the *Varanaka Samuchaya* by an unknown author is a Gujarathi work of AD 1520. This contains extensive lists of food ingredients and prepared items (all jumbled together, unfortunately) of Gujarat. Meals could consist of rice, jowari, bajra (made into palev or

palao with mirch, ginger, turmeric, pipaliya and vasudiya), served with dhokla, idari, khandvi, raitha and puran, the meal ending with dahi or chhas. Rice items are numerous and include several shali rices (maha, pancha-, pill-, rati-, and thatia) and the curd-rice preparation karambho flavoured with camphor, cardamom, rai, jeera, green ginger, and asafoetida. Apart from the common dhals are listed peas and vali (hyacinth bean), and a pulse-based kadhi flavoured with asafoetida. Numerous vadas and their spicing are listed. The vegetables noted include many green legumes (valor, chaulai, guar, papdi) and fruit-vegetables (tindora, kankoda, and thuraiya).

Distinctive to Gujarathi cuisine are certain rotis, and fried snacks called farsan and nasto. The khakda is very thin, brittle and large, rolled out from a dough that is kneaded with milk. The rotlee is another very thin roti of Gujarat. The vedhami is a circlet of spiced besan with a touch of sugar, which is rolled in wheat flour before it is baked on an earthen plate; it is described in the *Manasollasa* of AD 1130.

A rich Gujarathi khichdi called lazizan, consisting of rice, pulses, ghee, spices and nuts, was a favourite with Jahangir on his days of abstention from meat.

Nasto and farsan are classes of Gujarathi fried snacks, distinctive and never eaten together. Nasto comprises many types of fried crisp items that travel well in air-tight tins. One of them, ganthia, describes a class of besan-derived crisps, like the papri wafer, the solid cylindrical bhavnagri, the long, flat fofda, and the slim and spicy masala. Sev is also made from besan, and fried crisp either as thick long strings, thin long strings or wafers. Chevda is beaten rice, deep-fried to crispness, and then mixed with salt, spices, groundnuts, almonds, and raisins. A mixture of almost anything crunchy constitutes bhoosoo.

Farsan consists of items that can be eaten as a snack, or as part of a major meal. The fluffy dhokla is a mixture of rice and besan that is fermented with curd and then steamed, and khaman is a coarser version. There are numerous types of vadas. Khandvi is a tender, rolled-up pancake made from besan batter rolled out extremely thin, and sprinkled with mustard seeds and green coriander sprigs. Bhajiyas denote deep-fried spice balls, and the delicate muthiyas are dumplings of bajra or other flour introduced into

Gulab Jamun

a dish of mixed vegetables flavoured with saunf and methi, which is then steamed and finally lightly cooked in coconut milk. Kachori are deep-fried, vegetable-stuffed puffs, circular or crescent-shaped. Colocasia (arvi) leaves, coated with besan paste, steamed and lightly fried in the form of a roll, yield arvi-na-patra.

gulab-jamun Balls of chhana, or of khoa and paneer, kneaded using maida, deep-fried till dark brown on the surface, and then gently boiled in a medium-thick sugar syrup, sometimes flavoured with rose essence.

gur *See* jaggery.

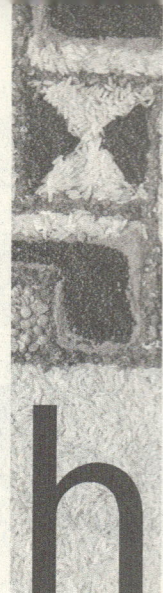

h

halal *See* Islam and food.

haldi *See* turmeric.

haleem, harees(a) Items of Middle Eastern origin, consisting of spiced, pasty preparations of ground meat and wheat. They were popular in the Sultanate and Mughal courts (being mentioned in the *Ain-i-Akbari*) and are delicacies among Muslims in Hyderabad and elsewhere.

halwa An Arabic word, which when first used in English denoted a Turkish confection of ground sesame seeds and honey. In India it connotes pasty or softly firm desserts made from a range of materials: wheat flour, wheat grits (rava, q.v.), wheat strainings (*see* gluten) and vermicelli, Bengal gram flour (besan, q.v.), fruits like the banana and date, vegetables like the carrot and white pumpkin (dudhi), and nuts like the almond (badam, q.v.).

handa, handva A cooking pot, usually made of clay; the term is also used in Gujarat for a dish of mixed vegetables cooked in a clay pot.

health and food *See* ayurveda; dosha.

hearth, domestic *See* cooking; chulah.

hemp For hemp, *Cannabis sativa*, *see* bhang.

The sann(sunn)-hemp is *Crotolaria juncea*, whose stem furnishes a valuable fibre used for cordage, and which also bears edible flowers.

hen *See* chicken.

honey A tasty product made for their own purpose by honeybees, honey is a very ancient food. The Bhimbetka paintings in the caves near Bhopal, from about 6000 BC, show man in the act of despoiling bee-hives built on rocks. The *Rigveda* (*c.* 1500 BC) has several references to honey. Honey is used to sweeten the fried barley delicacy apupa; it is interdicted, perhaps because of a perceived aphrodisiac connotation, for students and widows; and an opinion is expressed that the honey from small bees (saragha) is superior to that from larger bees (arangara). Later, three types of honey came to be commonly recognized. Maksika was honey made by the common honeybee, *Apis cerana indica*, itself called maksika. From the large black rock bee, *A. dorsata* or brahmara, came honey of the same name. Ksaudra honey was from the dwarf ksudra bee, *A. florea*. Both Charaka and Sushrutha list eight types of honey, including the above. The others are pauttika (from the tiny puttika bee), chatra, arghya, auddhalika, and dala, all of which have been identified in modern terms.

Even as early as in Rigvedic times, the Rbhu brothers are credited with building artificial hives of reeds and straw, in which were fixed sections taken from a natural hive. A year later, four sections were removed and the rest left in. In later times, hives were kept in logs or pots in a horizontal position, or on four-legged stools (perhaps to prevent insects from intruding), or in a hole in the wall. This last procedure is still in use in Kashmir, both ends of the hole being stopped with easily detached covers. When ready, the bees are smoked out, a few combs removed,

Honey bees

and the ends replaced, when the swarm soon returns.

As a food, honey enjoyed enormous esteem. It was a component of the ambrosial panchamrutha and also of the ritual concoction madhuparka. A paramanna of boiled rice, milk, ghee, and honey was the first solid food given to a child at the annaprasanna ceremony of weaning. Honey was by itself a relish, and down the centuries it was the sweetening agent of choice for the elite. After about 500 BC, sugarcane products became widely available, and honey is mentioned less frequently as a sweetener. The Puranas in fact do not mention honey at all. It is no coincidence that it is only in recipes found in the *Manasollasa* of the twelfth century AD, written by a king, that honey is used to stuff wheat rotis to give madhumeslaka and madhushirsaka, and to fill the pupalika envelope.

While the Buddha recommended honey as one of the pure foods, 'full of soul qualities and devoid of faults', the Jain canon banned honey 'since it was pressed out of the young eggs in the-womb of bees, and resembled the embryo in its first stages of growth (yasashthilaka)'. The Quran lists honey as one item of food, along with dates, figs, olives, milk, and buttermilk, with which to break a fast.

The Sanskrit word madhu for honey later became generic for sweetness. Even so, in the ayurvedic view honey is classed not as a sweet but as an astringent (kashaya) material, energy-giving, cooling, and a digestive stimulant. It reduces kapha (q.v.) and with it obesity. Fat people are recommended honey and water for weight reduction, and it is best employed as a rainy-season food. For treatment of loss of appetite, debility, and thirst, honey is added to a suspension in water of parched barley or rice.

Honey being a valuable product, accessible in south India to mountainous people, the Kuruvar, it was a prime object of barter for produce from other regions in Sangam times. It was also converted into liquor and matured underground in the hollows of bamboo stems. In Sanskrit literature there is mention of madhira and madhvikasava, wine and spirits of high quality derived from honey, to judge by their names; these liquors were permitted to kshatriyas who were not allowed spirits distilled from flour-based brews.

The collection and sale of honey, despite references to some degree of commercialization even in very early times, remained for centuries an unorganized, family activity. Just prior to the Second World War, the government of Bombay appointed a bee expert to train workers and set up apiaries in the Presidency, while the All-India Khadi and Village Industries Commission promoted efforts in the same area. In 1947, six bee-keeping centres with 68 registered beekeepers were functioning; the output in that year was only 74 kg, but just four years later, production had gone up 250-fold.

horse Indus Valley excavations show no evidence of horse saddles or clay representations of the horse, and the bones found are those of small, country-bred animals. The powerful equine that struck such terror into adversaries is associated with the conquering Aryans and their chariots (rathas), which later reflected a kingly ambience. The elaborate horse sacrifice (*see* ashvamedha) culminated in the ritual slaughter of the animal and distribution of the meat for consumption among priests and partakers in the ceremony. But before long, horse meat was forbidden, as Xuan Zang noted in the seventh century AD.

Early European visitors like Hans Schiltberger (*c.* AD 1410) and Domingo Paes (*c.* AD 1520) express surprise that horses in India were fed with human foods like cereal grains and pulses. Rather strangely, fine breeds of horses were never developed in India; they were always imported, both in north and south India, from across land and sea borders.

horsegram Grains of kulthi, *Dolichos uniflorus*, have been found in later Indus Valley sites, in Daimabad (*c.* 1800 BC) and slightly later at Tekkalakota, further south. The word khalakula occurs in the *Brhadaranyaka Upanishad* (*c.* 1000 BC), while the term gamut which figures in the even earlier *Yajurveda Samhita* has been identified as the horsegram. The first to use the word kulattha was Panini (*c.* 600 BC), and Sushrutha (*c.* AD 200) mentions a wild variety, vanya-kulattha. Archaeological findings in the Dekhan plateau indicate an early presence, and Sangam literature records that kollu was intercropped in agricultural sowings with the cereal varagu (*Paspalum scorbiculatum*).

Soup extracts made from several pulses, which include the kulthi, were termed yusa during the *Sutra* period (800–350 BC), and such soups are still popular as rasam in south India. Vadas made from the horsegram are listed in the Gujarathi work *Varanaka Samuchaya* of AD 1520. As its English name indicates, horsegram is considered a superior fodder crop. In the Indian ethos, unlike several other pulses, it is not an auspicious food, and a sweet payasam of kollu is a common shraddha food item.

host *See* guest and host.

hotels The austere brahmin of Vedic and even of much later times would not even have considered eating at a public place, but other sections of society had less inhibitions. Even in early times eating houses were a common feature of town life, serving 'cooked rice and prepared food ready for eating, whose pungent odours assailed the nostrils'. In south India in the early centuries of the Christian era, eating out was much in vogue. In the town of Madurai we read: 'The hotels and restaurants are now, in the cool of the evening, crowded by visitors who feast upon such luscious fruits as the jackfruit, mango, and banana, and on sweet candies, tender greens, edible yams, sweetened rice or savoury preparations of meat.' Plying their trade on the seashore were kaazhiyar and kuuviar, vendors of snacks like the appam, idi-appam, adai, and moodagam.

'hot' food *See* 'cold' food.

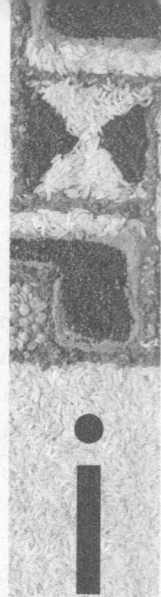

ice Evaporative cooling in really porous clay jars was the time-honoured technique of cooling water. In the *Harshacharita* (seventh century AD), whey for use as a gargle by the king's dying father is kept 'in a new vessel besmeared with wet clay'. Also 'buttermilk was kept very cold (shishirakriya) in pails packed with ice'. This may have been brought, as it was in much later Mughal times, from Himalayan heights by river or overland. According to the *Ain-i-Akbari* (AD 1590): 'Out of the ten boats employed for the transport of ice, one arrives daily at the capital (then Lahore), each being manned by four boatmen ... twelve pieces of ten to four seers (a seer was about a kilogram) arrive daily ... All ranks use ice in summer; the nobles use it throughout the whole year.' A perennial source close to Delhi was the mountain called Choori Chandni-ki-Dhar, near Kasauli. According to Abul Fazl, it was Akbar who introduced saltpetre for cooling water in India. Travellers like Francois Bernier describe how 'the higher sorts of people' cooled Ganges water by pouring it into tiny flagons, which for the span of seven or eight minutes were placed in water into which three or four handfuls of saltpetre had been thrown. The British colonial in India in the eighteenth century did the same: 'Every family had its abdar, the servant who stayed up all night constantly moving an earthenware jug of water in a larger vessel containing saltpetre and water, which produced a chilled liquid by morning.'

In the middle of the nineteenth century, a persevering American, Frederic Tudor, who had experimented for twenty-eight years with shipping ice from America to the West Indies, succeeded in transporting huge chunks of frozen water from Wenham Lake in Massachusetts to South America and beyond, using as packing materials 'felt and sweet-smelling pine sawdust'. On 6 September 1833 the ship *Tuscany* arrived in Calcutta from Boston with 180 tonnes of its ice-cargo (two-thirds of that loaded) still intact, and icehouses for storage of the precious commodity were set up in Calcutta, Madras, and Bombay. Referring to this, Thoreau in his *Walden* poetically remarks that 'soon the waters of my beloved Walden will blend with the sacred waters of the Ganges'. These massive imports led to the appointment of the first American Consul-General in Bombay in 1838.

In 1874, the International Ice Company started manufacturing ice in Madras by the 'steam process' and in 1878 Calcutta followed suit. Alongside, for domestic cooling and preservation, newspapers advertised cabinet refrigerators of polished oak, in which a block of ice was held in a galvanized iron tray at the top, and items of food placed in the lined, cooled cabinet below. While travelling in trains, blocks of ice could be ordered from certain railway stations to be kept in the compartments to cool them.

By Independence, block ice was being manufactured in 270 factories, chiefly situated in Calcutta, Bombay, Delhi, Madras, and Kanpur. The commodity could be bought for domestic use, or to pack fish, milk, and other produce for rail or road transport.

ice-cream Marco Polo is credited with having brought back to Italy, in the thirteenth century AD, not only noodles (which became vermicelli) but recipes for various water-ices that had long been consumed in Qiina. Cookery books of the eighteenth century in France and England had recipes for butter ice and cream ice, but the term ice-cream first appeared in America in May 1777 in the *New York Gazette*, the author being Philip Lenzi who described himself as a confectioner from London. The same Frederic Tudor (*see* ice) who brought ice from America to India, made ice-cream in the West Indies in 1810

Ice-cream

using milk, cream, and fruit juices, in an effort to establish a trade in ice that would help to render 'a beverage ... or tepid water ... palatable' in a hot climate. He had enormous success in selling both ice and ice-cream in South America, Iran, and India. The first commercial production of ice-cream was in 1851 by one Fussel in Baltimore, and soon after in Washington DC, Boston, and New York. To make the product in the home using a freezing mixture of ice and salt, churning pails cranked by hand became popular soon after the turn of the century in Europe, England, and the colonial empires.

idi-appam Fine noodles of a mash of boiled rice grits extruded in a press through brass dies constitute idi-appam, which is mentioned in the *Perumpanuru* (fifth century AD) as a snack being sold by vendors on the seashore, along with the appam, adai, and moodagam. A common breakfast item, it was accompanied, then as now, with sweetened coconut milk. The Syrians of Kerala and the Kodavas of Karnataka (where it is called nu-puttu) eat it with a meat stew or chicken curry. In Sri Lanka it is termed string hoppers, the latter word being an anglicization of the term appam.

idli A common breakfast food of south India, the idli is a white, spongy, swollen circlet about 10 cm across. Rice grits and urad dhal (in a 2:1 proportion) are ground together to a thick batter and left to ferment naturally overnight. Portions are placed on pieces of muslin held in depressions on a metal tray, and steamed in a closed vessel till cooked. Idlis are eaten with a coconut chutney (q.v.), or with sambhar (q.v.), or with a spiced pulse-based gritty powder called molaga-podi, doused with ghee or oil.

The first mention of the idli in literature seems to be as iddalige in the *Vaddaradhane* of Sivakotyacharya, a work in Kannada in the year AD 920, where it figures as

Idli

one of eighteen items served to a brahmachari who visits the home of a lady. Thereafter it is a frequent item in Kannada literature down the centuries. In AD 1025 Chavundaraya describes it in some detail as urad dhal soaked in buttermilk, ground to a fine paste, mixed with the clear water of curd, spiced with cumin, coriander, pepper, and asafoetida, and then shaped. The Sanskrit *Manasollasa* written in AD 1130 describes the iddarika as made of fine urad flour fashioned into small balls and then spiced with pepper powder, cumin powder, and asafoetida. In Karnataka, a century later, the idli is described as being 'light, like coins of high value'. In Tamil the itali makes only a late appearance, in the *Maccapuranam* of the seventeenth century AD.

In all these references, up to *c.* AD 1250, three elements of modern idli-making are missing: the use of rice grits along with urad dhal; the long fermentation of the mix; and the steaming of the batter to fluffiness.

In AD 1485 and AD 1600, the idli is compared to the moon, which might suggest that rice was in use; yet urad dhal flour is itself off-white, and moreover there are references to other moon-like products made only from urad flour. The Andhra area still has cakes of steamed urad flour called vasina-polu. The Indonesians ferment a variety of products (soybeans, groundnuts, fish) and have product very similar to the idli, called kedli. It has been suggested that the cooks who accompanied the Hindu kings of Indonesia during their visits home (often enough to look for brides) between the eight and twelfth centuries AD, brought innovative fermentation techniques to south India. Perhaps the use of rice along with the dhal was an essential part of the fermentation step which requires mixed microflora from both grains to be effective.

Some idli variations have, developed. The Kanchipuram idli served at the Devarajaswami temple is a huge (1.5 kg) preparation of ground rice spiced with pepper, cumin, ginger, and asafoetida, and fermented using curds before it is steamed. Idlis that use wheat rava (grits) in place of rice are also often spiced and contain cashewnuts. The kadubu (q v.) is related to the idli, but has a denser texture.

Iguana A large lizard which was eaten both in the north and south of the country. The Ramayana lists it, and the Tamil Sangam literature talks with obvious relish of a dish of 'iguana red meat big with ova resembling chank shell beads'.

Indrajau *See* Job's tears.

Indus Valley civilization As the earliest civilization of India, spanning the millennium 2500–1500 BC, life in the Indus Valley is naturally of enormous interest. Starting around 2500 BC, a thousand settlements arose in an enormous area along, and then spreading away from, the great rivers of Punjab, covering eventually Gujarat and parts of Rajasthan. The two major river-based metropolises were Mohenjodaro and Harappa, while other large settlements were those at Kalibangan, Ropar, Chanhudaro, Lothal, and Rangpur. All had close cultural affinities.

Agricultural operations included ploughing, furrowing, inundation, irrigation, and raising water from below the surface with water-wheels. It is likely that the area was then much more forested, though the rainfall patterns may not have altered significantly.

Among the foodgrains actually found in excavations, or as toy clay models, were, in different regions, barley, wheat, oats, rice, kangni (*Setaria italica*), amaranths, jowar, sesame, linseed, mustard, coconut, peas, chickpeas, masoor, mung and horsegram; besides these were dates, pomegranates, and perhaps bananas. Bones of numerous animals attest to extensive meat eating, and fish hooks and bones of both river and sea fish have been found in abundance.

Very large storage structures (*see* granary) were established, obviously as a state enterprise, in Mohenjodaro, Harappa, and Lothal, of surprising degrees of sophistication in terms of aeration and rodent control.

Adjacent to the granaries were placed grain-pounding platforms. Domestic storage was in partly buried pottery jars. Grain-pounding cylinders and spice-grinding querns (*see* food,

Granary at Mohenjodaro

utensils) are of designs still in common use, as were hearths and baking ovens. Cooking and dining vessels (*see* utensils) were made of clay, shell, chert, bronze, and copper. Alcohol was brewed, and apparently even distilled (*see* beverages, alcoholic).

The Indus Valley civilization went into a decline as rivers changed their courses through tectonic shifts or became silted, or as the soil turned saline. Some settlements lingered on, while from others people moved outwards. Aryan incursions described in the *Rigveda* may have played a part in bringing the civilization to a close.

irrigation *See* agriculture.

Islam and food Dietary injunctions for Muslims derive both from the Quran and the Sunnah, which embody the recorded words of the prophet Muhammad. Swine flesh is prohibited, but seafood allowed. Except for fish, it is mandatory to slaughter the animal ritually by halal: the jugular vein is cut, or a hollow pierced in the throat, using a sharp knife, while uttering the name of Allah. Alcohol is forbidden, along with games of chance, since according to the Quran 'in both there is great sin and harm'. Wine is referred to indirectly elsewhere as khamar (which means to cover up) since it clouds the brain.

Islam enjoins that no food be wasted, even leftovers being saved and eaten; it also stresses zakat (q.v.), the obligation to share food with others, especially on Id-ul-fitr (fitr means charity). Fasting is enjoined on all the faithful during Ramzan, the ninth month of the Muslim lunar year, with a meal before sunrise (fatoor or sahri) and one after sunset (sahoor or suhoor), which should preferably commence by eating some dates. Indeed dates, honey, figs, olives, milk, and buttermilk are items of food specially recommended in the Quran. It has four Sanskrit-derived words for food items: ambar, resin; kafur, camphor; mushk, musk, or kasturi; and zenjabid, srngavera, or ginger.

In practice, regional, cultural, and social practices influence the choice of food. Three examples of regional social influences may be cited. Nearly a century ago, a British official noted that after a death, no meat or fish is consumed, and in the house of mourning, for forty days no food served. In West Bengal, a black dot is applied to a child's forehead to ward off evil spirits, and the mother gives up 'hot' foods for the first five days. For forty days both mother and child are considered polluted, and she can neither touch the Quran nor offer namaz. In exact parallel with the annaprasanna (q.v.), the child is given its first solid food at the Mammar bath ceremony in its seventh month. In the far south, in

Nellore, turmeric is applied to the face of a bride (an auspicious Hindu ritual), and astrology is extensively used to find a spouse or go on a journey.

However, the actual foods eaten in these households, while to some degree regional, have a distinct Islamic connotation. Some of these are maleeda (broken bread with sugar and ghee), palao, biriyani, shola (a rice-dhal khichdi with meat), and haleem (q.v., a ground meat-wheat porridge), which is eaten with roti. Two breads are fairly distinctive: sheermal, a sweet, baked, bun-like type, and khajur, a sweetened crisp bread with poppy seeds and copra shavings. Kababs of several kinds, called sheekh, sharnmi, husseni and tikka, are eaten, and the distinctive sweet concoctions include fruit juices and sherbets, phirni (a kheer made from ground rice, with added raisins, nuts, and rose essence), and seviyan (fried sweetened vermicelli). Kheer, laddu, jilebi, halwa, sohan-halwa, and burfi are sweets that cut across religion and are common to the entire community. So are many raithas, chutneys, morabbas, and pickles eaten as food relishes in Nellore, and indeed all over the country.

Italian millet *Setaria italica*, kangni in Sanskrit and Hindi, and thennai in Tamil, is an exceedingly old grain. It has been excavated, on the one hand in prehistoric sites in Switzerland; and on the other, it was, even in 2700 BC, one of the five sacred grains of China, where indeed it may have been domesticated. In India it has been found in 2300 BC layers in Surkotada in Kutch (this may have been a wild variety), and in several early south Indian sites. In Tamil literature thennai is mentioned as a grain of the mountainous areas. In the *Perumpanuru* the cooked grain of the thennai is poetically likened to 'a swarm of the tiny young of crabs'.

Italy, trade with *See* Rome, contacts with.

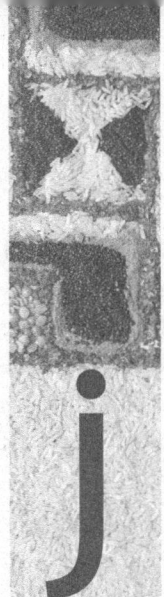

j

jackal A wild, gregarious scavenging animal related to the dog. Charaka lists it as an edible meat. The *Manasollasa* of King Someshwara describes a composite spiced dish of pulses and vegetables, to which could optionally be added brinjals, jackal meat or bone marrow.

jackbean The bada-sem of Hindi is botanically *Canavalia ensiformis;* it is a large bean with a pronounced white hilum along the edge that is native to the West Indies and Central America. It does look like a large sem, but the latter belongs to a different family, and is moreover indigenous (*see* sem).

jackfruit The genus *Artocarpus* has fifty species, and one each has found food favour in specific regions. In India and Indonesia it is the jackfruit, *A. heterophyllus;* in Malaysia and Oceania the bread-fruit, *A. communis;* and in South-East Asia the champedak, *A. integer,* a smaller version of the jackfruit. The jackfruit probably originated in India. Resembling the jackfruit, but unrelated, is the malodorous durian of South-East Asia.

The word jack is a corruption of the Malayalam chakka; the Tamil word for the fruit, sakkei, which means abounding in refuse, is exceptionally appropriate. The Sanskrit term panasa for the jackfruit is thought to be of aboriginal Munda origin. The first foreigner to mention the fruit, Xuan Zang, in the seventh century AD, used this Sanskrit word in his Chinese writings.

Ludovico di Varthema (AD 1508) was tantalized by the taste of the jackfruit. He declared it to be 'sweet and delicious; when it is eaten it seems to be as though you are eating musk melons, and it appears to resemble a very ripe Persian quince. It appears also as though you were eating a preparation of honey, and it also has the taste of a sweet orange'. Ibn Battuta called it the best fruit in India, but Babar was less enchanted, saying it was 'like a sheep's stomach stuffed and made into a gipa (haggis) … sickeningly sweet'. English official, Robert Orme, noted in AD 1743 that the jackfruit was 'rich, glewy and nutritious' and like several other Indian fruits was 'at once a delicacy, and no contemptible nourishment'.

Jackfruit tree

The abundance of the jackfruit all over India is repeatedly noticed by visitors, notably in Delhi by Amir Khusrau (*c.* AD 1300), by Ma Huan (*c.* AD 1300) in Bengal, and by Fernao Nuniz in the markets of Vijayanagar in the sixteenth century.

In northern literature the panasa figures, rather late, in the Buddhist and Jain canon, but a couple of centuries earlier, it is even depicted in Buddhist sculpture in Bharhut. Varahamihira' s *Brhat Samhita* (*c.* AD 505) notes that the jackfruit is amenable to grafting, and the operation is accurately described. Early south Indian literature has many references to the familiar jackfruit, which grew in mountainous marudam terrain. Commonly jackfruit seeds are put aside, chopped up and curried, or roasted to bursting on an open fire and eaten.

Unripe jackfruit, kathal, when cooked with dry spicing, strongly resembles a chunk of fibrous meat. To cut open the huge ripe fruit a sharp, strong knife smeared with oil is needed to deal with the gummy latex. The bulb-like yellow fruits have a strong odour not agreeable to everyone, and are eaten as such or mashed to a drink (panaka). In Kerala a mash of the ripe fruit with roasted rice powder and jaggery is packed in a vazhana leaf and steamed to give a product called unni-appam, which constitutes a prasad in some Ganesha temples in Kerala. In

Kodagu, mashed jackfruit has been replaced in this concoction by mashed banana, but it is still called koovale- or koale-puttu, the koovale being a soft and juicy kind of jackfruit. The flavour of jackfruit is one of many used in making sandesh in Bengal.

In medical parlance, the jackfruit and mango are textbook examples of 'hot' (ushna) foods, to be eaten along with a tempering 'cold' food like milk.

jaggery The gritty brown sugar of India is guda in Sanskrit, gur in Hindi, vellam in Tamil and jaggery in English. Though the sugarcane itself is mentioned even in the *Rigveda*, the viscous phanita and solid guda made by boiling down its juice first occur only a millennium later in *Sutra* literature. A major sugarcane-growing area has always been Bengal or Gauda, from which according to Charaka the word guda derives. The English word jaggery is drawn from the Sanskrit sharkara for sugar, by way of the Malayalam chakkara and the Portuguese xagara (first used in AD 1516 by Duarte Barbosa), jagara, and jagra. Indian medicine regards jaggery as a 'hot' food, growing increasingly 'colder' and less digestible as it is refined. Rice or barley water sweetened with jaggery is prescribed for debility as also in kidney disorders.

All through history, jaggery has been the low-cost sweetener with a distinctive flavour. Laddus (q.v.) of sesame seed, wheat rava, puffed rice, besan granules, coconut shreds, groundnuts, and the like are fashioned using thickened jaggery syrup. These items are also made into chikki when the sweet matrix is further evaporated so that it sets hard. The palala, now a sesame chikki called tilkut, goes back to Vedic times. Jaggery is used to stuff wheat paratas, as mentioned in the *Manasollasa* of the thirteenth century AD, to yield purana and polika, the modern puran-poli and holige. Annaji in Karnataka (*c.* AD 1600) describes the obattu-garige as being 'round as the earth, and made of wheat or rice flour with jaggery'. The rice-based sakkarai-pongal of the Tamil country is brown in colour through the presence of jaggery, as is the dark-brown fried athirasam or unni-appam based on rice grits. In Goa, baked yams are coated with melted jaggery to yield an unusual dessert.

Jaggery is also made from various palms. In south India, this is from the sweet juice of the spathe of the palmyra palm, *Borassus flabellifer*. It is collected in pots smeared with slaked lime to arrest fermentation (an ancient practice), then boiled down till the 'strike' occurs, and poured to set in moulds. Bengal uses the exudate from the trunk of the wild date palm, *Phoenix sylvestris*, and jaggery is poured to set in the halves of a coconut shell. The flavour of palm jaggery is relished in sandesh (q.v.) and mishti-doi (sweet curds, q.v.).

Fermented liquor and vinegar are also made from jaggery. Called sharkara-asara in Sanskrit literature, liquor made from jaggery was permitted to kshatriyas and vaishyas, along with liquor from honey and mahua flowers. Most Indian liquors, whether distilled or otherwise, were frequently preferred spiced and sweetened, the latter often with jaggery. Vinegar (q.v.), shirka or shukto in Sanskrit, is first mentioned rather late by Dalhana (c. AD 1100) in his commentary on the *Sushrutha Samhita*. It was made by placing jaggery solution in loosely covered jars, which were then buried underground to ferment for several months. Vinegar is used by Muslims extensively in medicine and to some extent in cooking, and by Hindus infrequently, and only in cooking.

In about 1947, nearly two-thirds of all the sugarcane grown in the country was used for the production of some 35 lakh tonnes of jaggery. Another 19 per cent of the cane was used for making crystal sugar, and the rest went for chewing and planting.

Jain food ambience Jainism counts twenty-four reformer-leaders or thirthankaras, of whom the most forceful was the last, Mahavira, a contemporary of the Buddha. Non-injury (ahimsa) was the cardinal tenet not only of the five drastic vows required of a Jain monk, but even of the thirty-five enjoined on a Jain householder. A Jain monk was expected to sweep the ground on which he slept to remove any living thing, as well as the path ahead of him as he moved along. Even waste material had to be deposited in a place free of organic life so that the latter would not be destroyed. Rigid food restrictions were based on avoiding injury to life, even when this was not apparent. No one could eat after dark (aratri-bhojana), preferably, all round the year, but at least during the four monsoon months when insects are abundant.

The question of eating flesh simply did not arise, only 'absolutely innocent food' being permitted. The prohibited foods included not only twenty-two 'uneatables', but 'thirty-two things that have infinite life germs in them'. This was explained as food which had the potential for life to manifest itself, such as putrid or rancid food vegetables like underground bulbs, roots and tubers that had germs in them, or pickles more than three days old.

To illustrate these prohibitions, pulses that split into two parts (like the chickpea) were not allowed; nor were brinjals, any fruit (such as the five kinds of figs) with abundant small seeds (bahu-bija), green turmeric, and ginger, carrots, the tender green leaves of any vegetable, and tender tamarind fruit before the seeds had formed. Honey was expressly banned on the ground that its removal from the comb implied the death of bees, and consumption of honey would destroy spontaneous creatures arising from it. All water had to be boiled, and reboiled every six hours; all liquids had to be strained before drinking, whether water, milk, or fruit juice. When drinking water from a tank or stream, and for a monk at all times, a Jain covers his mouth with a cloth, and drinks through it.

Mahavira Jayanti is one of the four major Jain festivals, and there are some minor ones. There are twelve pratimas or fasts, of various durations, when the community abstains from even permitted foods, which may include milk, curd, ghee, oil, salt, and sweetmeats. Jain monks are not allowed to eat even permitted fruit if it has fallen from the tree, or fruit that is kept for sale in a shop or on the roadside. Everything eaten has to be thoroughly washed and wiped. Juices from quite a number of fruits are permitted, but soured rice gruel (kanjika) is not. As for liquor, a Jain monk is not permitted to even stay in a place in which liquor is stored. States with a high proportion of Jains, like Gujarat and Rajasthan, and those with considerable Jain influence, like Karnataka, have a distinctly higher proportion of vegetarians than do other states. Jain writers on food include, in Gujarat, Nemichandra (eleventh century AD) who wrote *Lilavati*, Hemachandra who wrote *Abhidana-chintamani* (twelfth century AD), and Asadhara (thirteenth century AD). In Karnataka, Chavundaraya wrote the *Lokopakara* (eleventh century AD), and Gurulinga Desika the *Lingapurana* (AD 1594).

Jain monks begging for alms

Frequently it is early Jain canonical literature that carries the first reference in writing to certain food materials. Examples are the chickpea, alisandaga; the linseed, atashi; the sweet root, kaseruka (*Scirpus grossus*); the bittergourd, karavella; the watercress, mandakaparni; the spinach, palankya; and the brinjal, vrntaka.

jambu The rose-apple, *Syzygium jambos*, that has a thin sweetish fleshy layer with a pronounced rose flavour covering a large round seed. In historical literature it is the source of a wine, jambu-asava.

jamoon The purple jamoon or jamun or Java plum is *Syzygium cumini*, a fruit first mentioned in later Vedic literature. In fact there is a suggestion that the name may even be of Munda origin. In Tamil it is called naval. The taste is sweet but decidedly astringent, and children enjoy it with salt. The juice stains the mouth a deep purple. A decoction of the bitter seeds is prescribed for diabetics.

Jamoon juice is one of the acidic juices called raga by Charaka. It was a beverage permitted to Buddhist monks.

The jamoon was one source of fermented liquor, according to Charaka. It was also a raw material for making vinegar, called shirka in Sanskrit, and shukto or ambila in early Buddhist literature. The Bengali sweet delicacy, made from a deep-fried mix of chhana and maida, and shaped like a large jamoon fruit, is called gulab-jamun (q.v.), almost purplish-brown in colour and served in sugar syrup.

jeera *See* cumin.

Jewish food By and large Jews in India follow the food laws set out in the Old Testament (especially in Leviticus and Deuteronomy), and in the rabbinical regulations known as the Kashruth. Two strictures are the ban on the eating of pork, and the injunction that in killing an animal, the kosher system of cutting the jugular vein and allowing the blood (considered to be a part of life) to dram out thoroughly, must be followed. Orthodox Jews will not eat meat at the same meal in which dairy products are served, and even keep separate cooking, serving, and eating dishes for each type of food. Also, fish without scales which includes shellfish and seafood, is not permitted.

Jews came to make their home in India on four separate occasions. One of the lost ten tribes of Israel came to India, following persecution by the Greek overlord Antiochus Epiphanes, to form the Bene-Israel community. They arrived in Navagaon port in the Konkan, and now number distinguished professionals, mostly centred in Bombay, in their population of about 900. The Cochin Jews originally arrived in the port of Cranganore in Kerala in the first century AD, after the Second Temple

Jilebi

cone of some kind. The batter varies
in different areas. It could be ground
urad dhal with a little rice
flour as a binder, or
besan (q.v.) and
maida (q.v.),
both mixtures
sometimes
slightly
fermented
with curd. A
crisp texture and
golden colour
are sought.

Resembling the jilebi is
the jahangiri or imrati, in
which the batter of ground urad is
coloured with saffron and piped into
hot fat in symmetrical loops that
give it the appearance of a rose. The
product is soft and oozy and of a deep
orange colour.

The word jilebi is apparently a
corruption of the Arabic zalabiya or
Persian zalibiya. A Kannada work of
Jinasura dated AD 1450 describes a
feast at which the jilebi was served.
A well-known seventeenth-century
work on dietetics, Raghunatha's
Bhojana Kutuhala, composed in the
Maharashtra area, describes its method
of preparation. The *Soundara Vilasa*
of Annaji (c. AD 1600) in Kannada
accurately describes the jilabi (as he
calls it) as 'locking like a creeper, tasty
as nectar'. At a meal in south India it
would be served as the penultimate
sweet item, before the curd and rice.

in Palestine was destroyed by the
Romans. Persecution, first by the
Muslims and then by Portuguese
Catholics, caused them a millenium
later to flee to Cochin where a
synagogue was set up; today only a
handful of these Jews remain, mostly
as traders. Much later came a group
of Baghdad Jews who are now active
in business in Bombay, Pune, and
Calcutta. The fourth group consists of
European Jews who fled their homes
following Nazi persecution. Regional
Jewish foods reflect local influence.

jilebi Coiled strands which are crisp-
fried, then immersed in thickened
sugar syrup, and withdrawn for
serving. The strands are formed by
piping a batter into hot fat, using
either a coconut shell with a hole at
the base controlled with a finger, or a

Job's tears Botanically *Coix lacrymajobi*, Job's tears are small, hard, shiny grains that occur in many shades of brown and black, and are indeed even strung as beads. The related species *C. aquatica* and *C. gigantea* are also used as food in parts of South-East Asia. Called giral or kasi in modern times, the Sanskrit term gavedhuka (modem Hindi garahedua) goes back to Vedic times, with ritual significance as an uncultivated grain. It grows abundantly on mountain slopes, and even a century ago was an important cereal on the northeastern hills of Assam. The name kasi and its variations, and the association of the grain with those of Mongolian affiliation, suggests an eastern origin.

jowar Commonly called sorghum in English, jowar in Hindi and cholam in Tamil, *Sorghum vulgare* originated in or near Ethiopia, possibly from wild *S. propinquum*. Since sorghum cross-pollinates freely, it can diverge even by simple natural selection. Five basic races are recognized, of which Red Durra travelled, about 2000 BC or earlier, to the Near East and then to India, either by land along the Sabeaen Lane or by sea with the dhow traffic. Spikelets of jowar have been found in Ahar (Rajasthan) in strata dated 1725 BC and more profusely in 1550 BC and 1270 BC strata, and also in Daimabad (Maharashtra) in strata dated about 1700 BC. A drawing that resembles the sorghum, noted on a potsherd from Mohenjodaro could even be slightly older.

Yavanala and yavaprakara (which mean resembling barley) are clearly terms for jowar derived from the Sanskrit yava for barley. Other names are akara, parichaya, and jurna, from which the word juar or jowar derives. These Sanskrit names only appear extremely late, about the start of the Christian era, or perhaps a couple of centuries earlier, in the works of Charaka, Bhela, and Kashyapa. The localization of jowar essentially in western India, where rotis made from it are the staple diet, may explain this late identity in Aryan consciousness. The name sorghum is derived from the Italian word sorgho, meaning to rise, and is descriptive of the conspicuous height of the plant in a field.

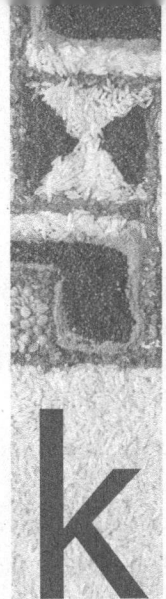

k

kabab Roasting marinated meat on spits while basting with fat is described both in Sanskrit and Tamil literature. At a picnic meal described in the Mahabharata, 'large pieces of meat were roasted on spits'. The *Manasollasa* written in the twelfth century describes the bhaditraka as 'pieces of meat, bored, stuffed with spices and roasted on spits'. Old Tamil literature has 'hot meats, roasted on the point of spits' and again 'large pieces of fat meat roasted on spits'.

Even so, the kabab has a distinct identity as a dainty from the Middle East which is particularly favoured by the Muslims in India. Spiced mutton, chicken, and beef are cooked, strung in small pieces with alternate bits of onion, garlic, and ginger, on metal or bamboo skewers, and rotated over glowing charcoal embers. Sheekh kabab, shammi kabab, tikka, and shashlik are variations. Husseni kabab is strung on skewers, but instead of being roasted it is deep-fried. Ibn Battuta records chicken kabab being served by royal houses during the Sultanate period. Even common folk ate kabab and paratas for breakfast, and in Mughal India a few centuries later it was still naan and kabab. In the *Ain-i-Akbari*, kabab is listed as one of a class of foods in which meat is cooked with accompaniments. Meat marinated in cream before roasting, called malai-tikka, is a food popular with Bohri Muslims.

The British anglicized the spelling and pronunciation to cabob, but preserved the essentials of its preparation, frequently employing the meat of wild game and animals of the chase.

kaccha food *See* cooking principles.

kadamba A moderately sized tree, *Anthocephalus cadamba*, bearing edible fruit and perfumed yellow globular flowers that look like the woollen balls used in playing ball badminton. A wine perfumed with the flowers was termed kadambari. Babar wrote that the kadam 'resembles a tumagha (a royal cap); the leaves are like those of the walnut, which the whole tree resembles'.

kadubu In AD 1485, Terekanambi Bommarasa describes the kadubu served at a royal feast in glowing terms: 'The kings are relishing the Kadubu made of black gram; it looked like a full moon; like a mass of mist set together; as if heavenly nectar had solidified into circles; or as if a drop of moonlight had hardened. The kadubu was attractive to the eye and pleasing to the mind.' Thus it was then an item based on urad dhal, but is now a fermented and steamed mixture of rice with half its weight of urad dhal. This is also true of the idli (*see* idli).

Later literature describes a number of variations. Tharagu-kadubu, which is kadubu steamed on leaves, is first mentioned in Kannada literature in AD 1430. Urad kadubu is noted in AD 1485, kadubu made from tiny sevage (vermicelli) in AD 1506, and in AD 1594, kadubu made from rava, chana (Bengal gram) or vermicelli, containing bamboo shoots. Thus the kadubu was apparently a generic term for a steamed product made of different pulses and cereals.

Tandoor

The kadubu is now a steamed slab of fermented rice-urad mix placed on a leaf, or more often a metal tray. Such steaming from only the top makes for a denser texture than in the porous, through-steamed idli based on the same ingredients. Stuffings, both sweet and savoury, can be placed between layers of kadubu, and the resulting sandwich cut up into smaller pieces for consumption. The denser kadubu is also amenable to further breaking up, followed by several possibilities recorded in Kannada literature, like frying; fashioning into a kheer in milk; reshaping into a ball or disc with jaggery; and roasting further to crispness to yield a product called uduru.

The Kodava thaliya-puttu, steamed on round metal plates, is mostly rice with just a little urad dhal. It is usually eaten with a curry of meat or chicken.

kahwah An aromatic Kashmir tea with cardamoms and almonds brewed in a special samovar. The term was originally employed in the Arab world in about the fourteenth century AD for a brew of coffee, which perhaps replaced an earlier sacerdotal wine of the same name used in Sufi circles.

kanji Current term for the resi-dual starchy water, from the Sanskrit kanjika, in which rice has been boiled, or even for a weak suspension of boiled rice in its water, a food for invalids in south India. Frequently the product was left to sour overnight and drunk as a morning beverage, either hot or cold. It was a beverage not permitted to Jain monks. The acidic liquor was even used, like vinegar, to preserve fruits like the mango, amla, and cucumber. In Gujarat, a dish of fried pulse lumps in soured rice water is also termed kanji.

kapha One of the three bodily humours or doshas (q.v.), kapha is composed of the elements earth and water, which give the body form and shape, stability, and resilience. The typical kapha prototype is strong, sleek, and supple, with abundant virility. An unbalanced kapha is marked by pallor, coldness, dullness, itching, and constipation. A marked psychological symptom is avarice.

In general, the site of kapha is the stomach, to which dietary therapy is applied. A disordered kapha is countered by foods that are pungent, bitter, and astringent, like pepper, garlic, ginger, mustard seeds, and aromatic foods. Foods that increase pitta (q.v.) and vata (q.v.) also serve to reduce kapha.

karela *See* bittergourd.

Karnataka, food of Historically, writings in the Kannada language go back about fifteen hundred years. During this period, there is a whole book on food, the *Supa Shastra* written by Mangarasa in AD 1516, and numerous chapters or references to food in no less than twenty-three others. Thus the historicity of food is exceptionally well documented, though this is confined to the brahmin and Jain ambience, which is of course totally vegetarian. However this does represent the mainstream of food in Karnataka, which even at present is 36 per cent vegetarian.

Rice had pride of place in Karnataka after the tenth century AD. Four varieties of a cooked rice–ghee combination flavoured with garlic and salt, called kattogara, are illustrative. Crushed papad was mixed in to yield one variation, crisp-fried sandiges made of the ash gourd another, and various cooked greens gave rise to yet other ogaras. A mung dhal khichdi is mentioned by this name. Further flavour changes were obtained by mixing in lime, huli (sambhar), turmeric, tamarind, or the powders of roasted rice and chana. Curd-rice that would keep for several days was made by cooking the rice in water in which, as a preliminary, the leaves of tulasi or madala (*Citrus medico*) were boiled. Despite being in the south, Karnataka, even today, consumes roughly equal amounts of rice, wheat, and ragi. Mucchala-roti was baked between plates, with live coals above and below, and kividhu-roti was made on a kavali (thava) with a little ghee. Several thava-roasted rotis could be stacked one upon the other with a pierced stick, and flavoured with ghee, sugar, edible camphor, and the thale

(palmyra) flower, to yield the chucchu-roti. A stack of ghee-smeared circles, savudu-roti, was baked on a griddle under cover of a cup. A cup cover above, live coals below, and a ball of dough within yielded uduru-roti, from which the blackened crust was peeled off before consumption. Mandige or mandage was a delicate baked product; when baked on a heated tile (kenchu) it was called white-mandige; and when overheated but still very soft it was ushnavarta-mandige, which when exposed to air became vayuputa-mandige. The stuffing could be varied. Sugar and ghee yielded khanda-mandige; multi-layered fillings of cooked chana, coconut shreds, dates, and raisins yielded a mandige variation called perane-hurige. Today the mandige or mande of Belgaum is a very large and fine parata made from a dough blended with finely ground sugar containing cardamom powder, baked on an upturned clay pot, and folded into a rectangle that sets moderately stiffen cooling.

True baking within a seal of wheat dough, called kanika in Kannada, is used to make the bhojanadhika-roti, in which the mandige, broken up into small pieces, is mixed with milk, cream, coconut milk, mango juice, and sugar, and pressed into a ball. This is placed within a covering of wheat dough, and baked under a seal on a hot tile with the vessel being turned frequently. When done, the upper crust is sliced off, and ghee and sugar are poured in before it is eaten.

Steaming is the last step in a complex operation in which whole wheat flour is first cooked in milk; spices, fried coconut gratings, and jaggery are added, and the mass is cooked again with water. Cooked banana flowers are put in, a seasoning of mustard seeds given, and the whole mass is steam-cooked to yield godhuma-ramba-kusuma, which literally means wheat-flowers mix.

Wheat dough made with sweetened milk or even cream, rolled out with coconut and bananas into circles and then deep-fried, yielded the yeriappa and the babara. Balls of dough made with wheat flour, curd, and sweetened cream were deep-fried to produce pavuda. A less viscous batter of rava prepared with sweetened milk was forced through a hole made at the base of a coconut shell cup (the usual extrusion device) directly into hot ghee to give the rope-like chilimuri.

As would be expected of vegetarian poets, descriptions of vegetable preparations are plentiful. Chavundaraya, even in the one chapter of his book devoted to food items, mentions thirty-one vegetables, and Mangarasa has a long chapter on ways of cooking numerous vegetables. Chapter 8 in the *Lingapurana*, written by Gurulinga Desika (AD 1594), is a long one, and the various ways of

cooking nearly a dozen vegetables are outlined. Thus brinjals could be seasoned with ghee, salt, methi, urad, and cream before being boiled. They could be roasted in ghee; spiced; placed on live coals and made into baji (bhartha); or cut into small pieces and cooked with jaggery. There were so many kinds of brinjals besides to do all this with! The bittergourd had first to be debittered with salt water and washed. Thereafter many ways of cooking were open. It could be stuffed with a favourite masala, tied with string and cooked; ghee-fried; cooked with jaggery syrup; cut into rounds and cooked with salt; cooked whole, stuffed or flavoured; and cooked with masala in a spicy juice in which the fruit would float. An unusual method that now seems to have been given up was to cook roots and greens in milk. Some preparations are frequently mentioned down the centuries. Melogara was a dish of pulses and greens in which tamarind was eschewed, and coconut gratings figured prominently. Eating pleasure, one poet says, comes from various kinds of melogara.

Relishes were of many kinds. The balaka (pronounced with a hard 'l') is now made by soaking large chillies in salt water, drying them, and frying them in oil when needed as a crisp and spicy accompaniment to food. Historically, some twenty kinds of balaka were prepared in the *Linga-purana* using various vegetables and their peels. The same work mentions five kinds of happala (papad) and fifty kinds of pickle (uppinkayi). Deep-fried items eaten as crisp and crunchy accompaniments to a meal were the chakkali (called murukku in Tamil), a coil built up of continuous widening rings extruded from a thick rice-urad batter, and numerous sandige (irregular lumps of spiced rice-urad batter, or sesame powder, or onion, or even vegetable skins like those of the ash gourd, all deep-fried to crispness in very hot fat). Curd-based relishes with greens and raw vegetables were known by various names, such as pacchadi, kacchadi, krasara-kacchadi (this had milk with the curd), palidya (one variety was called kajja), thambuli (with greens and coconut gratings) and rayatha (a word in common use today). Kosamris were uncooked relishes made from chana or mung, which were soaked in salt water to soften and swell, and then garnished with salt, mustard seeds, and fresh coriander.

There was a vast variety of sweet items and they alter little over a millennium. Sweet boiled rice, rice payasam in milk (of which paramanna was a prized kind that is repeatedly extolled), a rice-derived vermicelli payasam, mixed rice-wheat payasams, rice kadubu with a sweet filling, and deep-fried delicacies of rice flour and jaggery (now called kajayya) were all based on rice. Wheat was also used to make sweet dishes, especially in the form of rava grits, from which came shalianna (now called kesari-bath, flavoured with the fragrant stamens of saffron), a fried ball (ghrtapura), various payasams, and a ladduge. Wheat vermicelli from hard-wheat dough was extruded really fine as pheni, and usually eaten with sugared milk. Sweet wheat rotis, stuffed with a mash of boiled chana, jaggery, and coconut, constituted purige, later termed hurige and thereafter holige; a thinner, drier form was the obattu, and there was a rolled-up, cylindrical form called surali-holige. Rolled-out pieces of dough were fried in various forms and dusted with castor sugar to give several phenis and chirottis; madhunala was a small tube of dough (of wheat, rice, and chana, with added mashed banana) filled with sugar, sealed at both ends and deep-fried. Karaji-kayi was a half-moon puff with a sweet stuffing; if only sugar constituted the stuffing, the result was sakkare-burude. Pulse flour of chana and black gram was also used to make sweetmeats. Boondi grains of this flour were shaped with sugar syrup into ladduge, pinda, motichur, and mandhara-unde. The jilabi, 'like a creeper, tasty as nectar was made of chana flour; it was first mentioned by this name in AD 1600,' and as jilebi later (*see* jilebi). Milk was the major ingredient for sweet payasa, as also for hal-unde (balls of sweetened khoa) and halaugu (the halubai of today). Shikarini consisted of curd solids lightly spiced and sweetened, the modern term shrikhand first being used for the dish in Kannada in AD 1700. Fruit juices, called rasayasa, appear through the centuries. Chavundaraya gives elaborate directions for extracting the juice from several fruits by exposure to the sun. Another popular mix of ripe fruits or their mashes was seekarane, of which there were numerous variations in choice and combination of fruits.

No non-vegetarian food finds mention in these texts.

One can easily trace in these preparations and their names many that are now current. The majjige-huli is the historical palidya, the kootu is melogara, and chitranna, puliyodare, and bisi-bele-huli-anna are all forms of kattogara. Amvade or ambode, a vade of mixed dhals, is less frequent, as is the steamed nuchin-unde of thuvar dhal eaten with spiced curd, described in AD 1430 in the *Prabhulingaleele*. Other vadas, and the new bonda, are still here, as are all the forms of payasa, hdlige, obattu, and chirotti. Old sweets like the madhunala and sukhin-unde (of rice, jaggery and banana, deep-fried) are disappearing, but Mysore pak is still a favourite.

Kashmir, food of The French traveller, Tavernier, who visited India for twelve years during the reign of Jahangir, wrote of Kashmir: 'Meadows and vineyards, fields of rice, wheat, hemp, saffron and many sorts of vegetables, among which are intermingled trenches filled with water rivulets, canals and several small lakes, vary the enchanting scene.' Much earlier Xuan Zang had noted that the pear, wild plum, peach, apricot, grape, etc. have all been brought to India from the land of Kashmir, and this continued for centuries thereafter till the Mughals took steps to grow them in their own territories, while also establishing their rule in Kashmir.

Apart from temperate fruits, certain food ingredients are distinctive to Kashmir. Its wild grapes have repeatedly been commented upon (*see* grapes). The famous red chillies of Kashmir are intensely coloured, but with little pungency (*see* chilli). Saffron, mentioned by Tavernier, grows only in Kashmir (*see* kesar). According to Manucci, a white wine perfumed with flowers was imported from Kashmir for Jahanara Begum, Aurangzeb's sister. Historical works from Kashmir carry certain references to food. The *Nilamata Purana* of AD 550–650 mentions shali rice as the staple of Kashmir; the milk of both cow and buffalo was used, apupa and pishthaka sweet confections were made, meat and fish were important foods, and the first snowfall was celebrated with drinking. The *Rajatarangini* of Kalhana (*c.* AD 1200) notes the consumption of rice and barley by the poor. Mung (mudga) was eaten, but considered an inferior food, perhaps in comparison with meat, fish, and pork, which were all relished. With regard to alcohol, the nobility drank a light wine flavoured with flowers. Honey and fruits were widely consumed, and the spices used were asafoetida, onions, and ginger. Both salt and pepper are rarely mentioned. Products from both cow and buffalo milk are described.

Today even Kashmiri brahmins eat flesh, but the food of the Hindus and Muslims is differently spiced. Hindus use asafoetida, methi, ginger, and saunf; Muslims use onions (a variety called praan) and garlic, and both use Kashmiri chillies, intense in colour, but mild. Appropriate mixed spices are ground and shaped into discs with a hole in the middle, called alasadas or wadis, from which pieces are broken off for use either in cooking, or as a table spice. A festive feast is wazwan, cooked by specialists called wazas. Lamb dishes abound: yakhni (in curd); aab-gosht (cooked in thickened milk); roghan-josh (literally red meat, with 'Hindu' spicing, browned in ghee, then boiled in curd and coloured red with dried cockscomb); marzwangan korma, a mince; several meat balls, like goli and rishta; and goshtaba, a meat, loaf of very fresh mutton pounded in its own fat, large and silky in texture. There is even a special mishani dinner, served, say, for a wedding, in which exactly seven dishes, all made from lamb, are served. Rib chops, boiled and then fried, are tabakmaaz; there are fish (much) kababs, while fish with radish is gardmuf. Chicken is cooked with brinjals, and shikar is duck cooked with vinegar, garlic, and chillies. Before the advent of Islam, pork-eating was popular in Kashmir.

Rice is the staple food and is of course cooked in many ways, like the tursh, shulla, and zarda (sweet) palaos. Wheat breads include the kulcha, the sheermal (*see* rotis), the chewy girda, the sesame-encrusted tschvaru and the soft bakirkhani, all eaten for breakfast with tea. Tea is made in metal samovars, and is brewed either green, or with cardamom and almond to yield the richer kahwah, both of which are sipped all day long. Vegetables are grown in summer and dried in large quantities for use in winter. The unique floating gardens of Kashmir are water weeds bonded with lake mud on which are grown cucumbers, melons, tomatoes, radishes, and mint. In the lakes themselves are to be found lotus roots (rhizomes) called nedr which are cooked with meat, fish, and greens, or fried to crispness, or deep fried in a rice batter coating. Chutneys are made from fresh walnuts, sour cherries, yellow pumpkins and white radishes, and for dessert there is fruit like cherries, apples (amri and maharaji, *see* apples), peaches, pears and plums.

The Dogras are Rajputs from Kashmir who eat wheat, bajra, and maize as staple foods. Sri-palao and mutton-palao, made from rice, are popular with them. The other popular dishes are curried rajmah, a curd preparation called auria, and the relish ambal. Expert cooks are called siyan, and community meals called dhaam are served on large lotus leaves or stitched leaves (pattal) and in cups (doona).

kattha Water extract of the heart-wood of *Acacia catechu*, boiled down to a dark brown paste rich in astringent tannins. It is smeared on betel leaves before folding into a quid for chewing.

kedgeree An anglicization of the Hindi word khichadi which is a dish of rice cooked with dhal (usually mung) and ghee. The British kedgeree was the same dish, but often included fish, and was eaten for breakfast.

Kerala, food of Kerala was long known as Chera, historically part of the Tamil cultural ambience. Tamil literature notes that 'the sweetest toddy' came from Kuttanad (now in Kerala), and according to Ibn Battuta, the sugarcanes of Barkur were 'unexcelled in the country'.

Bananas of immense variety grow in profusion. It was near Kozhikode that Vasco da Gama landed in 1498, to die in Cochin twenty-six years later. Frequently, words for food items adopted into English from Malayalam were mediated by the Portuguese, like jaggery, betel leaf, areca nut, and the like. The *Mortis Malabaricus* was compiled between 1680 and 1700 by the Dutch governor, Heinrich van Rheede, in twelve volumes with 794 plates, with the help of a Carmelite missionary, Father Matheo, and a traditional Kerala physician, Itty Achyuthan. Many plants which entered India from the New World first found a home in Kerala, like the cashewnut, pineapple, tapioca, and cocoa.

Above all Kerala was the land of spices, the focus of European eyes. For centuries, long pepper, round pepper, cardamom, cloves, ginger, turmeric, and other spices had been shipped out from Kerala ports such as Quilandy (Tondi, Tyndis), Nileshwar (Nelkyanda), Cranganore (Muziris), and Kollum (Quilon), at first by the rulers there and later by the Arabs, Portuguese, Dutch, and British. Factories, ports and naval fleets were set up to facilitate this trade, supported by armed might.

Kerala has been the hospitable home to many exotic religions. St Thomas the Apostle, who arrived in about AD 50, made the first conversions to

Christianity on Indian soil in Kerala. Since the scriptures were written in Syriac, a dialect of Aramaic, Kerala converts came to be known as Syrian Christians. Jews also came into Cranganore during the first century AD, after the Second Temple in Jerusalem had been destroyed by the Romans. Persecution, first by the Muslims and later by Portuguese Catholics, drove the Jews a millennium later to Cochin, where a synagogue was set up in AD 1567. Arab traders had been active in Kerala even before the birth of Mohammad; after the coming of Islam, they formed the Kerala community of Moplahs, which grew by conversion.

The rice appam, a pancake also called vella-appam, is common to all Keralites (*see* appam for accompaniments and variations). The puttu consists of rice grits and coconut shreds, which are alternately layered in a bamboo tube. The latter is then affixed to the spout of a vessel in which water is boiled. The mass is pushed through after it has been steamed. Being rather dry, puttu is commonly eaten with bananas, or with a spicy dry chana. Another rice-coconut combination uses fried rice and is called avalose, a Syrian speciality. It can be moulded into an unda (ball) with sugar syrup. The churutta (literally cigar) is rice-based again; it has a crisp, translucent outer case, which is filled with rice grits and sweet, thickened palmyra juice (called pani). The unni-appam, eaten by all Keralites, consists of a mash of ripe jackfruit, roasted rice flour and jaggery, folded in an aromatic vazhana leaf (of the cinnamon family) in the shape of a triangle, and steamed. Jackfruit cooked with jaggery and some cardamom constitutes chakka-varathiyathu.

The Syrians eat beef, and eracchi-olathiyathu (fried meat) is a wedding speciality, a dry dish of beef chunks and coconut pieces fried in its own fat. To make eracchi-thoran, cubed beef is first boiled with vinegar and salt, then shredded on a grinding stone, lightly fried with spices, a coconut-masala mixture added, and the whole briefly steamed. Kappakari has pieces of tapioca (kappa) in the beef, and is finished by frying in oil. Most curries, including meat, always have a lot of coconut milk. Meen-vevichadu (cooked fish) is cooked differently in different areas even by Syrians. Both in Kottayam and Thrissur, river fish is used; this is cooked in Kottayam with the sour kokum fruit rind, called kodampuli, and is very red in colour with added chillies and even colouring matter; in Thrissur, tender mango as the souring agent and coconut milk are used. Meen-pattichadu uses very small fish like oil sardines, or even prawns, with coconut gratings. For Christmas there may be a wild duck, cooked as a mappas, or roasted with stuffing. Wild boar cooked with a strong masala, or pickled in oil, is also a Syrian speciality.

For pouring on dry dishes, buttermilk mixed with turmeric and spices is used; this is called kacchia-moru. Some sweet items have been mentioned earlier. A wedding speciality is thayirum-pazhampani, in which sweet palmyra juice is thickened by boiling down and poured on ripe bananas, mashed together, and eaten with curd. As a deep-fried savoury snack there is pakkuvada, a version of pakoda.

Though the usage of rice, coconut, and jaggery is common, there is evidence of Arab influence in the biriyanis and the ground wheat-and-meat porridge aleesa, elsewhere called harisa, of the Moplahs of Kerala.

The roti is the distinctive podi-patthiri, a flat, thin, rice chapati made from a boiled mash of rice baked on a thava and dipped in coconut milk. A wedding-eve feast could include the nai-choru, rice fried lightly in ghee with onions, cloves, cinnamon, and cardamom to taste, and finally boiled to a finish. A wedding dinner would necessarily mean a biriyani of mutton, chicken, fish, or prawn, which is finally finished by arranging the separately cooked flesh and the cooked rice in layers, and baking these with live coals above and below. Soups of various flavours are made from both rice and wheat, with added coconut or coconut milk, and spices. A whole wheat porridge with minced mutton cooked in coconut milk is called kiskiya. A distinctive and unusual sweet is mutta-mala (egg garlands), chain-like strings of egg yolk cooked in sugar syrup, and later removed from it; frequently this is served with a snow-like pudding

Seafood, an important part of Malayali food

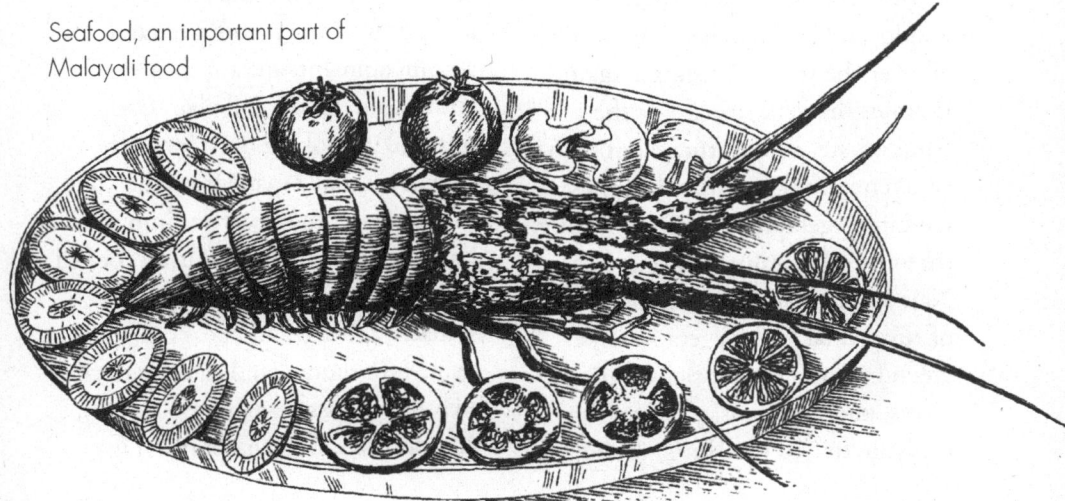

called pinnanthappam made from the separated egg whites, which are whisked up with the remaining sugar syrup, steamed, and cut into diamond shapes.

The Thiyas are a community that formerly tapped toddy but have now entered many other professions. Appam and stew are the breakfast fare, the stew being varied: fish in coconut sauce with tiny pieces of mango, mutton in coconut milk, or simply a sugared thick coconut milk. A bread speciality is nai-patthal, in the shape of a starfish. The curd pacchadi may be of pumpkin, and the sweet dessert may be one of several prathamans (q.v.), for example, mung dhal boiled in coconut milk and flavoured with palm jaggery, cardamom and ginger powder, and laced with fried cashewnuts, raisins, and coconut chips.

The Nairs are the Nakar, the original warrior class of Kerala, whose cooking skills have been employed by non-vegetarian families all over the south. Breakfast again is either the vella-appam or the bamboo-steamed puttu, eaten with sweetened milk and tiny bananas. Certain vegetable specialities, though eaten by all Keralites, have special Nair associations. The sambhar of tuvar dhal with vegetables like green bananas, drumsticks, various beans, and green cashewnuts (this is distinctive to the Nairs) is cooked in coconut milk and tossed with some coconut oil in spiced sour curd. Kalan is the same dish that uses green bananas alone, and olan is a dish of white pumpkin and dried beans cooked in coconut milk and coconut oil. A wedding feast of the Nairs will include several types of pacchadis, pickles, chips, and payasams based on milk, coconut milk, rice, dhal, and bananas. No meat is served at a wedding, though normally meat is eaten. Such domestic meat and chicken cooking, though spiced, uses a great deal of fresh coconut and coconut milk which tempers the dish to mildness. Small pieces of ash gourd or raw mango cooked with coconut, curds and chilli paste constitutes pulisseri, and puli-inji is fried sliced ginger.

The Nampoothiris are the brahmins of Kerala who may have first arrived there around the third century BC. They are strict vegetarians who favour for breakfast the idli, dosai, and puttu with a coconut or curd accompaniment, and eat their rice with kootu, kalan, and olan. Use of garlic in cooking is avoided. The thoran is usually made from the pods of green pay am (lobia) cut into small bits, stir-fried in oil and finally cooked in a little water. Green bananas, spinach, cabbage, and peas can all be made into thoran, and eaten with rice. Aviyal and erisseri, a pumpkin curry, are common. Chattha-pulisseri is a shraddha speciality, a sour buttermilk preparation of pepper, salt, and coconut paste, thickened by boiling down. All Kerala groups eat yellow banana chips fried in coconut oil and lightly salted. The best ones are reputed to be made in Kozhikode, which also boasts of a special sweet halwa made of bananas. The payasam of Kerala uses rice, and milk, but the prathaman (q.v.) has milk or coconut milk along with fruit or dhal, or with paper-thin shreds of a rice roll, cooked separately and added to the sweetened milk to give paladha-prathaman.

kesar Kesar is the gently dried stigma of the nargis (narcissus) flower, *Crocus sativus*. It is the kesara and kumkuma of Sanskrit, the zaffran of Persian and Arabic, and the saffron of English. It is first recorded in the fourth century BC, and is probably native to Greece. Its first mention in Sanskrit is in a medical dictionary, the *Bhava Prakasha*. Cultivation in Kashmir seems to have commenced in the sixth century AD. Bernier notes

Kesar

that saffron grows in Kashmir, and Jahangir records the production of '500 maunds by Hindusthan weight'. Thereafter cultivation was neglected till revived a century ago by Maharaja Ranbir Singh. The very dry alluvial plain of Rampur, and to some extent that of Paraspur, provides excellent conditions for the growth of the crocus. The purple blooms sit close to the ground, and are harvested for three to four weeks in October–November, very early in the morning before the sun comes up.

The powerful fragrance and orange colour of kesar are prized in Indian cuisine among the wealthy, Even a couple of stamens are sufficient to colour and flavour items like the kesari-bath (q.v.), palao, and the frozen kulfi (q.v.).

kesari-bath A confection of wheat rava (q.v.) lightly fried in ghee, with sugar added, and flavoured with kesar, sometimes called suji-halwa. In old Karnataka it was called shali-anna. It is an easily prepared dessert, popular all over India, and called by this name even when coloured and flavoured with other ingredients.

kesari dhal Even in AD 1590, Abul Fazl had noted the distressing effect of crippling (now called lathyrism) caused by consuming kesari dhal, *Lathyrus sativus*, either singly or in large quantities. Of the two types—a small-seeded dhal called lakhori and a larger one termed lakh—the latter is

believed to be the cause of lathyrism.
It is a very old grain, and has been
found in 6000 BC layers in Jarmo in
Turkey, and in various Indian sites
between 2000 and 1500 BC, such as
Chirand (Bihar), Atranjikhera, and
Nevasa (Maharashtra).

khadi A dish of spiced and diluted
curd beaten up with besan (q.v.)
powder, sometimes with balls of
fried pulse immersed in the liquid.
Frequently turmeric is used to
heighten the yellow colour.

The *Bimalprabhanda* written by
Lawanyasamay (*c.* AD 1200) in
Gujarat mentions themanam, which
resembles a khadi, and the *Varanaka
Samuchaya* (AD 1520) mentions
a pulse-based khadi flavoured
with asafoetida, both suggesting a
Gujarathi provenance for the dish.
Much earlier Charaka mentions a
dish of curds called khada acidified
with the pulp of the woodapple or
with changer! leaves (Indian sorrel).

khaman *See* dhokla.

khand Sugar in the form of large
crystals, which Alexander's party
in 326 BC described as 'stones the
colour of frankincense, sweeter
than figs or honey'. Along with
other forms of sugar, khand has
been known in India since at least
800 BC. Kautilya in the *Arthashastra*
(*c.* 300 BC) describes the whole
range of sugarcane products (q.v.).
The smaller, faceted crystals are
sometimes mixed with snacks

that are chewed, like grits of areca
nut (supari), crisp fried snacks of
flattened rice (chidva), etc.

Khand was traditionally obtained
by boiling down sugarcane juice to
incipient crystallization; the mass was
then placed in a basket lined with
fine cloth. Water in a finely divided
form, derived from moist aquatic
weeds placed on top of the basket,
served to wash away the molasses.
The layer of sugar crystals that
formed immediately below the weeds
was repeatedly removed and this
constituted khand. When redissolved
and crystallized, this yielded an
almost white crystaline sugar, called
misri or chini, or if in the form of
large crystals, khand, that varied in
size from a couple of millimetres to
solid blocks.

khandsari Later Hindi term for
rock sugar (*see* khand), which could
vary in colour from white to dark
brown. Before crystal pan sugar
was manufactured in India, large
quantities of khandsari (15,000–
20,000 tonnes in AD 1830) were
exported annually to England and
Europe for being further refined
to crystal sugar. At Independence,
about a lakh tonnes of khandsari was
produced annually in India.

khaskhas The tiny seeds from poppy
capsules, also called posto, a common
spice in Indian kitchens, and also
converted with jaggery syrup into
laddus (q.v.). Poppyseeds are also

crushed to give an oil of fine flavour (*see also* poppy).

kheel The puffed product obtained by stirring whole paddy grains with very hot sand; the product made in a similar way from rice is called murmura. Kheel is ground to yield a flour called sattu, a pottage of which is a popular breakfast item all over north India.

kheema A dry curry of minced lamb or beef. It is especially popular among Muslims as a breakfast item eaten with parata (q.v.) or naan. A more liquid form could accompany a rice meal.

kheer A sweet confection based on rice. When prepared as a ritual 'pucca' food, the rice is first lightly fried in ghee before boiling with sugared milk till the milk thickens (*see* cooking principles). A kheer of jowar is mentioned in the fourteenth-century *Padmavat* of Gujarat, and other cereals

Kheer

and cereal products (vermicelli, sev, pheni) may be used as well. A thinner product is payasam, and both are popular desserts, routinely as well as on festive occasions.

The Hindi word kheer derives from the Sanskrit ksheer for milk and kshirika for any dish prepared with milk.

khichdi, khichiri A composite dish of rice and mung dhal (occasionally other dhals may be used) cooked with ghee and some spices. The recipe for khichdi made in Akbar's kitchen specifies equal proportions of rice, mung dhal, and ghee, along with, certain spices. Jahangir's favoured food on his days of abstinence from meat was a very rich Gujarathi khichdi called lazizan, with both spices and nuts.

Much less ghee would be used in common versions of khichdi, repeatedly mentioned by visitors as the common evening (and occasionally morning) meal of Indian agricultural labourers. These include Ibn Battuta, Abdur Razzak, and Francisco Pelsaert, among others. Khichdi was even fed to horses, according to an early Russian visitor, Akanasy Nikhitin (c. AD 1470). The British adopted the item as a breakfast dish called kedgeree (q.v.)

khoa The solids of milk, obtained by boiling it down in a large metal pan called a kadhai, stirring the liquid at first, and constantly scraping it later with a flat ladle called a khunti to prevent caramelization. The light brown mass is finally shaped into a large ball or small pats. Khoa itself is a sweet concoction, sometimes further sweetened with a quarter its weight of sugar to yield burfis, and flavoured with cardamom to yield pedas. Khoa is the base of the frozen dessert kulfi (q.v.). The early Sanskrit term for khoa was shakarpaka, which is used in the *Shivatattvaratnakara* of King Basavaraja of Keladi. Khoa has a high content of all the three major nutrients, protein, fat, and sugar (lactose).

kidney bean *See* rajmah.

kitchens *See* cooking principles.

kneading pan *See* cooking utensils.

knives *See* cooking utensils.

Kodagu, food of Perched on the lush hilly highlands in the Kodagu district of Karnataka are a martial people, the Kodavas, with a distinctive cuisine. Rice is eaten boiled, or as a distinctive ghee-coated product (naikulu), or as a palao with the meat chunks firm, and every grain coated evenly with masala. Rice is transformed in numerous ways, and each has a distinct non-vegetarian accompaniment The akki-otti (rice roti) is based on a thick dough of ground rice rolled out on a wet cloth, roasted on a thava, and eaten with a spicy sesame seed chutney, or a dry and salty dish of bamboo shoot chiplets called baimblay (these shoots are also pickled). With the palao goes a pasty relish of ripe wild mangoes in a curd base called mangay-pajji. A paper-thin, soft handkerchief of rice (neer-dosai) is accompanied by a chicken curry into which is poured a lot of coconut milk. The nu-puttu of Kodagu is the strand-like idi-appam of south India, once eaten with jaggery water but now with any liquid (meat, chicken) curry. Steamed balls of mashed and cooked rice constitute kadambuttu, which is paired with a pork dish that has a very thick dark masala, in which an essential component is the black, sun-drawn extract of the yellow fruit of *Gracinia cambogia*. The acidity of this kacham-puli serves to keep the fat on the pork firm and chewy. A breakfast dish consists of a steamed thick batter of broken rice (than), liberally sprinkled with fresh coconut shreds, called pa-puttu, which is often eaten with ghee and the excellent honey so plentifully available in Kodagu. Another is thaliya-puttu, fine rice batter with a little urad dhal, steamed on metal trays, and eaten with meat balls (kyma-unde) in gravy.

Two fish are in use. One is the sardine, matthi-meen, and the other the tiny whitebait (koyle-meen), cooked dry and eaten bones and all. The two popular desserts are both based on the banana. Well-ripened fruit is mashed with the powder of roasted rice, to which a little methi is added, to give the uncooked thambuttu, eaten with ghee, fresh coconut scrapings and roasted sesame seeds. To make koale-puttu, a banana mash with small wedges of matured coconut is steamed in a banana leaf packet; when the packet is opened, a brown slab is obtained, eaten either hot or cold with fresh butter. The name is a corruption of koovale-puttu, which is the same dish that was earlier made not with banana, but with the ripe pulp of the soft, weepy variety of jackfruit called koovale.

kodhra The kodo millet, kodhrava or kodhra in Sanskrit, is *Paspalum scorbiculatum*. It was a sacred grain for the Aryans, and in *c*. 300 BC Kautilya mentions a cultivated form, kodhrava, and a wild form, daraka, which a century later Charaka refers to as uddalaka. Ibn Battuta in the thirteenth century records that among the grains stored in the stout walls that surrounded Delhi were 'kudhru grains' that had been placed there by Sultan Balban ninety years earlier. Excavations at many sites in the Dekhan plateau have revealed that the grain was in use even in 1800 BC. Varagu is frequently mentioned in early Tamil literature. It was a product of the forest areas termed mullai; the cereal varagu was sown along with the horsegram

Kulfi

kollu, and its straw was used to thatch houses. Kodhra grain is widely employed as cattle fodder.

Horsegram suppresses vata and kapha, and is constipative.

kosher meat *See* Jewish food.

kulfi A popular frozen dessert, probably brought by the Mughals from Kabul and Samarkand, or else developed by them in Delhi. It derives its name from kulfi, the conical metal vessel in which it is made. Its preparation is described in the *Ain-i-Akbari* (AD 1590) as freezing (probably in an ice-salt mixture) a mass of khoa (q.v.) containing chopped pistachio nuts and the essence of kesar (q.v.), in a metal cone, sealed with a plaster of wheat dough, a method followed to this day.

laddu A sweet confection popular all over India which takes the form of a ball of various materials held together with thick jaggery or sugar syrup. The base materials could consist of roasted sesame seeds, rava (wheat semolina), or fried globules (boondi) of the batter of various pulses, especially besan (q.v.). In early Sanskrit writings, the term modaka seems to signify the later ladduka, though at present the modaka (q.v.), modak, or moodagam signifies a sweet-stuffed envelope of dough. The term ladduka first finds mention in the Mahabharata and the *Sushrutha Samhita*.

ladles and spoons The Vedic sacrificial ceremonies entailed numerous libations of ghee, butter, water, and milk. For each of these, ladles of specific material, size, and design were prescribed. Large wooden ladles, with a yoni (oval)-shaped bowl ending in a lip, were collectively termed sruk, with individual items known as juhu, dhruva, upabhrt and pracharani. Small metal ladles with a long, slim handle, and lipless bowls, used for sprinkling ghee and water, were termed darvi, sruvi, sruva, tragbila and vitasi. Other ladles were the pariplupatra and antardhana. Spoons included the pariplava, a spoon without a handle for drawing out the soma juice; havani, a spoon used by the angihotr priest; and grahani, one used to hold prasadya (a mixture of butter in its own buttermilk after churning). A large, cup-like bowl with a handle, used as a decanting vessel, was termed prasaka. From being used for specific religious functions, some of these utensils passed into domestic service.

Early south Indian literature mentions three types of agappai spoons : thattai-, sanda-, and shirra-besides numerous ladles with such names as karandi (a scraper-spoon), sattuvam, muttai, thaduppu, maravai, thotti, kinnam, rnarakkal, and abanam, all doubtless of specific functional design. The vattal was a flat ladle made of either wood, stone, or metal. Some of these devices continue to be used in the kitchen to this day.

lady's finger The Sanskrit, bhina-daka, with a hard n, has been identified as the present Hindi bhendi, and Charaka mentions a plant bhandi. It was poetically called the lady's finger in colonial times in India, and okra in America. *Abelmoschus esculentus* is of African origin, and though perhaps a late entrant into India, is a popular mucilaginous vegetable, cooked in wet or dry form. It is a polyploid with 65 chromosomes, 29 from one genome and 36 from another, but even the basic chromosome number is uncertain.

Lady's finger (bhindi)

leaf plates and cups Many early societies must have used leaf plates and cups, but their use persisted in India because of the strong concept of cross-pollution that marked the Vedic food ethos (*see* etiquette of dining); this made disposable materials attractive even after those of clay, stone, wood, and metal became available. The Vedic sacrifices mention patravali (Hindi patroli), a plate made of leaves stapled together with slivers of cane or bamboo, while the purnaputra was a funnel made from a leaf of plaksha (palash, *Butea monosperma*) in which boiled ceremonial rice was hung on a tree. Apart from the palash and the large leaves of the lotus, leaves of the banyan and the teak, stapled together, are mentioned. In south India the choice was leaves of the lotus and the banana, both large in size, soft, and water-and-heat-resistant. Moreover banana trees were easily grown using waste kitchen water in every home. Kashmir has a community meal called dhaan, prepared by special cooks called siyan; this is traditionally served on huge round ambal (lotus) leaves, with the liquid items proffered in leaf cups called doona.

leather vessels Called kutuh or kutup in the *Amarakosha*, bags of leather are mentioned even in the *Rigveda* and *Mann Shastra* for storing liquids like water and oil. The skin of a whole goat is extensively used in India for transporting water, slung across his shoulders by a bihisti or bheesti. The latter word is of uncertain origin, but could be from the Sanskrit vish, meaning to sprinkle.

lehya(m) Category of foods that are meant to be licked, one of several food classifications (*see* etiquette of dining). In medical parlance it came to have the connotation of a medicated paste or viscous liquid, like the well-known restorative, chyavanapras.

lemon *Citrus limon*, oval in shape and yellow-green in colour, is an ancient Indian fruit. Excavations at Harappa (*c.* 2000 BC) revealed 'a pendant in the form of a lemon leaf in burnt steatite' and it is repeatedly referred to by Indian writers and foreign visitors as an acidulant in cooking both meat and vegetables, as the source of a refreshing beverage, and as an ingredient of tarts and puddings in British India.

lemon grass *See* ginger grass.

lentils *See* masoor.

lima beans A native of South America, the long, thin pods of *Phaseolus lunatus* are used as a vegetable in India.

lime The round, yellow, thin-skinned acidic Indian lime, kaghazi-nimbu, is *Citrus aurantifolia*. Though the Sanskrit term nimbuka is of Munda derivation (numbaka), the species is thought to be of Malaysian origin, though obviously known from very ancient times in India. A raga or juice from the lime is mentioned by Charaka. Babar listed the lime among the eight citrus fruits he encountered in India, and European visitors to Vijayanagar in the sixteenth century AD commented on the abundance of both lime trees and lime fruit. Francois Bernier carried with him on his travels a stock of lime for refreshment. Lime juice was one of the five components of the arrack-based drink, punch (q.v.), popular in colonial times; nimbu-pani, and later fresh lime with soda, was the supreme quencher of colonial thirst.

lime paste *See* chunam.

linseed The annual *Linum usitassimum* originated in Europe from a wild perennial ancestor, and was developed there to take the form of tall, unbranched plants that were utilized for the production of flax fibre and linen cloth. Sanskrit writings refer to kshuma and uma, which have been interpreted to mean linen, and which Manu considers appropriate wear for a student. Yet flax and linen have all but vanished in India, perhaps because the emphasis here is on the plant as the source of an oilseed.

Linseed oil has a strong odour, and finds very limited edible use. It is used to flavour, for example, a type of chutney in areas around Nagpur. A century ago, a dish called tisjauri, described as rice cooked

with linseed oil, was recorded in
Bihar. It is mentioned in ancient
agricultural writings as a dressing
used to nurse sick trees back to
health. Unani medicine (q.v.) makes
considerable use of linseed oil. In
the colonial period, its value as a
'drying' component in paints and
varnishes resulted in a sharp spurt in
production, largely for export.

liquor *See* beverages, alcoholic.

litchi *Nephelium litchi* (long
classified as *Litchi chinensis*) is a
native of southern China which
the Portuguese residents of Bengal
introduced into the area at the end
of the eighteenth century AD. The
spiny red fruit has a sweet pulpy
aril that surrounds a shiny oval
seed. It has rather exacting climatic
requirements, and does well almost
only in Ramnagar in north Bihar
and Dehra Dun in Uttar Pradesh.

lobia *See* cowpea.

loquat An edible yellow-orange fruit
not unlike a small apple, popular in
China and Japan, which Xuan Zang
in the seventh century AD did not
find in India. *Eriobotryajaponica*, also
called the Japanese medlar, was noted
in AD 1821 as 'growing extensively'
in Bangalore, but it is now rare and
confined to the hilly areas of Uttar
Pradesh and Bengal.

lotus The roots, seeds, stalks, and
tender leaves of *Nelumbo nucifera*,
kamal in Sanskrit and Hindi, have

Litchi

been consumed in India since the
dawn of history. Excavations at
Harappa yielded a 'representation
of a lotus root in faience', and the
Yajurveda (*c*. 800 BC) mentions
the edible lotus root as shaluka.
Today they are widely used as nedr
in Kashmir cuisine, either fried to
crispness, or coated with rice batter
and deep-fried, or cooked along
with meat, fish, or greens. In the
Manasollasa is described a dish of
pulses with pieces of lotus stalk. The
soft seeds are considered a delicacy, as
are the tender leaves. Full-grown lotus
leaves are very large in size, and their
use as serving plates at a kingly repast
has been described by Nemichandra in
his *Lilavati* (*c*. AD 1170). In Kashmir, a
special feast called dhaan is laid out on
a lotus *leaf* (*see* leaf plates and cups).
The Buddha remarked that water
meant for drinking should be 'clear,
cool, shining like silver and with the
fragrance of the lotus'. Indeed it was
common practice to grow the lotus
plant in tanks to purify water meant
for drinking.

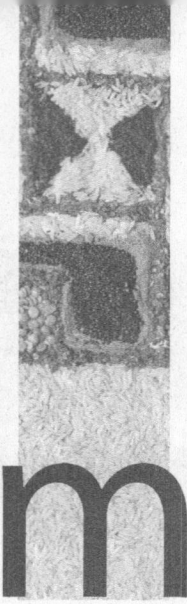

m

mace The fruit of *Myristica fragrans*, a tree originating in the Moluccas, yields a nut which is the nutmeg (Hindi jaiphal); this is surrounded by a scarlet aril, mace (Hindi jatri), which becomes visible when the fruit ripens and bursts open. The nutmeg is shredded for use, while mace is pressed flat, dried to a translucent red-brown and cut into strips for sale. If used in excess, both products give rise to nausea and even hallucinations. Linschoten (AD 1580) notes the consumption of both materials along with bhang, a narcotic, by poor people. Rather curiously, Xuan Zang was provided with twenty nutmegs daily during his stay at the Nalanda monastery in the seventh century.

madhu Sanskrit word for honey, which was later used for many items with a sweet taste, such as madhuka

(mahua) (q.v.), or *Madhuca indica*, with sweet flowers, and historical sweet confections such as madhumestaka, -parka, -shirshaka, -kroda, -golaka, -nala, -sarika, and -mada (*see also* honey).

madhuparka An auspicious ambrosial beverage made up of five ingredients, ghee, curd, milk, honey, and sugar. It was offered on solemn occasions: to a guest on arrival, to a woman after seven months of pregnancy, to a student when he left home for apprenticeship with a guru, to a suitor on arrival at the girl's house, and to a bridegroom arriving for the wedding ceremony. A dab of madhuparka was placed on the lips of a newborn male child. The madhuparka rite is set out in the *Ashvalayana Grhya-Sutra*.

madhya in ayurveda, madhya itself connotes any strong liquor, while madhya-varga signifies alcoholic beverages as a class.

maharaja A term frequently employed in north India to signify a cook, perhaps from the mythological story of Nala, a maharaja of Nishada, who, in reduced circumstances, entered the service of the king of Ayodhya and was renowned as an accomplished cook. Nalapaka signifies food of outstanding quality.

mahashali Shali itself connoted a fine transplanted winter rice, and mahashali was a plump variety of exceptional quality. Shaman Hwui Lui, a disciple of Xuan Zang, recorded this rice in the list of food items that his master was served when resident for some years in the seventh century at the great Buddhist monastery in Nalanda in Bihar. Even eight centuries later, the Gujarathi work, *Varanaka Samuchaya* (AD 1520), lists mahashali rice among numerous rice items, an astonishing persistence of the name, and perhaps of the variety itself.

mahua An ancient tree of India, *Madhuca indica* has diverse uses. It is mentioned in the later *Vedas*. The sweet flowers are noted as a source of sugar by Sushrutha, but were preferably either eaten as such, or converted into alcohol. Thus Grierson noted about a century ago in Bihar that a dish called mahuar contained mahua flowers, besan flour, and linseed, while another dish called latta was made of mahua flowers and parched grain. The flowers, when fermented, yielded a product that was distilled to make mahua spirit, described as having a 'mousey, foetid' odour.

Such distilled spirits were frequently sweetened and spiced, and mahua flowers themselves could be used for such saccharification. Colonial administrators stated that in about AD 1800 practically every village in Gujarat and Rajputana (Rajasthan) had its spirit shop, the number of these being 'absolutely incalculable'. In the middle of the nineteenth century, the production of distilled mahua spirit was licensed to a score of Parsi entrepreneurs on the island of Uran, near Bombay; in AD 1850, even the duty on produce amounted to £ 80,000.

In the seventh century AD, Xuan Zang noted the mahua as one of the fruits of India, and Ibn Battuta remarked on its sweetness centuries later.

The crushing of mahua seeds for fat is noted as early as in 300 BC in the *Arthashastra*. The seeds were cracked with stones, and the inner kernels crushed for fat in traditional ghanis and later in modern screw-presses. Tribals, especially those in central India, have always been associated with mahua products, and obtained the fat by crushing the boiled kernels between two wooden planks, or using the trunks of two trees as the lever and fulcrum respectively. The fat was used for cooking purposes.

maida This is the fine, white, inner flour of wheat obtained either by selective grinding in a chakki, or by segregation using specific gravity principles during the milling of whole wheat. It was traditionally favoured for making light-coloured fried products like the pun, bhathura, and lucchi, and in recent times for preparing bread, biscuits, cakes, and certain sweetmeats.

maireya *See* beverages, alcoholic.

maize Called in America Indian corn, and later simply corn, *Zea mays* was throughout history the staple food of both North and South America, with beans (rajmah) as the pulse complement.

There is little doubt that maize evolved in Mexico and South America. Yet there is some evidence that maize was grown in India before the inflow of New World plants in the sixteenth century AD.

Maize has found a place in Indian cuisine. Bhutta flour, makki, is converted in Punjab into rotis that are eaten with butter and a spicy relish of sarson (q.v.) leaves. In Gujarat, traditional rotlas of bajra are now sometimes made with maize flour. In Indian medical terms however maize is perceived as a 'cold' food in contrast to 'hot' bajra. Popped corn was noted even a century ago in Bihar

as a snack food called parmal, which later became a common urban snack all over the country.

makki The rather coarsely ground flour of maize (q.v.). Very fine cornflour for baking has limited traditional uses.

malabathrum An item that regularly featured in the trade between south India and Rome, which was at its height in the first two centuries of the Christian era (*see* Italy, trade with). In AD 1560 Garcia da Orta identified it as tejpat (q.v.), the aromatic leaves of *Cinnamomum tamala*.

mandarin orange *See* citrus fruits.

mango Inevitably, myth and legend have accrued around the ancient mango tree. It is thought by some Hindus to be a transformation of Prajapathi himself, the progenitor and creator of all creatures. Buddhists consider it sacred because the Buddha was accustomed to rest in a mango grove gifted to him by an admirer. On another occasion, the Buddha ate a mango fruit, planted the stone and washed his hands over it: a beautiful white mango tree sprang forth bearing flowers and fruit; it was looked after carefully, as shown in a tender medallion sculpted in Bharhut. In one legend, from a mango fruit appeared a daughter of Surya, the sun god, who was recognized by a king as his wife from a previous birth. The long racemes bearing mango flowers symbolize the darts of Kamadeva, the god of love, as depicted, for example, in the play *Shakuntala*, by Kalidasa (fifth century AD).

The literary record is ancient. The *Rigveda* itself mentions saha, but whether this is the term sahakara used for the mango in later literature is uncertain. From its very first mention as amra in the *Brhadaranyaka Upanishad* (*c.* 1000 BC) and in the slightly later *Shatapatha Brahmana*, the virtues of the mango fruit have been extolled for three thousand years. In later literature it also figures as chutha, rasala, and sahakara.

The hills of north-eastern India adjoining Myanmar are the likely centre of origin of the mango. Wild varieties still exist there, besides several other related species. In fact the amrataka, even now called the wild mango but belonging to a closely related species, *Spondias pinnata*, is also mentioned in the *Brhadaranyaka Samhita*.

In Tamil, the fruit is called manga, or man-kai, which is perhaps a euphonic transposition of am-kai (mango fruit) from the Sanskrit amra. The Tamil word manga was first used in a European tongue in AD 1510 by Varthema, and repeatedly thereafter. Using the current term mango for the first time in AD 1673, Fryer goes into superlatives over its taste: 'When ripe, the (legendary)

Apples of the Hesperides are but fables to them; for Taste, the Nectarine, Peach and Apricot fall short'. Practically every foreigner in India echoed these sentiments.

The mango is a highly heterozygous plant. Every tree raised from a seedling is potentially a new type, since seed is formed from the cross-pollination of a female cell of the flowers with the male pollen from other trees, with either one dominant or recessive. Vegetative propagation and grafting in the past helped to preserve superior types. Grafting was first used on the mango by the Portuguese, and yielded varieties like the Fernandin.

Mughal patronage also played a notable part in encouraging mango grafting. Noblemen could have all their revenues remitted by raising orchards. Mangoes of high quality were collected from all over India and grown by Muqqarab Khan in his garden in Kirana. Down the centuries, the selection of a superior variety that arose spontaneously, and its later perpetuation by grafting, led to nearly a thousand varieties of mango. Two types are distinguished, one with firm flesh for table use, and the other for sucking, with ample thin juice. Among those of north India are the dussehri (originating from a village of the same name near Lucknow), langra (which a lame fakir of Varanasi noticed growing in his backyard), chowsa and ratnal

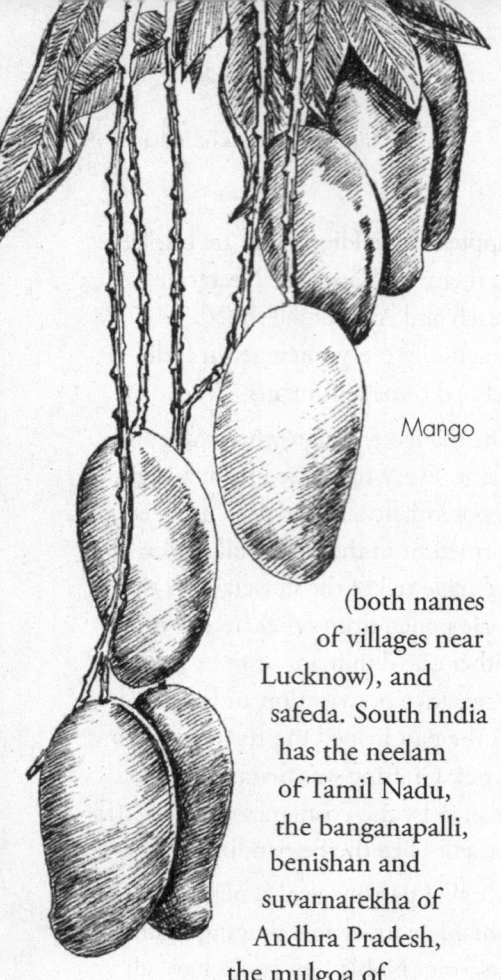
Mango

(both names of villages near Lucknow), and safeda. South India has the neelam of Tamil Nadu, the banganapalli, benishan and suvarnarekha of Andhra Pradesh, the mulgoa of several southern states, notably Karnataka, and the pairi and incomparable alphonso of Maharashtra. Recent hybrids of high quality are the amrapali, a dwarf but profuse variety that is a dussehri–neelam cross, and another that is a banganapalli–alphonso cross. Sucking varieties include a group from the village of Gangian in Punjab, and the rasalus of Andhra Pradesh.

Mango trees even a hundred and fifty years old have been known to yield fruit in profusion. A gigantic tree near Chandigarh, killed by lightning in AD 1955, yielded an enormous average of nearly 16,800 kg of fruit annually.

The mango fruit has been utilized in different ways. The ripe fruit is of course eaten, and is reported in ancient Tamil literature as being served in restaurants, and in Kannada literature as a component of ripe fruit mixtures called seekharane. Wild ripe mangoes are cooked in curd in Kodagu to give a sweet-sour relish called mange-pajji, and are also cooked whole, including the seeds, to a sweetish curry. When the juice is dried in thin layers on bamboo mats the delicious chewy am-papad or ambsath is obtained, and a mango 'cheese' called mangada has been developed in Goa. Mangoes when green are tart, and have their appropriate outlets. Meat cooked with mango pieces is described in the Mahabharata, and Kerala has a fish curry cooked in coconut milk along with tiny pieces of green mango. Lord Shiva, of choleric disposition, is appropriately depicted in the sixteenth-century Bengali work *Chandimangala* as being served sour mangoes for dessert. Semi-ripe mangoes, boiled, pulped, strained, and sugared, yield the delicious beverage now called mango-fool. Green mango is frequently ground into raw chutney used as an accompaniment to a meal. Pickles of unripe but tender mangoes abound, some using even the whole fruit with the seed. A wandering minstrel is served with 'tender mango pickle' in ancient Tamil, and it figures again in a feast in old Karnataka. Around

400 BC, Sanskrit literature records preserves of green mango in vinegar and soured rice gruel. Morabbas (q.v.) of ripe, sliced mangoes in spiced sugar syrup, and sweet versions of mango chutney (q.v.) in spiced sugar-vinegar bases, became popular with the colonial in India; sizeable quantities were commercially bottled for use in the country and for export.

Wine made from ripe mango juice was termed sahakarasura by Charaka. In medical terms, the mango had the very strong connotation of a 'hot' food, which had necessarily to be imbibed along with 'cold' milk to avoid boils.

Mango kernels are essentially starchy, and have been pressed into service as a famine food. Grierson described a bread made from mango kernel flour called anthi-ki-roti a century ago in Bihar.

A string of mango leaves is hung as an auspicious symbol across a household door. The characteristic mango fruit motif is widely used in sculpture, in fashioning utensils like plates and paan-holders, and in textile design, for example, sari borders. The shape of the mango was incorporated as the paisley motif in shawls and printed fabrics exported to Europe. The mango pervades the Indian literary corpus. Thus in an early Tamil work, the eye of a woman is compared to a very tender mango cut horizontally with a rusty knife, the stone resembling the pupil surrounded by the white of the eye.

masha *See* urad.

masoor *Lens culinaris* is masura in Sanskrit and lentil in English. The pink gram is one of the three Ms of Aryan literature (along with mudga or mung, the green gram, and masha or urad, the black gram). Masoor has been found even in the seventh and sixth millennia BC at many sites from Turkey to Iran, the earliest of these grains being much smaller than the present varieties. India has both an average and a small variety, called masoor and masari respectively. Masoor has been found in excavations at Navdatoli, Ter, and Chirand in periods dated between 1800 and 1000 BC. The literary record shows that masura, mangalaya, and khalva find mention in the *Brahadaranyaka Samhita,* the *Vajanaseyi Samhita,* and the *Taittiriya Brahmana,* all around 800 BC. Though there are several wild species, *Lens orientalis*, which has the same chromosome number (2n=24) and shows a series of intermediate types with *L. culinaris*, is believed to be its progenitor.

The name masura is believed to have an aboriginal connotation to it, suggesting an early presence in India. Tamil has no separate name for the pulse, only the derived maisur-paruppu, a product of the mountainous mullai areas of the

Tamil country. Everywhere masoor was a winter crop, grown in the north along with wheat and barley, and in the south with varagu, kollu or horsegram, and Bengal gram.

Being a plough-raised crop, masoor was classed as anna or kristapachya. Charaka includes it among the twelve pulses that comprised shamidhanya; its parched product constituted one of the bhrstadhanyas. However it is a food forbidden in a fast, or as a divine offering. In Bengal it is not eaten by staunch Vaishnavites. However the Buddha permitted it to his monks along with mudga and masha, all being considered 'full of soul qualities, but devoid of faults'.

mat, moth bean *Vigna aconitifolia* is in Sanskrit mat, matki, mankastha, and vanamudga, and in English the moth bean. A host of Indian names testify to its antiquity in India, though perhaps it was only domesticated after urad and mung. For long it was taken for granted that the moth bean originated from the wild species *V. trilobata*, but recent studies have shown that the two species are distinct from each other, and possess some isolating mechanisms. Wild forms are known in Mexico and Guatemala, which leaves wide open both the origin of the moth bean, and its very early presence in India. Two other members of the *Vigna* species, sutari

(*V. umbellata*) and lobia (*V. unguiculata*), are both indigenous.

mattar *See* peas.

meal, order of Indian medicine is in great measure based on appropriate diet (*see* ayurveda), and in turn health perceptions have set the pattern of Indian meals. Great stress is placed on taste or rasa (q.v.), and each taste is believed to be a combination of any two of the five fundamental elements of all matter, which are earth, water, fire, air, and ether. There are six 'pure' tastes, which are madhura (sweet), ami a (sour), lavana (salty), katu (pungent), tikta (bitter), and kasaya (astringent). Every meal was expected to include all the six tastes, and in the order just listed, according to Sushrutha. A meal would therefore, as stated in the *Shivatattvaratnakara*, start with a sweet item (though madhura has a very wide connotation, and includes cereals and pulses), continue with

Peas

sour and salty preparations, and finish with pungent, bitter and astringent items.

In practice, all six tastes (except perhaps for the distinctly bitter) can usually be savoured at, say, a formal wedding feast in most parts of India. However, considerations of texture and mouthfeel may overlie a purely taste progression.

In south India, a wedding lunch served on a large banana leaf has cold items laid out in specified positions, like salt, pickle, curd-based relish, papad, vadai, bdnda, a dry vegetable like beans, a dry sweet, and a small serving of say vermicelli payasam, which will be licked to start off the meal. In, say, Karnataka, rice is served, and small amounts are eaten with the curd relish, the dry vegetable, and a thovve (a yellow, practically unseasoned dhal). Ghee is then poured on the rice, which is eaten as a first course with a thicker dhal dish of huli (sambhar), and other mixed vegetables. Rice is served again and the second course eaten with a thin dhal extract, saaru (rasam), and vegetables. Occasionally a pre-mixed chitranna (lime rice) or bisi-bele-huli-anna (composite dhal and rice, in Tamil sambhar-sadam) could replace the boiled rice. Next is served the sweet item, frequently payasam in a leaf cup, or apasty sweet like kesari-bath (q.v.), or a solid sweet like jilebi (q.v.), or Mysorepak

(q.v.). All along a change of taste and texture is provided by pinching off and munching bits of the vadai or bonda. Finally, to soothe the palate and quench thirst will follow a fresh serving of rice eaten with curd or buttermilk, or a premixed curd-rice preparation like mosaruanna (thayiru-sadam in Tamil). A betel quid will frequently bring a heavy meal in south India (and indeed anywhere) to a close.

In Bengal a bitter item, shukto, is included at the start of the afternoon meal. Sweets are served at the very end. Meals are served on a circular thala of bell-metal, with side dishes placed around it in batis (bowls). Salt, chutney, lime, and various fried vegetables are always in place on the plate. Rice is normally eaten first with ghee, salt, and green chillies; then comes dhal accompanied by fried vegetables (bhaja) or boiled vegetables (bhate), followed by spiced vegetables like dalna or ghonto. Fish preparations follow, first lightly spiced ones like the liquid maccher-jhol, and then those more heavily spiced, after which comes a sweet-sour ambal or tauk (chutney), and fried papads. A dessert of either mishti-doi (sweet curds), accompanied by dry milk-based Bengali sweets (q.v.), or of a payesh (say, of rice and thickened milk) accompanied by fruits like the mango, ends the meal. A terminal digestive paan is certain to follow.

The night meal omits shukto, but could include deep-fried wheat lucchis (*see* roti), a palao, and a dalna of delicately spiced vegetables.

Other regional meals include their own characteristic preparations, but a variety of tastes and textures is always in evidence.

meat consumption Excavations in the Indus Valley have brought to light a wide range of animal bones: of zebu cattle, gaur, and buffalo, sheep, and goat, turtle, tortoise, and gharial, river and sea fish, fowl, and game birds. Clay models of many animals furnish further evidence of their presence. The Aryan civilization that followed from *c.* 1500 BC used animal flesh extensively in its early stages. The Vedas refer to more than 250 animals; of these about 50 were deemed fit for sacrifice and, by inference, for eating. These included domesticated animals like cattle and swine, wild animals, and some that were trapped or caught using decoys. Hooks, nets, and basket traps were in use to capture fish and turtles, whose flesh and eggs were relished. The marketplace had separate stalls for vendors of various meat: gogataka (cattle), arabika (sheep), shukarika (swine), nagarika (deer), shakuntika (fowl), and giddabuddaka (alligator and tortoise). It is strange that ducks, tame poultry, and their eggs do not find a place in these transactions, and a taboo against their consumption

is voiced in Sanskrit literature (*see* chicken; eggs).

In the *Rigveda*, horses, buffaloes, rams and goats are all described as being sacrificed for food. The elaborate ajapanchandam sacrifice of a male goat is laid down, the meat being cooked in cauldrons. The 162nd hymn of the *Rigveda* dwells on the elaborate horse sacrifice, ashvamedha (q.v.), with details of how the meat was to be shared by various priests and participants. Bulls and barren cows were favoured by Agni, a dwarf ox by Vishnu, a drooping-horned bull with a blaze on the forehead by Indra, a black cow by Pushan, and a red cow by Rudra. Indra is exhorted to cut down his adversaries 'just as cows are butchered at the place of sacrifice'. Both the *Shatapatha Brahmana* and the *Yagnavalkya Samhita* specify that for a special guest, a big ox or big goat be sacrificed. According to Panini, a new word, gogna, was coined by compounding the words for bull and kill to signify a guest so honoured. The *Taittiriya Brahmana* praised Agasthya for his sacrifice of a hundred bulls.

The *Jataka* tales at various points mention the flesh of the pigeon, partridge, monkey, and elephant as being eaten, and to this the *Brhat Samhita* (sixth century AD) adds buffaloes and lizards.

Meat was considered a nourishing food, particularly recommended by Charaka for the lean, for convalescents, for those subjected to very hard work, and for men. The meats that were highly rated were those of the goat, hare, tortoise, parrot, quail, partridge, peacock, alligator, and rohita fish.

Jains are strongly against taking any form of life, even of unseen forms like micro-organisms, so the question of meat consumption simply does not arise (*see* Jain food ambience). Buddha did not prohibit the consumption of meat, especially if it was offered to a monk as alms (*see* Buddhist literature and food).

In south India, meat consumption was widely prevalent prior to the arrival of the Aryans in about the sixth century BC. Even thereafter, the famous brahmin priest of the Sangam epoch, Kapilar, speaks with relish, and without fear of social ostracism, about consuming meat and liquor. Old Tamil had four names for beef, namely valluram, shuttiraichi, shushiyam, and padithiram, showing that it was widely eaten. The *Perumpanuru* talks of a fat bull being slaughtered in the open. Even buffalo meat was consumed. There were fifteen names for the domestic pig, and the wives of traders who lived in the coastal neydal regions are shown as relishing pork. Wild boar, rabbit, and hare were hunted using dogs and nets. Captured boars were fattened with rice flour and kept away from

the female to improve the taste of the flesh. Even meat from an elephant either killed in battle or hunted down was dried and stored for consumption. The Kuruvar class liked the meat of deer and porcupine, the Mallar fried snails, and the Meenavar the tortoise. A dish of 'iguana red meat big with ova resembling chank shell beads' is eaten with obvious relish. There was no taboo, such as prevailed in north India, on eating the domestic fowl (called karugu or kozhi). Another bird frequently mentioned is the pea-fowl, and both the quail and partridge were eaten. Fish was naturally relished by folk of the littoral: aral, varal, and the horned valai are mentioned, besides prawns that were captured by the fisherfolk, the Meenavar. In fact the Tamil word meen (q.v.) for fish even entered the Sanskrit language.

Right from the start visitors to India noted that many abstained from meat consumption. The Greeks mention a king who hunted for exercise, but, being a vegetarian, gave away all his spoils. Xuan Zang noted: 'Fish, mutton, gazelle, deer they eat mostly fresh, sometimes salted; they are forbidden to eat the flesh of the ox, ass, elephant, horse, pig, dog, fox, wolf, lion, monkey and all the hairy kind. Those who eat them are despised and scorned, and are usually reprobated; they live outside the walls and are seldom seen among men.' A very early European visitor to India, John of Monte Corvino (AD 1292), noted that the people of India ate no meat, and Francisco Pelsaert (AD 1625) reported that 'workmen in India know little of the taste of meat'. Yet Sebastian Manrique noticed in the bazaar of Lahore 'large spits bearing the flesh of winged creatures'. Francois Bernier commented on the abundance of meat and fish in Bengal, and numerous visitors said the same of Vijayanagar. (*see also* beef; meat dishes; fish).

meat dishes The *Rigveda* refers to meat being boiled in pots or roasted on spits, and the *Brhadarankya Upanishad* refers to meat cooked with rice. From *c.* 400 BC references are made to dressing meat with salt and pepper, to frying meat, and to broths or soups of meat. The Ramayana notes that rice cooked with venison and vegetables, termed mamsabhutadana, was a popular dish with Rama, Sita, and Lakshmana while exiled in the Dandakaranya forest, while broths of pork and mutton cooked in acid fruit juices, termed supa and nisthana, were preparations relished in Ayodhya. At the sacrificial rites of Rama's father, King Dasharatha, mutton, pork, chicken, and peacock were cooked in several ways: boiled in fruit juices, or fried in ghee, or simmered along with cloves, caraway seeds, and masoor dhal. In the Mahabharata,

a dish of rice cooked with minced meat is termed pistaudana. Roasted birds figure frequently in the epic. For a picnic dinner, meat was roasted on spits and cooked as a curry; young buffalo calves were roasted on spits while being basted with ghee; buffalo beef was fried in ghee and seasoned with acid juices, rock salt and fragrant leaves; haunches of venison were boiled in different ways with mangoes and spices, and sprinkled over with condiments; and shoulders and rounds of animals, dressed in ghee, were sprinkled with sea salt and powdered black pepper, and garnished with radishes, pomegranates, lemons, fragrant herbs, asafoetida, and ginger.

The *Sushrutha Samhita* describes seven types of meat preparations. The *Manasollasa* of King Someshwara in the thirteenth century gives pride of place to meat dishes in the chapter on food, annabhoga. Liver carved into the shape of betel nuts, was roasted on charcoal, fried with spices, and eventually placed in curd or in a decoction of black mustard. Roasted tortoise, seasoned fish, and fried crabs are noted. A whole pig was first roasted; subsequently pieces were carved out of the roast and charcoal-broiled. These sunthakas were eaten after being either seasoned with rock salt and black pepper, or sprinkled with sour lemon juice to yield chakkalikas. Other sunthakas could be carved out of the roast in several ways. One was in long strips 'resembling palm leaves' which were placed in spiced curds. Another was a preparation called mandilya made from pig entrails, by mixing them with marrow and spices, and broiling them on a charcoal fire. A marrow preparation ('khanda of vapa'), it is stated, should be kept in a roll 'like a panchanga' (an astrological document). In one of the recipes, meat pieces were mixed with a paste of gram pounded with spices and then fried; to this was added tender hyacinth beans (nishpava), certain berries, onions, and garlic, and the whole mass was mixed with some acid juice and flavoured. Kavachandi was a less acidic preparation, in which plum-shaped pieces of sheep mutton, mixed with gram or sprouted mung and powdered spices, were fried along with garlic, onions, and vegetables like the brinjal and radish. Another dish, puryala, specifies pieces of meat carved in the shape of amla fruits, which were cooked in spices, and cooked again with certain acid fruits, roasted pieces of pork, spices, and rock salt, flavoured with garlic and asafoetida. To make krishnapaka, sheep mutton (in the shape of betel nuts) and blood were cooked together to give a dark, dry dish. Bhaditraka was a roast product: pieces of meat were bored, stuffed with spices, roasted on spits and then spiced again; sometimes, after cooking, the roasted bhaditrakas were allowed to dry out, and later fried in ghee. Ground meat was used to stuff brinjals, which when fried yielded purabhattaka.

In south India, the earliest writings available are those in Tamil (q.v.), from about AD 300. An important component of meat dressing was black pepper; one of its names was kari, which was also used for the finished spicy dish. Meat was marinated in ground pepper and mustard seeds, and then fried in oil to yield thallitakari, or kuy. Fried meat had three names, one of which was porikari; hare meat was among those fried. Meat boiled with pepper and tamarind was pulingari or tuvai, and such meat could be ground and spiced to give a pasty relish. The meat of various animals was roasted extensively. We read of 'hot meat, roasted on the points of spits', and in the *Purananuru* of 'Ten large pieces of fat meat roasted on iron spikes'. Rice could be cooked along with fatty meat.

A new impulse and innovations in the cooking of meat came with the arrival of conquerors from across the north-western borders of the country, starting from about the second millennium AD. The food items that appeared at the royal court and among the nobility of the Sultanate empire in Delhi are described by Ibn

Battuta in the thirteenth century AD. At various meals were served shiwawoon (roast meat), roast mutton, and a roast of whole sheep. The birds that were roasted were chicken, quail, and sparrow (kunjshakka), and a dish of rice cooked in ghee, with a roast fowl (dojaj) placed on top, is described as 'palao with murg mussalam'. Meat is described as being cooked with ghee, onions, and green ginger, and a popular side-dish was 'samusak', a fried envelope of wheat stuffed with minced meat cooked with almonds, walnuts, pistachios, onions, and spices (*see* samosa).

We have considerable culinary details of Akbar's kitchen in the *Ain-i-Akbari* written by Abul Fazl (AD 1590). Of the three classes of food described, safiyana was meatless dishes for the emperor's days of abstinence from flesh, which were quite numerous. The second class was composite dishes of rice, or wheat, with meat, amonst which are ranked qabuli and Drzd-biryani. The third class of food described in the *Ain-i-Akbari* consists of various meat dishes, some of which may be noted. Yakhni needed meat, onions, and salt. To make musamman, all the bones of a fowl were to be removed through the neck, leaving the fowl whole, after which the recipe called for minced meat, ghee, eggs, onions, coriander, fresh ginger, salt, round pepper, saffron (this melange was clearly meant as a

stuffing). Dupiyaza called for meat (of middling fat), ghee, onions, salt, fresh pepper, cumin seed, coriander seed, cardamoms, cloves, pepper. Not long after this, Edward Terry, chaplain to Sir Thomas Roe, lauded the dish dupiyaza at the court of Jahangir. describing it as 'venison cut in slices, to which they put onions and herbs, some roots, with a little spice and butter: the most savoury meat I ever tasted, and do almost think it is the very dish that Jacob made ready for his father, when he got the blessing'.

Current regional cuisines have adapted these inherited legacies to local materials and tastes, sometimes incorporating external influences. Thus the Kodavas of Karnataka cook a wet chicken curry with a lot of fresh coconut. Pieces of pork are cooked slowly in a very thick masala in which an essential component is the black, sun-drawn extract of the acid fruit (*Garcinia cambogia*), locally known as kachampuli, the acid content of which serves to keep the fat firm and crunchy. In Goa (q.v.), the souring agent can be kokum, but vinegar is also widely in use, and the pork dishes show Portuguese influences. One is the distinctive Goa sausage, chourisam, developed by Portuguese monks. Vindaloo is a liquid pork curry of pork meat, liver fat, and blood, with vinegar and tamarind juice. Feijoada is pork cooked with beans, and pork that is to be pickled is first salted. A shallow-fried dish of meat or chicken is termed chacuti. In Kerala (q.v.), the Syrian Christians have created a range of beef dishes. A dry dish of beef chunks and coconut pieces fried with no extraneous fat is eracchi-olathiyathu (fried meat)—a wedding special. To make eracchi-thoran, cubed beef is first boiled with vinegar and salt, then shredded on a grinding stone, lightly fried with spices, and steamed after adding a coconut-masala mixture to it. Kappa-kari has pieces of tapioca in the beef, and is fried in oil. Many meat curries use a lot of coconut milk. Parsi food (q.v.) shows a blend of Gujarathi and Iranian cuisine. There is a distinctive sweet palao of rice and mutton, and dhansakh is a mixture of at least three (and even up to nine) pulses, distinctively spiced, with added meat, tripe, and vegetables. From the local vegetable dish undhiu, baked underground in a handa, has emerged the Parsi oberu, to which the meat of game like quail is sometimes added.

In many regions of India, Muslim communities have built on styles that stem from the imperial kitchens. Kababs (shammi, sheekh, tikka, husseni) are popular everywhere, as are regional-style palaos and biriyanis, haleem and shulla. Bohri Muslims in Gujarat have a special palao of rice with meat and split peas; lagania-sheekh is a baked dish of minced meat topped with a beaten egg;

and malai-tikkas are kababs of beef that have been marinated in cream. Hyderabad (q.v.) meat dishes have likewise developed a local ambience. An early-morning speciality is nahari, a stew of lamb trotters and tongue, cooked slowly all night, and eaten early in the morning with kulcha or sheermal rotis. In the kacchi-biriyani of Hyderabad the rice is firm and the chunks of meat cooked almost to disintegration, with an irregular saffron staining of the rice. Full-boiled eggs in a minced meat coating constitute nargisi-kofta; when cut in two, the golden yolk surrounded by egg white against an earth-brown meat edging recalls the narcissus flower (nargis) against bare earth. Chakna is a dish of offal, and dalcha is lamb stewed with beans and tamarind. Lukmi is like Italian ravioli, small squares of soft pastry filled with spiced meat, and deep-fried. Frequently, mutton and chicken, and almost always palao, will be baked in a seal of dough, a technique termed dumpukht (q.v.). Very rich meat dishes characterize Kashmiri cuisine. The Mughal lamb dish yakhni is cooked in curds, and aab-gosht in milk. Roghan-josh is flavoured with methi, ginger, saunf, and asafoetida, and coloured red (hence its name) with the dried flowers of the cockscomb. Minced lamb is marzwangan, and goli and rishta are balls of ground meat. Very finely ground minced mutton gives the silken meat loaf, goshtaba. At a special mishani dinner, prepared, say, for a wedding, exactly seven dishes, all of lamb, are made by specialist cooks. From rib chops is made the dish tabakmaaz, and shikar is duck cooked with vinegar, garlic, and chillies. The Dogras of Kashmir have a distinctive sri-palao (*see also* meat consumption, kabab, palao).

meen Tamil term for fish, which entered the Sanskrit language at an early date, to complement the earlier term matsya. Thus Meenakshi is the fish-eyed goddess of Madurai.

melogara A class of savoury preparations of various dhals with vegetables, which figures prominently in historical Kannada literature on food. According to Gurulinga Desika, in his *Lingapurana* (AD 1594), 'eating-pleasure comes from various kinds of melogara'. To make it, mung dhal, urad dhal, fresh chana, thuvar dhal, or avarai beans (*Lablab purpureus*) were first cooked with sesame seeds, then cooked again with greens, drumsticks, chakota (grapefruit), salt, and coconut gratings, and finally mixed with ghee and tempered with asafoetida and thick milk. Even thin strands of fried wheat dough could go into melogara. Each vegetable added to the melogara was treated differently. Certain leaves were washed in lime water before being cooked, other leaves in turmeric water, and yet others with common salt or saline ashes. The giant yam, surana, was first boiled with betel leaves, soaked in rice water, and then cooked with tamarind leaves. A melogara of this kind, with dhal and vegetables as basic ingredients, could be sweet, spicy, or sour in taste (*see* Karnataka, food of).

melons There are two main melons in India. The popular musk melon or kharbuza probably originated in Africa, but *Cucumis melo* exploded in terms of variety only after reaching India. The best melons in historic times seemed to have been grown from imported (Persian) seed, and were probably the ancestors of the two best-known types raised today, the Honey Dew of Lucknow and the Cuddapah melon of the south, both grown on the dry beds of rivers or lakes before the rains, with a lacy overlay on the creamy skin.

Seeds of some variety of melon

Melon bed

were found in a pot in Harappa. Xuan Zang mentions the fruit in India, and Patrick Copland while in Dhaka, received from the nawab a gift of 'Persian melons'. Linschoten remarked that the melons of India were less sweet than those of Spain, and needed to be eaten with sugar. Babar lamented the lack of good melons in India, and when one was brought to him, felt acutely homesick, and was 'close to tears'. Obviously the quality of melon improved over the years, probably through imports of quality seeds, because Jahangir mentions that in Kashmir they were 'very sweet and creased ... varieties of the best kind can be obtained', noting the same at Kistwar also.

The water-melon belongs to a different family, *Citrullus lunatus*, which again is of African-Indian origin. It must have come to India in prehistoric times, since even the Sanskrit name, kalinda, is thought to be of Munda origin. Early European visitors to India called it either by its Portuguese name pataca or its Arab name bathiec, which is probably of earlier origin, since it is also used in the *Ain-i-Akbari*. The origin of the Hindi name, tarbuza, is uncertain (*see also* gourds).

methi *See* fenugreek.

Mexico, food materials from For thousands of years Mexico was a cradle of plant development. Many of these plants then spread elsewhere in Central America, and onto the South American landmass as well. Once Columbus reached the New World, which almost coincided with the arrival of Vasco da Gama in India, many of these food plants (and at least one animal, the turkey, q.v.) were consciously carried on Spanish and Portuguese ships, with commercial intent, from the New World to the Old.

The Portuguese slave trade was between Brazil and Africa, and thence to Goa. The Spanish plied between Mexico, Brazil, and the home country, and from there to the orient. Once the Spanish had conquered the Philippines, the latter became an entrepot for merchandise from South America to areas being colonized, or to other eastern countries. Thus a commodity could enter India from a westerly or an easterly direction, and at different places and times: this certainly happened with the groundnut, papaya, and tobacco.

The food materials that entered India from the New World may now be noted; individual entries will furnish more details of: amaranths, cashewnuts, chilli, cocoa, some gourds, groundnuts, the haricot bean (*see* rajmah), maize, mat bean (?), papaya, sapota, sitaphal, sweet potato, tapioca, tomato, and turkey.

mice The *Manasollasa*, written in the twelfth century AD, mentions as an edible item 'peculiar mice that lived in fields near rivers'. In Kozhikode, Varthema (AD 1508) noted that as an item of food (besides venison, goat and fish) mice were permitted to the Nairs or landed gentry. In modern times, a sociologist has noted that mice are an off-season food of the villagers in the rural areas of Mandya district in Karnataka.

milk The Aryans have a strong association with cows and dairying. However, even before their arrival in India, there is indirect evidence of the prevalence of dairying in the magnificent bull and cattle seals of the Indus Valley civilization (2500–1500 BC). In particular, the famous seal of a hump-backed, heavily dewlapped bull, identical with the Kankrej breed of today, bears testimony to a well-developed animal husbandry, with almost certainly a knowledge of milk (and meat) as food. Thereafter, even the earliest Aryan Vedic literature is replete with references to dairying. Milk was an important food.

Milk was a food favoured even by breakaway sects like the Buddhists and Jains. As with all liquids, Jains were obliged to strain milk through a muslin cloth before drinking it. A novel procedure in use by Jains was to soak cloth in milk and then dry it, reconstituting this when needed to a product called kholas. Foods with which to break a fast have a special

place in the Muslim ethos, and milk is one of them.

Though the prime source of milk was of course the cow, termed vara or blessing, both the buffalo and goat are mentioned in Vedic literature. In addition to these, the *Sushrutha Samhita* refers to the milk of the sheep, camel, mare, elephant, and human being. Milk in medical terms was considered sweet, heavy, fat, and cooling, generally strengthening and tranquilizing. It contains the essence or rasa of many plants, and is a life-giver, particularly good for children and the elderly, the convalescent and the weak.

Milk has a very special conceptual niche in Indian cooking. Milk emerges hot from the udder, and is considered to be the sperm of Agni, the god of fire, and hence naturally cooked. Again, its further treatment by fire (heat) is believed not to alter its qualities, so culturally milk is neutral (this is also true of ghee). The use of milk as an ingredient in cooking results in food which has considerable restrictions on sharing. The two major divisions of Indian cooking are cooking without fire, and cooking with it (*see* cooking principles). Milk has a place in both. Thus the two great ambrosial beverages, madhuparka and panchagavya, use milk and both are uncooked. Yet another auspicious food, paramanna, is a cooked food of boiled rice, milk, ghee, and honey, which is given to a child at the weaning ceremony, annaprasanna. The capacity of milk to boil over gives it significance as an agent between man and god.

Historical literature contains a range of uses of milk. The ways in which it was used in Vedic times have already been mentioned. As an accompaniment to the main meal, vatakas (vadas) soaked in milk and curd were served at a feast described in the *Apabrahmsatrayi*. In south India, rice appams were served with sweetened milk, referred to in the *Perumpanuru*. In the Kannada work *Jaimini Bharata* by Lakshmeesha dated AD 1700, a milk–curd relish, kacchadi, is mentioned.

Milk could be used as a cooking ingredient. A sweet preparation of rice cooked in milk is termed payasa or kshirika even in Vedic literature. King Yudhisthira in the Mahabharata fed ten thousand brahmins with various choice dishes, which included cooked preparations of rice and milk mixed with ghee and honey. Kheer (q.v.) and payasam (q.v.) are even now exceedingly popular sweet confections in many homes all over India. In Rajasthan the item is termed bakir or rasiya, and in the Muslim ambience sheerbirinj. In the thirteenth century Ibn Battuta recorded that the grain shamak (shyamaka, *Echinochloa frumentacea*) was cooked in buffalo milk; 'it is pleasanter prepared this way than baked as bread: I used

often to eat it in India and enjoyed it'. A wandering minstrel in south India in ancient times was served by shepherds with millet cooked in milk, and elsewhere we read of 'vegetables cooked in milk', a practice hardly in use now.

For making various rotis from wheat flour, milk is sometimes used in the flour to yield distinctive products. The large, very thin and brittle khakras of Gujarat need milk in the dough to be rolled really fine. Milk is also added when kneading the flour to make sheermal, the sweetish and almost powdery flat bun of Hyderabad.

Derivatives of milk find mention throughout Sanskrit literature. Curds were dadhi, cream santanika, butter navaneetha, buttermilk udasvit, and ghee ghrta, and all were consumed daily. Classical Tamil literature of between the third and sixth centuries AD mentions most milk products: cream (edu or perugu), curds (thayiru), buttermilk (moru, and four other names), butter (vennai), and ghee (nai). The *Nachchinarkkiniyar* has a curious reference to the removal of all fat from milk using a 'medicine'; such milk was even sold, but pronounced 'worthless'.

Milk can be thickened to yield khoa or mava, a base for sweetmeats (*see* khoa). The boiling and cooling of milk causes a thick, creamy layer to form on the surface; this when skimmed off constitutes malai or cream, usually eaten as such. If the milk is not stirred when being boiled down, films of coagulated milk form on the surface, which are set aside using bamboo splints. This constitutes the delicacy rabbri (usually sweetened) which is described in Annaji's *Soundara Vilasa* (AD 1700) as 'milk thickened by boiling till it fell in flakes'. Elsewhere we read of kene-payasa, a sweet concoction of cream. A feast for King Shrenika described in the *Bhavissayatakaha* (*c.* AD 1000) has as the last item some 'half-boiled milk' containing sugar, honey and saffron, which could mean a thickened milk preparation. Khoa, the ultimate thickened milk product, was termed hal-unde (later pal-unde) in the work *Lokopakara* (AD 1025) written by Chavundaraya in Kannada. Early Bengali literature reveals the extensive use of khoa; the *Chandimangala* and *Chandidasa Padavali*, both written in the sixteenth century, mention numerous sweet items like manda, khanda, nadu, and sandesh, all probably made from khoa (q.v.). The precipitation of milk with slightly acid whey or other acidulants yields solids in the form of chhana; this is, especially in Bengal, the basis of innumerable sweetmeats (*see* Bengali sweets; chhana). Solids obtained either by dewatering curds, or by the acid precipitation of milk, pressed under a weight into a flat slab, and then cut into cubes, constitute

paneer (q.v.); this can be used as such, or fried to chewiness, or cooked in curries (say with peas).

Milk in course of time turns sour by fermentation and sets to a curd. Controlled fermentation yields a quality product, called dadhi in Sanskrit, dahi (q.v.) in Hindi and yoghurt in English. Dewatered curd, sweetened, spiced with cardamom, coloured with saffron and beaten smooth, gives the ancient confection shikharini; now called shrikhand, it is eaten as a sweet-sour dessert or as a dip for puris. It is first mentioned in about 400 BC in Sanskrit literature. In Kannada the word shikarini occurs even in AD 1025 in the *Lokopakara*, and shrikhand in AD 1594 in the *Lingapurana* written by Gurulinga Desika. When diluted and churned, curd yields buttermilk, now called chhas (*see* beverages) and butter (q.v.); the latter on boiling down yields ghee, the major milk product of India, which merits a separate entry.

millet Though originally used for the grain of *Panicum miliaceum* (the common or Proso millet, Sanskrit akusthaka, Hindi cheena, Tamil panivaragu) (*see* panicum grains), the term millet (often used in the plural) has acquired a general connotation of any small cereal grain, especially of the genus *Panicum* (gondli, samai), *Echinochloa* (shama, sanwa, sawank), *Setaria* (kangni, thennai, bandra), *Eleusine* (ragi), and *Paspalum* (kodra, varagu). Thus Ibn Battuta uses the Arab term meaning millet for *Echinochloa frumantacea*, shyamaka, which he terms shamak.

Millet has been grown in most parts of India. Strabo of Amnesia (*c.* AD 20) states that it grew in the fertile land between the rivers Jhelum and Chenab. A south Indian marketplace described in early Sangam literature vended sixteen kinds of grain, which included millet, and elsewhere in the Tamil country it is described as being eaten cooked in milk. Ma Huan, the Chinese admiral, remarked on the abundance of millet in Bengal in *c.* AD 1400, so did Fernao Nuniz in Vijayanagar a century and a half later. All millets are dwindling in importance at present as foodgrains.

milling A term applied to the grinding of cereal and pulse grains, oilseeds and sugarcane between hard, rough surfaces under pressure to effect either dehusking, or size reduction, or the expulsion of a liquid (oil or juice). The earliest crushing devices were stone saddle querns of various designs, flat, concave or convex, either shallow or deep. With these were paired separate stone grinders that were either round or cylindrical, and used either horizontally or upright. The early Indus Valley civilization (2500–500 BC) had two types. One was more or less flat and went with a cylindrical muller rolled with both hands, a common grinding device in an Indian kitchen even today. The other had a shallow circular depression, and was used for crushing grain, rather than grinding it, with a rounded stone held in one hand. A four-legged quern of the latter type is depicted in a sculpture at Sanchi dated around 250 BC. A later development consisted of a solid stone cylindrical base, on which revolved another heavy domed stone, which was operated by two women working a horizontal pole that passed through two holes opposite each other. Only as late as in the early Christian era was the upper domed stone replaced by the now-familiar heavy circular stone with a single wooden peg at its periphery called the chakki. This term clearly derives from the Sanskrit chakra for a turning device, by way of the Pali chakka.

Larger chakkis for commercial grinding consist of two heavy circular stones set slightly apart, one stationary and the other revolving. These could at one time only be worked either by hand for short periods or by using the power of running water, such as streams in the hills. From about AD 1880, chakkis that used oil engines at first, and later electric power, spread rapidly all over India for the commercial milling of both paddy and wheat. At Independence, there were some 10,000 powered chakkis for paddy processing, and 60 per cent of the wheat produced was processed in powered chakkis.

The second type of crushing device was the mortar and pestle pounder. Deep mortars firmly fixed in the ground and long poles for the pounding of grain were discovered even at Harappa and Mohenjodaro. A mortar in the shape of an hourglass, with a woman wielding a long pounder, is seen in a Sanchi sculpture (c. 250 BC) of a busy village scene. The *Dasakumaracharite* written by Dandin between the sixth and seventh centuries AD graphically describes the pounding of paddy in a mortar made of arjuna wood (*Terminalia arjuna*), using a heavy pestle of kadhira wood (*Acacia catechu*) tipped with an iron ring, while a Tamil work of the third century describes 'white rice, well-cleaned in pounders set in iron rings'.

Another grain-milling device, which uses the foot, is the dhenki (q.v.).

Literary records also reflect the antiquity of grinding devices. Sanskrit terms for the flat grinding stone (drshad), its partner (drshad-putra), the mortar (ulukhala), and pestle (musala) are all perhaps borrowings into Sanskrit from even earlier Munda usage.

In south India also, several neolithic sites of the second millennium BC have yielded grain crushers, milling stones, mortars and pestles.

Devices for milling sugarcane and oilseeds seem to have evolved out of the crushing devices just described. Current terms for these devices for milling both sugarcane and oilseeds are ghani, kolhu, and chekku, all of which stem from Vedic Sanskrit words like gravan, ulukhala, and chakra (*see* ghani). The other device for crushing sugarcane is a roller mill with revolving corrugated cylinders; this appears to have originated abroad around AD 1500, based on a similar mangle device for removing seeds from cotton. Modern oilseed crushers with a screw-worm working at high pressure in a barrel were developed about a century ago in America, and were first used in India in about AD 1914 in Navsari in Gujarat. At Independence over 600 factories using powered oilmills were in operation, which produced some 9 lakh tonnes of oil.

mint Indian mint, pudina, called field mint in English, is *Mentha arvensis*, a perennial herb native to hilly northwest India. European mint, now also grown in many parts of India, is *Mentha longifolia*. Mint goes into Indian chutneys and western-style mint sauces. Other *Mentha* species are the peppermint and spearmint, with mostly industrial outlets.

mirchi *See* chilli; pepper.

mishti-doi The sweet curd of Bengal. Milk is boiled down slightly,

Mirch

and caramelized sugar or palm jaggery is mixed in before setting the curd with a starter. This is often done in earthen vessels, which contribute a slightly earthy flavour and some degree of dewatering.

modak In earlier Sanskrit literature, modaka appeared to have the same connotation as ladduka, a sweetened ball of some sort (*see* laddu). It now signifies an envelope of rice or wheat, filled with a sweet stuffing, and fried or steamed. The term first occurs only as late as in the Mahabharata and *Sushrutha Samhita,* then around AD 1000 in the *Bhavissayatahaka* and again in the twelfth century in the *Manasollasa* by Someshwara. In Tamil, the early *Mathuraikkanchi* written in *c.* AD 450 terms it moodagam, and in sixteenth-century Bengali works it is modak. The modak is considered a favourite food of Lord Ganesha; it is specially prepared on his feast day, Ganesh Chathurthi, and representations of the god frequently show him with modakas or laddus held in one hand.

Mughal period, food of One may start with the emperors and the imperial cuisine of the palace. Arriving in India in the summer of AD 1526, Babar lamented that his new country had 'no grapes, musk-melons or first-rate fruits, no ice or cold water, no bread or cooked food in the bazaars'. 'The flesh of Hindustan fishes is very savoury,' he wrote, 'they have no odour or tiresomeness' (probably meaning a lack of bones). He commented most judiciously on the various food items that he encountered. The chironji (*Buchanania lanzan*), a small oily nut, 'is a thing between the almond and the walnut, not bad', he noted. He carefully listed eight citrus fruits in India, the orange, lime, citron, santhra, galgal, jambiri lime, amritphal (perhaps the mandarin orange), and the amal-bid. Babar lived for only four and a half years after coming to India, and remained an alien to its cuisine. His son Humayun was more acclimatized, to the extent of even giving up animal flesh for some months when he started campaigning to recover his throne, and deciding, after much reflection, that beef was not a food fit for the devout.

Akbar did not care for meat and took it only seasonally, 'to conform to the spirit of the age', according to Abul Fazl, 'and because he had the burden of the world on his shoulders'. He abstained from meat at first on all Fridays, subsequently also on Sundays, then on the first day of every solar month, then during the whole month of Fawardin (March), and finally during his birth month of Aban (November). He started his meal in true Indian fashion with curds and rice, and preferred simple food, though a variety of rich foods were prepared in the royal kitchen.

Three classes of cooked dishes are described in the *Ain-i-Akbari*. The first was called safiyana, meant for the emperor's days of abstinence from meat. The dishes were made from rice (zard-birinj, khuskka, khichri, and sheer-birinj), wheat (chikhi, essentially the strainings of wheat isolated by washing, and then seasoned), dhals, palak-sag (spinach), halwa, sherbets, and the like. The second class comprised those in which meat and rice were cooked together, like palao, biriyani (also a palao), shulla (rice, dhal, and meat) and shorba (thick soup), or meat and wheat together (harlsa, haleem, kaskh, and qutab, 'which the people of Hind call sanbusa'). The third class consisted of dishes in which meat was cooked with ghee, spices, curd, eggs, etc. to obtain such dishes as yakhni, kabab, dopiyaza, musamman, dumpukht, qaliya, and malghuba (*see* meat dishes). Bread was of two kinds: a thick variety made from wheat flour and baked in an oven (naan or tandoori), and a thin kind made from either wheat or khushka by baking on an iron plate (chapathi or phulka, 'tasting very well when served hot'). Rice for the royal kitchen came from Bharaij, Gwalior, Rajori, and Nimlah; ghee from Hissar; ducks, waterfowl, and certain vegetables from Kashmir; and fruits from all over the country and even from across the north-western borders. The delicious cold kulfi (q.v.) was made at court by freezing a mixture of khoa, pistachio nuts, and kesar (zaffran) essence in a metal cone after sealing the open top with dough.

Jahangir, unlike his father, enjoyed meat, especially that of the chase. He was willing to experiment; 'I found the flesh of the mountain goat more delicious than that of all wild animals, though its skin is exceedingly ill-odoured, so much so that even when tanned the scent is not destroyed.' 'Though the flesh of the wild ass is lawful food and most men like it, it was in no way suited to my taste.' He found the milk of the antelope 'palatable ... they say it is of great use in asthma'. On two occasions, Sir Thomas Roe, ambassador to his court from England, received gifts of game from the emperor: on one occasion this was 'a mighty elk' whose meat was 'reasonably rank', and on another a wild boar, with the polite request that the tusks be returned. Despite his love of meat, Jahangir kept to his father's schedule of abstentions, adding to them all Thursdays (the day of his father's birth), and banning the slaughter of animals on Thursdays and Sundays. He seems to have given up fish altogether. A rich khichdi from Gujarat called lazizan, made of rice cooked with pulses, ghee, spices, and nuts, was one of his favourite foods on days of abstinence from flesh. Another was falooda (q.v.), a jelly made from the strainings of boiled wheat mixed with fruit juices and cream.

Aurangzeb was of spartan habits. Jean-Baptiste Tavernier, who attended on him as a doctor, wrote that no animal food passed his lips; he became 'thin and lean, to which the great fasts that he keeps have contributed ... he only drank a little water, and ate a small quantity of millet bread ... besides this, he slept on the ground, with only a tiger's skin over him'. Nor did he ever use vessels of silver or gold, as was customary with nobility.

Wine had a strong attraction for Mughal royalty. Babar enjoyed liquor, but had periodic bouts of abstinence, when he would break up his flagons of gold and silver and give away the pieces, only to resume drinking and the use of bhang. Akbar rarely drank wine, according to the Jesuit visitor Father Monserrate, and preferred post (bhang). He enforced prohibition in his court, but relaxed rules for European visitors because 'they are born in the element of wine, as fish are produced in that of water ... and to prohibit them the use of it is to deprive them of life'. Of his sons, both Daniyal and Murad died young from excessive drinking. His other son, the, emperor Jahangir, was addicted to wine, but did not drink on Thursdays and Fridays. However, by the end of his reign, he consumed fourteen cups of double-distilled liquor by day and a further six at night. One kind of wine was made by steeping raisins in rice spirit for three or four days, straining it, and then keeping the liquid in an empty barrel for six to eight-months, adding an extract of dates for flavour and sweetness. In his *Memoirs*, Jahangir describes a strong wine called sir or achhi, ten years old, made at Pigli near Atruck, by fermenting together rice and bread.

Shahjahan drank, but never to excess. Aurangzeb was of course, a strict teetotaller, and in AD 1668 issued severe prohibition orders on all his subjects, Hindu and Muslim alike. On the other hand, his unmarried sister Jahanara Begum was extremely fond of wine; these were either imported from Persia, Kabul, and Kashmir, according to Manucci, or distilled in her own home, 'a most delicious spirit, made from wine and rosewater, flavoured with many costly spices and aromatic drugs', of which he was sometimes a recipient.

The Mughal emperors soon came under the mystique of Ganges water (q.v.). Akbar termed it 'the water of immortality', and 'both at home and on his travels he drinks Ganges water', according to the *Ain-i-Akbari*.

Jahangir was very particular about drinking only the water of the Ganges. The French visitor Tavernier muses that 'considerable sums of money are expended to procure Ganges water' and that 'by many it is constantly drunk on account of its reputed medical properties'. This was in the time of Aurangzeb. Francois Bernier spoke with revulsion of the water of Delhi: 'it exceeded my powers of description (being) accessible to all persons and animals, and the receptacle of every kind of filth.'

Babar, as we have noted, lamented the lack of first-.rate fruits in India, and took steps to grow melons and grapes which, when they bore fruit, 'filled me with content'. By the time of Akbar, about fifty years later, the *Ain-i-Akbari* notes: 'Melons and grapes have become very plentiful and excellent; and water-melons, peaches, almonds, pistachios, pomegranates, etc. are to be found everywhere.' Prices in the Delhi market of a remarkable number of fruits are quoted, including some like the pineapple (ananas) that must have come only recently to India from the New World. Fruits in Delhi came largely from Kashmir, with some from Kabul, Kandahar, and Samarkand, all of which had been at one time ruled by Babar. Jahangir noted that the 'sweet cherry, pear and apricot, so far imported, are now being grown in Kashmir through the efforts of my nobleman, Muhammad Quli Afshar', and that the oranges, citrons and water-melons raised at Kistwar were all of superior quality. Grafting was applied to numerous fruits to improve their quality (*see* grafting; mangoes).

Even the nobility in Mughal times lived in great splendour, as remarked upon by visitors. Sir Thomas Roe noted that they kept luxurious tables, with twenty dishes, and even up to fifty, being served at a time.

However the visitors also commented on the lot of the poor peasantry. Thomas Roe remarked: The people of India live like fishes do in the sea—the great ones eat up the little. For first the farmer robs the peasant, the gentleman robs the farmer, the greater robs the lesser, and the king robs them all.' His chaplain Terry noted that the poor ate rice boiled with green ginger to which they added a little pepper and butter; it was their principal dish, but even so was seldom eaten. Their ordinary food was not made of wheat flour but of a coarser grain (possibly jowar) baked on small, round iron hearths (the sigris of the present) to give round, broad and thick cakes (rotis) that were 'both wholesome and hearty'.

Water was the common drink, but sometimes it was converted into sherbet with lemon juice and sugar. Humbler Muslims had naan for breakfast, frequently with kheema or kabab as an accompaniment, with plenty of onions, desserts of phirni, and sheer-birinj (kheer of rice and milk), halwas, and dried fruits. The practice of chewing the betel quid was widely prevalent. Ordinary Hindus had fried buns and bhathuras for breakfast, along with various vegetables and green leafy preparations (saag). The common Indian dish noted by most visitors was rice cooked along with pulses (khichdi, q.v.), eaten as an evening meal.

moley, moile A liquid curry of, say, fish with plenty of fresh coconut, called by this name in the Tamil country, in Sri Lanka, among the east Indians of Maharashtra, and by the British colonial. The word is thought to be a corruption of the term Malay, from where perhaps the dish originated.

morabba, murabba A preserve of boiled fruit (mango, amla, citron) held in a spiced thick sugar syrup. The preparation is linked with the Unani system of medicine, the word itself being Arabic for preserved and domesticated. By Independence, a sizeable morabba production industry had developed in Delhi, Amritsar, and elsewhere to cater to domestic and export demand.

mosambi *See* citrus fruits.

moth bean *See* mat.

motichur A sphere of fine globules (moti = pearls) of fried besan (q.v.) held together with thickened sugar syrup. A laddu would have coarser granules. It is mentioned in the Kannada literature of a few centuries ago, and as a food item of Bihar about a century ago. The sculpted or painted figure of Ganesha frequently holds in one hand what appear to be balls of motichur, as in the great Lingaraja temple at Bhubaneshwar.

mulberry The black mulberry, *Moms nigra*, is a native of Iran and the white mulberry, *M. alba*, of China. Both have long been grown in India for their fruit and leaves, which find use as a food for silkworms. Charaka refers to the mulberry as tuda. In Mughal times, figs were grafted on mulberry trees. During his travels in India around AD 1610, William Finch observed that 'from Agra to Lahore the way is set on both sides with mulberry trees', and not long after this Bernier noticed in Bengal 'small mulberry trees, two or three feet in height, for the food of silkworms'.

mulligatawny Literally, pepper-water (milagu-thannir) in Tamil; this was the rasam (q.v) of south India, which was adopted with such modifications as the addition of meat stock as a soup by the colonial.

A British prisoner of Hyder Ali in
AD 1784 sang mournfully:

In vain our hard fate we repine.
In vain our fortunes we rail;
On Mullighu-tawny we dine,|
Or Congee, in Bangalore jail.

In fact the colonials who lived in
Madras were derisively referred to as
Mulls, and those in Bombay as Ducks
(from the fish).

Munda A loose term used (along
with Austrics) for the very early
inhabitants of India. Once widely
spread all over the country, the
Mundas now comprise tribals who live
mostly in Bihar, Orissa, West Bengal,
Madhya Pradesh, and Tripura, with
a particularly high concentration in
the Ranchi district of Bihar. Vedic
literature terms them nishadas (nisha =
turmeric, ad = to eat); in the *Yajurveda*
this term included such groups as
the svanin (dog-keepers), chandala
(dog-eaters), and punjistha (fowlers),
who had domesticated the dog, fowl,
and elephant. Numerous food words
believed to be of Munda origin were
absorbed into the Sanskrit language.
These may be listed in groups. Fruits
included the kadali (banana), panasa
(jackfruit), dalimba (pomegranate),
narikela (coconut), nimbuka and
numbaka (lime), and nagaranga
(the Seville orange). Pulses with
names of Munda origin include the
masha (urad), mudga (mung), and
masura (masoor); and the vegetables
are vartaka and vrntaka (brinjal),
alabu (pumpkin), tundli (tinda),
patola (parwal), aluka (tubers), and
pundarika (lotus, with edible parts).
Oilseeds like lila (sesame), sarshapa
(sarson), and perhaps atashi (linseed)
also sound non-Sanskritic, while
several spices are distinctly of Munda
provenance, like srngavera (ginger, in
Tamil injivera), haridra (turmeric), and
chincha (tamarind). So is the betel leaf
(thambula) and the areca nut (guvaka).
Words for utensils like drshad
(grinding stone), ulukhala (mortar),
and musala (pestle) probably have a
Munda origin, as has the term kukkuta
for a chicken. Though ragi for the
cereal *Eleusine coracana* derives from
the term riga (red in Sanskrit), the
grain itself has numerous tribal names.
Of course a Munda-derived Sanskrit
name would imply the presence of the
item in India from ancient times.

mung The Sanskrit mudga,
botanically *Vigna radiata* and mung
in Hindi, is certainly of Indian
origin. An old, lost plant form first
gave rise to two forms of *Vigna
sublobata*; one of these then evolved
to the urad (black gram) and the
other to mung (green gram). It is
mentioned in Sanskrit literature
from the *Yajurveda* (c. 1000 BC)
onwards, and is one of the 3-M
trio, mudga, masha, and masura.
Early archaeological finds date from
c. 1800 BC–500 BC, in Navdatoli-
Maheshwar (Maharashtra) and
Paiyampalli (the Dekhan plateau).

Mung is used in numerous ways. Buddha recommends it in a group of foods 'full of soul qualities' and 'devoid of faults'. However, in Kashmir in the *Rajatarangini* of Kalhana (*c.* AD 1200) it is rated as an inferior food. In ayurvedic terms all pulses increase vata (wind), but mung is now recognized as the least flatulent of the common pulses, which can even be given to children, and is recommended by Sushrutha for eating daily. A soup of mung, generically termed yusa, features in medical literature. Pulses cooked with greens, called melogara (q.v.) in old Kannada literature, feature the mung. Mung can be puffed to a crisp bhrstadhanya; this product is ground to a flour which in Rajasthan is the batter of choice for a whole range of deep-fried snacks. A laddu made of puffed mung is referred to in the Gujarati work *Varanaka Samuchaya* (AD 1520). Perhaps the widest use of mung dhal, apart from direct consumption, is in a khichdi (q.v.) with rice. This is frequently mentioned by visitors to India, like Ibn Battuta, Abdur Razzak, and Tavernier, as the common evening meal of peasants in India.

murmura, muri Puffed rice, pori in Tamil, is a plump, shining, white, crisp product obtained by tossing soaked or parboiled rice on very hot sand, when the grains expand and burst. Puffed rice can be munched as such, or dressed with a little salt, and in Bengal with pungent mustard oil. Other additions are chopped onions, chiplets of fresh coconut or copra, roasted groundnuts, and even sugar crystals.

murukku Tamil term for a crisp snack, made by extruding a thick batter of rice and urad dhal through star-shaped dies into very hot fat in the form of a flat whorl. It is termed chakkali (perhaps from its coiled form) in Kannada, and is mentioned in a work of AD 1560.

Muslims, food of *See* Islam and food; Mughal period, food of.

mustard leaves *See* sarson.

mustard oil While mustard seeds find early mention in Sanskrit literature, only in later Vedic literature is there a contemptuous reference to the extraction of oil from these seeds by the aboriginal inhabitants, termed nishadas (*see* Munda). The Buddhist canonical literature mentions the oil, while the *Arthashastra* of *c.* 300 BC lists mustard among the major oilseeds crushed. The *Charaka Samhita* describes the class of food preparations with mustard oil as a hot commodity. Both Xuan Zang and I Ching in the seventh century AD make many references to the use of mustard oil in cooking; perhaps this was common around the Nalanda monastery in Bihar, where they resided. The use of mustard oil to dress puffed rice in Bengal is also mentioned by Xuan Zang. In a commentary on the *Charaka Samhita* written in AD 1060 by Chakrapani Datta, the many virtues of mustard oil are expounded; appropriately, this work emanates from Bengal, where mustard oil has always had pride of place in cooking and pickling. In the *Chandimangala*, written in the sixteenth century by Mukundram Chakravarti, the tamasic nature of Lord Shiva is reflected in the fact that his food is cooked not in ghee, which is a luminous sattvika product, but in pungent mustard oil. The *Khanar Vachana*, a very early Bengali work of the eleventh century, recommends foods appropriate to various seasons, and includes free use of mustard oil in Magh, a cold month.

Another outlet for the oil is as a body massage prior to taking a bath, the so-called oil bath, which the *Sushrutha Samhita* recommends for both adults and infants. The oil is absorbed and reaches every organ of the body, particularly benefiting the skin, hair, and eyes, and the muscles and joints.

mustard seeds Carbonized seeds of rai, *Brassica juncea* subsp. *juncea*, have been discovered at the Indus Valley site of Chanhudaro dated about 1500 BC. Even today this seed, called mustard in India, is the major Indian brassica species. Next in terms of output is brown sarson, which is *B. napus* var. glauca, followed by reddish-brown toria, *B. napus* var. napus. There is also a minor crop of yellow sarson. All these are oil-bearing seeds; however, they are never

Mustard field

crushed singly for oil, but always in a judicious admixture so as to yield a 'mustard' oil of distinctive taste and flavour in high yield, to which each seed type contributes something distinctive. In countries abroad it is sarson and toria types, there called rapeseed, which is processed for oil, yielding in turn rapeseed oil.

Sanskrit literature used in this context the term sarshapa, believed to be of even earlier aboriginal origin (*see* Munda). Two kinds of seeds are mentioned. Rajika is certainly the rai of today, a reddish seed, and siddhartha (also called sveta-sarshapa and gaura-sarshapa) is probably yellow sarson. In Indian rituals, mustard seeds have a connotation of disinfection. In the *Apasthamba Dharmasutra* it is enjoined that at ancestral ceremonies the practitioner rub the powder of white mustard seed on his hands, feet, ears, and mouth. Red mustard seed is sprinkled on a fire to subdue evil spirits, and in the *Matsya Purana* it is stated that before undertaking certain vows, a man should have a bath with panchagavya (q.v.) and mustard paste. A paste from white mustard seeds was used to wash linen garments; the seeds were also scattered in a birth-chamber, and put into the mother's bathwater during the tenth-day ablution. In the *Atharvaveda*, the word abhaya, meaning fear-inspiring, is used for mustard seeds.

Rai itself is of two kinds. In India the oilseed-spice form is important, whereas in China it is the vegetable leafy form. The leaves eaten in India as a spicy relish are the sarson variety. All these brassicas are the result of accidental crossings in the remote past of two simpler species. One of them still exists; this is *Brassica nigra*, the black mustard, Banarsi rai, or kadugu, which finds use only as a condiment. It may be used in one of two ways. Commonly, all over India, the initial baghar operation begins with the frying of mustard seeds in hot oil till they cease to splutter, followed by the frying in the same oil of chopped onions and perhaps other spices; after this comes the frying of meat, fish, or vegetables; the mustard pungency is here mostly lost. The baghar can also be used to top a finished dish, of say, cooked dhal or even curds. The second way of using mustard seeds is to crush them into a paste in which meat, fish, or vegetables are marinated before being cooked into distinctly spicy dishes. The *Naishada Charita* (*c.* AD 1000) describes a bowl of curd spiced so pungently with mustard that the diners were obliged to scratch their heads!

In ayurvedic terms mustard seeds have a decidedly 'hot' connotation. External poultices are used for abscesses, itch, and rheumatism. Taken internally, mustard seeds aggravate pitta conditions, but are helpful in vata and kapha disorders (*see* ayurveda, doshas).

mutton Mutton in India connotes both goat and sheep meat, which in about equal amounts is the commonest form of meat eaten in the country. Stray references to mutton occur throughout literature, though not with the frequency expected from its present widespread use. Mutton was served at a sacrificial feast of King Dasharatha described in the Ramayana. The *Manasollasa* of King Someshwara in the twelfth century mentions kavachandi, a spicy dish of fried pieces of mutton in the shape of plums, cooked with pulses, garlic, and onion, with vegetables like the brinjal and radish also included sometimes. Xuan Zang notes that mutton in India was mostly eaten fresh, and sometimes salted. When he visited the Khan of the Turks in Su-Yeh, the monarch consumed wine, mutton, and veal (young beef), but ensured that his distinguished guest was given 'pure articles of food such as rice cakes, cream, sugarcandy, honeysticks (?), raisins, etc.' Amir Khusrau in the thirteenth century notes mutton among the food of the Muslim

aristocracy, and in Mughal India, Edward Terry remarks that the flesh of the 'sheep with great bob-tails', as he puts it, was 'altogether as good as ours'. A mutton-pie was one of the numerous items served at a colonial lunch in Calcutta by Mrs Elizabeth Fay in AD 1780.

Current Kashmiri cuisine boasts of a whole array of mutton dishes, especially lamb. Yakhni is mutton cooked in curds (*see* Mughal food), and aab-gosht in milk. Roghan-josh, literally red meat, is coloured with dried cockscomb, marzwangan is a mince, and goli and rishia are meat balls. A meat loaf, ground fine and silky in texture, constitutes gosh-taba. Exactly seven dishes, all of lamb, are prepared by specialist cooks for a mishani dinner. There are references to eracchi in old south Indian literature in Tamil which most often means mutton (*see* meat dishes).

Mysore pak A sweet crumbly confection of roasted besan (q.v.) cooked in a moderately thick sugar syrup, and finished with ghee. It is popular in the former state of Mysore, from which the name may derive. It does not seem to figure in the historic literature of Karnataka.

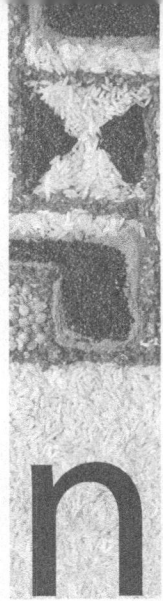

n

naan A roti of fine white maida (q.v.), leavened, rolled out oval in shape, sprinkled with nigella (kalonji) (q.v.) seeds, and baked in a tandoor (q.v.) or ordinary oven. Small, mud-plastered ovens 'closely resembling present-day tandoors' have been excavated at Kalibangan, an Indus Valley site. In about AD 1300, Amir Khusrau notes naan-e-tanuk (light bread) and naan-e-tanuri (cooked in a tandoor oven) at the imperial court in Delhi. Naan was in Mughal times a popular breakfast food, accompanied by kheema or kabab, of the humbler Muslims. It is today associated with Punjabis, and is a common restaurant item, rather than a home-made one all over India.

Nalapaka *See* maharaja.

navy bean *See* rajmah.

neem Every part of the neem tree has a utility value, but in medicine

Neem

and for health rather than in food. The bitter leaves arc edible, and on Ugadhi or New Year's Day in Karnataka and Andhra Pradesh, a few neem leaves are chewed with jaggery, as a symbol of acceptance of the bad with the good during the year. In Bengal, the leaves could be a component of the bitter shukto dish. In fact in a sixteenth-century Bengali work, the *Chandimangala*, a dish of brinjals cooked in neem leaves is offered to Lord Shiva, who is of a tamasic (q.v.) temperament. The ends of neem twigs are chewed to create a toothbrush, with which the teeth and gums are cleaned.

neera Incisions made on the spathes of the palmyra palm, date palm, coconut palm, and sago palm all yield an intensely sweet juice called neera, collected (usually early in the morning) in earthen pots tied in a place below the cut. If the pots are coated with slaked lime, fermentation is delayed, and the neera is then boiled down to palm jaggery (q.v.), or is drunk as a beverage; if not used in these ways, the juice rapidly ferments to toddy (q.v.). The *Purananuru* written in the sixth century AD in Tamil mentions munnir, a favourite drink with women, which was made of equal parts of neera, coconut water, and sugarcane juice.

nigella seeds In Hindi these tiny black seeds are called kalonji or kala-jeera, and in English black cumin or small fennel; botanically they are termed *Nigella sativa*. Nigella seeds are used as a condiment in cooking, and are sprinkled on naan before it is baked.

niger Botanically *Guizotia abyssinica*, niger seeds resemble those of sesame (tila in Sanskrit); indeed in many Indian languages the names for niger seeds are akin to names for the sesame: in Sanskrit ramtila and kalatila; in Telugu (in which sesame is ellu) garellu; and in Kannada hucchellu. The seeds are usually crushed to obtain an edible oil.

nigger fowl *See* chicken.

nutcrackers *See* arecanut.

nutmeg *See* mace.

nutrition The act or process of nourishing, as nutrition is defined, is well recognized in such historic Sanskrit terms as aharatattva, poshana, purshi, and palan. In fact a major part of ayurvedic medicine is based on setting right an imbalance of body doshas (q.v.) through corrective foods (*see* ayurveda). Variety in food, a cardinal concept of nutrition, was ensured by an insistence that every meal contain all the six tastes or rasas. The foods named for everyday eating by Sushrutha, and the quantities of major ingredients noted in the *Arthashastra* (*see* balanced diets), reflect sound nutritional principles. Ayurveda went even further in

Walnut

Badam

insisting that such diets should take into account the temperament (prakruthi) and digestive power (agni) of each individual.

nuts Among the older nuts of India are the almond (Sanskrit vatama), pistachio (pishtha), and walnut (akshota). Much later arrivals from South America are the groundnut and cashewnut (*see* individual entries for details).

Two other nuts of antiquity are the chironji (*Buchanania lanzan*) and chilgoza (*Pinus gerardiana*). Chironji kernels were noted by Babar as 'a thing between the walnut and the almond, not bad! (They are) rather smaller than the pistachio and round ... people put (them) in custards and sweetmeats'. The chilgoza (abhisuka in Sanskrit) is the nut of the neosia pine, an evergreen tree of the dry interior and arid north-eastern Himalayas that grows at heights of 2000–3000 metres. The ripe cones are picked in October before they open; when heated the scales expand, and the nuts can be removed.

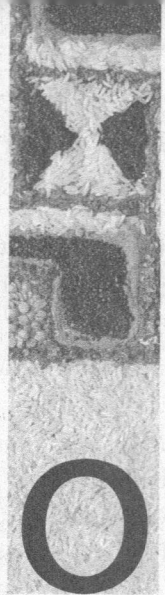

O

oats Originally native to the Mediterranean countries, oats, have been found in layers dated in the millennium after 4000 BC in Mehrgarh, beyond the north-west frontiers of India, but never within its boundaries. Oats, jai in Sanskrit, are now grown mainly as food for horses in the western Himalayas.

oils, oilseeds Oilseeds like the sesame, mustard, and linseed were known in the Indus Valley, and the Sanskrit names are believed to be of Munda origin (*see* Munda). The coconut has always been familiar to south Indians. Knowledge of these oilseeds almost certainly implies a knowledge of their oil, which is released merely by boiling the mashed seed. By about 500 BC crushing devices had developed (*see* ghani; milling) for commercial, as opposed to domestic, operations. The following individual entries may be consulted for details of both oilseeds and oils: coconut, linseed, mahua, mustard, neem, niger, safflower, and sesame.

Reference may be made to the entry, fats in cooking, for various facets of the edible uses of oils; the term fat is a generic one used in nutrition to denote both solid and liquid products, though in common speech it connotes a solid material.

oil pressing *See* ghani.

olive *Olea europacea* is essentially a Mediterranean tree. The fruit has worldwide, usage, and is also the source of an edible oil of distinctive flavour, particularly employed as a salad oil. The Indian olive is *O. ferruginea*, with an edible fruit, kau, found in the Himalayas. It is grown in India to a very limited extent for use as a vegetable, especially in

Bengal. Neither species is particularly important in India.

onion *Allium cepa*, the onion, belongs to the same family as the garlic (*A. sativum*), and both are believed to be native to the Afghanistan region. It is a very ancient plant, being described in the funerary offerings of Egypt dated 2800 BC, and actually found in mummy stuffings. Even by the fifth century BC, many forms of the onion, long, round, white, yellow, and red, had been described by Greek writers. Neither the four Vedas nor the sixteen Upanishads mention the onion, and when the palandu does appear in Aryan writings, it is as a food of the despised native population, the mlecchas, and of foreigners (yavanas), to be shunned by those seeking an austere life, as well as on ceremonial occasions. Both the onion and garlic were believed to stimulate the baser instincts, and always headed the

Onion

lists of foods forbidden to students, widows, those under a vow, followers of Vishnu, and the like. The Buddhist travellers in India, Fa Xian and Xuan Zang, note these views. Fa Xian wrote (*c.* AD 400): 'Throughout the country no one kills any living thing, nor drinks wine, nor eats onion or garlic.' And Xuan Zang, two and a half centuries later, noted: 'Onions and garlic are little known, and few people eat them; if anyone uses them for food, they are expelled beyond the walls of the town.' These statements reflect the Buddhist and brahmin viewpoint.

Among other sections of society the onion was in general use. Charaka classes it among the harid or underground materials, and its physiological effect was that of a pungent but noticeably 'sweet' material, which was stimulating, diuretic, and expectorant. Both Hindu and Muslim royalty consumed onions extensively. The *Manasollasa* (twelfth century AD) written by King Someshwara describes numerous meat dishes in which onions were fried in the initial baghar (q.v.). Ibn Battuta describes samosas stuffed with (fried) onions served in the Sultanate court in the thirteenth century AD. Almost all the numerous recipes used in Akbar's kitchen, described in the *Ain-i-Akbari*, employ onions; thus yakhni has, for 10 seers of meat, one seer of onions and half a seer of salt, and dupiyaza has 10 seers of meat and 2 seers of onions, besides ghee, and spices (*see* meat dishes; Mughals, food of). This latter dish, served at the court of Jahangir, and replete with onions (piyaz), was extolled by Edward Terry as 'the most savoury meat I ever tasted'. In Kashmir today, Muslims and Hindus use distinctive spices in cooking, and a special kind of onion called praan is used only by the former. Even in Mughal times, visitors noted that while humbler Hindu peasants ate a khichdi of rice and pulses, humbler Muslims would do with rice and raw onions. The missi-roti has finely chopped spinach, fenugreek, and onions mixed into the wheat dough. The initial frying of mustard seeds followed by chopped onions is an extremely common practice all over India (*see* baghar) in the preparation of both meat and vegetable dishes.

opium *See* poppy.

Orange

orange The origin of various orange varieties is noted under citrus fruits. Two types of the orange group are common in India. One is the narangi (first mentioned as naga-ranga by Charaka, and also called airavata in Sanskrit) which is *Citrus aurantium*, and the other is the mosambi or sweet orange, which is *C. sinensis*. A third common citrus, which belongs to the mandarin/tangerine group, is the loose-jacketed santhra, *C. reticulata*, which is of Chinese origin. Babar carefully describes these common types and several lesser kinds, but most visitors either use the loose term orange, or describe them as sweet or sour oranges; these include Xuan Zang, Varthema, Domingo Paes, and Pelsaert. In about AD 1680 Tavernier records that he received from the Nawab at Dhaka a gift of 'Chinese oranges', perhaps the loose-jacketed santhra variety.

oregano Brought to India from Mexico, and called sathra and miranjosh in Hindi, the dried green leaves of this herb are used to flavour Mexican foods like chilli con carne, taco, and tamale. Its flavour resembles that of marjoram, sage and thyme, all of which again are exotic to India.

ovens *See* cooking utensils.

oxen *See* cattle.

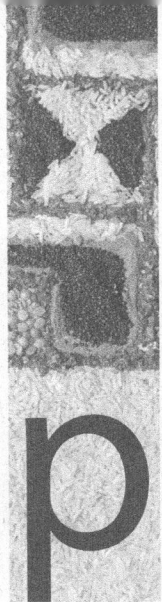

p

paan Hindi term for the betel quid (*see* areca nut).

pak From the Sanskrit term pak, meaning cooked, come the names of several sweet cooked confections, like shakarapaka (made by boiling down milk), Mysore pak (q.v.), and methipak, and gunderpak (medicated Gujarathi confections).

pak, pakku Term used for the betel quid in the Tamil/Kerala area, as noted even in AD 1560 by Garcia da Orta (*see* areca nut).

pakoda, pakauri Irregular lumps of besan batter (with, say, cashewnuts), or slices of brinjal, potato, tomato, onions and the like dipped in a besan batter and deep-fried to semi-crispness. A methi-spiced product in Bihar is termed methauri.

palak Hindi term for the spinach. *Spinacia oleracea*, from the Sanskrit palankya, first mentioned in the *Sutra* literature (800–300 BC). It is native to south-west Asia, and had a long history of edible use in India before it was known in the West. It is cooked with dhals to a liquid curry, or to a pasty mash with paneer or potatoes. The Parsi akuri is a baked dish of greens, frequently spinach, topped with fried or full-boiled eggs.

palao A dish of rice cooked with spiced meat and ghee. The word is ascribed to the Persian and Arabic pilav, pulao and pallao, yet it would appear to have found its way long ago into both Sanskrit (in the *Yagnavalkya Smriti*, as pallao-mevach) and early Tamil literature of the third to the sixth centuries AD. Biriyani (q.v.) is quite similar to palao, the word being derived from the Persian term birinj for rice.

The *Ain-i-Akbari* specifies, for a palao of minced meat (kheema), 10 seers (each about a kg) each of rice and meat, 4 seers of ghee, 1 seer of dehusked gram, and 2 seers of onions, besides fresh ginger, pepper, cumin seed, cardamom, and cloves. More commonly pieces of goat, sheep, and chicken would be used. A chicken palao was noted at the Sultanate court in Delhi in the thirteenth century. The multicoloured navratan palao with saffron, sultanas, paneer, and nuts, was designed to honour the nine intellectual gems of Akbar's court. Bohri Muslims use split peas with meat, and Kashmiris and Parsis eat a sweet, zarda (saffron)-flavoured palao with raisins and nuts. Tejpat leaves are frequently added for flavouring, besides raisins and almonds for taste. While the biriyani of Hyderabad is irregularly stained, and the meat is cooked extremely soft, in the palao of Kodagu the meat is firm and springy, and every grain of rice is fully coated with ghee and brown masala. The Dogras of Kashmir have a distinctive sri-palao, besides a mutton palao. There are innumerable other local variations in the preparation of palao. Even a dish of rice cooked with vegetables and spices is loosely called a vegetable palao.

palms A large genus of tropical plants, the Palmae, have three species of importance in India: the coconut, the palmyra, and the date, which are

Coconut palm tree

individually listed in this volume. Of lesser importance is *Caryota urens*, the caryota palm; this yields a sweet sap used to make jaggery or toddy, while sago from the starchy interior of the stem was a source of food for the poorer classes along the Malabar coast a century ago. The talipot palm, *Corypha umbraculifera*, has enormous fan-shaped leaves as much as 3 metres across, and hard, ivory-coloured fruit/ seeds used to make beads, buttons, and even small bowls; a sago is derived from the pith.

palmyra Known as thalpatra in Sanskrit, *Borassus flabellifer* or the toddy palm has a crown of fan-like leaves. In the purple, woody nuts are embedded three translucent pulpy fruits of doughnut shape, filled with a sweetish juice that soon turns alcoholic. It is beautifully depicted in Buddhist sculpture. From the inflorescences an intensely sweet sap is tapped into clay pots. These pots are smeared with slaked lime if fermentation is to be retarded either for use as a beverage or for boiling down to jaggery (q.v.). Fermentation yields a toddy with a strong aroma, and distillation a potent arrack.

A popular drink with ladies and described in the *Purananuru*, a work of Sangam Tamil literature, is munnir, made of equal parts of sugarcane juice, tender coconut water, and fresh palmyra sap. In Kerala, the fresh sap on thickening after being boiled down yields the syrupy pani; this is mixed with rice grits and filled into a translucent tube of rice to give the confection, churuttu (literally cigar).

A Tamil proverb ascribes to the palm '801 uses which meet almost all the wants of man'. The name palmyra derives from the Portuguese palmeira, meaning the palm par excellence.

panchagavya *See* beverages.

panchamritha A sweet, ceremonial, five-component confection. In medical literature, this comprised three sweet fruit juices along with honey and water. The panchamritha offered as prasadam in the Murugan temple in the Palani hills of Tamil Nadu consists of crystal sugar, honey, ghee, cardamom, and fruits (banana,

dates, raisins); it does not go rancid even for six weeks.

panchphoron A mixture of five condiments in equal quantities employed in Bengali cooking (q.v.).

paneer *See* milk.

panicum grains Till recently, several small grains were included in the *Panicum* family, but some of these are now included in the families *Echinochloa* and *Setaria* (*see* millet). Even in the *Samhitas* of the *Yajurveda*, these grains were collectively called shyamaka, with such prefixes as ambah- (or toya-), rajah-, and hasti-. They were regarded, for example by Apasthamba, as uncultivated food-grains that were permitted to hermits.

The two major panicums are *P. sumatrense* (synonym *P. millare*), otherwise the little millet, shavan, gondli, and samai, and *P. miliaceum* or the Proso millet, akusthaka, cheena, and panivaragu. Samai is still an important crop in the Eastern Ghats of south India, the husked grain being cooked like rice or ground to a flour. Proso millet is a very old grain, cultivated even by the prehistoric Lake Dwellers of Switzerland, and domesticated perhaps in the eastern Mediterranean or even in India. Panivaragu has been excavated *c.* 1000 BC in Adichanallur, and was an important food-grain in the Tamil country during the Sangam period. It is a crop of very short duration, as well as hardy, and hence was frequently cultivated before and after the main kharif and rabi crops. It is widely grown in Bihar, and used like rice, or after parching as a gruel, or in the form of a chikki.

pao A sort of bun baked in four sections (hence the name, meaning a quarter) that can be broken apart. It is often sold on city streets for on-the-spot consumption with cooked vegetables, meat, or chicken. It is believed to be of Portuguese origin (*see* roti).

papad Pulse flour doughs rolled out very thin into circles and deep-fried or roasted to crispness, used as an accompaniment to meals. The parpata is first mentioned in about 500 BC in Buddhist-Jain canonical literature, and the medical authorities note that they are made from pulses like urad, masoor, chana, and the like. Professional papad-makers called kagal-kutas soon developed, and are mentioned in the fourteenth century as part of a king's army in Rajasthan. This state has both thin and thick papads, called kheladas. The Tamil term is appalam or pappadam. The Kannada word happala occurs in the *Siddaramacharite* written by Raghavanka in about AD 1200, and again in the *Sanatkumaracharite* written by Terekanambi Bommarasa (AD 1485), in which happalas are described as 'being broken into pieces' at a feast for kings.

papaya A fruit-bearing tree that seems to have come to India from South America by way of the Spanish East Indies (Philippines) and Malacca, or, according to Delle Valle, from Brazil. In AD 1550 a European visitor to Peru mentions papaie in use there, while in the Caribbean it is called ababai. Writing of it in India in AD 1598, Linschoten uses the word papaios, while pawpaw and papeeta are employed by several English writers in succeeding centuries. Papayas in India grow on female plants, and, in plantations, about 15 per cent of male plants suffice to effect pollination and fruit setting.

papdi Crisp, deep-fried wafers of besan that incorporate jeera and methi, popular in Gujarat and Rajasthan. The item termed purika mentioned in the *Manasollasa* in the twelfth century AD answers to the description, not of the puri of today, but of the papdi.

paramanna A ritual confection of rice and milk with honey and sugar given to a child as its first solid food at the annaprasanna ceremony (q.v.). Though older, the term occurs as a food item in a work in Kannada written in AD 1485, and is repeatedly extolled as the finest type of payasa (q.v) in subsequent writings.

parata, paranta Wheat dough rolled out, with frequent folding over, while smearing with fat, to a square or triangular shape, and pan-fried using a little fat to a layery texture.

Paranta

Cauliflowers, potatoes, spinach, or methi leaves can be mixed into the dough before frying, and the product eaten with curd. A stuffing of besan flour yields the birahi, with an unusual taste and texture. The sweet poli, holige, and obattu of Maharashtra and Karnataka are stuffed with boiled and mashed pulses and jaggery, while a stuffing of finely powdered sugar, coconut shreds, dates, raisins, and the like yields various forms of mande and poli (q.v.). Many of these are of considerable antiquity, both the purige (later termed holige) and the mandage being mentioned in a Kannada work of AD 920, the *Vaddaradane* of Shivakotyacharya.

parboiling Parboiled rice is termed pulungalarisi in Tamil, and the term first occurs in the *Siruppanarupudai* of the late Sangam period. Paddy was soaked in cold water for a few days, then boiled till the grain softened, after which the grain was dried in the sun. Subsequent milling in a pounder, or on a chakki between stones, yielded parboiled rice with a distinctly better yield of unbroken grains than when paddy itself is milled. Modern studies reveal that during the operation many surface nutrients are driven into the grain; these are not lost by leaching when the rice is subsequently cooked, making for distinctly better nutrition. Improved parboiling processes recently devised call for quick steaming of the grain, followed by cold steeping for a few hours, and a second quick steaming, a process which saves time and improves the sensory quality of the product.

parching Soaking grain in water, roasting it in hot sand so that the grain swells but does not burst, and finally pounding it in a mortar yields a parched and flattened product. Even the *Rigveda* (1500 BC) mentions lajah or parched barley, which was reduced to a coarse flour called saktu (the modern sattu) and eaten with ghee, milk, curds, and even soma juice. Parched rice is later referred to as chipita, a name that survives in the crisp fried snack, chivda or chidva. Other Sanskrit terms for parched grains are ulumbah and prthuka, while Charaka refers to parched grains as a class as bhrshta-dhanya. Distinct names were current in Bihar a century ago for parched products from various grains: lai from rice, chiuri from barley, lawa from maize, and pavaral also from maize (this was also a general term). Old Tamil literature describes parched rice by the term even now in use, aval.

In ritual terms, parched grains made by professionals can be bought and used even by an orthodox brahmin without the stigma of pollution. Indeed parched nee or chura is an auspicious food, and in the wedding ceremony of the highly orthodox Kanyakubja brahmin community of Uttar Pradesh, where Vedic ritual is still maintained, the bride will throw it with both hands into the fire during the marriage ceremony. In Indian medical understanding, parched grains are considered to be more easily digested than the ordinary products, and are recommended for use by diabetics in place of cooked or fried grains. Visitors to India in Mughal times note that the morning nourishment of peasants was a handful of parched grain dressed with a little pungent mustard oil. A crisp-fried chura seasoned with salt, turmeric, groundnuts, and copra shreds constitutes the popular snack chidva. In south India an uppuma (q. v.) of aval is eaten for breakfast, and a milk-based payasam (q.v.) as a dessert.

Parsis, food of Islam was established in Iran after the fall of the Sassanian empire; sacred Zoroastrian fire temples were destroyed, and religious persecution drove its followers first into the mountains and then to the port town of Hormuz. Around AD 850, a group seeking a new home set out in seven junks; they arrived first at the island of Diu, off Gujarat, and then entered the mainland. After a couple of decades, the small migrant community led by Dastur Nariosanj again set sail, and after a violent thunderstorm landed in Sanjan port in the Thana kingdom of Jadi Rana (Vajjadeva). He welcomed them and allowed the first fire temple in India to be set up. Once again persecution by the invader Sultan Mahmud Bagda drove the Parsis with their sacred fire into the mountains. Later they were able to settle in Navsari and Udweda, and to thrive as a mercantile community with strong religious and social ethics based on 'good thought, good word and good deed'. Today Parsis are to be found all over India, but total only 100,000.

In about AD 1325, an early European visitor to India, Odoric of Pordenone, was in Surat, and described the fire worship of the community of Parsis. Father Monserrate, who was in India in c. 1600 AD, remarked that the 'diet of the Parsis consists of milk, ghee, oil, vegetables, pulses and fruit, they drink no wine', which is rather inaccurate. In fact there are few food restrictions on the Parsis, but some Hindu customs have been adopted voluntarily, such as the prohibition on beef. The cuisine reflects both an Iranian ancestry in its strong non-vegetarian component and local Gujarati influence. The Iranian influence also shows in the free use of nuts, raisins, and sultanas. Parsis relish the distinctive sweet fried noodle dish called seviyan (q.v.), the rich drink falooda (q.v.) made from sago granules, the mutton-barbecued shoojan, and a distinctive zard or sweet palao (q.v.). At least three dhals, and even up to nine, are cooked together with subtle spicing to give dhansakh, but into it also goes pieces of fatty meat, tripe, and vegetables. From the local undhiu, a mixed dish of soft vegetables (beans, sweet potato, brinjal, red pumpkin) baked underground in a handa, has evolved the Parsi oberu or umberio, to which quail meat is sometimes added. Chutneys, morabbas, and snacks have been freely borrowed and adapted. The coconut with a dab of vermilion is an auspicious symbol among both Gujaratis and Parsis, and its soft pulp is extensively used in cooking. Fish, freely available in Gujarat, is baked with a thick coconut paste in a banana leaf packet to give the delicious patra-ni-machi. Patia is pomfret in a dark vinegar sauce, and there are several dry fish-preparations

besides. Eggs are a great favourite; they are baked on a green layer of pot herbs, with added ingredients like potatoes, tomatoes, almonds, raisins, cream, and butter, to yield the dish akuri with various names like akeedar, tharkari, and bharuchi. The sources may be diverse, but the unifying Parsi touch is distinctive.

partridge A common bird of the Indian scrubland, which constitutes a table delicacy. It is mentioned in the Buddhist *Jataka* tales, and Charaka rates the thitther or chakora highly as meat. In about AD 1520, Domingo Paes notes that three kinds of partridge were available in the Vijayanagar market. The British colonial considered the Indian partridge good eating.

parwal Botanically termed *Trichosanthes dioica*, the Sanskrit name patola of this tender spherical gourd is believed to be of even earlier Munda origin, which makes it an ancient food item. The medical authorities prescribe its juice during a fever. It has always been regarded as a delicious and delicate vegetable, served, for example, to the mystic Chaitanya by his admirer Sarvabhauma. Again in the sixteenth-century Bengali work, *Chandimangala*, Lord Vishnu who demands only pure sattvik food is given 'tender potola browned in ghee'. Parwal is a favourite food all along the Gangetic basin, dusted with turmeric and pepper, and lightly cooked in its own juice.

passion fruit *Passiflora edulis* is a climbing vine with purple fruit, native to southern Brazil, while the yellow fruit is *P. laurifolia.* The loose jelly-like pulp makes a beverage with a distinct and pleasant flavour. It is not known when the vine was brought to India, but it now runs wild in the Western Ghats of south India.

payasa(m), payesh A sweetened dish of rice cooked in milk, the payasa first finds mention in Buddhist-Jain canonical literature in *c.* 400 BC. Since common ingredients are used, the dish could well be very much older. It seems unchanged to this day, being called payasam in south India and payesh in Bengal. A sarvaligeya-payasam made with vermicelli figures in a work in Kannada written in AD 1222, and a 'bead-like' payasam (perhaps made from sago granules) in a work of AD 1235. A dish of clotted cream flakes in sugar and milk is mentioned as kene (cream)-payasa in the *Manasollasa*, written in the twelfth century AD. Similar to payasa is the kheer (q.v.) of north India and the prathaman (q.v.) of Kerala, while the ritual paramanna (q.v.) represents an extension.

peach *Prunus persica* developed from the same ancestral materials as the cherry, plum, apricot, and almond; the diversions occurred somewhere in western China, where the peach was developed. Xuan Zang pointed out the Chinese origin of the peach during his travels in India in the early seventh century AD, and stated that it was then being brought into India from Kashmir. The Sanskrit name chinani reflects this origin. The Mughals made efforts to grow this

Peacock

semi-tropical fruit in the country, and by the time of Akbar, according to the *Ain-i-Akbari*, 'peaches ... are to be found everywhere', while its grafting on plum trees was also being explored. It is a hill plant, now cultivated not only in Kashmir, but in Himachal Pradesh and the Kumaon Hills.

peacock The spectacular plumage of the Indian mayura naturally excited the attention of foreign writers. Megasthenes (*c.* 300 BC), Aelian (*c.* AD 80-140), and Varthema (*c.* AD 1508) all remarked on tame peacocks kept in royal palaces and gardens. Al-Biruni noted that the peacock was a bird that was allowed to be killed and indeed the Indian medical authorities, Charaka and Sushrutha, endorsed its meat highly. The term peafowl is used for both the cock and hen, and finds frequent mention in early Tamil literature. Roast peacock was sometimes served at a Christmas meal in India.

pear *Pyrus pyrifolia*, var. culta, the hard country or sand pear, has two Sanskrit names, urumana and nashpati, and a Tamil one, berikai, and must have entered the country long ago from China or Japan. The soft, sweet European pear, *Pyrus communis*, was not well known, and Xuan Zang mentions that the fruit was brought into the country from Kashmir. Under the Mughals, pears were imported during the time of Akbar from Kashmir and Samarkand but were stated to be 'grown also in Hindusthan'. Jahangir states in his memoirs that pears 'so far imported, are now being grown in Kashmir [which formed part of the Mughal empire] through the efforts of our nobleman Muhammad Quli Afsar'. Juicy pears are still a product of the hilly northern terrain.

pearl millet *See* bajra.

peas The common cultivated garden pea, kalaya and vatana in Sanskrit, mattar in Hindi, and pattani in Tamil, is *Pisum sativum*. It is an exceedingly ancient food material, and was domesticated in the area of the Fertile Crescent as early as in 7000 BC. A second centre of domestication of the pea (along with the pepper, areca nut, cucumber, bottle-gourd, and almond) came to light recently, by way of 10,000 BC layers in the Mekong Valley in Thailand. Carbonized peas have been found at very early dates in Hacilar (Turkey) and Jericho (Israel). One ancestor suggested for the garden pea is *P. aravense,* the small, marbled field pea; this form is still in use in India, and has been found in Harappa, Kalibangan, and Daimabad in 2000–1500 BC sites, and later (1500– 750 BC) in Inamgaon, Navdatoli, and Jorwe in western-central India. The pea is mentioned considerably later in literature, in about 400 BC, but frequently thereafter. Three varieties are mentioned, satina, khandika, and harenu. Peas are a market item noted in the *Mathuraikkanchi* of early Tamil literature. It is a crop harvested in spring, according to the *Arthashastra*, and in medical terms is a cold, dry, sweet food. Green peas are cooked as a vegetable, or along with rice, or made into a soup or used as a parata filling.

pepper, long Pippali or long pepper, *Piper longum*, is probably native to India, and was an export item from south India to Syria as early as in 1400 BC. It is mentioned in the *Atharvaveda* (*c.* 1000 BC) and, slightly later, in the *Shatapatha Brahmana* as usana. Charaka notes that minced meat to be used for stuffing could be spiced with both long and round peppers.

Today long pepper is a minor commodity, obtained from creeping shrubs that grow untended in Kerala and Assam. The name comes from the long fruit pods, which, by an odd coincidence, resemble in outline the thin, curved green chillies that came to India from Mexico in the sixteenth century AD. A woodcut of the long pepper shrub published in Basel in AD 1543 brings this out strikingly. An equal mixture of long pepper, round pepper, and ginger, called trikatu, is prescribed in Indian medicine for kapha and vata disorders (*see* pepper, round).

pepper, round The dried berries, of a climbing vine, *Piper nigrum*, constitute round or black pepper, termed

maricha in Sanskrit and milagu in Tamil. Wild pepper vines, which occur in Kerala, bear both male and female flowers, whereas the cultivated forms bear a one-sex inflorescence.

Round pepper is referred to in the Sanskrit works, *Apasthamba Dharmasutra*, and *Arthashastra,* and is also mentioned in the Pali work *Mahavagga*. The *Periplus Maris Erythyraei*, written in about AD 50 by an anonymous Greek sailor, notes the export of pepper from the port of Muziris in south India to middle-eastern sea ports, and about the same time Pliny in Greece mentions both black and white pepper (obtained by depulping), perhaps drawing his information from the lost writings of Megasthenes. Tamil literature of the same period—the early Christian era—is replete with references to pepper, a product of the then Chera country (now Kerala). The marketplace, in the *Mathuraikkanchi*, has 'sacks of pepper', while 'the brokers move to and fro with, steelyards and measures in their hands weighing and measuring the pepper and grains purchased by the people'.

One word used for both pepper and pepper-dressed meat in Tamil is kari (anglicized in colonial times to curry, q.v.). To obtain thalittakari, or kuy, meat was marinated in ground pepper and mustard seeds, and then fried in oil. Meat boiled with flavourants like pepper and tamarind was termed pulingari or kava, which in turn could be ground to yield a pasty relish. The spiced Kanchipuram idli contains whole peppercorns, which are also used both in the deep-fried urad dhal snack medhu-vada, and the bonda, to impart a light flavour.

The use of pepper in cuisine is well illustrated in the *Manasollasa* written by King Someshwara in the twelfth century AD. This work was written in Kalyana, about 160 km west of modern Hyderabad, and reflects the influence of both southern and northern food styles. The iddarika, a forerunner in name of the present idli (q.v.), and the purika used pepper. An elaborate dish was prepared by seasoning a mixture of mung dhal, pieces of lotus stalk, and priyala (chironji) seeds with green ginger pieces and asafoetida, frying the lot in oil, and boiling it to a curry; to this could be added pieces of brinjal, mutton, jackal meat or even animal marrow, the dish being finally dusted with black pepper or dry ginger. A beverage termed phanta consisted of diluted molasses sprinkled with pepper, and another beverage, majjika, consisted of churned buttermilk dressed with black pepper and mustard seeds. Chakkalika were pieces carved out of a whole roast pig, eaten after seasoning with either lemon juice, or with rock salt and black pepper.

Further north, the use of pepper was less common. The Mahabharata describes a feast in which was served 'shoulders and rounds of animals dressed in ghee, sprinkled over with sea salt and black pepper, and garnished with radishes, pomegranates, lemons, fragrant herbs, asafoetida and ginger'. The *Sushrutha Samhita* describes seven types of meat preparations. Vesavara, ground meat used for stuffing, uses pepper. Pepper was of course an important item in the health-medicine repertoire, classed as having a pungent taste as well as a pungent aftertaste. It strengthens the dosha pitta, increases

Pepper vine

the metabolic rate, improves blood circulation and stimulates bladder function. Pepper is of outstanding value in treating coughs and colds, and a mixture of lemon, honey, and pepper controls hiccups and mitigates gas discomfort. Trikatu, the triple combination of equal amounts of ginger, long pepper, and round pepper, is prescribed for ailments that relate to deranged kapha (shown in body stability, firmness, and flexibility) and deranged vata (which has to do with such states as breathing, animation, and inspiration).

Pepper was a spice greatly valued in medieval England and Europe, being used to preserve meat when all animals had to be slaughtered, as winter closed in, for lack of fodder. Thus early visitors to India from the West showed great curiosity about pepper. Odoric of Pordenone, a Franciscan friar, sailed around the tip of south India to China, and described the climbing pepper plant, which resembled 'a vine in its growth and its clusters of fruit, and an ivy in its leaves'.

A German soldier, Hans Schiltberger, in about AD 1410, detailed three types of pepper in the south of India. The lure of spices brought Vasco da Gama to India in AD 1498 and the produce that he took back with him was said to have paid for his entire expedition six times over. The *Camera da India* was established for the regular

export of spices to Portugal, and one shipment alone consisted of 1500 tonnes of pepper, 28 tonnes of ginger, 8 tonnes of cinnamon, and 7 tonnes of clove, the value of which must have been astronomical in Europe. In about AD 1700 Manucci noted that south Indians 'sip a concoction which is some water boiled with pepper', doubtless a reference to rasam (q.v.). The British colonialist adopted this preparation as a spicy soup which was called mulligatawny (q.v.), a literal translation of the Tamil pepper-water.

Persian words To start with, there is rice itself. The old Persian virinji (later birinj) is only a short step from the Sanskrit vrihi and varisi, and in turn the Tamil arisi, besides the meat-rice dish biriyani. Wheat in old Persian was gandhum and in Sanskrit godhuma. The cumin seed, zira in Persian, is jeeraka in Sanskrit, while the Persian-Arabic zaffran (which in Sanskrit is kesar) is saffron in English. The almond, vadam in old Persian, became vatama, which Charaka and Sushrutha used for the sweet almond (the bitter form was vatavairi), and which became badam in Hindi.

When food is cooked in a seal of dough it is termed dumpukht, literally air-cooled in Persian, and is frequently shortened simply to dum, as in dum-aloo. The word palao (q.v.) has entered every language in the world: it figures in Sanskrit as palao-mevach in the *Yagnavalkya Smriti* (first century AD) and stems from the Persian-Arabic pilav or pullao. The word achar (q.v.) for pickle is of similar origin, though various others have been put forward (*see* pickle). The delicious jilebi (q.v.), a term first used in India in a Jain work of about AD 1450, and a later Kannada work of about AD 1600 is, according to Hobson-Jobson, apparently a corruption of the Arabic word zalabiya or Persian zaliblya.

pestle *See* milling.

pewter An alloy of tin and lead, almost unknown in India. In the fourteenth century, the traveller Ibn Battuta describes a meal at the Sultanate court in Delhi in which a post-prandial drink of sweetened barley (termed fuqqa) was served in pewter tankards. These were perhaps imported.

phala Literally, and in common parlance, the term phala (Hindi phal) means fruit, and both Charaka and Sushrutha have, in their classification of edible materials, categories of phala-varga (fruits) and shaka-varga (vegetables). But the word is used in a larger sense in ritual terms to denote all foods that are not raised with the help of the plough, in contrast to foods that are so raised, termed anna. Uncultivated foods may include wild cereals, millets, fruits, vegetables, green leaves, roots and tubers, and forest produce. Only such foods

are permitted to those who have renounced the world as ascetics, and frequently to householders who observe vows or are on fast.

In the taxonomy of orthodox cooking, phalahar refers to the product obtained by cooking phala using ghee, fire, and milk products.

phalsa Of indigenous origin, *Grewia subinaequalis* yields a small, sour, purplish berry from which is made a refreshing acidic drink. It was one of the eight beverages permitted to Buddhist and Jain monks. The *Charaka Samhita* lists it among the sour fruits from which can be made the class of drinks termed raga.

pheasants Around 300 BC, Megasthenes describes tame pheasants in the walled-in park of the royal palace of Chandragupta Maurya, along with wild peacocks, ornamental trees, and lakes full of sacred fish. Four centuries later, Aelian repeats this in his monumental *Collections of History*.

pheni Exceedingly thin, extended strands of wheat dough extruded from certain hard wheats and vended in bundles, termed pheni in Sanskrit and Hindi, and seviyan in Muslim circles. They are commonly made into desserts with milk and sugar. The *Manasollasa*, written in the twelfth century, refers to pheni, and Annaji, in AD 1400, refers in Kannada to 'delicious strands of pheni' served at a meal. It figures in Gujarati historical literature as phenaka (sutar-pheni), and pahalika (khaja-pheni), while the *Varanaka Samuchaya* of AD 1520 mentions 'thin pheni'. Grierson in Bihar a century ago describes pheni as 'a frothy sweetmeat'.

In Mughal times the humbler Muslims ate desserts of pheni. A century ago, the Muslim community in Nellore first boiled strands of pheni in milk and sugar, and then fried the product in ghee to obtain a rich dessert (*see also* seviyan).

phulka A thin circle of rolled-out wheat dough roasted dry on a thava (griddle) yields a chapati; this, when placed immediately thereafter on hot embers, puffs up to yield a phulka; which is best eaten piping hot.

pickle The Sanskrit sandan or sandin, Gujarati athanu, goondas, and chundo, Tamil urukai, Kannada lippinkayi, and Hindi achar. The origin of the word achar is obscure. In AD 1563, Garcia da Orta describes a conserve of cashew fruit in salt, 'and this they call Achar'. About thirty years later Linschoten, writing in Dutch uses the same word. In AD 1687, bamboo-achar and mango-achar are noted in Thailand and Indonesia, which leaves the origin of the word open. Though commonly ascribed a Persian origin, Hobson-Jobson hints that it may even have originated in western Asia from the Latin acetaria. Considerable prior use

Raw mango pickle

of the word achar does not support the view of Rumphius in AD 1750 that achar derives from the Spanish word axa for the chilli, which the Portuguese write as achi.

Pickling frequently falls into the ritual category of 'cooking without fire', only the heat of the sun being employed to create an edible product. In the seventeenth century, the *Shivatattvaratnakara* written by King Keladi Basavaraja, refers to relishes as a class as uppadamsha; this consists of five types, of which one is pickles cooked without fire. A Kannada work of AD 1594, the *Lingapurana* of Gurulinga Desika, describes no less than fifty kinds of pickles. By far the most important material for pickling is raw mangoes (whole baby fruit, wild mangoes, cut slices, or the hard, fibrous avakkai). Others are limes, lemons, small onions, brinjals, chillies, karaunda berries, pork, wild boar, prawns, and fish.

Mustard oil in the north and east, and sesame oil in the south and west, are the two vegetable oils popular in pickling for their long keeping qualities. The avakkai of Andhra is an uncooked pickle. In current practice, it is customary to make use of the fire to make a pickle. Thus mustard seeds may first be fried in the oil of choice; then the mango or lime pieces dressed with turmeric and salt are put in and fried till tender, after which powdered spices (chillies, methi seeds, asafoetida) are added, and the mass mixed thoroughly and put by to mature. There are of course numerous variations (*see also* achar; chutney; morabba).

pig Both Fa Xian in the early fifth century AD, and Xuan Zang in the mid-seventh, note that fowls and pigs were not reared in India, and that pork was a forbidden meat to many inhabitants. Literature well before the Muslim advent shows that kshatriya rulers were always partial to pork. In the Mahabharata, King Yudhisthira fed 10,000 brahmins with, pork and venison. Even in recent years the Rajput nobility performed the sholgava sacrifice in which young pigs were first roasted whole; strips of this roasted meat were then marinated in spiced curd, placed with ghee in a wrapper and baked, followed by a final grilling on a skewer. The *Manasollasa* written by King Someshwara in the twelfth century gives two methods for dehairing a pig: by covering the carcass with a cloth and pouring boiling water over it to soften the bristles, or by covering the body with clay and then burning the skin away with a fire made of grass. To prepare tasty sunthakas, a whole pig was first roasted on an open fire. Pieces were then carved out and eaten after being seasoned with rock salt and black pepper, or sour lemon juice. As an alternative, long strips ('resembling palm leaves') were carved out of the roast and placed in spiced curds before consumption. Another dish, called mandaliya, was made from the entrails, mixed with marrow and spices, and broiled again on a charcoal fire.

In about AD 1640, Father Sebastian Manrique noted that in Bengal tame pigs were not eaten, but that wild boar was 'considered a great delicacy by Sikhs and Rajputs'. In south India there were no reservations, and indeed its early literature contains no less than fifteen names for the domestic pig. Wild boar was hunted using dogs and nets; captured animals were fattened with rice flour and kept away from the female to improve the taste of the flesh. Much later, Domingo Paes describes in Vijayanagar 'pigs in some streets of butcher's houses so clean that you would never see better in any country'.

Currently, certain areas of the country have distinctive pork dishes. Goa has the sorpotel, a curry of pork blood, meat, liver, and fat soured with vinegar and tamarind sauce, and the vindaloo, a more liquid curry that uses the rind of the kokum fruit (*Garcinia indica*) as the souring agent. Feijoada is pork cooked with beans, and salted pork is pickled. The Kodavas of Karnataka make a dry pork dish with a dark, thick masala which derives its colour from the black, sun-drawn extract of the kokum fruit. Wild boar meat is smoked, and also pickled. It was rated highly as meat by the British colonial (*see also* boar).

pigeon The Buddhist *Jataka* tales refer to the use of pigeons as food, as does Sushrutha. A Sanskrit work that originates from Assam, the *Kamampa Yatra* (*c.* AD 600–800), specially commends to the upper classes the meat of the duck, pigeon, tortoise, and wild boar. Domingo Paes notes pigeons on sale in the markets of Vijayanagar in the sixteenth century AD. Writing about Bengal in about AD 1640, Father Sebastian Manrique notes however that 'pigeons are not generally eaten, as being of a blue colour they are held sacred to Shiva, but doves are generally eaten'.

pigeon pea *See* thuvar.

pineapple The development of the pineapple is attributed to the Indians of the lowlands of South America. The word pineapple derives from its remarkable resemblance to the large stone-pine of southern Europe, and in fact the term pineapple was already in use for this pine cone long before the discovery of America. While the pineapple is called ananas in most Indian languages, in Malayalam the term used is poruthu-chakka, or the Portuguese jackfruit, because of a resemblance in size and shape, and perhaps in flavour, between the two fruits.

In AD 1564 the fruit is described in India, nearly a hundred years before it was seen in England. In AD 1616 Edward Terry describes its 'taste to be a pleasing compound, made of strawberries, claret-wine, rose-water and sugar, well-tempered together'. The *Ain-i-Akbari* in AD 1590 quotes its price in the Delhi market as 4 dams each, an amount that could then buy 10 mangoes. A decade later Jahangir calls it a fruit of the 'European ports' in India, but adds

Pineapple

that 'some thousands' were being grown in gardens in Agra. In about AD 1665, Bernier notes in Bengal 'the innumerable islands abounding in fruit trees and pineapples'.

There is no evidence whatsoever of the presence of the pineapple in India prior to Columbus (*see* maize, sitaphal).

pishta From the Sanskrit, meaning ground or powdered, arise words like pishtaka for a cake of flour, pishataka for flour mixed with water, pistaudana for a dish of rice cooked with mince meat, and pishtak, an early Bengali sweetmeat.

pistachio *Pistachia vera* is a small evergreen tree of ancient Mediterranean provenance, with centres of diversity in Turkey and Kirgisthan. The hard, white nuts, which split open when they ripen, have always been imported after salting into India. Charaka refers to them as abhlsikha.

Ibn Battuta notes samosas stuffed with pistachio nuts in the Sultanate court, and Abul Fazl in the time of Akbar lists them as items earlier scarce but now 'found everywhere'.

pitta One of the three bodily humours or doshas (q.v.), pitta is composed of the single element fire. Accordingly, pitta influences the metabolic processes of the body like digestion, combustion, body temperature, and skin colour, besides contributing to intelligence, memory,

Pistachio

enthusiasm, and high ideals. The main location of pitta is considered to be the small intestine in the upper abdomen. Accordingly, an increase in pitta is treated with laxatives. Fierce heat and over-exposure to the sun, and grief, fear, and rage can all bring on an upsurge of pitta. It can be pacified by foods that are sweet, like sugarcane juice and coconut water; by astringent foods like the amla, figs, honey (which in ayurveda has an astringent aftertaste), and barks of certain trees; and bitter foods like turmeric, coriander, bittergourd, and neem leaves.

A reduced pitta is revealed in a loss of body heat, poor appetite, and loss of skin glow. Pitta strengtheners are foods that are sour, salty, and pungent like chilli, pepper, nutmeg, acid fruits and curd (*see also* kapha; vata; dosha).

plantain *See* banana.

plates, leaf *See* leaf plates and cups.

plum The
Prunus family
includes the
cherry, plum,
peach, apricot, and almond, all
of which are believed to have
diverged from an ancestral
cherry species of Central
Asia. The cultivated plum,
alucha and alubukhara
in Sanskrit, represents the link
between the various members of this
family. Plum varieties were developed
independently by natural selection
in Central Asia, the Middle East,
China, Europe, and North America.
Xuan Zang notes in the seventh
century AD that wild plums brought
from Kashmir were found 'growing
on every side' in India. Among the
Mughal experiments on grafting was
that of peaches on plum trees.

poli(ka) Pan-fried paratas (q.v.)
stuffed with a ground paste of dhal
(usually mung) and jaggery to yield
a soft, mildly sweet product, eaten
hot or cold with milk or ghee.
They are described in the twelfth-
century *Manasollasa* as polikas or
pahalikas, and in the Kannada work
Parshavanatha Purana, written by
Parshva Panditha (dated AD. 1222),
as holige. This word, even now in use
in Karnataka, had superseded earlier
terms like purige and hurige.

A related product is puran-poli. A
brief description in the *Manasollasa*
of the item purana suggests an

Pomegranate

item similar to the poli. At present
puran-poli denotes a loaf of wheat,
mashed dhal, and jaggery baked in an
oven, thought by some to be a Parsi
adaptation for making the poli in a
form that could be baked and cut like
a cake and eaten with a fork.

pomegranate *Punica granatum* is
an ancient fruit native to Iran, and
indeed the old Persian name dulim
is echoed in the Sanskrit dhalimba
and the Kannada dhalambi. It came
to India very early; excavations at
Harappa in the Indus Valley
(*c*. 2000 BC) yielded 'two polychrome
earthenware vases, the former
shaped like a pomegranate and the
latter shaped like a coconut'. The
Mahabharata describes a picnic meal
in which the cooked animal food was
garnished with pomegranate. Charaka
notes two varieties of pomegranate,
and lists it as one of the sweet fruits
from which a panaka beverage was
derived. The pomegranate was a
fruit permitted to Buddhists. It
is mentioned frequently in early

south Indian literature; a wandering minstrel was fed, for example, by a brahmin with cooked animal flesh garnished with pomegranate.

Even in the seventh century AD, Xuan Zang notes that pomegranates and sweet oranges were grown everywhere. Ma Huan observed it in Bengal in the fourteenth century AD, Ibn Haukal in Kasdar, and Ibn Battuta generally in the country. In Vijayanagar, Domingo Paes noted 'many pomegranates' and Father Monserrate remarked on 'the goodly gardens (of Surat) with pomegranates, lemons, melons and figs continuing all the year'.

As early as in AD 1300 Amir Khusrau remarked on the excellent flavour of the pomegranates in Jodhpur, and a couple of centuries later Sikander Lodi declared these to be superior to the pomegranates of Iran.

In ritual terms, the pomegranate is classed as a 'fruit for chewing', along with grapes and ber, and these fruits formed the first course at a meal served to King Shrenika, described in the *Bhavissayatakaha* of *c.* AD 1000.

Dried seeds of the pomegranate, termed anardhana, are used as a mild souring agent in north India. Anar juice is greatly relished.

pomelo *See citrus.*

pongal The south Indian New Year, when the sun turns north in about mid-January, is called Pongal, an agricultural festival when cows are garlanded with mango leaves. A pot of rice is placed on the fire, and just when it is about to boil over (pongu means to boil), cries of 'pongal' rent the air, and the pot is offered to Lord Ganesha. In the matu-pongal rite, the milk should actually boil over.

The dish pongal(i) is a rice-mung dhal preparation in ghee, with a spicing of jeera, pepper, green ginger, and asafoetida. These spices would be avoided in the sweet version, sakkarai-pongal(i), and jaggery, cardamom, powder and cashewnuts would be used instead.

poppy The small black seeds of the poppy, *Papaver semniferum*, constitute the khaskhas or posto condiment in an Indian kitchen, particularly in use in Bengal. An item in which it is used is the sweet leavened bread khjuru or khajur, to the dough of which both sugar and poppy seeds are added before fashioning into small slabs that are deep-fried in ghee. Khjuru is described in Mughal times by Father Sebastian Manrique as being of a delicate flavour.

The capsule of the poppy flower is the source of the narcotic opium, in Greek opion and in Arabic ofyun, from which derive the Sanskrit ahiphena and the Hindi afin. A knowledge of this drug was brought to India in about the eleventh or twelfth century AD by the Arabs, and Uttar Pradesh and Malwa regions became centres of opium production. In AD 1511 Giovanni di Empoli recorded that the Portuguese admiral Albuquerque found opium in the cargoes of eight ships from Gujarat that he had captured. In AD 1516 Barbosa noted that opium was an export item from India, and both Acosta and Linschoten, before the end of the sixteenth century, described at length Indian indulgence in opium. In AD 1668 Bernier observed that the Rajputs consumed it as a stimulant on the eve of a battle.

Father Monserrate described the preparation of opium, referring to the poppy not as khakhas, then its common name, but by the old word posto (*see also* bhang).

porcupine Porcupine as a food item is noted in the Ramayana and Charaka and Sushrutha list it under edible meats. It is mentioned as a meat favoured by the Kuruvars of south India during the early Christian era.

pork *See* pig; boar.

Portuguese impact The three visits of Vasco da Gama to Kerala commencing in AD 1498 established Portuguese presence in Kozhikode, Kochi, and Kannur. In about AD 1512 Albuquerque took over Goa, and developed it into a thriving metropolis, a bastion of Catholicism and a cultural centre. After about AD 1650 the Portuguese presence waned, yielding to Dutch, French, and British influence. By then over 20,000 Portuguese had settled in Bengal at Hughli and Rajmahal, influencing local practices in this area.

The Portuguese adapted into their language Indian names for the new food items they encountered from whence they passed into English. Noting the great value of numerous products derived from the toddy palm, the Portuguese named it the 'excellent palm' or palmeira, which later came to be written as palmyra. The 'face' on a coconut, stripped of its outer fibre to reveal two eyes, a nose, and a mouth, led to its being dubbed cocos (monkey-face or hobgoblin), which was anglicized to coconut. The Malayalam chakka became jackfruit, while the plantain (a word used only in India for the banana) derived from the huge leaf, planta. In Portuguese grao means a grain; this was first used for the Bengal gram, and soon the word gram became synonymous with pulses. The Malayalam vettile leaf became the betel leaf, and the nuts chewed with it, adakka in Malayalam, was Europeanized to areca (*see* individual entries).

Brought to India were terms for food materials in use in other countries. The acaju of the Tupe Indians of Brazil became kaju in many Indian languages and cashew in English, while the Tepi Indian term nana for the pineapple crossed the seas as ananas, which entered several Indian tongues. The fruit papaya came with a variant of that name from

South America to the Philippines and thence to India, along with such variations as pawpaw and papeeta. The term sapota derives from the word sapodilla in use for the tree and fruit in its native Mexico and Central America; another name for the tree in the New World was chicle, which was Indianized to cheeku. Tomato (tamatar in Hindi) is from the South America tomatl, and potato is from the word batata (which entered several Indian languages directly), itself a case of mistaken identity (see potato). Cacao in the Mayan tongue of South America was smoothened out to cocoa. The chilli in all its forms came to India from Mexico with its name intact, but Indian languages simply adapted the word for pepper (which already existed in that language) to describe the new pungent material (see chilli).

So much for mere nomenclature. There were actual plants of perhaps even greater subsequent impact which the Portuguese and Spanish brought to India from the New World. Groundnuts came to more than one coastal location; they were first cultivated only in about AD 1860, but then rocketed to become the dominant oilseed crop of India (see groundnut). The tapioca (q.v.), also from South America, is today a major staple food in Kerala and Assam. The great historical staple of America,

maize (q.v.) or corn, has established a considerable presence in India as a food for humans and animals, and as a source of industrial starch.

Interaction in Goa between the existing Saraswath food and the strong Portuguese presence soon gave rise to a striking and distinctive cuisine, as described elsewhere (see Goa, food of). The curries of the neighbouring East Indians, a small but distinctive Catholic community that speaks not Konkani, as in Goa, but Marathi, also felt the Portuguese presence, in the use of vinegar for cooking pork and fish, in the stuffing of roast suckling pigs, and in the delicate salted tongue relish that uses vinegar, jaggery, lime juice, saltpetre, and salt.

In Bengal, the Portuguese presence first stimulated the preparation of sweet fruit preserves. A more lasting effect was by way of creating a demand for cottage cheese, which in turn gave the Bengali sweetmeat maker a new raw material, chhana, that set off a fantastic array of Bengali sweetmeats (see Bengali sweets).

Two Portuguese botanists who lived in India wrote classic volumes that incorporated a great deal of information on Indian plants and herbs. Garcia da Orta published in AD 1563 from Goa his *Colloquios dos Simples e Drogas e Cousas Medecinaes da India*, and Christoforas Acosta published in 1578 his *Tractado de las Drogas y Medecinas de las Indias*

Orientates, both mines of information on food and medicinal plants.

pot herbs *See* green leafy vegetables.

potato *Solanum tuberosum* is believed to have been domesticated by native American Indians on the high plateau of Bolivia-Peru in the general region of Lake Titicaca, sometime between 5000 and 2000 BC. Though termed papa in South America, they were incorrectly called batata (the name for the sweet potato) when John Gerard first described them in English in 1597, and this name stuck. As a result of this confusion in nomenclature, it is doubtful whether the potato mentioned in the well-documented dinner given in Ajmer by Asaf Khan to Sir Thomas Roe in 1615, and again noted by Fryer in 1675 as constituting a garden crop (along with the brinjal) in Karnataka and Surat, was really the potato at all, and was perhaps the sweet potato, known much earlier in India. However the identity of the 'basket of potatoes', considered worthy enough to be offered as a gift to Warren Hastings around AD 1780, is not in doubt, since he even invited members of his

Council to dine with him and partake of the unusual gift.

In about AD 1830, potatoes came to be grown on terraced slopes in the Dehra Dun Hills through the efforts of a Captain Youns and a Mr Shore, who simultaneously developed the hill stations of Mussoorie and Larjdour. By 1780, potatoes, peas and beans, according to an 1860 report, were in high repute as foods in Calcutta; the report adds that 'the Dutch are said to have been the first to introduce the culture of potatoes, which were received from their settlement in the Cape of Good Hope. From them the British received annually the seeds of every kind of vegetable useful at the table, as well as several plants of which there appears to be much need, especially various kinds of pot herbs'.

Potatoes in India were first accepted only by Europeans, and then by Muslims. But with rapid general acceptance, the potato is now grown all over the country, though at first it grew especially well in elevated terrain. A major breakthrough in the control of viruses spread by aphids enabled very high yields of potatoes even in the plains. It has literally invaded the Indian kitchen. A dry potato bhaji is a perfect accompaniment to the chapati, parata, puri, and pao, and makes excellent stuffing for a masala dosai in the south. It constitutes a dry

Potato

Puffed grains

stuffing for paratas, samosas, and kachoris, and is cooked with, say, peas to a wet curry. Rings, fingers chips, and crisps are deep-fried potato variations, while potatoes may themselves be stuffed and cooked, or boiled and placed in curds as a raitha relish. On ceremonial occasions, when plough-grown anna is interdicted, the potato may be eaten as a staple food. Even potato peels are crisp-fried to relishes in Bengal and Karnataka.

pots *See* cooking utensils.

poultry *See* chicken; game, wild.

pounding *See* grinding devices.

prasad(am) Food that is first offered in a temple to the presiding deity, and then given to devotees, is termed prasad. In the Hindu belief, such prasad is pure essence or rasa, which when consumed is convened totally into mind or manas, the finest form, and leaves no dense residues (to be eliminated as faeces) or residues of medium density (that are transmuted into flesh). Each temple has its own form or forms of prasad, which will usually reflect the food of the region. In the Padmanabha temple in Thiruvananthapuram, this is an aviyal, in the Thirupathi temple of Venkateshwara the prasad is a laddu, and in the Vishnu temple at Kanchipuram, a spiced idli. In smaller temples, it may simply be a sweet boiled rice (*see* festival and temple foods).

prathaman A generic class of sweet confections in Kerala based on milk or coconut milk. In a pazha-prathaman, fruit (bananas, jackfruit) are fried in ghee before boiling them in milk and sugar. Alternatively mung dhal, and coconut milk and jaggery, could be used to yield parippu-prathaman. A special palada-prathaman will carry paper-thin shreds of a rice-roll, separately prepared, in milk sweetened with sugar; the ada-prathaman is similar, but is sweetened with jaggery, and uses coconut milk.

preserves Traditional Indian preparations for the preservation of fruit and other materials include pickles, chutneys (sweet), and morabbas, also a sweet form of preserves.

pucca food *See* cooking principles.

puffed grains When rice is tossed on very hot sand it swells to a plump, glistening product, called murmura, muri, and pori. If paddy with the husk on is used, the product is termed kneel. Parboiled rice and paddy puff particularly well. Both chana (Bengal gram) and mung are puffed to crunchy, porous products, and the former product is ground to the versatile flour, besan (q.v.).

Parched grains (q.v.) are made by partial puffing, followed by a pounding operation for flattening.

In Sanskrit ulumbah refers to puffed chana and mung grains. The terms missita and dhanidaka also appear to mean puffed, rather than parched, grains. Charaka probably refers to both, as a class, as bhrshta-dhanya. The Tamil word pori, which is still in use for plump puffed rice, occurs in the Sangam literature of between the third and sixth centuries AD; it figures in the *Karuntogai* as a favourite food eaten with milk or as a sweet confection (possibly as a laddu bound with jaggery, as at present). All over India, crisp puffed rice, called muri or murmura, is eaten as a snack after it is dressed with a little pungent mustard oil, or in a mix with wedges of fresh coconut, puffed Bengal gram, roasted groundnuts, and raw onions (*see* murmura).

pulses A collective term for the edible seeds of leguminous plants like grams, beans, lentils, and peas; about a dozen are in common use in India, several from remote antiquity. To take the archaeological record first, green peas were found in Harappa, Kalibangan, and Daimabad in 2000 BC sites. Masoor, dated about 1800 BC, has been found at Navdatoli, Ter, and Chirand. Mung and kulthi (horsegram) grains occur in only slightly later phases at

Navdatoli-Maheshwar; and so does urad, which also occurs at Daulatpur. Further south kulthi has been found at Tekkalakota (*see* individual entries for specific pulses).

The obnoxious kesari (q.v.) has been found at sites dated between 2000 and 1500 BC in Chirand (Bihar), Atranjikhera, and Navdatoli (Maharashtra).

The literary record is of course even more extensive. Masha (urad) occurs even in the *Rigveda* and from the *Yajurveda* onwards the 'three Ms', masha, mudga (mung), and masura (masoor), are constantly in evidence as the three most commonly used pulses of their time. Soon after appears kulattha or kulthi, while the literature of the Buddhist-Jain period records a host of other pulses—kalaya (peas), adhaki (arhar, thuvar), chanaka (chana, the Bengal gram), alisandaga (perhaps the large kabuli-chana, stated to come from Alexandria), and nishpava (the cowpea, lobia or karamani). The rajmasha is mentioned by Charaka; this is not the present rajmah (which only came to India from South America in the eighteenth century), but some large, masha-like grain, perhaps the nishpava. Much later the name rajmah was transferred to the New World kidney bean. The moth or mat bean, makusthaka, finds mention in the *Taittiriya Brahmana* (*see* individual entries under these pulses). Other pulses of more recent origin are the guar-phali or cluster bean, the bada-sem (jackbean or sword bean), the bhakla or broad bean, the lima bean, the rajmah (haricot or kidney bean) from South America, and the winged bean, a recent entrant (*see* individual entries).

Apart from being cooked into liquid or drier forms eaten with rice and rotis, numerous means of using this array of pulses is reflected, though without much detail, in Sanskrit literature. The kulmasha was perhaps a dish of parched pulses dressed with jaggery and oil (the present ghugri), and had the connotation of a poor man's food in the Vedic period. Several pulses, in the *Sutra* period, were extracted to yield supas (soups), and the grits of fermented masha and other dhals were fashioned into various shapes for frying to vatakas (vadas). To supas and vatakas during the Buddhist-Jain period are added parpatas, the modern papads (q.v.). After about 350 BC, pea soups appear to be a popular item.

Charaka described more than twenty-four kinds of pulse extracts, termed yusa, drawn mostly from mung and kulthi. Parpatas (papads) continued to be fashioned from various pulses. Puffed chana and mung yielded products called ulumbah, while parched and puffed products as a class were termed bhrshtadhanya. Pulses in general are sweet and astringent foods in ayurvedic terms, except for the horsegram which is considered pungent. Urad, kulthi, lobia (cowpea), and hyacinth bean (sem, avarai) are all classed as hot, but the thuvar, chana, mung, masoor, and rajmah are cold. Consumption of pulses by those who are of the vata type is not recommended.

The *Manasollasa* of AD 1130, written by King Someshwara of Kalyana, records numerous pulse-based dishes: vidalapaka, vatakas (the fermented and fried urad vadas of today), manahvataka, gharika (perhaps the present garage of Maharashtra), vatika (was the wadian or vadi of today), purika (the papdi of today), parika, veshtika, and iddarika. Pulses could be blended with both vegetables and meat to yield curries.

In old Tamil literature, of roughly between the third and sixth centuries AD, references to pulses are surprisingly meagre. While horsegram, beans, and lentils are stated to grow in mullai forest areas, there is scant mention of the two pulses, ulundu (urad) and thuvaram (arhar), which are so important at present in fashioning common dishes like the dosai, idli, rasam, sambhar, and pongal. There is a stray reference to pastoral people imbibing an aromatic tamarind soup, perhaps a thuvar rasam.

There is about nine centuries of writing in Kannada, from about the tenth century AD onwards, which reflects enormous diversity in the use of pulses. An important class of cooked food all through was melogara, dishes of pulses cooked with greens in which tamarind was not used but coconut gratings were important. Papads in the Karnataka area are termed happalas. Crisp rice–urad relishes were the sandige and chakkali (termed murukku in Tamil). Several pulse-based vadas find mention through the centuries: one from chana, another of colocasia leaves in a chana batter, and a steamed nuchin-unde based on ground, spiced thuvar dhal, and eaten with curds in a work dated AD 1430. The common daily item huli, better known by its Tamil name sambhar, was of course based on thuvar dhal, with various soft vegetables cooked in it (brinjal, lady's finger, drumstick, etc.). An intriguing item is a dish of chana dhal cooked with soma: could this possibly have been wine? Raw chana and urad feature in kosamris, uncooked dishes of pulses soaked in water to soften them, and garnished with mustard seeds and coriander.

Several sweets in the Kannada-language area are based on pulses. Deep-fried pellets of besan flour could yield either a savoury snack after being salted and spiced (now called boondi), or a sweet product by being soaked in sugar syrup in various ways to yield the ladduge,

pinda, motichur, and manoharada-unde. The jilebi (q.v.) is essentially a pulse-based (urad or besan) product, first deep-fried and then soaked in sugar syrup, which finds a place in a Kannada work of AD 1600. Mysore pak (q.v.), the antiquity of which is uncertain, is a besan-based sweet confection cooked in hot ghee.

Combination dishes of pulses and wheat also feature in Kannada literature: purige and hurige, now termed holige, surali-holige (see poli), and mandiges, rice could of course be cooked with pulses: a mung-dhal khichadi (q.v.) is mentioned by this name in AD 1648 even in a Kannada work. The spicy rice-thuvar dhal blend, bisi-bele-huli-anna, is a modern form of the kattogaras abundant in historical Kannada literature.

The historical literature of Gujarat also reflects the enormous diversity of pulse usage in that area. The *Varanaka Samuchaya*, a posthumous work of AD 1520, has fairly extensive lists of both ingredients and prepared items, which are unfortunately mixed up together. Apart from the commoner pulses are listed vatana (peas) and val (sem, the field bean), and a dish of khadi (possibly of curd and besan) spiced with asafoetida. Other historical literature in Gujarati, much of which is of Jain origin, records many more items that contain pulses. The well-known dhokla (q.v.) made of fermented and steamed besan flour is first noted as dukkia in AD 1066. Ground, cooked pulses constituted avaranna or varan, and the baked product vedhami, based again on besan, is first mentioned as veshtika. Numerous fried vadas are noted, from mung, kulthi, and urad; the last was also dipped in sour liquid bases like rice kanji, buttermilk, and curd (the modern dahi-vada). Also from urad is the gharika with holes, fried to a deep brown. The purika, which today has pride of place as the muthiya and chopade, is usually made from besan, though other pulse flours may be used. The vatika was the current vati; urad flour is fermented, spiced, shaped, dried, and put aside, to be fried when needed. The well-known undhiu is a five-vegetable stew which is often served with steamed balls of besan placed on top. Many Gujarati sweetmeats are milk based, but pulses also find a place here. There is a sweet, pulse-stuffed ghari-puri based on maida, and the mohanthal is a halva of besan. Puran-poli is a parata stuffed with a paste of sugar and arhar (thuvar) dhal, an item common to many states of the central belt of India (*see* poli).

While crisp deep-fried snacks, frequently based on besan, are popular all over India, Gujarat has a special generic term for them, nasto. Besan crisps are ganthia, and wafers constitute papdi. The Bhavnagri crisp is solid and cylindrical, the fofda long and flat, and the masala slim and spicy. Sev, made from besan, can be either in the form of long, thin wires, or thicker, short strands, or wafers. A mix of several fried. Another class of rather more substantial snack items constitutes farsan, again largely based on pulses. The fluffy dhokla (q.v.) and

Pumpkin

khaman are fermented rice-besan flour batters, thereafter steamed. The tender, rolled-up besan pancake khandvi is sprinkled over with mustard seeds and green coriander. Deep-fried balls of pulse are termed bhajiyas. Colocasia leaves, coated with besan batter, are first steamed and then fried to yield the rolled-up arvi-na-patra.

pumpkins *See* gourds.

punch Panch in Hindi means five, and first paunch, and then punch, was the name that eventually settled on the five-component drink made up at first of arrack, spices, sugar, lime juice, and water. It was first noted by Mendelslo in AD 1638 as palepunzen in Dutch, and became punch about forty years later. In course of time, numerous recipes for the drink developed, including one with milk in it, described in AD 1823 in Madras. Punch houses were set up in Goa by the Portuguese, and later in Calcutta and Madras.

puri Rolled-out circles of wheat dough, about 10 centimetres across, are deep-fried in hot fat to get swollen puris, which are either eaten hot as part of a meal, or as a snack with dry vegetable preparations like potato bhaji, or with shrikhand. Tiny gole-gappas are almost globular puris, eaten as a festival or roadside snack in north India with a cold, fiery pepper-mustard liquid concoction. The Sanskrit word pura, meaning blown up or filled up, may have occasioned the name; the Sanskrit term purika denoted deep-fried wheat-based or pulse-based snacks (papdi) of a different kind.

puttu A general term for steamed rice items in Kerala and Karnataka. The puttu of Kerala is a breakfast item consisting of alternate layers of rice grits and coconut shreds that are through-steamed in a tube of bamboo or metal, and then pushed out to be eaten with sweetened coconut milk and tiny bananas. The Kodavas of Karnataka have several puttus. A steamed rice mash extruded as fine noodles constitutes nu-puttu (nul means string), once eaten with jaggery water but now with any liquid curry. Steamed balls of mashed, cooked rice constitute kadambuttu, traditionally paired with a spicy pork preparation. Pa-puttu (pal is milk) is a thick batter of rice grits (thari) liberally sprinkled with fresh coconut scrapings and steamed in a metal tray; it is eaten with ghee and honey, or with liquid curries. A dish of finely-ground rice batter also steamed in a tray is thaliya-puttu, which is eaten with a liquid curry of minced-meat balls (kyma-unde).

quail The Sanskrit varthak or varthika, and Hindi bather, meat of the quail is highly rated by Charaka. Amir Khusrau (AD 1253–1325) describes it as a food of the Muslim aristocracy in Delhi, and it figures in early Tamil literature as a delicacy.

Plump, tender quails in season were praised by the British as 'flying pats of butter', eaten after light roasting or poaching so as not to ruin their delicate flavour.

querns *See* grinding.

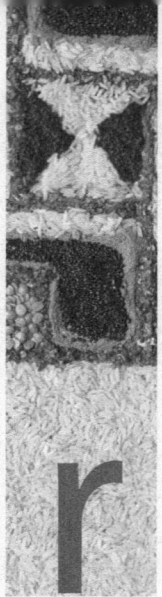

r

rabbit Rabbits as food find scant mention, though old Tamil literature has a reference to poets being feasted by kings on a dish of ragi, with roasted rabbit as a side-dish. The British trapped them wild, or fattened them up in their own gardens for use either in curries or palaos.

radish The radish is a very ancient plant, probably developed in the Fertile Crescent area of domestication. It occurs in later Vedic literature as mulaka, an item to be chewed by way of a digestive after a heavy meal. There are four varieties of *Raphanus sativus*. The type developed in India has little or no fleshy root; it is called the greater radish in Europe, and is conical in shape and white in colour. The types developed in Europe were purple, red, and white, globular in form and with roots, and these are now also grown in India.

The so-called rat-tailed radish is also found in India, with such names as sungra, mungra, and singri; it seems to have originated in South-East Asia, where it is called mougri.

The use of radish as a vegetable is described in literature through the ages. A meal described in the Mahabharata notes a dish of venison, sprinkled over with radish, pomegranate, lemon, and spices. The *Manasollasa* of the twelfth century describes a dish of fried meat and pulses termed kavichandi which incorporates both radish and brinjal. Radish is grown in Kashmir in floating gardens of water-weeds bound with mud from the lake. A current Kashmiri delicacy is gardmuf, which is fish cooked with radish. Radish can be cooked with potatoes, or grated and fried with spices.

In Charaka's classification, the radish belongs to harid or underground food materials. Radish juice is prescribed for fever, while asuta connotes a preserve of radish or gourd in vinegar. Leaves of the mulaka or muli are a valued pot herb, described, for instance, in the *Bhela Samhita* of *c.* AD 100, and commonly eaten fried with spicing.

ragi *Eleusine coracana*, appropriately called the finger millet, derives from Uganda in East Africa where numerous tribal rituals and religious ceremonies are attached to it, and where six of the nine species grow. The cultivated ragi species that came to India was *Eleusine coracana*, a tetraploid form with round seeds. This does not cross with the native Indian wild form, *Eleusine indica* subsp. *indica*, which is diploid and has oblong seeds, and so cultivated ragi developed in isolation in India.

Radish

Wild ragi grains have been found in Surkotada in Kutch, a late Indus Valley site, and in about 1800 BC both wild and cultivated grains were discovered in Hallur on the banks of the river Tungabhadra. Paiyampalli in Tamil Nadu showed ragi at 1390 BC levels, perhaps the cultivated form. Many other food plants of India, jowar, bajra, and lobia, also originated in West Africa and appeared in India around 2000 BC. They may have come to India in several ways: landward across the Sabaean Lane, up the seaward ledge of Africa, by way of the dhow traffic from Arabia, or as part of the direct monsoon-propelled traffic across the Indian Ocean in both directions.

The numerous tribal names for ragi, probably the wild variety, listed in Watt confirm the ancient provenance of this millet. A charming Sanskrit name is nrtta-kondaka or the dancing grain. Sanskrit references to the grain, as rajika or markataka (ragi, from raga or red, is probably colloquial) are rare, but the Bower manuscript (q.v.) of the eighth century AD does have a reference to ragi. It was mentioned as umi, a food in Bihar, a century ago. It was a common grain at one time in the Tamil country, and there are several references to it in early literature. In medical terms ragi is a cold and sweet food.

Ragi is consumed as nachni in southern Maharashtra, and widely as a staple food in Karnataka. The grain is gently roasted (sometimes after it is sprouted and dried), ground, and sieved, and the pinkish flour eaten as a ball or gruel, either sweetened or salted. This flour is also a popular weaning food.

rainwater Sushrutha recommends that cleanly collected rainwater be filtered and stored in a container of gold or silver, or in a boiled clay pot. It was recommended by him for everyday consumption.

raisins The fourteenth-century traveller Ibn Battuta notes that raisins and almonds were products imported from Khurasan into the country, and accordingly he took some along as gifts to the governor of Multan. Indeed both black and white kishmish have always been imported from across the north-west border, the name itself being that of a grape grown around Quetta and Kandahar. To make raisins, bunches of black or green grapes are hung in a darkened room to dry slowly. Sultanas are derived from greenish-brown Thompson seedless grapes; if exposed before drying to burning sulphur for disinfection, the sultanas have a transparent, off-white appearance.

Raisins are used to dress such food items as palao, samosa, halva, kesari-bath, and the like. In medical terms raisins are sweet and cold foods.

Historical literature refers to the use of raisins to temper the raw edge of distilled liquors. Pedro Texeira (AD 1587) says that 'raisins are thrown in arack (arrack), which takes off its roughness and sweetens it'. In Jahangir's court a wine was made by steeping raisins in rice spirit for three to four days, straining the material, and then storing it in an empty barrel for six to eight months; an extract of dates could finally be added to further improve the sweetness and flavour.

In colonial times, Parsi distillers set up units in the island of Uran, near Bombay, to distil liquor from mahua flowers. Occasionally other materials like raisins were also distilled. Vinegar, doubtless of an expensive kind, was made from raisins in Rawalpindi in colonial times.

raitha A class of relishes with a spiced, lightly beaten curd base, with added salt, raw onions, chillies, ginger, and fried mustard seeds, into which may be folded raw diced cucumber, tomatoes, and even banana, pumpkin, and fried besan (boondi) granules. It is an invariable accompaniment to palaos and biriyanis. Rayatha is referred to in the *Manasollasa* of the twelfth century, and regularly in Kannada literature from AD 1485. The palidhya, pacchadi and kicchadi of Karnataka, and the kacholi and kocchumber of Gujarat, are similar curd products.

rajasic One of the three types of guna or inherent temperament, the others being sattvik (q.v.) and tamasic (q.v.). Rajas means energy, which can work either positively towards sattva by the consumption of certain cold, energy-giving foods, notably milk products, or negatively towards tamas, expressed in violence and eroticism, by the regular consumption of hot, spicy, sour, and bitter foods. Lord Brahma, the creator, exemplifies the rajasic temperament.

Rajasthan, food of On the rolling sand-dunes of the dry riverbed of the river Ghaggar (believed to be the fabled lost river Saraswathi), archaeologists uncovered a perfectly prepared field, ploughed in two directions at right angles to each other—dated 2800 BC! Even today in the area horsegram is grown in the wider-spaced north-south furrows, and low mustard plants on the more closely spaced east-west furrows, so that shadows of the tall plants do not stunt the growth of the shorter ones. Of course the actual crops grown nearly five thousand years ago may have been different. Hardy crops have always been grown in the area. Excavations in the Indus Valley town of Kalibangan revealed the hardier crop barley in much greater quantity than wheat, whereas the reverse was true for sites slightly more northern, like Harappa and Rupar. Jowar, another hardy crop, has been found at Ahar in 1725 BC strata and more profusely in 1550 BC and 1270 BC

layers. In even later strata (1200–1000 BC) another sturdy crop, bajra, was recovered, Both these are still major staples in the area.

An early text from Rajasthan, the *Kanhadade-Prabanda* written by Padmanabha in AD 1455, describes the food served at the table of this ruler as 'sev, suhali, manda, papads, khajor, salan, badi, lapsika of the panchadari variety, kansar, dhan and many other delicious dishes'. Perhaps the ruler was a Jain or Vaishnavite, which would explain the lack of animal food. The cuisine of the area at present has numerous rotis. Bhakri are crisp products made from bajra or jowar on a griddle, and there is even a besan roti with just a little wheat flour added to bind the dough. Dopatris are thin, soft rotis that come apart in two circles because of the style of rolling the dough. Dough with

An assortment of Rajasthani food

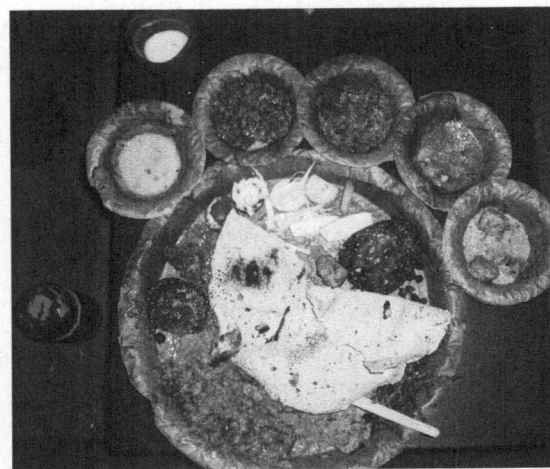

spinach, green chillies, and onion is rolled out to yield the thava-roasted missi-roti. Also thava-roasted are the round, slightly flattened phefras which are finished on live coals, and eaten with ghee. A distinctive type is the batti, a word derived from vatya in Sanskrit, a hard, roasted ball of wheat which is cracked open and eaten with plenty of ghee. Mung and besan flour are the basis of numerous crisp-fried savouries like the mangodi, gatti, and papdi, sometimes with methi incorporated. Khelada is thick or thin papads, and kachori is a spicy, stuffed wheat envelope. Both vadas and dahi-vadas are made, besides spicy farsan snacks, as in Gujarat (*see* Gujarat, food of). Many vegetables are sun-dried for year-round use as gattey-ke-sag, as are certain berries (like khair and debra), fruit (bijoda), stems and roots (garmar), and even certain aromatic twigs (sanghar). Sweet items are mostly pulse-based, like besan-burfi, sheera of mung dhal, and churna laddus. Rajasthan has an exceptionally high proportion of vegetarians—about 60 per cent of the population. But members of the royalty in Rajasthan are Rajputs who have always eaten meat and have a partiality for pork. The *Manasollasa* written by King Someshwara of Kalyana, himself a kshatriya, describes how a whole pig was roasted on an open fire. Pieces of the roast were then carved out, broiled on

live charcoal, and eaten after being seasoned with rock salt and black pepper, or with sour lemon juice. In medieval Udaipur, it was customary for a young pig to be roasted on a spit called shula in a sacrifice known as the shulagava. Strips of meat were then carved out, marinated in spiced curd, placed with ghee in a wrapper and baked, followed by grilling on a skewer. Such elaborate preparations of pork dishes are described in detail in the *Manasollasa*, and yield various items like sunthakas, chakkalikas, mandaliya, or 'khanda of vapa (*see also* meat dishes).

rajmah *Phaseolus vulgaris* is the commonest bean of South America, going back 7000 years in Peru and Mexico. It is not even mentioned in India a century ago by Watt in his exhaustive works. It was first grown by French colonialists in their Indian settlements, and then by the British, first as a garden and later as a commercial crop. The name rajmah appears to be one instance of transfer of an already existing term, namely the Sanskrit rajmasha (q.v.), to a new variety which it somewhat resembled. Similarly, the soybean when it first came, again about a century ago, was for a time called raj-shimbi, from shimbi, used for the hyacinth bean (sem, avarai). The rajmah commonly grown is a large, shiny bean which is black, brown, white, or mottled, but over a hundred varieties with an extraordinary range of variations in colour, shape, and size have been raised in India. The rajmah is cooked and eaten as a pulse, and canned as baked beans in tomato sauce. It has also been called the haricot bean, kidney bean, and navy bean.

rajmasha A grain first mentioned in literature around the start of the Christian era or slightly earlier, and then by the medical authorities, Charaka and Sushrutha. Literally meaning large-masha (that is, urad or blackgram), rajmasha is thought to refer to the lobia or cowpea. When the new kidney bean, *Phaseolus vulgaris*, came from South America to India about a century ago, it came to be called rajmah (q.v.) in Hindi.

rape-mustard *See* mustard.

rasa Rasa or taste is the keystone of Indian dietetics. There are six rasas: sweet (madhura), sour (amla), salty (lavana), pungent (katu), bitter (tikta), and astringent (kasftya). Each taste is believed to consist of a combination of some two of the five basic elements, namely earth, water, fire, air, and ether, and these pairs have been worked out by observation of their action on the body. Thus the sweet taste, madhura, is made up of earth and water; it is a builder of body tissues, which are themselves formed from earth and water. The dosha (q.v.) kapha is also made up of earth and water, and a sweet-tasting substance will strengthen this dosha, but will weaken the dosha pitta (made from the single element fire) and the dosha vata (made from air and ether). A sour substance (earth and fire) will similarly strengthen the kapha and pitta doshas, but will weaken vata. The final outcome depends on the interaction of the elements present in the six tastes with those present in the three doshas in the body.

A second important concept is that of after-taste or vipaka. This is the rasa that is left after digestion. The six original mouth tastes are reduced to just three after the process of digestion. Sweet and salt tastes both become sweet. Pungent, bitter, and astringent tastes all turn into a pungent vipaka. The sour taste remains sour. A sweet vipaka will strengthen kapha attributes, a pungent aftertaste vata qualities, and a sour vipaka will boost pitta characteristics (*see also* ayurveda, dosha).

rasa, rasam Rasa in Sanskrit means extract, and Charaka, for example, applies the term to extracts of sugar-cane and cereals. Rasam in the Tamil country is a thin extract of thuvar dhal spiced in various ways, such as with pepper, tamarind, lime, tomato, curry leaves, etc. It is poured on rice as the first course of a south Indian meal; rice and sambhar (a thicker pulse preparation with vegetables) constitute the second course, and rice and curds the last one. Rasam is also called saar, saaru, chaaru and pulusu in other southern languages. The British colonial adopted it as a pungent soup called mulligatawny (q.v.).

rasogolla, rasmalai *See* Bengali sweets.

rava Grits of wheat, which can be in coarse or fine form for different end-uses. Other names are suji, semolina, and cream-of-wheat. Rava was traditionally made in stone chakkis by soaking wheat for six to twelve hours, then drying it partially, and grinding it, followed by winnowing or sieving. When mechanized roller flour mills came into India about a century ago, their settings could be adjusted to yield different proportions of various wheat products. The outturn of rava could for example be varied from about 5 to as much as 18 per cent, depending upon the extent of local demand.

Rava can be employed in several ways. In south India, it is lightly roasted and then cooked with some water to make uppuma, generally eaten for breakfast. For another breakfast item, the rava dosai, equal parts of rava and rice flour are made into a batter, and then shallow pan-fried. A steamed item is the rava idli (*see* idli). Sweet items from rava include a rava unde or rava laddu of toasted rava bound with sugar solution, a halva, a rava payasam with milk, and, perhaps commonest of all, a kesari-bath (q.v.). In old Kannada literature, the payasam is termed payasa, the laddu ghrtapura, and the kesari-bath shali-anna.

relishes Variations in taste and texture in an Indian meal are provided by relishes of several types. Pickles (q.v.) can be hot, sour, or sweet. The chutney (q.v.) is usually a freshly ground and uncooked item, though in later colonial terms it came to stand for certain sweet preserves (q.v.), which included the morraba (q.v.). Among crisp-fried relishes are papads (q.v.), vadas (q.v.), and murukku (q.v.). Special Karnataka relishes are the crisp balaka, sandige, and happala, and the raw kosamri (*see* Karnataka, food of), while Gujarati food (q.v.) has the kocchumber and pralehaka.

rice A primitive wild aquatic grass is postulated to have existed in the huge land mass called Gondwanaland which, some 10 million years ago, split up to yield the present land areas of Africa, India, Australia, and South America. From this grass arose two cultigens, *Oryza glaberrima*, which is African rice, and *Oryza sativa*, Asiatic rice. The latter was derived from an annual wild form termed *O. nivara* (given to it from the Sanskrit terra nivara for wild rice); this annual itself arose from a wild perennial form called *O. rufipogon*, which is widely distributed in deep-water swamps all over south and South-East Asia, south China and Oceania. There are also numerous intergrading hybrids between *O. saliva*, the cultivated form, and its two wild relatives. The continuous distribution of all these forms over so enormous an area had led to many conflicting claims in the past regarding the origin of rice, but it is now believed that 'the area including north-eastern India, northern Bangladesh, and the triangle adjoining Burma, Thailand, Laos, Vietnam, and southern China appears to be the primary centre of domestication'.

In the event, three ecogeographic races developed, named indica, japonica, and javanica.

The terraced fields of Kashmir, so typical of rice cultivation, have been placed at 10,000 BC. Was rice grown on them then, or was it perhaps colocasia tubers? Wild rice grains have been found at Chopani-Mando, and both wild and cultivated rice has been found at 5000 BC levels (by radio-carbon dating) in Koldiwha, near Allahabad. Regionwise, the earliest finds of cultivated rice (apart from the very early Koldiwha find) occur in the north and west of India dated about 2300 to 1900 BC, a couple of centuries later in the Indo-Gangetic plain, and at a distinctly later date—1400–1000 BC—in the Dekhan, suggesting a rather late arrival of rice in south India, after its domestication in the well-watered Himalayan plains. Thereafter the rice plant spread all over India wherever there was a fertile alluvial plain, helped in its spread by

the efforts of humans attracted by its prolific grain yields. Also, the discovery of rice as the only staple in 1300 BC layers at Hastinapura near Meerut suggests that there was enough water then to support the growth of rice in places where only wheat now grows.

Rice is not mentioned in the *Rigveda*, but innumerable names turn up in Sanskrit literature after its first mention in the *Yajurveda*, reflecting the sustained development of rice varieties. The greatest praise was reserved for the winter varieties called shali, which were all transplanted. There is mention of rakta-shali, of kalama-shali which was hard, white, and flavoured, and of mahashali, the most highly regarded of all varieties of rice. This plump rice was grown in Magadha and reserved for royalty or honoured guests. As early as in 1900 BC long-grained rice, a type highly prized even today, was cultivated at Ahar near Jaipur. There is a tradition that fragrant basmati rice varieties were brought to the Dehra Dun valley by Amir Dost Mohamad of Afghanistan when he was exiled there by the British in 1840. South India has fairly long-established fragrant rice varieties called jeerige-sambha, rascadam, and chingari.

A medieval text from Bengal, the *Shunya Purana*, states that fifty varieties of rice were even then grown in Bengal. More recently

1500 morphologically distinct varieties of rice have been found in just one district (Jeypore) of Orissa. The varieties in India may well number 200,000.

To early European visitors, rice was an unusual crop. Aristobolus, who accompanied Alexander to India in 327 BC, described it as 'a strange plant, standing in water and sown in beds; the plant is 4 cubits in height, has many ears and yields a large produce'. Megasthenes, who shortly after that was in Chandragupta Maurya's court in Pataliputra (Patna), noted how rice was eaten: 'When Indians are at supper, a table is placed before each person, this being like a tripod. There is placed on it a golden bowl, into which they first put rice, boiled as one would barley (the Greek dish chondros), and then they add many dainties prepared according to Indian recipes.' Edward Terry noted that the principal dish of the poor was 'rice boiled with some ginger, to which they add a little pepper and butter', while wealthier people had 'rice boiled with pieces of flesh, and boiled many other ways'. And Bernier, in about AD 1666, spoke of 'fields of rice' in Kashmir, and, in Bengal, of 'the endless number of channels, cut in bygone days from that river with endless labour lined on both sides with extensive fields of rice, sugar, corn ...'

Once rice spread across the subcontinent it became the dominant cereal staple, displacing barley in the north and millet elsewhere. In Vedic times, it was cooked with water to yield odana (later called bhatka, and currently bath), or with milk to give kshira (now kheer, q.v.), or with sesame seed and milk to yield krsara (perhaps a forerunner of the khichdi of the present).

By the start of the Christian era, works by the Indian medical authorities show that rice reigned supreme, with barley a distant second, and wheat barely mentioned except as a winter food. Winter, summer, and autumn rice was catalogued. While all varieties of shali or winter rice were extolled, disease-curing properties were attributed to red or rakta-shali. Shastika, the short-duration summer variety, was considered nourishing, while the poorest in nutritional terms was the monsoon rice vrihi. Old rice was more easy to digest than new rice, and raw rice the least easy to digest.

The *Manasollasa* of the twelfth century AD reflects a resurgence of numerous wheat-based items. Indeed rice in the form of flour appears only as a supplementary item, to be mixed with acid-precipitated milk solids, fried in ghee, and coated in sugar to yield kshira-prakara. When this mass was shaped into the likeness of peacock eggs an item called morendaka was obtained. The

Shivatattvaratnakara written by King Basavaraja of the Keladi kingdom, which ran along the west coast, notes eight kinds of shali, here used as a synonym for rice. In the kanji (or liquid residue) of ordinary rice was boiled the rare bamboo (q.v.) rice (called rajannaakki or the rice of kings) to yield shudodana, which is thought to resemble thumbe flowers. Tamarind cooked in oil with a dash of asafoetida was recommended for pouring over rice as a 'finish'. Ordinary boiled rice could be exalted to a feast dish by dressing it with papads, pumpkin peel crisps, coconut gratings, lime juice, roasted urad dhal, and the like to give various katta-yogaras. These ogaras (*see* below) also feature prominently in Kannada literature. A crisp relish described by the royal author was puri-vilangayi, to make which grits of rice and mung dhal were roasted together, spiced, flavoured with camphor, made into marbles the size of areca nuts using rice flour as a binder, and then deep-fried. Brinjal, fried with rice grits and chopped onion, could form one style of filling in a folded turmeric leaf, which when steamed yielded a class of dainties called pude.

The adjoining Kannada-speaking area has a rich literature in food from the tenth to the eighteenth centuries AD, and rice of course features extensively. Four variations of a cooked rice-ghee combination, flavoured with

garlic and salt, called kattogara, are illustrative. Crushed papad was mixed with the dish to yield one variation, crisp-fried sandiges (q.v.) made of ash gourd peels another, and various cooked greens yielded yet others. A mung dhal khichadi is mentioned by the latter name. Further changes were obtained by mixing in lime, huli (sambhar), turmeric, tamarind, and the powders of roasted rice and chana. Curd rice that would keep for several days was made by cooking the rice in water, in which the leaves of tulasi (*Ocimum sanctum*) or madala (*Citrus medico*) had earlier been boiled, before folding in the curd. Other rice–pulse combinations of Karnataka were the steamed idli and kadubu (these are listed as separate entries). Sweet items based on rice included various payasas (q.v.) of rice, rice-wheat, and rice-vermicelli, and a deep-fried delicacy of rice flour and jaggery, now called athirasa.

Tamil literature (q.v.) goes back to slightly before the start of the Christian era, with the bulk of it spanning the third to the sixth centuries AD. Rice is of course the main cereal, mostly eaten boiled, but sometimes with aromatics sprinkled on it. A dressing of tamarind yielded puli-kari (puli-sadam), and a dressing of sesame seeds and sugar yielded chitrannam. Rice could be cooked with pulses (the present pongal, q.v.), or with 'fatted meat', or could be 'well-cooked with ghee'. Rice stored for three years was considered healthy. Pungalarisi was paddy parboiled by immersion in hot water, which was dried and then pounded. Both the ageing of paddy, and its parboiling, were probably means of hardening the product to obtain better yields of whole rice on milling. Cooked rice was kept overnight in cold water; the rice was consumed, and the liquid drunk as the first input of the following day. Rice gruel was soured overnight to yield a beverage; this practice, in the Aryan view, was tantamount to eating stale food and, according to the *Baudhyayana Dharmasutra*, was very specific to southern brahmins. In the home of an Andanar or Aryan brahmin, 'rice which bears a bird's name (rajannan)' was served with 'chips of the green fruit of the kommatimalula shrub, peppered and spread with curry leaf and fried in fresh cow butter ... with excellent sliced tender mango pickle'.

Rice was also transformed into a series of appetizing foods. The appam (q.v.), mentioned in the *Perumpanuru* was a pancake baked on a concave clay vessel, a popular food eaten drenched in milk. So was the idi-appam, thread-like extrusions of a dough of boiled and mashed rice, which in Chola times (*c.* the tenth century AD) was eaten, as it is now, with sweetened coconut milk. Other forms of shallow pan-fried snacks were the dosai (q.v.) and adai, both based on rice combined with pulses. The *Mathuraikkanchi* contains a reference to the deep-fried sweet-filled moodagam with its rice casing. In slightly later Chola times appears the athirasam, a dark-brown, deep-fried patty of rice flour sweetened with jaggery. The idli (q.v.), though a popular breakfast food today, is an extremely recent entrant in Tamil literature. (For other rice products, *see* parching, and puffed grains.)

Rice gruel, kanjika or kanji, fermented slightly to acidity overnight, constituted a beverage particularly popular in the south and east of the country. The cereal was also a source of alcoholic beverages (q.v.). Sura was probably made in the Indus Valley from barley and rice flour. In Vedic writings, it is spoken of in derogatory terms as a drink of the mlecchas or natives. The word later acquired the generic connotation of a strong distilled liquor. Masara was likewise rice or barley flour fermented with added spices and then filtered clear; it may also have been pre-Aryan in origin. Kilala was a cereal-fermented, sweetened drink, and kashaya a fermented extract of rice meal and flowers. Prasanna, whose name suggests that it was a clear drink, was fermented rice flour with spices, tree barks, and fruit. In Surra limes spirits derived from the flour of cereals were not permitted to kshatriyas and vaishyas, and were thus obviously regarded as non-elite products. Rice liquor could be strong. Thus in Jahangir's court, rice spirit was put into empty wine casks from Europe together with water and sugar; dregs from other barrels were added, to yield in due course a clear spirit. This was called a 'made' wine and when given to Sir Thomas Roe, the British emissary, made him sneeze, to the amusement of the court. Jahangir in his memoirs describes a strong rice liquor called acchi which he first tasted in Pigli near Attuck, which was fermented for two to three and even for up to ten years. In south India, apart from palm toddy and arrack, rice was also a source of wine. Liquor was brewed in 'strong-mouthed jars' from both paddy and rice; pounded, germinated paddy was stated to yield 'after two days and two nights a high-flavoured wine'. The flavour of wine was enhanced by burying it underground after it had been filled in the hollows of stout bamboo stems. Thoppi was home-brewed rice liquor, and wealthier folk fermented rice in the presence of fragrant flowers such as the dhataki (*Woodfordia fructicosa*).

In medical terms, rice was the classic 'sweet' food and generally a 'heavy' one; only varieties of short-duration rice and red rice were classed as 'light'. Rice strengthens all the three doshas (q.v.) and is considered cooling, diuretic, and strengthening.

Only diabetics and those with stomach ulcers are advised to reduce their consumption of rice. In relation to the Indian cooking ethos, rice is the prime example of a plough-raised food, anna or krista-pachya. When cooked in a ritual cooking pot, the sthali, in the sanctum of the kitchen, it yields an everyday kaccha food (q.v.) which can be eaten in the same area only by the family. When observing a fast, or when under a vow, rice will frequently be given up in favour of wild or uncultivated food items. Rice plays a part in most domestic rituals. At an orthodox Kanyakubja wedding, white rice is offered to the silvery moon. At every wedding, rice will be sprinkled on the couple as a symbol of good fortune and fertility. A mixture of rice, turmeric, and vermilion, termed akshata, is specially auspicious. At an annaprasanna ceremony, feeding a child rice and milk is believed to enhance its future glory. There are festivals associated with the sowing, transplanting, and harvesting of rice. The Pongal festival of Tamil Nadu (*see* pongal), the Onam festival of Kerala, and the Huthri of Kodagu are all harvest festivals that centre on rice. The *Jataka* tales have references to the payment of rice as wages to both agricultural and domestic labourers, and as tax by farmers to the king.

ridge gourd Probably native to India is the Sanskrit koshataki, first mentioned in the *Arthashastra* and now called (kali-) thorai and pirankai. *Luffa acutangla* is a strongly ribbed, green, tender vegetable, which when dried yields a fibrous skin brush. An even larger sponge brush is derived from *L. aegyptiaca*, the (ghia-) thorai or dilpasand.

roasting Roasting meat on spits is an ancient Indian practice. The Vedic sacrifices detailed in the *Sutras* employed, among a host of other utensils (q.v.), shulas or roasting spits in the shulagava rites. The 162nd hymn of the *Rigveda* describes in detail the ritual steps to be followed in sacrificing a horse, in roasting it whole, and finally in serving and distributing the roasted animal (*see* ashvamedha). The Mahabharata has a graphic depiction of a picnic meal at which young buffalo calves were roasted whole on spits while being basted with ghee. The *Manasollasa* written in the twelfth century AD by King Someshwara of the western Chalukya dynasty gives elaborate directions for roasting a whole pig, after which pieces were carved out and dressed in different ways to get several spicy dishes. Till recent times, royal rulers in Rajasthan continued this tradition (*see* Rajasthan, food of).

Literature in the Tamil language from between the third and sixth centuries, the Sangam period, is full of references to roast meat. Poets talk of 'hot meat, roasted on the points of spits' and in the *Purananuru* of 'fine large pieces of fat meat roasted on iron spikes'.

Elsewhere we learn that whole roasted animals were valued for their taste.

Grilling on a griddle, as in making a chapati, also constitutes a form of roasting (*see* griddle; grilling). So does exposure to heat of material kept in a potsherd or a clay vessel, as in baking an auspicious purodasha cake on a garhyapatya in different shapes (*see* baking).

rock salt One of the five important types of salt (q.v.) in India recognized by medical authorities was saindhava-lavana, meaning salt from Sindh. Such rock salt was probably always obtained by simple open mining from the vast salt ranges in Punjab and the north-western frontiers of the country. A picnic meal mentioned in the Mahabharata describes a dish of buffalo meat 'fried in ghee, seasoned with acids, rock salt and fragrant leaves'. A dish of pork described in the *Manasollasa* specifies the use of rock salt for salting the meat. Sushrutha prescribes rock salt as the salt of choice for everyday consumption, since in the medical view it has the best therapeutic effects of any form of salt. Though most salt forms are considered 'heavy' and slightly 'hot' in ayurvedic terms, rock salt is described as 'light' and 'cooling', with a calming effect on all the three doshas (q.v.). It is reputed to strengthen the eyesight and stimulate the digestion.

Around the time of Independence, rock salt constituted about 9 per cent of the total salt production in the country (*see* salt).

Rome, contacts with The incursion of Alexander in 327 BC brought the Greeks to India from across the land borders, though earlier too there had been some trade contacts with the north-western part of India (*see* Greek contacts). In AD 40, a Greek sailor, Hippalos, came to realize (for the first time for a European), the phenomenon of the monsoon winds to and from India (the word itself being the Arabic mausam), which resulted in fanning the trade that already existed between south India and Europe. The *Periplus Maris Erythraei* or *Circumnavigation of the Erythrean Sea*, written in the first century AD by a posthumous Greek sailor posted in Alexandria, contained a graphic description from personal knowledge of how India's 'seas ebb and flow with tides of extraordinary strength, which increase both at new and full moon, and for three days after each, but fall intermediately'. The exports described in the *Periplus* were ivory from Dosarene (Orissa), muslin from Maisolia (Macchilipatnam), pearls from Korkai in the Pandyan kingdom, and pepper from Muziris, the port in the Chera kingdom. The

other items exported were perfumes, herbs, sesame oil, coconut oil, and butyron (q.v.) packed in leather skins (to be used by wealthy people in Europe for cooking and sacrifices), gold from Kongunadu, sandalwood and betel from the west coast, spikenard grass (*see* ginger grass) from the Ganges, diamonds, rubies, coral and tortoise shell, aghil (a black aromatic wood), and salt. The cloth exported was particularly fine, being described in Tamil literature as 'webs of woven wind' 'sloughs of serpents', 'vapours from milk', and 'silk in the web'. This trade was with Greece and Rome, and the term yavana (q.v.) was applied to people of both countries in Tamil literature written in the first few centuries of the Christian era. They were described as people of 'fine physique and strange speech', whose 'well-built ships rode the waves of foaming rivers', loaded (among other things) with 'different kinds of grain, white salt, sweetened tamarind and salted fish'. This description is contained in the *Mathuraikkanchi* while the *Pattinapalai* talks of 'well-weighed goods in abundance being exported with the Tiger mark (of the then ruling dynasty) impressed on them so as to recover customs duty'.

Against these exports were imported gold (always an item of insatiable demand in India), brass and lead, topaz, fine horses and Italian wine. Tamil poetry speaks of the kings of the south imbibing 'cool, green and fragrant (Italian) wine, served in golden goblets held by bright-bangled girls'. About fifty years ago was excavated at Arikamedu near Pondicherry (the Pouduke of early Roman writers) a Roman warehouse 50 metres long, with a ramp running from it to what was probably a quay. Found in the warehouse in large numbers were two-handled Roman amphorae used for transporting wine; some of these bore the marks of Roman potters, like VIBII, CAMURI, and ITTA, which firmly dated the warehouse to the first and second centuries AD.

After a lull of almost a thousand years, Italians started to visit India again. John of Monte Corvino, who was afterwards appointed by the Pope as Archbishop of Peking, came overland by way of Iran in AD 1292, and spent thirteen months here. He described south India as a land of 'perpetual summer', noted ginger with its enormous roots, cinnamon bark from a tree that resembled the laurel, and the 'wonderful Indian nuts', obviously coconuts, growing on trees that resembled date palms. The people of India were scrupulously clean, consumed milk and rice, ate no meat and drank no wine. Marco Polo (AD 1 294) noted that the best quality of ginger came from Kollam; both cinnamon and ginger grew in the Pandya country, while Bengal

produced spikenard (q.v.), ginger, and sugar. Odoric of Pordenone, a Franciscan friar, was in Surat around AD 1325, after which he sailed round south India to China. He described the fire worship of the Parsis, the veneration of the ox by the brahmins, the pepper plant (which resembled a vine in its growth and its clusters of fruit, and the ivy in its leaves), the ginger of Kollam, and the preparation of sago from palms in Borneo. Another traveller, Giovanni di Marignolli, on his return from China overland with two others, all sent by the Pope, spent sixteen months in Kollam 'where all the pepper in the world grows'. He described its growth in gardens, and the steps involved in its ripening and gathering, 'struck down with staves and collected on linen cloth spread out beneath'.

The next few Italian visitors had Vijayanagar, then in the heydey of its glory, as their objective. Nicolo dei Conti, a Venetian merchant, came with his wife and children, and noted that it was a great city, with a circumference of 60 miles and walls that carried up to the mountains. Ludovico di Varthema, who was in Vijayanagar from AD 1505–8, took a sole, ten-year copyright from the Pope before he left home for an account of his travels, well aware of the blatant plagiarism of earlier writers. He noted the abundance of produce in Kananoor, and observed that while brahmins could not eat animal food without losing caste, the Nair or landed gentry was permitted venison, goats, fruits, and fish. All other castes ate any kind of meat, even mice, but not beef, and all classes were very fond of chewing betel leaves. Varthema described a number of fruits: the sweet orange, three varieties of banana (long, short-and-sweet, and bitter), and the jackfruit, the taste of which intrigued him (*see* jackfruit). So small and delicate were the scales and weights in use that even a hair would turn them. Buying and selling prices were negotiated under cover of a cloth, using finger pressures alternately by both parties. The practice continues to this day at oilseed auctions. Of Vijayanagar itself he wrote: 'There are immense parks for hunting and fowling, with the best of air, great fertility, wealth of merchandise, and abundance of all possible delicacies, a second paradise.' And of Kozhikode: 'The orderly nature of the town and people and the manner in which justice was strictly administered, was most admirable.'

roselle *Hibiscus sabdariffa*, red roselle or lal-ambadi, is a beautiful plant with shining green leaves and stems which set off the glossy red calyces. These are used as a souring agent in curries, as a thickening material in jellies, and as the source of a pleasant, red, acid beverage. It seems to have been domesticated as early as in 4000 BC in western Sudan. Later two varieties evolved, one a bushy shrub for the purpose of eating, termed var. sabdariffa, and the other, var. altissima, a 5-metre tall, unbranched shrub for use as a source of fibre.

A related species is *Hibiscus cannabinus*, called nalida, ambadi, and gonkuru in India, and mesta and kenaf elsewhere. It appears to have originated in Angola, Ethiopia or Sudan, though its fibre is given such names as Deccan Hemp and Bimli Jute. The leaves are used in the Andhra region to make the popular sour gonkuru chutney.

roti The generic Indian name for baked, grilled, or roasted products mostly based on wheat flour, but also applied to such products derived from rice, jowar, bajra, maize, and so on. The word roti resembles the word karoti mentioned in the medieval *Ramcharitamanas* (*c.* AD 1600) of Tulsidas, while the sixteenth-century *Bhavaprakasa*, a medical text written by Bharatamishra has the Sanskritized rotika, so the word roti may only be of recent colloquial origin.

Some unusual kinds of rotis made from wheat which are described in Kannada literature of between the tenth and eighteenth centuries AD are of historic interest. The methods of roasting were themselves quite unusual. Baking between plates,

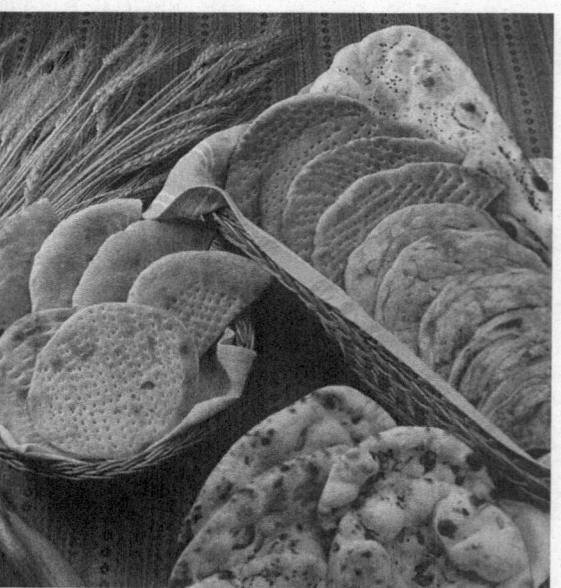

An assortment of rotis

with glowing embers both below and above, gave the mucchala-roti, while the kivichu-roti was roasted on a thava (called kavali in Kannada) with a little ghee. Several thava-roasted rotis could be stacked one over the other using a stick to pierce them, and these were flavoured with ghee, sugar, edible camphor, and palmyra (male) flowers to yield the chucchu-roti. A stack of ghee-smeared circles mounted one over the other, savudu-roti, was baked under cover of a cup. A cup cover above, live coals below and a ball of dough within, yielded uduru-roti, from which the blackened crust was peeled off before consumption. Mandige or mandage was a delicate baked product; when baked on a heated tile (called kenchu)

it was termed white-mandige; when overheated and still very hot it was ushnavarta-mandige, which when exposed to air became vayuputta-mandige. The stuffing could be varied; sugar and ghee yielded khanda-mandige, and multi-layered fillings of cooked chana, coconut shreds, dates, and raisins yielded a mandige version called perane-hurige. Other huriges, puriges, and holiges of the Karnataka area are described elsewhere (see poli). The mandige or mande made today in Belgaum is a very large and fine parata stuffed with finely ground sugar containing cardamom powder, baked on a large upturned clay pot, and folded when hot and flexible into a rectangle that hardens as it cools. Yet another sweet-stuffed wheat roti is made by placing, in a ball casing of wheat dough, a mixture of broken-up mandige pieces with milk, cream, coconut milk, mango juice, and sugar; the ball is baked on a hot tile within a seal of dough (a process termed kanika in Kannada), and when done, the upper crust is sliced off and ghee and sugar added before eating the delicacy, called bhojanandika-roti. Wheat dough made with sweetened milk or cream, rolled out in circles and deep-fried, yielded the yeriappa and babara.

Wheat-based rotis in current Indian cuisines fall into three categories. First are the kinds dry-roasted on thavas, then come those either pan-fried using a little fat, or deep-fried in a kadhai. Finally there are products which are leavened and baked in ovens and tandoors. Dry-roasted forms of roti include the common chapati, roasted dry on a hot thava (griddle), and sometimes puffed out to a phulka by brief contact with live coals. A very thin chapati of Gujarat is the rotlee. The rumali (literally scarf) is also thin; it is pressed out with the fingers and tossed, never rolled, till it achieves an enormous size, after which it is roasted on a large upturned thava, and then folded over many times to a manageable size. Also thava-roasted are the round, slightly flattened phefras of Rajasthan which again are placed briefly on live coals and eaten with ghee. The bhatia of the same state is a popular peasant food, and do-patris, also of Rajasthan, are soft, thin rotis that come apart as two circles because of the style of rolling the dough. Dough that contains spinach yields distinctive rotis; the missi-roti, roasted dry on a thava and flaky in texture, has, besides spinach, green chillies, and onions in the dough. The khakras of Gujarat are kneaded with milk and water, and are very thin, brittle products that keep well and are carried by Gujarati travellers. Rajasthan has the unusual ball-like batti, roasted dry in an oven, and then on live coals; it is broken open and doused in ghee before

consumption. Bafflas are cooked in a soup of masoor dhal and then roasted.

Wheat products, after being rolled out, can be either pan-fried using just a little fat, or deep-fried. Paratas are the commonest form of the first kind, often rolled out square or triangular in shape rather than round. The dough can be mixed with seasoned vegetables like potatoes, cauliflower, spinach, or methi. Or a stuffing of vegetables or chopped eggs may be placed on the parata which is then folded over and lightly fried. Both types are frequently eaten with curds. A stuffing of besan gives birahi, with an unusual taste and texture. Deep-fried products are exemplified by round, swollen puris, and the tiny, almost globular gole-gappas which are a delectable relish when eaten with a fiery pepper-water liquid. The lucchis of Bengal are larger and thicker and not as fully puffed as puris, since some fat is kneaded into the dough. They can also be stuffed, for example with a mash of cooked urad dhal placed at the centre of the ball of dough before it is rolled out. The dough of the bhathura is allowed to ferment using yoghurt, and then rolled out to give a layery fried product. The khjuru or khajur is made with added sugar and poppy seeds, and deep-fried to crispness, resembling in effect fried slabs of a western bread loaf.

The third class of wheat products is those which are leavened and baked, either in closed and heated ovens, or in Indian-style tandoors, which are open, lined, glowing ovens with live coals placed at the bottom. Naan is made of maida (q.v.), the white inner flour of wheat, which is leavened before baking to yield a thick elastic product, sometimes sprinkled with tiny black kalonji (nigella) seeds. Use of more ghee in the batter gives the even more elastic kulcha, which is also sometimes stuffed; use of milk in the dough yields the sweetish and more powdery sheermal, rather like a round, flat bun. Both are eaten in Hyderabad, Amritsar, and Kashmir, which also has the chewy girda, the sesame-encrusted tschvaru and the soft bakirkhani, all eaten for breakfast with tea. Enriched with butter, and crisp, is the khasta, a word also used to designate a type of parata.

Western-style oven baking has yielded leavened breads that are unique to this country. Ordinary loaf bread is called double-roti in India, since it was made in jointed sections. Pao is a Portuguese contribution, rather like an elastic bun, which is baked as four sections that can be broken apart. The gutli is a very hard, round, or rectangular well-risen roll with a brown crust, and the crusty peti-pao (literally box-bread) looks like an ancient treasure chest. There is a large commercial naan which is vended after it is cut into wedges. In fact all these oven-baked items are sold on the street for consumption as on-the-spot snacks, with vegetables (bhaji), boiled eggs, minced meat, or chicken as an accompaniment (*see* also poli).

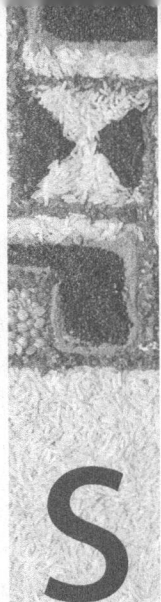

S

sacrifice Sacrifice was a basic component of Vedic life, which gave way in later Hinduism to the puja. Kings and chieftains performed the great sacrifices described in the *Rigveda*, which involved the use of soma juice (q.v.), like the rajasuya at the start of a reign or the asvamedha (q.v.) towards its end, or the ajamedha at intervals. These were expensive and elaborate rites which could even spread over a year or more. The ordinary householder was expected to perform five sacrifices daily. These were the worship of the world spirit, Brahman, by recitation of the Vedas; of the ancestors, by libations of water and periodical shraddhas; of the gods, by libations of ghee; of living things, by scattering grain for their consumption; and of fellow-men, through hospitality. These did not involve animal sacrifice, but the latter was sometimes carried out to appease the gods and spirits on special occasions, such as at a funeral, at harvest time, when building a house, before felling a tree, and so on.

In relation to food, the purpose of animal sacrifice was to sanctify the meat and render it suitable for later consumption. The Vedas describe fifty animals as fit for sacrifice and by implication for consumption. The elaborate aja-panchandam rite of the *Rigveda* describes the sacrifice of a male goat (*see* ajamedha), and its 162nd hymn details the ritual for the sacrifice of a horse (*see* ashvamedha). Various gods were propitiated with specific animals, like a dwarf ox for Vishnu or a red cow for Rudra. The *Yajurveda* is no more than a compilation of mantras or prayers to be recited by a priest at various sacrifices. The *Brahmana*s relate the ritual to the sacred text, and the *Aranyakas* explain the symbolism of the sacrifice. Thus the *Brhad Upanishad* explains: 'Dawn is the head of the sacrificial horse, the sun its eye, the wind its breath, fire its mouth ... and sound its voice.' Domestic rituals are delineated in the *Sutras*; thus the sacrifice of a cow at a cremation is described in the *Ashvalayana Sutra*, with details of how the various dissected organs are to be placed on the corpse just before its immolation.

Animal sacrifices in rituals were condemned by Buddha and Mahavira, and to strong effect by the Buddhist emperor Ashoka in his far-flung edicts. Ingenious prohibitions on the killing of animals found their way into the *Dharmasutra* texts, and eventually Vedic thinkers like Shankara, Madhva, and Ramanuja substituted pumpkins, coconuts, and animals made of flour in the Vedic animal sacrifices. Only in the Shaivite Kali cults in Bengal, centred on Durga, did animal sacrifice before an icon (though shorn of ritual), and the use of fresh blood, still prevail.

safflower There are no really early archaelogical finds of safflower (*Carthamus tinctorius*) in India, though Egyptian mummies of 1600 BC have been found with long garlands of cloth or papyrus on which were sewn florets of the safflower. Nor are there any early records in India of the use of the dye from the flowers, though a century ago it was a major industry for both internal use and export. Mention of the seed as a source of oil occurs in early Buddhist literature, and the *Arthashastra* (*c.* 300 BC) lists the kusumbha seed as one that was crushed in oilmills (*see* ghani). The Sanskrit name survives as kusuma in south India, though karadi is the more general term.

Two wild plants, *C. lunatus* in Kashmir and *C. oxyacantha* in Pakistan and Uttar Pradesh, may have been the ancestors of the safflower, and two distinct types developed. One was a non-spiny type with orange or yellow flowers tinged scarlet, used as a source of dye. The oily type, with yellow flowers, was grown in areas in the present southern Maharashtra and northern Karnataka, where the seed is an important source of edible oil. At the time of Independence, however, the safflower did not figure among the seven major oilseeds in the country.

saffron *See* kesar, kesari-bath.

sag *See* green leafy vegetables.

sago Sago granules were for long a product imported from the Indonesian islands, manufactured from starch derived from the stem of the sago palm. Called sabudana in India, it was used to make food for invalids, translucent milk-based payasams (q.v.), beverages like falooda (q.v.), and the like. A Kannada work of AD 1025 describes one dessert as a 'pearl-like padalige'; this could well refer to a sago payasam, which was certainly popular in the area in later times.

Tapioca starch, abundant in south India, was found suitable for granulation to sago, and at Independence, about 5000 tonnes of the product were being manufactured annually, mostly in the Salem district of the Tamil country.

salt Certain pottery moulds with convolutions on the inside found in the Indus Valley were probably salt moulds of a kind still in use in India. Salt is not mentioned in the *Rigveda*, but occurs frequently thereafter. Strabo of Amnesia (65 BC–*c.* AD 25) in his *Geography* mentions salt as a product of the country of King Sopithes (Saubhutu). Five of the more important types of salt are first mentioned in the Buddhist *Vinaya Pitaka* and later by Charaka. These are rock salt (saindhava), sea salt (samudra), black salt (vida), earth salt (pansuja or ushasuta), and audvida (efflorescence salts). Sushrutha has nine others, but these are mostly other mineral salts of both sodium and potassium. Kautilya in the *Arthashastra* also refers to saindhava, 'salt from the Sindhu country'.

Salt quickly assumed ritual significance. In the *Sutra* literature its use is forbidden to students, to widows, and to newly married couples for the first three days. Black or vida salt was interdicted at an ancestral shraddha ceremony. In certain types of fasts, ordinary sea salt has to be replaced by rock salt. Certain dishes in historic literature note specific salts, such as rock salt for a dish of meat in the Mahabharata, and for a pork dish in the *Manasollasa*. An amusing sidelight is given by Niccolao Manucci: chewing a betel quid for the first time in India as a very young man, his head swam and he fell down: a little salt placed on his tongue brought him to his senses.

In medical terms, salt in general is considered heavy, hot, pungent, moistening, emetic, salivatory, and peristaltic. Salt stimulates pitta and kapha, and reduces vata (*see* dosha). Sea salt is heavy and not heating, and does not cause a burning sensation on consumption. Rock salt has a superior therapeutic effect, calming all three doshas. Other forms of mineral salts, like vida, increase appetite to an exceptional degree and so are of value in digestive disorders and all vata diseases.

The production of sea salt is described in historical literature. Sea water was evaporated in long, shallow beds and the salt simply raked off. In Kautilya's *Arthashastra*, the lavanadhyaksha (superintendent of salt) scrutinized salt manufacturing practices and regulated trade, using a system of licenses for which either a fixed fee was paid, or a share of the output retained. The Superintendent also sold salt that was received by the government, which was one-sixth of the produce, as its share; profit was ensured right at source by the 5 per cent difference between the king's balance, the ayamani, and the public balance, and by further differences between buying and selling prices. Salt was an expensive commodity, inviting no less than six taxes, four paid by the seller and two by the buyer.

Early south Indian literature bias frequent references to the activities of salt producers and vendors. Five names for salt beds are recorded, namely nannugupalam, alkkar, uvarkkalam, uvalagam, and kazhi. The places where salt was manufactured were Markanam, Kanyakumari, Variyur, Aythurai, and Bapatla. Poets describe 'white salt manufactured in clayey beds' and 'hearths of stones left by salt vendors'. Salt was widely vended slung in two bags across the backs of oxen, or by 'salt sellers who enter villages crying out the price of salt', or by entire families creaking along in carts called vandi-chattu. The *Pattinapalai* notes that, as a pastime, young girls kept count of the numbers of such carts that passed along the highway. Salt was a principal measure of value, and could be bartered to advantage. Sea salt was of course used in cooking, and for salting and preserving fish and meat.

During the colonial period, salt production from saline incrustations in the Bengal area first attracted British attention, but after numerous attempts at organization, was finally abandoned as uneconomic. Alongside, control was slowly gained over the production of sea salt in Gujarat, Bombay, and Madras, of lake salt in Orissa and Rajasthan, and of rock salt in Punjab and the north-west. The quality of salt produced was also greatly improved and the prices were lowered. Mahatma Gandhi in 1930 led a salt march to the seashore at Dandi to protest against the payment of excise duty for salt manufacture, which was resolved by the Gandhi-Irwin pact of 1931 which permitted salt manufacture to anyone, provided the salt was not sold. At Independence, of the 21,000 tonnes of salt annually produced, 15 per cent was lake salt, 9 per cent rock salt, and the rest sea salt.

sambhar A fairly thick spicy extract of thuvar dhal soured with tamarind, frequently containing soft vegetables like the brinjal, drumstick, gourd, and lady's finger. It is served in south India with rice as a middle course, after a course of rice with rasam (q.v.), and before a course of rice with curds. Sambhar is also eaten as an accompaniment to the idli and vada. The Kannada term for the dish is huli and the Telugu, pulusu. The Tamil country has a pre-mixed sambhar-sadam, convenient for travel, and Karnataka the bisi-bele-huli-anna, best eaten with ghee.

samosa A deep-fried snack, consisting of a crisp, triangular and layery wheat casing filled with spiced meat or vegetables. In about AD 1300 Amir Khusrau describes, among the foods of the Muslim aristocracy in Delhi, the 'samosa, prepared from meat, ghee, onion, etc'. About fifty years later Ibn Battuta calls it samusak, describing it as 'minced meat cooked with almonds, walnuts, pistachios, onions and spices placed inside a thin envelope of wheat and deep fried in ghee'. The *Ain-i-Akbari* lists, among dishes of meat cooked with wheat, the qutab, 'which the people of Hind call the sanbusa'. All these descriptions suggest that the samosa was not an item brought by these courts from their parent lands, but was an existing indigenous product, perhaps enriched in its stuffing to cater to royal courts.

samovar The spouted copper or silver urn of Central Asia and Europe which is used to brew either an aromatic tea called kahwah flavoured with cardamoms and cloves, or a green tea using un-fermented leaves.

sandal The heartwood of *Santalum album*, which when dried has an exquisite perfume. In Sanskrit chandana (from which the word sandal is derived) appears to be a generic term covering srikhanda, the

true or white sandal, pitachandana, the inferior yellow type, and even raktachandana or red sandal, a different, mildly scented species.

Sandalwood was exported to Europe even 2000 years ago. Xuan Zang relates that its powder was used in the Nalanda monastery in the seventh century, to perfume washed hands after a meal. Though the perfume is obtained by steam distillation and widely employed in cosmetics and even in medicine, it is probably not compatible for use in food items. A lone reference is to a sandal-flavoured vermicelli payasam which was served as sattvik food to a group of advanced Shiva devotees in Karnataka

Samovar

(*Lingapurana* of Gurulinga Desika, *c.* 1594).

sandesh *See* Bengali sweets.

Sangam literature *See* Tamil literature.

sann-hemp *See* hemp.

Sanskrit sources A great deal of the early history of food in India is enshrined in Sanskrit literature, as is evident in numerous entries in this volume. A brief chronological account of the major works would therefore be helpful.

Some caution is called for. Thus while the great Kurukshetra battle of the Mahabharata has been placed from several considerations at 1424 BC, the core of the epic itself was written a thousand years later from oral tradition, and references to food would thus reflect the habits that prevailed not when the event occurred, but at the time of its compilation. An even greater difficulty is with texts like the *Samhita*s of Charaka and Sushrutha, which represent accretions over several centuries to the original works, which makes the dating of a specific food or food item uncertain. Some primary Sanskrit sources in approximately historical order now follow.

PERIOD 1700 BC TO 1500 BC

Rigveda: A collection of 1017 hymns plus 11 others, totalling 1028 suktas. Each is subdivided into 8 ashtakas (octaves) or khandas (sections), and each of these have 8 further divisions called adhyayas (chapters). Further dissection yields 2006 vargas (classes), 10,417 riks or verses (hence the name), and 153,826 padas (words). Another division yields 10 mandalas (circles or classes) and 8 anuvakas (sections). Of the 10 mandalas, numbers 2 to 7 are attributed to single families, and are probably the oldest nucleus. Mandala 9, which contains the famous soma (q.v.) hymns, was probably introduced into the collection later.

PERIOD 1500 BC TO 800 BC

Samaveda: A song book with 1547 stanzas, all but 75 of which also occur in the *Rigveda.*

Yajurveda: A prayer book of mantras for a priest to recite at sacrifices. There are two texts, the black and the white. The latter is attributed to the sage Yagnavalkya Vajasaneya, and consists of 40 chapters, of which 15 are of a later date than the rest.

Atharvaveda: This is in two recensions or samhitas. It consists of 20 books containing 731 hymns, many drawn from the *Rigveda.* These hymns consist of charms and spells against maladies, accompanied by the use of herbs and dietary injunctions. The hymns are attributed to the first physician, Dhanvantari.

Brahmanas and Aranyakas: These are books of prayer designed to relate the ritual to the sacred text. Each Veda has its own *Brahmanas*, such as the *Aitareya* and *Kaushika Brahmanas* of the *Rigveda*, the *Taittiriya Brahmana* of the *Yajurveda*, and the *Gopatha Brahmana* of the *Atharvaveda*. At the end of each *Brahmana* is placed the *Aranyakas* or forest books, explaining the symbolism of the sacrifices.

Upanishads: These are philosophical writings attached to the Vedas, and the source of Vedanta philosophy. The *Rigveda* has the *Aitareya* and *Kaushitaki Upanishads*, and the white *Yajurveda* has the *Brhadaranyaka* and *Isha Upanishads*. The authorship of the Upanishads is obviously very diverse.

PERIOD 800 BC TO 350 BC

Sutras: These consist of 8 vedangas or manuals of instruction in phonetics, grammar, metrics, astronomy, astrology, and ritual (kalpasutra).

Puranas: Eighteen later non-religious works which record ancient Aryan ruling dynasties. Parts of these are thought to be very old, while others came much later.

Paninlyam: The great grammar of Panini, which has been described as a 'natural history of the Sanskrit language'.

Nighantu: A treatise on medicine a later Dhanvantari, perhaps ruler of Varanasi.

Buddhist canon: These consist off three *Pitakas* written in Pali, a provincial dialect of Sanskrit, and are termed *Vinaya, Sutta,* and *Abhidamma*. Also of value are the *Dhammapadas*, 423 verses expounding Buddhist ethics, and the *Jatakas*, consisting of some 500 tales relating to the previous births of the Buddha which contain information on the social customs of the time.

Arthashastra: A manual of statecraft by Kautilya who was also called Chanakya. He lived around 300 BC in the court of Chandragupta Maurya.

Mahabhashya: A commentary by Patanjali (written around 200 BC) on the grammar of Panini, defending it against the criticisms of Katyayana.

Ramayana: One of the great epics, originally written by Valmiki in about 400 BC, with later accretions over many centuries.

Mahabharata: The other great epic. It consists of 18 parvas (books), being accretions over several centuries on the original tale of Vyasa (written around 400 BC).

Manusmriti: The Institutes or Codes of Manu, in Sanskrit *Manava Dharmashastra*, a digest in 2685 verses of the creeds and laws of behaviour of various social classes current at the time (around 200 BC).

PERIOD AD 100 TO AD 800

Charaka Samhita: The original work of perhaps the fifth century BC has been much amended subsequently. The *Charaka Samhita* consists of 120 chapters, with great emphasis on the fundamentals of ayurveda, the science of life. The effects of various foods are described in relation to their physiological impact, the temperament of the eater, the way of cooking the food items, and the seasons, based on actual observation. As many as 341 medicinal plants, 177 drugs of animal origin, and 64 drugs of mineral origin are so described.

Sushrutha Samhita: A work that was originally composed about a century after Charaka by Sushrutha, but is available for use in the recension of Nagarjuna of about the third/fourth century AD, with further information in Kalhana's commentary of AD 1100. The emphasis is on surgery, but dietary injunctions for health are included.

Ashtangahrdayasamhita: Written by Vaghbhata (mid-seventh century AD), this is a concise synthesis of the two earlier medical *Samhita*s.

Manasollasa: Meaning refresher of the mind, this work was written in about AD 1130 by King Someshwara of the western Chalukyan dynasty based in Kalyana, about 160 km west of modern Hyderabad. Its 100 chapters are divided into 5 books, of which the third describes the pleasures to be enjoyed by royalty. One of the chapters, entitled Anna-bhoga, contains a large number of concise recipes for both meat and vegetarian dishes.

Shivatattvaratnakara: An encyclopaedic work covering the whole range of human knowledge, combined with personal information. It was written by King Basavaraja, who from AD 1696 to 1714 ruled the kingdom of Keladi that stretched along the coast from Goa to Kannur. The chapter entitled Society and Amusements deals with the royal kitchen, the preparation and serving of food items, meal accompaniments, drinking water, and the like.

Sanskrit words Most current Hindi words in the area of food (as of course in other spheres) are obviously derived from Sanskrit, and a classified list of these follows. It seemed convenient to place first the common Hindi term, next the Sanskrit word, and finally the English usage. (*See also* individual entries.)

Cereals: cheena, cheenaka, amaranthus § jowar, jurna, sorghum § ragi, raga, finger millet § rajgeera, raj-geera, amaranthus § shama, shyamaka, panicum.

Pulses: arhar, adhaki, *and* thuvar, thuvarika, *both* pigeon pea § chana, chanaka, chickpea § kesari, vetch § kulthi, kulattha, horsegram § masoor, masura, lentil § mung, mudga, green-gram § sem, shimbi, hyacinth bean.

Oilseeds: alsi, athasi, linseed § kusum, kusumbha, safflower § til, tila, sesame § sarson, sarshapa mustard.

Tubers, etc: alu, aluka, tuber (potato) § gajar, garjara, carrot § manakanda, manaka, alocasia § muli, mulaka, radish § piyaz, palandu, onion § shakarkand, madhvaluka, sweet potato § surana, suran, elephant yam.

Fruits: akrot, akshota, walnut § am, amra, mango § amla, amlaka, Indian gooseberry § bael, btfva, Bengal quince § bfir, badari, jujube § draksha, drakshaka, grape § jambu, jambu, roseapple § jamoon, jambula, Java plum § tarbuz, kalinda, water-melon § kamrakh, kamaranga, star fruit § panas (kathal), panasa, jackfruit § keia, kadali, banana § kharbuza, kharbuza(?), musk melon § pgtha, kushmanda, ash gourd § mahua, madhuka, mowrah § ndrangi, nagaranga, Seville orange § nimbu, nimbaka (numbaka), lime.

Vegetables: baingan, vrntaka, brinjal § bhendi, bhinadaka/bhandi(?), lady's finger § karela, karavella, bitter gourd § chachinga, chachinda, snake gourd § khira, chirbhita, cucumber § parwal, putulika, pointed gourd § sajuna (shaonjana), shaubanjana (singru), drumstick.

Leafy and aquatic materials: bathua, vasthuka, pigweed § kamal, kamal, lotus (water-lily) § padma, padma, lotus § palak, palankya, spinach § pat, pathua, jute § singhada, singhataka, water chestnut.

Nuts: badam, vatama, almond § nariyal, narikela, coconut.

Spices: adrak, ardhraka, green ginger § dalchini, darugandha, cinnamon § elaichi, ela, cardamom § haldi, haridra, turmeric § imli, amlika, tamarind § jaiphal, jatriphal, nutmeg § jatri, jatri, mace § jeera, jeerika, cumin § kesar, kesara, saffron § lassan, lasuna, garlic § lavang, lavanga, clove § methi, methika, fenugreek § mirchi, maricha, pepper (round) § paan, pama, betel leaf § sunti, smgavera, dry ginger § tambul, thambula, betel leaf § tejpat, tvak, Indian cassia,

Flavourants: gur, guda, jaggery § karpur, karpura, camphor § khand-sari, khand, candy sugar § shakkar, sharkara, sugar.

Utensils: chakki, chakra, grinding-stone § chulah, chulli, stove § ghani, gravan (ghatani), oilpress § kadhai, kataha, deep frying pan § kolhu, ulukhala, oilpress § patra, patra, vessel § shurpa, shurpa, winnowing tray § shula, shula, spit § thali, sthali, metal dinner plate.

Prepared foods: afin, ahiphena, opium § chatni, chatahi, chutney § chidva, chipita, parched rice § khichdi, krsara, rice-pulse dish § muri (murmura), missita, puffed rice § panch, pancha, punch § sattu, saktu, grits of parched cereals § shirka, shirko, vinegar § sura, sura, distilled liquor § tali, tan, toddy.

sapota The sweet, brown globular fruit of *Manilkara achras*, called sapodilla in its native Mexico and Central America. The exudate from the bark was called chicle, from which came cheeku, the other name in India for the sapota fruit. This latex was used as a chewing gum, both in its place of origin and later commercially in Europe, but has today been replaced by synthetic resins. The species was brought either from Mozambique to Goa, or from the Philippines to Malaysia and thence to our east coast. Today it thrives best in southern and western India, and very large-fruited varieties have been developed.

sarson In the group of *Brassica* seeds now internationally termed rape-mustard, the main variety in India is the dark-red seed rai, *Brassica juncea* subsp. *juncea* (*see* mustard). Next in order is brown sarson, *B. napus* var. glauca, and lastly there is toria, *B. napus* var. napus. A minor crop is yellow sarson. Brown sarson is thought to have arisen a very long time ago in the north-west of India as a subspecies of the very ancient *B. campestris.* Simple human selections from this yielded toria on the one hand, and yellow sarson on the other. Brown sarson is termed sarshapa in Sanskrit, and the word is supposed to be of pre-Sanskritic Munda origin. Yellow sarson is termed siddhartha in Sanskrit, and as early as in 1000-800 BC was clearly distinguished from both rai (rajika) and sarson (sarshapa).

The seeds of rai are preferred as a condiment. In crushing seeds for oil, it has long been the practice to crush mixtures of rai, sarson, and toria, with the greater proportion being rai; this is done to achieve an optimum in terms of oil yield, flavour, and taste. This oil was called sarson-ka-tel in India, and alluded to as mustard oil in English.

The leaves of all three species are cooked in north India to a popular spicy mash called sarson-ka-sag, eaten with fresh butter as an accompaniment to rotis of makki (maize). This leafy mash is first mentioned as long ago as in the *Acaranga Sutra* (*c.* 500 BC), and again much later in the *Charaka Samhita.* The *Ashtangahrdayasamhita* written by Vaghbhata does not rate these leaves very highly as food. Sushrutha describes how in Suhma country (Bengal), the tender leaves were boiled, the water squeezed out, and jeera and rai seed added before shaping the mass into a delicacy called sindhaki.

sattu From the Sanskrit saktu, which originally meant the coarse flour obtained by grinding parched barley and later parched rice. These were then made into balls for chewing, or a paste for licking. Sattu is now applied to the coarse flour of any parched grain, including pulses. The *Varunaka Samuchaya* written in Gujarat in the sixteenth century speaks of laddus made from sattu, and a century ago Grierson records in Bihar a sattu of chana flour, boiled to yield a dish called pittha. The parallel term dalia refers to coarser grits or brokens of various grains.

sattvik One of the three types of guna or inherent temperament, the other two being rajasic (q.v.) and tamasic (q.v.). Sattva means essence, and represents serenity and refinement. A sattvik nature is best served by foods that do not disturb the body elements and conduce to serenity and spirituality. Examples are milk and its products, jaggery, honey, fruits, deer meat, rainwater, and the like. The list of foods with 'soul qualities' enumerated by the Buddha (*see* Buddhist food and literature) represents a range of sattvik food materials. Lord Vishnu, the preserver, exemplifies the sattvik temperament.

saunf Native to the Mediterranean, *Foeniculum vulgare* or fennel has been widely grown in India from early times. It is used as a food flavourant, for example, in a Bengali dish of urad dhal, or in the muthiyas of Gujarat, or in the spicing of food made by Hindus in Kashmir (q.v.). Saunf water is a home remedy for stomach upsets, and the yellow-green seeds are commonly offered as a digestive after a heavy meal.

seafood Though prawns, shrimp, crab, and other food from the sea and river must certainly have been in use all through history, references to seafood in literature are scanty. Manucci in the seventeenth century AD makes a suggestive remark: 'As for shell-fish, they are classed among the most impure of things, and are not used except by the pariahs.' Early Tamil literature talks of prawns caught by Meenavar, the fishing community, and elsewhere of 'white rice served with curried crabs and vegetables'. Fried crabs are noted in the *Manasollasa* written by King Someshwara. Like the flesh of other creatures living near or in water, namely in anupana terrain, these foods are considered sweet, fat, and heavy, and help to reduce the digestive fire and regulate kapha (q.v.) (*see* meat consumption, rasa).

seasons and months In the *Arthashastra* three seasons were noted. Rice was raised in the rainy season and harvested at the onset of winter. Pulses, lentils, and peas were harvested in spring, and barley, wheat, linseed, and hemp (cannabinus) were all sown in winter and reaped early in the following summer. Eventually finer gradations were made into six seasons (rtu), each of two months duration; these were vasantha (spring, March–May), grishma (summer, May–July), varsha (the rains, July–September), sharad (autumn, September–November), hemantha (winter, November–January), and shishira (cold season, January–March).

The year itself had twelve months. Starting from mid-March to mid-April, which was Chaitra, there followed Vaishakha, Jyaistha, Ashada, Shravana, Bhadrapada, Ashvina,

Karthika, Margashirsa (or Agrahayana), Paus, Magha, and Phalguna (from mid-February to mid-March).

sem The hyacinth bean, *Lab lab purpureus* (Sanskrit shimbi, Tamil avarai, Gujarati valpapdi), is thought to be indigenous to India, though wild forms have never been identified. It is a particularly popular vegetable in Karnataka, the Tamil country, and Gujarat.

sesame *seed:* There is now fairly conclusive evidence that the sesame, rightly called *Sesamum indicum*, is indeed of Indian origin, its progenitor being the wild Indian species, *S. orientale* var. malabaricum which still exists all over the country. This was probably the wild sesame, or jartila, first mentioned in the *Taittiriya Samhita* as an uncultivated grain permitted to ascetics. It is also listed in the twelve-volume *Hortus Malabaricus*, which was compiled in Kerala between AD 1680 and 1700 by the Dutch governor Heinrich van Rheede, with 794 plates sketched for him by an artist from Kochi.

Both archaeological and literary evidence support the antiquity of the sesame in India. A 'charred lump of sesame' was found in *c.* 2000 BC layers in Harappa, along with burnt grains of wheat and peas. Though tila is not mentioned in the *Rigveda*, the word pala does occur, which in later writings was employed in compound forms to denote sesame products; for example palala denoted a confection of sesame seeds and jaggery. From the *Atharvaveda* onwards, tila finds abundant mention in both secular and religious contexts. Sesame seeds find a place in every major life event. It has an important function in the naming ceremony of an infant, in the annaprasanna or weaning ceremony, in the tonsure ritual, and in the initiation ceremony of a student. At the sacred thread ceremony, sesame seeds are scattered in the four corners of a room to ward off evil spirits. The seeds are used in several rites connected with death and cremation; after everything is over, the relatives are given balls of sesame seeds, boiled rice, and jaggery, called tillanna. At the ancestral shraddha (q.v.) ceremonies, sesame seeds in the form of pindas (balls) are offered as pitr-tarpana to the manes or pitr.

While edible items that contain sesame have a ritual significance, there were of course numerous other items with sesame seeds eaten simply for pleasure. A Vedic dish of rice, sesame seed, and milk was called krasara, and in south India, in early times, a dish of rice, sesame seed, and sugar was termed chitrannam, perhaps from its speckled appearance. Rice cooked with sesame seed was tilaudana; it could also be cooked with vegetables, besides being roasted, pounded, and fashioned into crisp parpatas (papads). A flour of roasted sesame seed (or of the oilcake), when mixed with rice flour and jaggery, yielded the shaskuli. This was an item permitted to Buddhist monks, which on one occasion was denied to one of them since he had committed a transgression. An unusual dish of dressed curds called kambalika is described by Sushrutha; curds were acidified with woodapple (kapittha) pulp and dressed with jeera and pepper, and finally sesame seeds and roasted urad dhal were added.

An item that occurs throughout the centuries, and is still widely eaten, is the laddu fashioned from sesame seeds and thickened jaggery, called palala in *Sutra* literature. An early Greek writer, Aristobolus, who was one of Alexander's party, describing laddus as 'cakes of sesamum and honey' (sugarcane products being unknown to him), noted that brahmin priests simply helped themselves to these sweet cakes in the markets without payment. The sesame plant, the Greek noted, was grown in the rainy season along with wheat and millets, to which Ibn Battuta adds the sugarcane nearly sixteen centuries later. Early Tamil literature notes that it was a product of hilly country, and was harvested when the pods turned dark. The rattling of the dry seeds in the pods gave rise to the Arabic term juljul or jeljel (meaning jingling of bells), from which originates the term gingelly that is used for the sesame in south India, and even by early British writers. The Hindi til is of course from the Sanskrit tila.

Sesame oil: Sesame oil has played a seminal role both in north and south India. The oil drawn from the sesame seed, tila, was thaila, and before long this had become the generic term in Sanskrit, and later in Hindi, for all vegetable oils. By coincidence, the same thing happened in south India. An early Tamil word for the sesame seed was ell, and both the commodity and the name was transported to the Euphrates valley, and are listed in the Chicago Assyrian dictionary. The oldest Tamil grammar has enn for me sesame, nai for an essence (oil), and ennai for sesame oil. In course of time, ennai came to denote any vegetable oil, with a prefix to indicate its origin. Thus thenga-ennai was coconut oil, and sesame oil itself was termed ell-ennai.

Sanskrit literature reveals that from about 500 BC or so, oil was extracted from sesame seed in an animal-drawn mortar-and-pestle device. This was at first called thaila-peshana-yantra ('oil-crushing-machine'), and later colloquialized to terms like ghani and kolhu in north India, and chekku in Tamil (*see* ghani). A Tamil work, *Purananuru*, of about the second or third century AD, refers to the nurai or froth on the surface of oil extracted from the sesame seed. This is typical of what happens in a chekku, which was therefore probably in use. Three or four centuries later, the *Naladiyar* and *Nalayira Thivya Prabhandhan* refer to the chekku by this name.

Long before this, at the start of the Christian era, sesame oil packed in leather skin bags was an article of export from south India to Greece and Rome (*see* Rome, contacts with). It was also extensively used in south India as a 'sweet' oil with exceptional preservative qualities, for example, in making pickles. It is noteworthy that while most other Indian vegetable oils, like the coconut, mustard, safflower and niger, were strongly regional in terms of growth and hence in terms of crushing and usage, the sesame was grown all over the country, and its oils used everywhere. Early Sanskrit writings do not reflect this, since ghee was almost the only cooking fat consumed by the brahmins, and vegetable oils were for non-Aryans to use (*see* oils, oilseeds). But by the time of Charaka, more balanced views prevailed, and of all the vegetable oils, sesame oil was rated the highest, and particularly recommended for use in the rainy season; its use every day was not advised.

A further use of sesame oil in south India is for body massage. For making perfumed oils, as well as medicated oils, sesame was the oil of choice (*see* oils).

Sesame oilcake: This was always a valued cattlefeed. As already described, it could be pounded fine and mixed with rice grits and jaggery to yield a tasty concoction, shaskuli. Sesame seeds, deskinned after soaking in water, yielded a fine, white oilcake which was specially relished. Among the items that could be eaten as a purificatory rite for the crime of killing a cow was sesame oilcake.

sev First mentioned as sevika in the *Manasollasa* of the twelfth century, but probably much older, sev is the term for crisp-fried noodles of besan flour, extruded either thick or thin from a batter through dies into very hot fat. It is a popular snack food all over India, and stores well (*see* Gujarat, food of).

seviyan The thicker and shorter form of vermicelli, long made in India from hard wheat (q.v.). Seviyan is used to make a payasam by boiling it with milk and sugar, or a drier sweet, fried brown in ghee, a Parsi delicacy. In south India the product is called semiya, and is used to make a payasam or an uppuma (q.v.).

Seville orange The Sanskrit nagaranga and Hindi narangi, botanically *Citrus aurantium* and probably native to north-east India (*see also* citrus).

shaka Collective Sanskrit term for uncooked vegetables, the corresponding Hindi term being tharkari. One of Charaka's food classes is shakavarga, under which eighteen items are listed.

shali Generic term for fine winter varieties of rice (*see* rice).

sheep Sheep meat always figures in lists of edible flesh in Sanskrit literature, as in the Mahabharata. Charaka lists it, but not with such superior meats as venison, goat, and hare. However, in the *Vishnu Purana* of about the third or fourth century AD, it is classed with other meritorious meats that are served at a shraddha ceremony. Strabo records that Alexander received 10,000 sheep and 3600 oxen as a gift when he was in Takshashila, presumably for feeding his army. At a royal meal during the Sultanate period, Ibn Battuta noted that a 'whole roasted sheep (each) yielded 4 to 6 pieces', an enormous serving. The fat-tailed sheep, dumba, was thus described by Edward Terry in about AD 1620: Their sheep exceed ours in great bobtails, which cut off are very ponderous ... the flesh of them both is altogether as good as ours.' In colonial times it was not uncommon for sheep to be reared and fattened for the table, to obtain good mutton, which was rarely to be had from the butcher. In fact, the term mutton is used in India for both sheep and goat meat, with even less distinction between the young of each species, lamb and kid (*see also* goats).

shellfish *See* seafood.

shraddha Ceremony performed by a son at every anniversary of the death of his father, now a pitr or manes. Relatives are invited and feasted, but strict rules govern the ritual itself and the food that is served. Fried apupas are auspicious. Both the Ramayana and the Mahabharata note that the use of black salt (vida) is interdicted, and also, according to the *Vishnu Dharmasutra*, the use of black mustard seeds. On the other hand the use of black sesame seed is mandatory. Some vegetables, like green bananas, are allowed, but others are not. In the south a payasam of horsegram (kollu, kulthi) with jaggery as a sweetener must be served, and in the north boiled mung. Various authorities differ on the excellence of the meat to be served, when such a practice was followed. The *Apasthamba* and *Baudhyayana Dharmasutra*s extol the use of rhinoceros flesh (khadga), and the *Manusmriti* describes the periods of the year when specific meats must be served to really propitiate the manes. Today only vegetarian food would be served at a brahmin shraddha.

shrikhand A sweet-sour concoction of curds, dewatered by 'hanging overnight in a muslin bag, and then sweetened with sugar, coloured yellow with saffron and flavoured with cardamom powder'. It popularly accompanies a meal of small fried puris (q.v.) in the Maharashtra area, and elsewhere is a dessert.

shukto A dish with a bitter taste, derived from, say, the bittergourd or neem leaves, which forms one constituent of a meal at lunchtime in Bengal (*see* Bengal, food of).

shula *See* roasting; cooking.

sigdi A small, portable iron stove, with a detachable slatted iron plate to hold embers in place below the cooking vessel. The simple iron sigdi and clay chulah (q.v.) have been the two main forms of the stove all through India's history.

Sikhs, ceremonial food of The holy book, the Adi Granth or Granth Sahib, was compiled by Guru Arjan, the fifth guru of the Sikhs, and the tenth Guru declared that the Book itself was hereafter the Guru that would provide leadership to the community. This is a collection of writings by twenty authors who span six centuries, with those of six Gurus forming the bulk. It has many exhortations to high principles of conduct, but does not concern itself with laying down ceremonies or rituals or any earthly code of laws, though in practice some have emerged. Khalsa tradition is also embodied in the *Rahatnamas* or Codes of Conduct compiled by several contemporaries of Guru Gobind Singh. Thus after a child is born the Guru administers a few drops of water and sugar on its lips, and at baptism the candidate has to accept sixteen conditions among which are abstinence from all intoxicants and from tobacco in any form. At the engagement ceremony of a couple, sacred food of kaval prasad is prepared. This is a special wheat halwa, which also figures in ceremonies after a cremation.

Food figures in some of the selections in the Adi Granth, but even these offer advice more than laying down definite rules. 'Cursed is such a living which induces one to eat and fatten his belly.' 'Even the dry grains of saints are treasured by all; but the thirty-six kinds of food prepared in the house of a follower of Mammon are like poison.' 'Which place can be considered pure, where I can sit and take my food?' In practice alcohol is forbidden, and so is beef, but not pork. Slaughter is performed by cutting the jugular vein at the throat.

Sikhs now constitute 15 million, or about 2 per cent of the population, largely centred in Punjab, Haryana, and around Delhi.

singhada *Trapa natans* var. bispinosa is an exceedingly ancient plant, a fossil even several million years old having been found. It occurs in early Vedic literature as mulali and saphaka, and is a floating aquatic weed which bears under water letrahedral starchy nuts that are boiled and eaten. In the Indian view it is an uncultivated food which accordingly is permitted during abstentions and to ascetics. In about

AD 1611, William Finch described the water-chestnut as being 'green and soft and tender, white, of a mealish taste, being exceeding cold in my judgement, for always after eating it I needed (to drink) *aqua vitae* (water)'. It was even cultivated in Bengal as a food crop. William Sleeman wrote in AD 1844 that 'the holdings are staked out and so much paid per acre ... The nut grows under water after the beautiful white flowers decay, ripening in September and eatable up to November.

A century ago, it was described as being cultivated in Kashmir, and three types were distinguished: basmati, a small nut with a thick shell (and presumably of fine flavour); dogra, a larger nut with a thicker shell; and kangar, with a thick shell and projecting horns.

In Bengal a small tetrahedral samosa (q.v,) with vegetable stuffing is also called singhada, and the term samosa is reserved for one with meat stuffing.

sitaphal A globular, green, knobbly fruit with numerous shiny black seeds embedded in a sweet, custard-like pulp. The first description of this fruit in India is by P. Vincenzo Maria in AD 1672: 'The pulp is very white, lender, delicate, and so delicious that it unites to agreeable sweetness a most delightful fragrance like rosewater ... if presented to one unacquainted with it he would certainly take it for blancmange.' An error of translation

Sitaphal

has led to the mistaken belief that the custard apple was available in Delhi as early as in AD 1590; the word sadaphal in the *Ain-i-Akbari*, translated by Blochmann as custard apple, means only a perennial fruit, and had indeed been employed earlier by Babar himself for a citrus fruit.

The sitaphal is *Annona squamosa*, and the family certainly derives from Peru and Ecuador, from where the species had long back reached Mexico. The genus is supposed to have come to India from the West Indies by way of the Cape of Good Hope, and there are several species. The sitaphal in India is also called sharifa (meaning noble fruit), as well as custard apple. Kami phal (*A. reticulata*) was called bullock's heart in British India, but in the West Indies is called the custard apple. It is a large, reddish-yellow, faceted fruit with a smooth flesh and odd flavour that does not appeal to everyone. Two other less-known species are the hanumanphal or lakshmanphal, *A. cherimola*, and the very large and prickly *A. muricata*, called the mamphal or sour sop.

Stray facts could suggest an earlier presence of the sitaphal in India. The sculptures in Bharhut (second century BC) and the fresco paintings of Ajanta (seventh century AD) show fruits with a knobbly appearance; however Watt is of the view that these are not the sitaphal but conventionalized representations of either a jackfruit or a kadamba flower head.

snails There is a lone reference in old Tamil literature to the community of Mallars relishing fried snails.

snake gourd An ancient Indian vegetable in the form of a striped 2-metre long pod, whose name in English is singularly appropriate. In Sanskrit it is called chachinda and in Telugu pottalakaya, and botanically it is *Trichosanthes anguina*. The snake gourd is used in sambhars, in a dry curried preparation, or fried in sections with a stuffing of minced meat or mashed vegetables.

soma Common to the priestly practices both of the ancient Iranian Aryans and the early Vedic Aryans was an exhilarating drink called hoama in Iran and soma in India. The drink was offered to the gods, and imbibed by the priests and proponents of the sacrifice. It was clearly distinguished from a mere alcoholic stimulant. In course of time soma had become the moon goddess, and almost the entire ninth mandala of the *Rigveda*, consisting of 114 hymns, is addressed both to the libation and to the goddess. An individual who imbibed soma was exhilarated beyond his natural powers, and the juice itself was described as being 'primeval, all-powerful, healing all diseases, bestower of riches, loved by the gods, even the supreme being'. Indra was exhorted to destroy enemy strongholds after fortifying himself with soma juice.

Several attempts have been made to identify the soma plant. One guess was *Sarcostemma acidum*, a leafless shrub, still called somalata in several Indian languages, but containing a constituent that is toxic to animals and man. Another was *Asclepias acida*, the American milkweed, which contains a poisonous glucoside; the leaf juice is used against worms and to combat bleeding, and the roots to induce vomiting. A third candidate is ephedra, a genus which carries an adrenalin-like alkaloid called ephedrine; two species, *E. gerardiana* and *E. major*, are densely branched but almost leafless shrubs, the dried stems of which are employed in allergic conditions and as a cardiac stimulant. A fourth claimant is the Indian bhang (q.v.) plant, *Cannabis saliva*, whose leaves are chewed, or crushed to obtain bhang. Each of these identifications has obvious loopholes and is unsatisfactory.

A strong case has been made for the fly agaric mushroom, of a deep red colour with white spots, which is *Amanita muscarita*. This was widely used all over Central Asia in the third and second millennia BC, notably by the Koryaks and Chuckchis in Siberia. The fly agaric mushroom exerts the kind of effects described in the Vedas, where Indra is exhorted to destroy enemy strongholds after fortifying himself with soma juice. Much of the poetic if rather cryptic imagery of the texts seems to fit the mushroom. Thus it is red, udder-like and powerful; has a head like a cap, and a single, seeing eye, like a stud or a knob; has a hide of wool, and the dress of a sheep, and is by day red, by night silvery, like Agni and like Surya. The *Amanita* mushroom is an Old World species, and its active principles are now known: it contains the hallucinogen ibotenic acid, which, on drying, releases two other compounds, muscimol and muscatine, that repel flies. Incidentally, the New World mushrooms of Mexico are *Psilocybes*, with hallucinogenic effects of a different kind caused by psilocybin and psilocin.

sooty fowl *See* chicken.

sorghum *See* jowar.

sorrel The Sanskrit changeri and Hindi amrul, botanically *Oxalis*

corniculata, the sorrel is a shrub with sour leaves that are used as an acidulant. Medical literature describes a dish called khada (perhaps resembling the khadi [q.v] of the present) in which curds are acidified using sorrel leaves, followed by seasoning with jeera and pepper.

soups As early as in 500 BC, extracts of pulses are described in Sanskrit as supa or yusa, and in succeeding centuries we read of extracts not only of pulses, but of cereals like rice and wheat, and of meats of various kinds. Many of them have a medical connotation. One is a rice soup, flavoured with long pepper, dry ginger, and pomegranate, and the kanji (q.v.) left over from boiling rice was a base for soup-like beverages. Soups of meat were prescribed for vomiting, and of the chicken, pigeon, and wild fowl for asthma. Medically, un-spiced soups were pronounced superior to spiced ones. In south India, a soup still in daily use is rasam (q.v.), a tamarind-flavoured extract from thuvar dhal adopted by the colonial living in Madras which he called mulligatawny (q.v.).

South America, foods from *See* Mexico, food materials from.

south India *See* Karnataka, food of; Kerala, food of; Tamil literature, food references in; Rome, contacts with.

soybean China is the home of the soybean. It probably originated in the eastern half of north China in about

1200 BC, perhaps from *Glycine soja*, a wild form related to the cultivated *Gycine max*, which is soya. The present name may spring from the shu or sou used by Confucius. It spread by 300 BC all over South-East Asia, but not to India, and as late as in 1908 was described as 'having only recently been introduced into India' and 'growing as a garden rather than a field crop in hilly eastern India'. However a thorough survey in 1911 showed fairly extensive soybean cultivation up to heights of 2000 metres all the way from Punjab to Manipur. In the 1930s, Mahatma Gandhi wrote about the excellent nutritional qualities of the soybean and of his own experiences of eating it after steam cooking. The popular name was bhat, and the Sanskrit term rajshimbhi, shimbi itself being the sem. Many states, and notably the princely state of Baroda, looked into the possibilities of growing the soybean plant both for fodder and for food. These efforts made little headway, and even in 1948, soybean production was estimated at only a thousand tonnes. The big spurt in soybean production in Madhya Pradesh had its beginnings only some twenty-five years later.

spikenard *See* ginger grass.

spinach *Spinacia oleracea*, spinach in English, palankya in Sanskrit, and palak in Hindi, is an ancient plant in India, first mentioned in the *Sutra* literature of *c*. 500 BC. Long before it was known in the West, the spinach has been extensively used in India as a green leafy vegetable in various ways. It can be incorporated into the dough used to make a parata (*see* rotis), or cooked soft with spices, sometimes along with paneer, and eaten with a blob of butter to accompany chapatis. The Parsis serve eggs on a bed of greens as akuri, and spinach is a popular choice. Bengal has a climbing spinach, called puin, which may be cooked with a vegetable like pumpkin. Names like Malabar spinach and Chinese spinach have been mistakenly applied in America to several *Amaranthus* species that were taken there recently from India.

spit The ancient Sanskrit term shula was used even in Vedic sacrifices, in which whole animals were roasted on spits (*see* Rajasthan, food of; ashvamedha; meat dishes).

spoons *See* cooking utensils.

squash Squash is American usage for fruits that are termed pumpkins and gourds (q.v.) in India, all of which belong to the *Cucurbita* family. Thus the American winter squash, *C. moschata*, is known in India by such names as lal-kumra, kaddhu, and kumbalakayi; fruits are round to oval, bluntly ribbed, with a yellow or reddish flesh. Other winter squashes of America are here termed dudhi and dumbala, some smooth and oblong, others fluted, and either spherical or flattened. Another winter squash is *C. mixta*, called cushaw in the New World and the African gourd in India; it has a prominent peduncle, and is used to make the supporting bowls of the veena and thanpura, both musical instruments. The American summer squash, *C. pepo*, called marrow and pumpkin there, is a green, deeply ridged pear-shaped fruit, which in India has names like safed-kaddhu, kumra, and surai-kayi.

The *Cucurbita* species have been traced back ten thousand years in Mexico and Guatemala, and were fully developed there. Yet many carry Sanskrit names of considerable antiquity, which is probably explained, not necessarily by human intervention, but by the ability of these dried gourds to float across the seas from continent to continent without losing seed viability.

stale food A cardinal concept of the Hindu food perception is that boiled or kaccha food (q.v.) cooked in the sanctity of a home kitchen using ritual codes has necessarily to be cooked afresh for every meal. Leftover food, termed ucchista in Sanskrit, and basi or jutha in Hindi, is likely to become ritually polluted, and cannot therefore be eaten later.

star fruit The mildly acidic, juicy fruit of *Averrhoea carambola*, with a star-shaped cross-section, is kamaranga in Sanskrit and kamrakh in Hindi. It is a native of the Moluccas, but has long been in India, though never regarded here with the same esteem as in South-East Asia.

steaming Though Xuan Zang blandly stated in the seventh century AD that Indians 'do not know the steamer used for cooking rice', the prevalence all over the country of numerous steamed dishes like the idli, dhokla, modak, and puttu indicates that steaming was a familiar domestic practice. No specific vessel was really needed, since simple means suffice. Steaming vessels did develop in south India a couple of centuries ago with names like the idli-patram in the Tamil country and sekala in Kodagu (*see* idli; dhokla; Kerala, food of; cooking practices).

Stone Age paintings Paintings are found at several places in India, notably in the caves at Bhimbetka about 40 km south of Bhopal, and at Singhanpur near Raigarh, and Benakar near Hampi. The earliest paintings were made in about 8000 BC and continued for the next few millennia. Early man's quest for food is reflected in these paintings, with scenes of hunting with spears, trapping deer, stalking game with bows and arrows, and spearing fish or catching them in nets. The animals shown being hunted, probably for food, are the bison, gaur, peacock, and rhinoceros, besides giraffe and ostrich which exist in India no more. Paintings at Bhimbetka show groups of dancers linked arm in arm performing what appear to be magic rituals, aimed perhaps at gaining control over the desired prey. Elaborate masks and head-dresses are depicted, which perhaps sought to imitate or emulate animals and birds. Enormous bows even taller than the hunter himself are shown, besides traps made of pliant materials like reeds and ropes. The quest for food was clearly an ardent and incessant activity.

Of particular interest at Bhimbetka are the activities of women. They are shown gathering fruit, with long baskets hanging on their backs. Women are frequently shown kneeling down or standing up, mixing something in a device that is shaped like a shallow letter 'w', perhaps a section of a dried gourd. One woman has her hands on a ball (of dough?) placed on a ledge in front of her. What exactly is being done can only be guessed at. Another woman is clearly pounding grain

Sugarcane

using a long (wooden?) pounder in a deep, V-shaped vessel. Here are food-processing activities painted by contemporaries with verve and economy.

sugarcane The likely progenitor of *Saccharum officinarum*, the sugarcane, is *S. robustum* (2n = 80), which, starting several thousand years ago, was subject to human selection in or near Papua New Guinea for sweetness and lack of fibre. These so-called noble canes then migrated north-west to the Asian continent, and hybridized, probably in India, with the wild kasa grass, *S. spontaneum* (2n = 40 to 128), to yield thin but sweet canes. These are now called *S. barberi* (2n = 64 in India, and from 80 to 120 elsewhere), which were the varieties grown throughout the centuries all over India for chewing and for processing into products.

Indus Valley cities have yielded charcoals that have been identified as originating from some *Saccharum* species, but whether this was the sugarcane is uncertain. The kusara of the *Rigveda* is thought to refer to it, and ikshu, which is certainly the sugarcane, is mentioned thus at a sacrifice in the *Atharvaveda*: 'I offer you dried sugarcane, white sesamum, reeds and bamboos.' All the *Samhitas* also contain references to ikshu. The *Mahabhashya* of Patanjali (*c.* 600 BC) mentions sharkara repeatedly. Charaka describes two varieties of sugarcane, the superior paundraka growing in north Bengal (Pundra), and the inferior vainsaka. He even derives the word guda, meaning jaggery (q.v.), from Gauda, as Bengal was then called. Sushrutha mentions twelve varieties of sugarcane, and Vaghbhata lists five; the best kind in his view was vamshika, with thin reeds, and the next best the paundraka of Bengal.

Visitors to almost every part of India have commented on the sugarcane. To the Greeks, it was a totally new and curious article. Nearchos of Crete, who was in Alexander's entourage, talked of a 'a reed tree that produced honey without the association of bees'. This was in the Punjab area, and in Sindh in AD 1080 Al-Idrisi noted that the country produced dates and sugarcane in abundance. Ibn Battuta in the thirteenth century AD was of the opinion that the sugarcanes of Barkur in Kerala 'were unexcelled in the rest of the country'. Bernier who visited Bengal talks of the extensive fields of sugarcane. Early Tamil literature poetically describes the river Kaveri, 'along whose banks the sweet cane's white flowers wave, like pennoned spears rising from the plain', and indeed the sugarcane was always associated with river valleys. A homely touch is provided by the observation in the *Agananuru* that when carts got stuck in the mud, stalks of sugarcane were heaped beneath the wheels to provide a grip. It was a valuable regional item of barter, for example, for venison or arrack.

In colonial times, thick or noble sugarcanes, *Saccharum officinarum*, were brought into India from the West Indies and the East Indies. In 1912, the Sugarcane Research Station was founded in Coimbatore as a result of the efforts of Pandit Madan Mohan Malaviya to stop the huge drain of currency incurred through the import of sugar into India from Java. At this centre, research efforts were made to cross Indian sugarcanes with a species of wild grass, *S. spontaneuin*, found growing wild in the vicinity. Later sorghum (jowar) and bamboo were also introgressed to yield a series of hybrid sugarcanes that excelled existing products in terms of thickness, sugar content, and resistance both to disease and adverse climate. In five short years, between 1930 and 1935, these sugarcanes developed by T.S. Venkataraman led to a doubling of cane production in the country.

sugarcane products Sanskrit literature at the start mentions only honey as a sweetening agent, but by the Buddhist period a millennium later it had been all but displaced by guda (jaggery or brown sugar). Buddhist literature also refers to the crushing of sugarcane in a yantra (machine), an ancestor of the kolhu or mortar-and-pestle press used till very recent times. Even the name of this device seems to have a connection with the sugarcane, which in Sanskrit is ikshu. This yielded to later words like ikh and ukh for the sugarcane, and to ukhli andokhli for a small mortar. The residual mass from the crushing is termed khali or khalli in Marathi. Finally, the original mortar in the *Rigveda* for crushing soma juice was the ulukhala, itself not a far cry from the current term kolhu for the sugarcane press.

After the expression of sugarcane juice in a kolhu, it was boiled down to a series of products. *Sutra* literature (800–300 BC) mentions thickened phanita and then solid guda. In 326 BC, Alexander's party speaks of 'stones the colour of frankincense, sweeter than figs or honey', an unmistakable reference to large Indian crystal sugar lumps, khand. Indeed Kautilya in his *Arthashastra* of almost exactly the same period describes the whole range of products from sugarcane juice, namely phanita (thickened juice, now called rab), guda (jaggery), sharkara (brown sugar or bura, which was gur crystals thoroughly drained of molasses but not refined in any way), matsyandika (literally fish eggs or roe, which must have been crystalline sugar of some sort), and khand (sugar in the form of large lumps or small, faceted crystals).

The mode of preparing khand, later termed khandsari, is not described, but it was later made by an ingenious process. Thickened rab was held in a basket lined with a fine cloth. Water in a finely diffused form, derived from moist aquatic weeds placed on top of the basket, served to gently wash away the mother liquor. The layer of sugar crystals that formed and grew immediately below the weeds was repeatedly removed, and this constituted khand; it could be redissolved and refined to yield almost white crystalline sugar, called misri or chini, or large crystals. It is instructive that in about AD 627, there is a record of a Chinese delegation to Emperor Harsha to study the manufacture of crystal sugar. The widespread Hindi term chini for sugar current even today may have resulted from the import from China at some time in the past of superior white crystal sugar. In British India, an enormous expansion occurred in the area under sugarcane after AD 1800; gur and khandsari production went down, while the quantity of modern crystal sugar produced in vacuum-pans went up dramatically.

In one classification of Indian food, as things to be licked, sucked, and chewed, sugarcane pieces are a prime example of foods to be sucked, and are served as a second course at a meal. Sugarcane juice is a beverage (q.v.) which may be spiced with ginger, for example. It was a food permitted to Buddhist monks, and even sugarcandy was served to Xuan Zang by Su-Yeh, the king of the Turks, as a 'pure food'. Guda or jaggery (q.v.) is a major sweetening agent, which may be thickened in solution over a fire to yield a binding material for soft laddus (q.v.) and hard chikkis (q.v.). Khand crystals are mixed in both for taste and textural variety with various crisp snacks, betel nut grits (to yield supari), and saunf (q.v.).

In ayurvedic terms, the sugarcane and sugar not only taste sweet, but also have a sweet aftertaste (vipaka), and are dry, light, and cold. Sugar has a mild digestive and aperient action; it promotes the excretion of waste products, and is recommended in kidney and liver complaints. Sushrutha is of the view that as sugarcane products are purified, they become 'colder' but more difficult to digest; in fact, even sugarcane juice pressed out between wooden rollers is rated nutritionally inferior to chewing sugarcane itself.

Sultanate, food of The Sultanate rule in Delhi lasted three centuries, starting from AD 1206 with the so-called Slave dynasty of eleven rulers, then the house of Balban (two rulers), six Khaljis, three Tughlaks (including Muhammad bin Tughlak, AD 1324–51), four Saiyyids, and three Lodis. It ended when Babar from Afghanistan set up Mughal rule in India in AD 1526. Amir Khusrau (AD 1253–1325)

spanned six reigns, of both the Khalji and Tughlak sultans. The food of the Muslim aristocracy could include very sweet sherbet, light and tanduri rotis, samosas (prepared from meat and onions), mutton, birds like quails and sparrows (kunjshakka), halvas, and a sweet beverage, subunisakar; wine was drunk with meals, which was followed by the betel quid (tambula). The master-muster of Sultan Balban in Sindh fed his entire secretariat every midday with large trays loaded with fine naan, goat meat, chicken, biriyani, fuqqa (a drink of wine or barley), sherbet, and betel leaves. When nobles had eaten together, the unconsumed food would be distributed to fakirs and beggars.

Khusrau also described how grain was stored in a khatee or deep pit lined with straw and sealed when absolutely full with clay and cowdung; except for a change in colour, the grain remained edible for years. Some fifty years later, Ibn Battuta describes rice brought out from storage in the walls of Delhi fort, where it had been held for ninety years, and 'although it had gone black in colour, it was still good to the taste'. Ibn Battuta was born in Tangier and spent twenty-nine years in India (AD 1325-1354), writing his *Rehla* or Travels after returning home. He wrote that at the tables of the rich were served rotis, roasted meat (shiwawoon), chicken, rice, samusak, and round pieces of bread split and filled with sweet paste. At a grand dinner given by Sultan Muhammad bin Tughlak to a distinguished visiting qazi or judge, the food items served in order were khubi (probably chapatis); roasted sheep cut into very large pieces, four to six to a whole animal; round cakes of bread soaked in ghee, called subunia, in the middle of which was placed a mixture of almonds, honey, and sesame oil; a brick-like sweet cake called khisti made of flour, sugar, and ghee, each placed on a piece of bread; dressed meat cooked with ghee, onions, and green ginger in dishes of china; four or five samusaks; next a dish of ghee-cooked rice with a roasted fowl (dojaj) on top; and finally sweet items like hashimi and al-qahiriya (a pudding from Qahira).

Both private and public dinners were held. Private dinners were attended by the Sultan and about twenty people, dignitaries whom he had summoned. He would send a roti to a person whom he specially wished to honour, who received it with his left hand and bowed, with his right hand touching the ground. Public dinners, which could also be attended by the Sultan, were larger affairs headed by the chief palace officer, who held a gold mace in his hand. All except the Sultan stood up when he entered and gave a call. After the dishes had been served on the floor, the chief police officer

eulogized the Sultan, followed by his deputy, who ended by bowing to him, as did everyone present. When they had taken their seats, the Sultan would appoint one of the great amirs to supervise the feeding of the people.

A rigid seating order prevailed at these feasts. The judges (qazis), orators (khatibs), jurists (shorfa), saiyids, and dervishes (mashaik) sat at the head of the Simat (dinner carpet). Then came the Sultan's relatives, the great amirs, and the rest of the people, and since everyone sat strictly at his appointed place, there was no confusion. Each person had his own servings, and there was no sharing. These meals were eaten twice a day, in the forenoon and afternoon.

sura A term repeatedly used in the *Rigveda* for a distilled alcoholic drink manufactured from barley or wild rice flour, whose consumption by the despised local population was strongly condemned. Components fashioned in clay found in Indus Valley excavations have been assembled to form a distillation still, a key component being a plate with perforations at the base. This was placed on top of a pot in which fermented liquor was boiled; alcohol passed through the perforations and was condensed on the cold under-surface of a vessel placed on top, to fall in drops into the annular space of a basin. Thus a strong spirit, sura, would have been available to the community.

suran The huge elephant-foot yam, *Amorphophallus campanulatus*, can weigh as much as 10 kg. The common names are suran in Hindi and senai-kizhangu in Tamil, and there are three Sanskrit names, vajrakanda, surana, and arsogna (literally, destroyer of piles). Till recently, dried slices were sold as madana-mast in bazaars as a remedy for piles and dyspepsia. The *Manasollasa*, written in the twelfth century AD, describes an acidic pralehaka relish made with curds, fruit juices, and pieces of surana. The suran originated in India, and then moved eastwards and westwards even as far as America.

Sushrutha Samhita See Sanskrit literature.

Sutras See Sanskrit literature.

sweet lime The mitta-nimbu, *Citrus limettoides*, is of Indo-Iranian origin, and is represented in India by the rather insipid chikna of Saharanpur (*see also* citrus).

sweet potato Cave remains which go back to between 10,000 and 8000 BC leave no doubt that *Ipomoea batatas* is of Peruvian-Mexican origin. Despite this, archaeological sites in Hawaii, the Easter Islands, and New Zealand have yielded remains of the tuber. In India the evidence is of a literary kind. The pindaluka mentioned, in the Ramayana could be the sweet potato, and Sushrutha employs the more specific madhvaluka.

The current Hindi term is shakarkand. The early Tamil work *Purananuru* alludes to the tubers of the sweet potato (sakkarai-kizhangu) 'descending from the (foot of) the creeper'. Perhaps the sweet potato came to India eastwards from the South Pacific rather than from South America.

In AD 1615 Edward Terry mentioned potatoes, and so did John Fryer in AD 1678, but since potatoes had not by then reached India (*see* potato), these were probably sweet potatoes, which were equally strange to the English visitors.

The sweet potato in ayurvedic perception is hard to digest.

sword bean The sword bean is *Canavalia gladiata*, termed bada-sem and makkan (butter)-sem in Hindi. It is the product of a large climbing plant found throughout India and is cooked as a soft vegetable.

A more recent entrant to India from the New Word is *Cunavaliti ensiformis* of the same family This is called in English the horse bean and jack bean and in India the French bean. It is large, thin, and flat. resembles the sword bean, and has unfortunately also been termed bada-sem in India.

The sem (q.v.) itself is the hyacinth bean, a very ancient product called shimbi(?) in Sanskrit, valpapdi in Gujarati, and avarai in Tamil. It has a white hilum running along one edge, as do the two bada-sem beans.

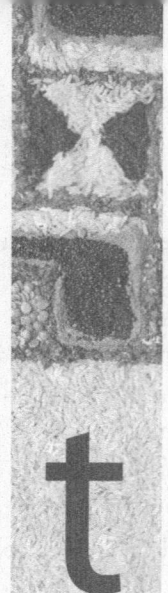

t

tamarind *Tamarindus indicus* is
native to the tropical savannah of
Africa, but has grown in India since
prehistoric times. In AD 1298 Marco
Polo refers to it as tamarindi, a name
that derives from the Arabic thamar-
ul-Hind or tamar-ul-Hindi, the date
or fruit of India. It has an ancient
aboriginal name, chincha, in Sanskrit,
and another, amlika, from which
comes the Hindi imli. In Tamil it is
termed puli, which later became the
generic word for tartness.

The tamarind figures extensively in
old Tamil literature. Rice dressed with
it was puli-kari (current puli-sadam),
and meat boiled with tamarind
and pepper was pulingari or thuvai.
Pastoral people are described as
imbibing an aromatic tamarind soup,
perhaps akin to the rasam (q.v.) of the
present. Two sour fruits, the tamarind
and the nellikayi (amla), were blended

Tamarind

to make a drink. A Kannada work of
AD 1485 by Terekanambi Bommarasa
notes a tamarind side-dish.

Tamarind is used more widely in south
India, but is not unfamiliar elsewhere.
The *Manasollasa*, compiled in central
India, describes a beverage made from
whey with sugar and cardamom,
which was blended with fruits and

roasted tamarind seeds. The latter item was at one time a regular adulterant of coffee powder. Sorpotel, the pork dish of Goa, uses both vinegar and tamarind. A dark brown tamarind sauce is poured as a dressing over curd-based dishes like the dahi-vada (q.v.).

tamasic One of the three types of guna or inherent temperament, the other two being rajasic (q.v.) and sattvik (q.v.). Tamas has the connotation of coarseness and roughness, and of quick and thoughtless action. Tamasic foods include pork, beef, non-scaly fish, and strong liquors. Lord Shiva, the destroyer, exemplifies the tamasic nature.

Tamil literature Many entries in this book carry references to ancient Sangam Tamil literature, which will now be described. In ancient times, Tamil poets were believed to have gathered at three Sangams to recite their works, which were then put together in collections. There is some dispute about the dates of these three academies of letters, but periods of 300 to 100 BC, 100 BC to AD 300, and AD 300 to AD 700 are now commonly accepted for the three Sangams on grounds of both internal and external evidence.

No works of the First Sangam have survived. From the Second, there are only fragments of the *Tholkappiyam*, a grammatical treatise in the form of aphorisms that is attributed to the sage Agasthya. From the Third Sangam a mass of material has come down by way of both collections of works, and of stories. The nature of these is tabulated below.

ANTHOLOGIES

(a) *Ettuthokai* (Eight Collections): Some of these may be of the second and third centuries AD, the others of a later date.

(b) *Patthupattu* (Ten Idylls): The first four of these are dated to the third and fourth centuries AD, and the last six to the sixth century AD. These ten idylls included the *Pattinapalai, Porunararu, Perumpanuru,* and a long poem of 782 lines, *Mathuraikkanchi,* dated about AD 450.

(c) *Pathinenaru-Killkannaku* (Eighteen Minor Didactic Poems): These are placed in the sixth and seventh centuries AD.

INDIVIDUAL POEMS

(a) *Nedunalvadal* by Nakkirar.

(b) *Thirukkural* by Thiruvalluvar.

COLLECTIONS

(a) *Agananuru* or *Akam-nanuru*: Some of these pieces may be older, but most are dated between the fourth and sixth centuries AD.

(b) *Purananuru*: A collection of the works of 150 poets, including Kapilar, Avvaiyar, and Korur-Kilar. The earliest of these stem from before the fifth century AD, the others being of a later date.

EPICS

(a) *Silappadikaram* (Story of the Anklet): This is by Ilango Atikal, a prince, and is dated around the sixth century AD.

(b) *Manimekhalai:* This is by Seetalai Sattanar, and is contemporary with the above epic.

(c) Five other epics have survived, while three have been lost.

LATER LITERATURE

(a) Nayanar mystics: These collections date from between the seventh and the twelfth centuries AD, and include the *Thiruvachchakam, Thevaram*, and *Periyapuranam*.

(b) Alwar mystics: There is a collection of 4000 stanzas, of the same period as the above, by poet-mystics like Nammalwar, Thirumangai, Kulasekara, and others.

The references to food in old Tamil literature in the present book belong mostly to the fourth, fifth, and sixth centuries AD.

tandoor At the Indus Valley site of Kalibangan were found small, mud-plastered ovens with a side opening 'very strongly resembling the present-day tandoors'. Live embers are placed at the bottom and fanned briskly so that they glow, raising the temperature of the clay sides. Thick, slightly leavened wheat rotis called naan and tandoori are slapped on to the sides to cook, with some puffing and surface charring in patches. Meat and fish can also be tandoor-grilled; chicken is glazed a brilliant orange-red through a turmeric and lime rubbing, and even artificial colouring. Tandoori products are very dry. Till recently the tandoori style of grilling was confined only to north and north-west India, but has now spread by way of restaurant food all over the country.

tangerines Also called mandarins, botanically the species is *Citrus reticulata*; in popular terms it is the loose-jacketed santhra, which is probably of Chinese origin. There is a Japanese tangerine species, and mandarins with names like Satsuma, Mediterranean, and spice (*see* citrus).

tapioca The tapioca tuber is a staple food only in Assam and Kerala, being eaten elsewhere as a tuberous vegetable, like the sweet potato and potato. Outside India it goes by such names as cassava and manioc. Though wild *Manihot esculenta* is not known, maximum diversity has been noted in north-east Brazil and south Mexico. Even as far back as in 3000 BC, tapioca flour was an important trade commodity in the north-west part of South America. The crop is stated to have come into India only around AD 1800. There may have been more than one point of entry. An early ingress may have been to Malabar from Africa, to which it had been transported from Brazil with the slave trade, and a later one from the Philippines to Assam and Bengal.

About a century ago, following the failure of the rice crop and widespread distress, the Travancore ruler Vaishakam Thirunal (1880–1885) investigated several plants in terms of future food security. He decided on the tapioca, which could be grown in every backyard in lush Kerala and kept in the ground till required. The ruler personally conducted demonstrations to show how the bitter principles should be leached out of the tuber before consumption. Such bitterness varies in degree; long duration varieties tend to be bitter, and are therefore chosen for the industrial production of tapioca starch, since the plants can simply be left untended in forest areas without danger of animal depredation. Moisture stress, and the location in which the plant is raised, also influence the development of the bitter constituents. Tapioca contains very little protein, unlike common Indian cereal staples. Its consumption is on the decline in Kerala.

tastes *See* rasa.

tea The tea plant is indubitably Chinese, and both common terms for tea that are in use the world over— teh and cha—are of Chinese origin. Cultivation has been practised for two thousand years, and at first the leaves were probably eaten as a green vegetable. Brewing is first described in a Chinese book of AD 220–265. I Ching, a Chinese traveller in India in the fifth century AD, described the tea brew.

Tea garden

Mendelslo, in AD 1662, noted the medicinal use of the tea brew: 'At our ordinary meetings every day we took only thay, which is commonly used all over the Indies, not only among those of the country, but also among the Dutch and the English, who take it as a drug that cleanses the stomach, and digests the superfluous humours, by a temperate heat particular thereto. In AD 1665 Jean de Thevenot notes that the brahmins drank nothing but water 'wherein they put coffee and tea', and in AD 1689 Ovington records that tea was drunk by the banias in Surat without sugar, or mixed with a small quantity of conserved lemons, and that tea with some spices added was consumed as cure for headache, gravel, and gripe. The source of the tea leaves then in use is not clear.

There are two major forms of tea. *Camellia sinensis* var. sinensis is a Chinese variety with small leaves, and *C. sinensis* var. assamica is almost a tree, with large coarse leaves. Modern plants in India are mostly hybrids of the two. A secondary centre for tea plant diversity was Kampuchea.

In 1830, when the Chinese tea trade with England collapsed during the Opium Wars, commercial tea planting was proposed by the British in India. Plants brought in from China did badly, but a few years earlier Major Charles Bruce had reported seeing tea plants with thick leaves being cultivated in Assam. Growth trials with both plants in Assam, and on the Himalayas and the south Indian hills, showed the Assam varieties to hold the most promise. An opinion poll in England in 1838 confirmed the quality of the tea leaf, and in 1841, two parcels of tea, one of 95 chests from the Luckimpore plantation, and another of 30 chests of tea that had been traditionally raised in Assam by the Singfo tribe, whose chief was Ningrolla, commanded high prices at a London tea auction, and commercial interest was aroused. In 1864, £ 3 million and in 1875 £ 26 million worth of tea was auctioned in London at Mincing Lane. The Assam Company had been formed in 1840, and between 1835 and 1853 tea plantations sprouted all over Assam and later in the Kumaon Hills, around Dehra Dun, and then in the Kangra Valley and Darjeeling. In south India Christie and Crew laid out the Ketti Experimental farm near Ooty (Udhagamandalam);

Tejpat

Mann planted tea near Coonoor, and by 1839, tea was reported to be 'growing luxuriously in the Nilgiris'. Sri Lanka, where coffee plantations had been wiped out by fungal disease by 1887, 'was saved from absolute bankruptcy by the substitution of tea for coffee'.

With rapidly expanding production, tea was actively promoted both within India and abroad. Production at Independence was about 245,000 tonnes, of which a major proportion was exported.

tejpat The aromatic leaves of the Indian cassia, *Cinnamomum tamala*, used as a flavourant in palaos and biriyanis. At the beginning of the Christian era, tejpat leaves were exported to Rome under the name malabathrum (q.v.). The Sanskrit name tamali occurs in the *Raja Nirghanta*. Tvak is mentioned by Sushrutha and Vaghbhata; this was the bark of the same tree, and an inferior substitute for cinnamon, used, for example, to perfume drinking water.

temple foods It is usual in a Hindu temple to prepare foods that are first offered to the deities, and left in their presence for a while to satisfy their spiritual hunger. Thereafter the food becomes a sanctified prasad (q.v.), which is distributed or even sold to the assembled devotees. Each temple has its own special prasad(s) established over a long period of time,

and the quantities cooked daily at the popular temples are enormous. In south India, the Padmanabhaswami temple in Thiruvananthapuram has a special aviyal that uses traditional vegetables, fresh coconut, and coconut oil, and no mustard seeds. The Ganesha temples of Kerala have the unni-appam, which are spongy-brown fried pieces made of a melange of rice powder, banana, jackfruit, and jaggery. The Muruga temple of the Palani Hills has its own panchamrita of crystal sugar, honey, ghee, cardamom, and fruits (bananas, dates and raisins), which does not go rancid for even as long as six weeks. The great Vishnu temple of Devarajaswami in Kanchipuram has a prasad of a giant idli weighing a kilo and a half; this is spiced with pepper, jeera, ginger, and asafoetida, fermented with curd, and then steamed. The Vishnu temple at Srimushnam has a confection prepared from the sweet root korai, which is held to be dear to Varaha, the boar incarnation of Vishnu.

In the great Thirupati temple dedicated to Lord Venkateshwara, laddus are given as prasadam to the pilgrims after it has been offered to the deity. As many as 70,000 of these are made every day in the inner kitchen by thirty cooks, who use 3 tonnes of urad dhal, 6 tonnes of sugar and 2.5 tonnes of ghee, besides large amounts of raisins, cashew-nuts, and cardamom. Smaller quantities of other sweets are also made, besides 30,000 each of the vada, dosai, and rava-appam. In the inner kitchen, some 400 kg each of various rice-based dishes, like savoury and sweet pongal, sour rice, curd rice, and sweet payasam are cooked every day to be served to pilgrims, who eat in large dining halls. At the Dharmasthala temple in Karnataka, food is served every day to between 30,000 and 50,000 people.

Some of the most elaborate preparations of temple food are perhaps those at the Jagannatha temple in Puri in Orissa, where every day a thousand persons manning 750 chulahs and ovens turn out a hundred varieties of dishes using rice and wheat and their flours and grits, urad dhal, indigenous vegetables, jaggery and spices, with cow ghee as the cooking medium. The gods are served ritually five times a day, and pilgrims can eat at the spacious bhoga-mandapa, or buy mahaprasad at a huge market within the temple walls. In these very traditional temple foods, many recently arrived food ingredients will be avoided; thus only sweet potatoes are used at Puri, though potatoes are in common local use.

tempura These are strips of vegetables or fish dipped in batter, deep-fried and served piping hot one by one in Japan. They closely resemble the well-established bajjiyas of India which use a batter of besan (q.v.), and indeed appear to have been introduced into Japan by Catholic Portuguese missionaries who were accustomed in India to eating fish fried in batter on days of abstinence from meat, such as Fridays.

thali The sthali was a ritual cooking pot used in a domestic Vedic kitchen to boil rice, the everyday kaccha food (q.v.). The name survives in a modified form in the thali of today; however, this is not a pot but a circular metal dining plate with raised edges, often accompanied by deep, small circular metal bowls called katoris in which are placed

Thali

accompaniments to the meal, like dry and wet curries, curds, and even desserts like payasam. Earlier used mostly in the northern parts of the country thalis are now popular everywhere, both in the home and in restaurants. At large gatherings, as for a wedding feast, disposable leaf plates (q.v.) would still be preferred.

thava *See* griddle.

therapeutic diets Certain specific items of food suggested for various conditions by Sushrutha may be briefly recorded. Coconut water was recommended for biliousness (deranged pittha), and barley water for fever, thirst, and indigestion. In convalescence or slight fever, boiled rice with lightly-seasoned meat was recommended, and during fever, the juices offered are radish, parwal, and neem. Loss of appetite, debility, and thirst could be counteracted with a suspension of parched barley or rice in water, sweetened with honey or jaggery, or with buttermilk containing bitter juices. In dysentery, milk was as valuable as ambrosia. For tuberculosis, it was animal meat all the way; the flesh of the crow, vulture, mongoose, cat, cormorant or beasts of prey fried in mustard oil, or, as an alternative, the flesh of the camel, ass, elephant, mule, horse or forest-dwelling herbivores. Vomiting called for milk, or soups of meat, or light cereals, and tender vegetables. Asthma needed extracts of chicken, pigeons, and wild fowl,

cooked with large quantities of acid juices, salt and ghee. When intestinal worms were present, milk, meat, ghee, green leafy vegetables, curds and sweet or acid substances were all forbidden. Dyspepsia called for fruits, cooked roots, tasty beverages, and sweetmeats made with acid juices. These injunctions can hardly be faulted even in the light of present hindsight.

The accent was always on the preservation of good health through a well-adjusted diet. 'Without proper diet, medicines are of no use; with proper diet, medicines are unnecessary' sums up this attitude very pithily.

thuvar The thuvar or arhar (pigeon pea, *Cajanus cajan*) is an important pulse in the country. It is called adhaki in early Buddhist literature (*c.* 400 BC) and is the thuvarika mentioned by Charaka. It had long been held to be of African origin, since no wild form could be found in the country. However, careful work in India showed that the progenitor of thuvar was a species of *Atylosia*, of which seventeen species grow in India; this includes wild species on the Western Ghats of the Dekhan plateau. Thuvarai crosses easily with at least three species of *Atylosia* to give a fertile first-generation and later crosses, and this involves no change in the chromosome number of 11. A southern origin also seems likely from the southern name thuvarai or thuvari which travelled northwards. Even today two distinct varieties are recognized. Arhar in north India is a tall shrub with yellow flowers streaked with purple, and long, hairy, maroon pods that bear four or five seeds. The southern thuvar is a short plant, with pure yellow flowers and short, green pods with three seeds.

Thuvar dhal is the base for the sambhars and rasams of south India, and indeed has second place among the pulses of India, after the chickpea (chana). It is surprising therefore that it does not seem to be mentioned in old Tamil Sangam literature. In the twelfth century AD, the *Manasollasa* of central India describes a dish called vidalapaka made from five pulses, of which one was parched thuvar. A pulse called krishnadhaki or black thuvar, of uncertain identity, is referred to in the *Shivatattvaratnakara* (*c.* AD 1700) of the western coast. A work of AD 1648 AD by Govinda Vaidya refers to a dish of thuvar dhal cooked with vegetables, the current huli or sambhar (q.v.) which has a place in every southern meal.

tiffin In colonial India, when the evening dinner became a heavy daily repast, only a light afternoon meal was necessary. This was called tiffin, a word which first appears in AD 1807 in Anglo-Indian writing. It meant a light family meal of salads, done-over remnants of the meats of the previous day in the form of minces, pies, and even curry, fruit fools, jellies, and ice-creams. The word tiffin itself is a colloquial English term, which comes from the word tiffing for eating or drinking out of mealtimes, and the word tiff, which was to eat the midday meal. The word tiffin has been adopted particularly in the Madras area for a light afternoon snack of items like the uppuma, dosai, and vada, to the extent that many take it to be an Indian language word.

tobacco Shredded tobacco leaves, Indianized to thambaku, are frequently chewed in India packed in a betel quid, making the product a food of sorts. The tobacco plant is of South American origin, but was introduced into India as early as in the sixteenth century. This seems to have been at two locations, the Surat-Broach area in Gujarat and the Andhra Pradesh coast round Macchilipatnam. Both plantations progressed so rapidly that exports were recorded as early as in AD 1619 from the former location and in AD 1622 from the latter. Akbar was presented a pipeful of tobacco by his courtier Asad Beg, and took two or three puffs, strongly against his physician's advice. So rapidly did the habit of smoking spread that Jahangir issued a ban against it in AD 1619, but to little effect. Revenues from tobacco were considerable almost from the start.

Tomato

toddy A simple anglicization of the Hindi term tari (itself from the Sanskrit tala), the fermented sweet sap of the tar or palmyra palm (q.v.). It was referred to as tala by Megasthenes as early as in 350 BC, and by numerous later European visitors. The Tamil term is kallu, and the pot in which the exudate is collected from incisions is termed kall(u)-kundam in old Tamil literature (*see also* beverages, alcoholic).

tomato In AD 1880, Watt remarked that tomatoes were grown chiefly for the European population; Indians, he added, were beginning to appreciate the tomato, and 'Bengalis and Burmans to use it in their sour curries'. The tomato (tomatl in the Nahua tongue of Mexico) seems to have originated either in Mexico or Peru, and great morphological variation exists between the forms in Mexico, Central America, and coastal Peru. The tomato was well diversified when Europeans reached the New World, and from just one sub-species is believed to have sprung the four common varieties of the tomato *Lycopersicon lycopersicum*, namely the common, cherry, large-leaved, and pear tomatoes.

The tomato reached Europe in AD 1550, and was first adopted in Italy as an excellent partner to pasta dishes. Because of its relationship to poisonous plants like the belladonna and mandrake, its acceptance in England was slow; this was not helped by the name love-apple, with aphrodisiac connotations, that became attached to it. Unlike several other plants from the New World, the tomato did not come directly to India, but by way of England at a late but uncertain date, perhaps around 1850.

tools, prehistoric The Palaeolithic period in the evolution of civilization started about 250,000 years ago and lasted a long time, to be succeeded in about 10,000 BC by the brief Mesolithic period, and from about 7500 to 2000 BC by the Neolithic or new stone age. Each was characterized by man-made tools of increasing sophistication and diversity.

Some thirty sites of the Palaeolithic age have been discovered all over India. Early tools here take the form of what are called cleavers and hand-axes, which are massive stones used to club down animals. Gujarat is especially rich in such tools, probably because there was a land bridge with the African landmass before the sea level rose in the last warm period after a glacial age. Tools of the next period consist mostly of pointed oval-shaped stones of various kinds, which were used as axes, spears, scrapers, and knives. In both these phases, the kinds of tools suggest that while man must have been a vegetarian in the simian phase (as apes still are), meat has now found a place in his diet. In the Neolithic stage, the tools become more finished and polished. Flakes are chipped off from a pebble singly to give a single sharp edge, or repeatedly to give a serrated one. Hand-axes are now pear-shaped or oval, up to even an arm in length, and cleavers are similar but oblong in shape, with a long chisel edge. Such tools, found all over the country, connote an essentially meat diet. But some tools are clearly meant for digging, probably for food articles like roots and tubers. Besides these foods, natural items like honey, berries, fruits, and nuts were eaten.

The next step in tool evolution took the form of small, sharp stone flakes called microliths, which have been found in particularly large numbers in southern and western coastal India after about 7500 BC. These were small chips struck off from rocks of fine-grained stones like jasper, agate, flint, and crystal. Microliths could

be affixed with resins to an arrow to greatly increase hunting skills, to lances, and to spears for fishing. Affixed to wooden handles, microliths were made into scrapers, scythes, and knives, which gave a new dimension to the gathering and processing of vegetable foods. From a food hunter, man, through the refinement of tools, became a food gatherer and agriculturist.

A special development in south India around 4000 BC was the teri or sand-dune fishing culture of the sea coasts, which used microliths extensively. Rather later came another unusual development in the south, the megalithic culture of about 750 BC, which lasted about a century, and saw the wide use of iron tools (much before anywhere else in India) for agriculture, and perhaps also to put up the huge stone structures of uncertain import called megaliths.

toothpicks At the Nalanda monastery in the fifth century AD, the Chinese pilgrim I Ching was given tooth sticks after every meal, and he later exhorted his countrymen in his writings to rinse the mouth after a meal, then chew tooth wood and cleanse the tongue and teeth. In *c.* AD 1000, after dining, King Shrenika cleaned his teeth with tooth sticks and fragrant powder, then washed his hands with water and fragrant powder. The *Shivatattvaratnakara* written by King Basavaraja of Keladi, in *c.* AD 1700, mentions that small toothpicks, called vati and ghutika, were made from pichumani wood, or from bamboo, grass, or metals. To make scented toothpicks, the slivers were marinated in bovine urine mixed with the powder of the haritaki myrobalan (*Terminalia chebula*) for a week, then immersed in scented water, smeared with spices and flavours, and dried.

tortoise, turtle Tortoise shell was an export item to Europe noted in the Tamil literature of the early Christian era, and its flesh was relished, we are told, by the Meenavar or fishermen. Charaka lists tortoise meat as edible, and Sushrutha rates it highly. It is also extolled in an Assamese work, the *Kamarupa Yatra* of AD 600-800, along with the meat of the duck, pigeon, and wild boar. The twelfth-century *Manasollasa* written by King Someshwara refers to roasted tortoise.

tubers Tubers come under the class of uncultivated foods, and hence are permitted to ascetics and people who have taken a vow or are fasting. Charaka terms roots mula, and bulbous tubers kanda. Old Tamil literature echoes these in words like mulam and kandam, and others like vem, shadai, shivai, and thuri. Tubers are particularly abundant in wet terrain, such as Bengal, Assam, and Kerala, where they are cooked as vegetables, or along with greens or meat. In health terms, tubers are sweet and heavy, providing energy and building up tissues. They depress vata and kapha. Yams are rated the best among tubers; they improve digestion, whereas sweet potatoes are hard to digest (*see* aroids; yams; individual tubers).

turkey The turkey originated from wild forms in Mexico, from where it was taken to England. Here it was given the name turkey in error for some large eastern bird, such as the peacock or guinea fowl. It became the accepted item for a traditional Christmas lunch, and for this purpose the turkey was brought by the colonial to India. It was never very successful here, and was often replaced by the peacock, which in one view 'combines the flavour of the pheasant with the juiciness of the turkey', besides having a meat of an attractive white colour. A traditional Thanksgiving meal in America, on the fourth Thursday of every November, would include the indigenous turkey.

turmeric *Curcuma longa* is an ancient yellow rhizome, probably native to India. It is a triploid (2n = 42), but various polyploids (2n = 32, 62, 64, etc.) have been recorded, and even the basic chromosome number is not known. Its striking orange-yellow colour and dyeing ability soon gave the turmeric root an important place in magic, ritual, and cuisine in India. Its name in Sanskrit, haridra (haldi in Hindi) has an aboriginal connotation.

The *Yajurveda* mentions a community of despised nishadas (nisha = turmeric, ad= to eat), comprising people in such low occupations as svanin (dog keepers), chandala (dog eaters), and punjistha (fowlers). Old Tamil literature also has numerous references to turmeric as manjal, a word that came to be also used for the sacred orange colour of the spice.

Turmeric in the Hindu view is a highly auspicious material, whose use is banned in a house of mourning. It is considered auspicious to apply it on the face of a bride, and many women apply turmeric paste as a depilatory and to ensure a smooth, shining skin. Xuan Zang notes of Indians: 'Every time they perform the functions of nature they wash their bodies and use perfumes of turmeric and sandal-wood.' Jains do not permit the use of fresh green turmeric, since it is an underground product liable to harbour life forms.

In cooking, turmeric powder is almost an indispensable part of the mixed curry powders that are freshly ground using a roller and flat slab. It is used in the cooking of vegetables, meat and fish to impart both colour and a slight sharp taste and flavour. In health terms turmeric is tikta (bitter) but also pungent and astringent, dry, light, and keen. Medicinally it is warming, a good stomach and appetite regulator; boiled in hot milk, it helps cure sore throats, colds, coughs, and chills.

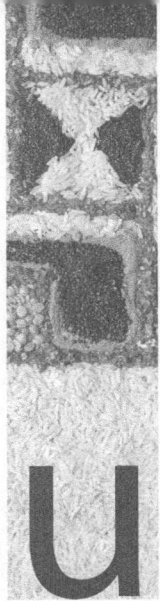

Unani medicine The Unani (or Greek) system of medicine owes its origin to Hippocrates (460–377 BC), but was later extensively developed by Arab doctors. Al-Razi dealt in detail with smallpox and measles, and Al-Majusi with dietetics and materia medica; prominent among writers was Ibn Sina (Latinized to Avi-cenna), whose book *Al-Quandom*, written in about AD 1025, deals extensively with both physiological and psychological matters.

Unani medicine is based on the Hippocratic theory that a perfect balance between the elements (arkhan), humours (akhlat), and temperament (mizaj) is necessary for good health. Every individual has inherent powers of self-preservation, called quwat-e-modabira. The four humours present in the human body are dum (blood and other red body fluids), balgham (phlegm and other colourless fluids), safra (yellow fluids like bile), and saoda (black bile and other black fluids). The preponderance of these humours determines an individual's temperament or mizaj, which could be of four kinds: damvi (sanguine or plethoric), safravi (choleric or bilious), balghami (cold or phlegmatic), and saodavi (melancholic).

In diagnosis, the pulse (nabz) is extensively employed, besides an examination of the urine (baul) and stool (baraz). In examining the pulse, numerous aspects are looked for, like volume, tension, blood volume, pattern of movement, rest, rhythm, irregularity and so on. Treatment for simple diseases is mainly through diet in the initial stages, followed by the administration of a single drug, failing which compound preparations may be administered. Each drug is placed under four categories, based on potency and efficacy.

There are four treatment therapies employed in Unani medicine. These are regimental therapy (venasection, diuresis, Turkish bath, massage, purging, exercise and so on); pharmaco-therapy (use of herbal, animal and mineral drugs); surgery; and dieto-therapy (quantity and quality of food). Thus for diabetes, several bitter and astringent items (stones of the jamoon fruit, phalsa fruit, bittergourd juice, tender neem shoots, bilva leaves, and cottonseed kernels) are prescribed. Incompatible combinations, which should never be taken together, are rice and water-melon, rice and sattu (flour of parched rice), pomegranate and hareesa (ground wheat and meat), and fish and milk.

urad The black gram, urad, is botanically *Vigna mungo*; the Sanskrit term, masha, is probably of even earlier Munda origin. It is one of the three Ms of Sanskrit literature from the *Yajurveda* onwards, the others being mudga (mung) and masura (masoor). The Buddha endorsed all the three Ms for regular use, and the *Brhadaranyaka Samhita* includes it as one of 'the ten food-grains'. Urad is thought to be indigenous to India, and shares a common ancestor with mung. The pulse has been found around 1500 BC in archaeological excavations at Navdatoli and Daulatapur.

Historical literature indicates a wide range of usage. One of these, from the very start, is as a pulse accompaniment to rice, a practice now confined to the north. In the south it has other outlets. An early form of the idli described by Chavundaraya in AD 1025 was made by soaking ground urad in buttermilk, grinding it again to a fine paste with spices, and finally deep-frying the shaped masses. A century later, the *Manasollasa* written by King Someshwara has essentially the same recipe (*see* idli). Even the kadubu (q.v.) of the Karnataka area is thus described by Terekanambi Bommarasa in AD 1485: 'The kings are relishing the kadubu made of black gram ... (it was) attractive to the eye and pleasing to the mind.' Thus both the idli and kadubu were then products based entirely on urad dhal, whereas today, to make both, a mixture of two parts of rice grits and one part of urad are ground and fermented together overnight, after which a thicker batter serves to make the steamed idli, and a thinner one the pan-fried dosai. In fact it is puzzling that the urad, or ulundu in Tamil, so important an ingredient in these common breakfast items, is hardly even mentioned in old Tamil Sangam literature (q.v.).

Urad has always been the pulse of choice for making papads and vadas. The *Manasollasa* mentions a crisp-fried snack called gharika. Old Gujarati literature describes an urad vada with holes in it that was fried to a deep brown shade, and in Bengal, a meal served to the mystic Chaitanya by his admirer Sarvabhauma included a boda of urad. The current medhu- or uddina-vada of the Karnataka area is a disc with a hole in the centre, soft and elastic inside and crispy brown on the surface; when soaked in curd the dahi-vada (q.v.) is obtained, with a salty spicing of the curd base in south India, and a sweet touch in the west and north. A rice batter with some urad, when deep fried, yields the crisp coiled murukku and chakli, crunchy seedai marbles, and bonda balls. Almost pure urad flour, with just a little rice as a binder, yields the crisp jilebi (q.v.), which is later soaked in sugar syrup. Roasted urad dhal grits give textural variety to an uppuma, and to red chilli-based molaga-podi, eaten with a little oil poured on it as an accompaniment to the idli. A sweet laddu of urad figures in a Gujarati work of AD 1520, the *Varanaka Samuchaya*.

utensils *See* cooking utensils.

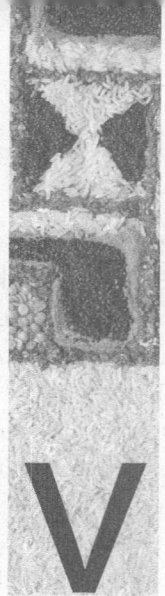

V

vada Termed vataka, the vada is fully described even in the *Dharmasutras* (800–300 BC) as soaked, coarsely ground and fermented pulses (especially masha or urad), fashioned into various shapes, and deep-fried in ghee. Patanjali (second century BC) notes a special vatakini Paurnamasi day, when only this item was eaten. The *Apabrahmasatrayi* (*c.* AD 1000)

Vadas

mentions vatakas of several kinds dipped in milk and curd, perhaps the first reference to the current dahi-vada. The *Manasollasa* (twelfth century AD) describes fermented urad vatakas, soaked either in milk to give kshiravataka, or in sour rice water, kanjika. Kannada literature mentions a chana vade in AD 1025; urad-based products were served at a domestic meal (Annaji, AD 1600); and in AD 1606, both a sukhin-vade (today a rice-banana-jaggery deep-fried product) and a vade of colocasia leaves were served. The Gujarati work *Varunaka Samuchaya* written in AD 1520, has a rather jumbled list of pulse-based items, in which may be discerned a mirchi-na-vada, magna (mung) and kulattha (horsegram) vadas, and a kanji-vada. While several pulses may be used to make a vada, urad remains a favourite; the uddina-

(or medhu-) vade of the present in Karnataka, soft inside and crunchy outside, is excellent for eating as such, or after soaking it in curds flavoured with salt, green ginger, and coriander leaves. The vada of Hindi is termed vade in Karnataka and vadai or vadam in Tamil Nadu.

varagu *See* kodo millet.

vata One of the three doshas (q.v.) or temperaments, which in ayurvedic theory is a combination of the elements air and ether. These elements give vata the quality of mobility or movement in space, both in the universe and within man. It is responsible for perception, assimilation, and reaction, converting sensory experience to psychosomatic reactions. Sushrutha describes vata as the driving force that keeps everything going, but also as the main cause of disruption. Vaghbhata describes a vata temperament as one of instability in thought and action. Dry and cold are the two important vata characteristics, for which a diet of grain, fruit, milk, and meat broth is best suited; pungent, bitter and astringent foods such as pulses, hot spices, tea and coffee are best avoided. The seat of disturbed vata is frequently the colon (*see* kapha; pitta).

Vedas *See* Sanskrit literature.

vegetables The major foodgrains are those raised by the plough, namely cereals, pulses, and oilseeds, and hence references to agriculture in Sanskrit Vedic literature are mainly to these foodgrains, and indeed especially to rice. We do learn however that supplementary foods were raised on the outskirts of villages. Banks of rivers, 'beaten by foam', were considered suitable for growing pumpkins and gourds. Vegetable root crops were raised in the vicinity of wells. Low grounds, like the moist beds of lakes, were suitable for leafy crops. Marginal furrows between rows of other crops were recommended for planting fragrant plants and medicinal herbs.

The collective term for vegetables was shaka, which comprised six kinds. These were ripened vegetables, leaves, tubers, roots, flowers, and pods (shimbi). Of these, there are other entries in this volume under green leafy vegetables; aroids; and melons, pumpkins, and gourds. It is mainly the fruit-type of vegetables that are discussed here, with some excursions where called for.

The first vegetables mentioned in the *Rigveda* are the lotus stem (visa), and the cucumber (urvaruka). The later Vedas refer to several others, like lotus roots (shaluka), the bottle-gourd (alabu), the water-chestnut (saphaka, mulali), two other aquatic plants (avaka and andika), and the bittergourd (karivrnta, later kara-vella). Uncooked shaka were cooked to give products termed bhaji and shrano. The Buddhist and Jain canonical literature refers to yams (aluka), two convolvulus roots (etaluka and kadambu), and several leafy vegetables (*see* green leafy vegetables). Kautilya in his *Arthashastra* refers to the rajdhana or ksiri (now kauki, *Manilkara kauki*) and to the cucumber as chidbhita. The Ramayana speaks of the surana or elephant yam (vajrakanda), the pindaluka (possibly the sweet potato), the bottlegourd (kalasaku), the sleshmataka and lasora (both *Cordia* species that bear fruits which can be cooked or pickled), karira (*Capparis decidua*, with edible sour berries), and sudarshana or vrspani (unidentified). Medical literature refers to the patola (parwal) and vartaka (brinjal), which are praised as good vegetables. Early Tamil literature has references to brinjals and bittergourd (pagal), unripe bananas, and a variety of tubers (q.v.)

After AD 1500, several new vegetables came in from Mexico and South America through the efforts of the Portuguese and Spanish (*see* Mexico, food from). These included some vegetables that greatly influenced Indian food, namely the tomato, potato, tapioca, and capsicum, one of several forms of the chilli. Also, with colonialism came temperate European vegetables like the cabbage, cauliflower, lettuce, long orange carrots (which differ from the indigenous variety; *see* carrot), French

or sword beans, haricot or navy beans (rajmah), and, quite recently, the winged bean. (Separate entries may be referred to for several of these.)

In ayurvedic terms, many of the fruit-type of vegetables are sweet. Most of them (gourds, brinjal, cucumber, radish) reduce pitta and kapha, with mixed reactions on vata (depressed by ash gourd, snake gourd, and cucumber, aggravated by the bottlegourd, ridge gourd, and large radish). Specific vegetables are recommended for specific symptoms. Thus the ash gourd, bittergourd, peas, and radish all purify the blood, but have different reactions. The brinjal is strength-giving and a heart tonic, and the bittergourd is a laxative that also increases the appetite; the brinjal is not recommended in a cough, fever or lethargy, in all of which the bittergourd is useful. The snake gourd is appetizing, strength-giving, and very useful in tuberculosis.

In the Aryan view, vegetables were not anna or cultivated grains, but phala. They had to be washed in the home to render them of sufficient rank to enter the cooking area. In fact, when recovering from childbirth, the new mother could not enter the cooking area for fear of pollution, but could, for a few months, undertake to peel and cut phala elsewhere.

Vegetable preparations are hardly ever described in Sanskrit literature. A late reference is to a small cucumber, chirbhita, which was cut into pieces, dried, and fried to constitute a delicacy. The *Manasollasa* uses the generic term pude for a delicacy of mixed fried vegetables folded into a turmeric leaf and then steamed; one example of such a filling was brinjal fried with rice grits and chopped onion. A bartha (mash) of brinjal was termed baji. Palidhya was a class of spiced vegetables cooked in curd and then given a baghar seasoning. Both brinjal bartha and palidhya also feature in a Kannada work of AD 1485. Chavundaraya's *Lokopakara* mentions thirty-one vegetables in one chapter on cooking, and Mangarasa's *Supa Shastra* has a long chapter on the cooking of vegetables. Chapter 8 of the *Lingapurana* written by Gurulinga Desika (AD 1594) is a long one, and numerous ways of cooking each of a dozen vegetables are outlined.

Current cuisines show considerable variety in the use of vegetables. The sambhars of Tamil Nadu and Kerala based on thuvar dhal employ soft vegetables like brinjals, lady's finger, drumsticks, gourds, and yams. The distinctive aviyal of Kerala employs green bananas, drumsticks, various beans, and the like cooked in coconut milk and then tossed with coconut oil in spiced sour curd. Kalan is a similar dish that uses only green bananas, and olan is a dish of ash gourd and dried beans cooked again in coconut milk and coconut oil. Small pieces of ash gourd or raw mango cooked with coconut, curds, and chilli paste is called pulisseri. Erisseri is a similar preparation from pumpkin. Kootu is a dish of various mixed vegetables. Thoran is usually made from payaru (lobia) cut into small bits, stir-fried in oil, and finally cooked in a little water. Green bananas, spinach, cabbage, and peas can all be cooked in this way.

Bengali food has innovative vegetable combinations, like pumpkin with climbing spinach (puin), gourds with whole chana, and sponge gourd with poppy seeds. Raw jackfruit, tender drumsticks, parwal, and tubers are imaginatively cooked, and even peelings of potato and pumpkin are utilized. The bitter shukto item can contain bittergourd, neem leaves, brinjals, potatoes, radish, and green bananas, along with turmeric, ginger, mustard and radhuni (celery seed) in the form of ground pastes. Dalna is a dish of delicately spiced vegetables; fried vegetables are bhaja, boiled vegetables bhate, and spiced vegetables ghonto. Flowers of the pumpkin and banana are eaten, as is the pith of the banana (called thod). Gujarat has a handva or mixed vegetable stew, often served with steamed besan cakes placed on top. From this dish has sprung the Parsi oberu, to which meat may sometimes be added. The sun-drying of several vegetables, berries and greens for year-round storage and cooking is characteristic of arid Rajasthan (*see also* individual vegetables).

vegetarianism About a quarter of the population of India is reckoned on census data to be vegetarian. The states with a high proportion of vegetarians (shown as percentages) are Gujarat (69), Rajasthan (60), Punjab–Haryana (54), and Uttar Pradesh (50). At medium-high levels are Madhya Pradesh (45), Karnataka (34), and Maharashtra (30). Medium-low levels prevail in Tamil Nadu (21), Andhra Pradesh (16), and Assam (15), and low vegetarian levels (6 each) in Kerala, Orissa, and West Bengal. Part of this vegetarianism is economic in origin, since animal foods are comparatively expensive. But a more compelling force is the ethical one against the consumption of food that necessitates the taking of life. Such perceptions have a long history in India.

The early Aryans ate meat of many kinds, over fifty being listed in the Vedas as fit for sacrifice, which was always a prelude to their being consumed (*see* meat consumption). The cow, because of its utility and being practically a household pet, was especially an object of concern right from the very start (*see* beef). Prohibitions, starting with various members of the bovine species, gradually begin to be expressed in the *Sutra* literature. Thus the *Manusmriti*

(*c.* 200 BC), a veritable code of living, has formidable lists of forbidden meats in no less than fifty-four chapters.

It has been said that this battle against Vedic animal sacrifices was really won by the Buddhists and the Jains. The Buddha was strongly opposed to ritual sacrifices as a means of personal salvation practised by the brahmins, but he allowed Buddhist monks to consume cooked meat if it was given to them as alms. His contemporary Mahavira, the 24th thirthankara of the Jain community, went much further. Not only did the question of killing an animal for food simply not arise, but great care was taken to ensure that even unseen but potential forms of life were spared. Only food that was 'absolutely innocent' was permitted, and the prohibitions included twenty-two unsuitable things and another thirty-two with life potential (*see* Jains, food of). These feelings found a responsive echo among the people, to which weight was added by the edicts of Emperor Ashoka, a devout Buddhist. Brahmin priests were obliged to follow suit, and influential reformers like Shankara, Madhva, and Ramanuja altered the sacrifices by substituting, for the animal head, objects like coconuts and pumpkins smeared with vermilion powder.

Brahmins in India in general are vegetarian, with the exception of those in Kashmir (q.v.) and

Bengal (q.v.), and the Saraswaths of Karnataka, who are believed to hail from Kashmir. Followers of Vishnu, even in Bengal, are always vegetarian, as are Jains and Buddhists. Some communities follow vegetarian habits as a means of gaining social esteem, others from genuine conviction. Quite frequently an older person seeking spiritual serenity will give up eating meat. Being a vegetarian occasions little surprise in India. And even as long ago as in 1000 BC, so extensive was the range of cereals, pulses, oilseeds, vegetables, fruit, milk, condiments, spices, and sweetening agents available, that vegetarian meals of high nutritional quality, and with gustatory and aesthetic appeal, could be fashioned. Perhaps nowhere else in the world except in India would it have been possible 3000 years ago to be a strict vegetarian.

venison *See* deer.

vinegar Shuktha and ambila in Sanskrit (in Hindi, shirka) is first mentioned in early Buddhist literature. Sugar and wheat were added to buttermilk in a jar, which when kept warm in respiring grain yielded vinegar. Sushrutha has a class of preparations called asuta, which are vegetables like gourds and radish preserved in vinegar. Dalhana (*c.* AD 1100) in his commentary on the *Sushrutha Samhita*, mentions jaggery, sugarcane juice, and honey as sources of vinegar. Vinegar came

to be used mainly in medicine by the Hindus, and in both medicine and cooking by the Muslims.

In colonial times, a variety of materials were used to make vinegar in different locations, like jaggery, sugar, grapes, raisins, jamoon fruit, the sap of the palmyra palm, and mahua flowers. These were stored underground in loosely covered jars for about six months, and then decanted or filtered. A quick-fermentation outfit was devised in the 1930s, in which the fermentation was carried out continuously in sections, after first charging the unit with enzymes from an earlier batch. Vinegar has a special place in the cuisine developed by Portuguese monks in Goa, in such dishes as pork vindaloo, sorpotel, and prawn balchao (*see* Goa, food of).

visitors to India From very early times, visitors to India left vivid records of India and her food and customs. These have frequently been referred to in this historical dictionary, and for convenience, a list now follows of these writers arranged chronologically according to their country.

Dates given after each name are followed by either S (period of stay in India) or L (lifespan). An asterisk placed before the name refers to writings with an exceptional degree of information concerning food in India.

GREECE

Scylax of Charybanda, 510 BC (S)

Herodotus 484–431 BC (L)

Ktesias 416–358 BC (L)

Alexander 327–325 BC (S)

Nearchos of Crete 327–325 BC (S)

Onesikritos 327–325 BC (S)

Seleukos Nikator 327–325 BC and 306 BC

* Megasthenes 305–302 BC (S)

Apollonius of Tyana 295 BC–? (L)

Diodorus Sicilus c. 85 BC–15 BC (L)

Strabo of Amnesia 65 BC–AD 25 (L)

Quentin Curtius-Rufus c. 30 BC–AD 30 (L)

All succeeding dates are in years AD

Pliny the Elder, 23–59 (L)

* Anonymous author, *Periplus Marts Erythraei c.* 50 (S)

Aelianus Tacitus (Aelian) 80–140 (L)

Flavinus Arrianus (Arrian) 96–160 (L)

Athenaios 3rd century (L)

Marcus Junianus Justinus (Justin), 3rd century (L)

CHINA

* Fa Xian 399–14 (S)

* Xuan Zang 629–645 (S)

* I Ching 671–695(5)

Ma Huan 1406 (S)

ARABIA

Ibn Khordadbah, died 911

Al-Masudi 915–916 (S)

Ibn-Haukal 950 (S)

* Al-Biruni 1017–1030 (S)

Al-Idrisi c. 1140 (S) (, [5]

Amir Khusrau 1253–1325 (S)

* Ibn Battuta 1325–1354 (S)

Abdur Razzak l470 (S)

EARLY EUROPEANS

John of Monte Corvino (Italy) 1292 (S)

Marco Polo (Italy) 1294 (S)

Odoric of Pordenone (Italy) 1316–1330 (S)

Friar Jordanus (France) 1328 (S)

Giovanni di Marignolli (Italy) 1357–1358 (S)

Hans Schiltberger (Germany) 1410 (S)

Afanasy Nikhitin (Russia) 1466–1472 (S)

Vasco da Gama (Portugal) 1498–1524 (3 visits)

VISITORS TO VIJAYANAGAR

Nicolo dei Conti (Italy) 1420 (S)

* Ludovico di Varthema (Italy) 1508 (S)

Duarte Barbosa (Portugal) c. 1518 (S)

* Domingo Paes (Portugal) 1518–1524 (S)

Fernao Nuniz (Portugal) 1536–1540 (S)

LATER EUROPEANS

* Garcia da Orta (Portugal) 1534–1569 (S)

St Francis Xavier (Spain) 1538–1546 (S)

* John Huygen van Linscnoten (Holland) *c.* 1596 (S, 6 years)

Henrique Henriques (France) second half of the 16th century

Goncalves Rodrigues (Portugal) second half of the 16th century

Father Frois (France) second half of the 16th century

Michael Pinheiro (Portugal) second half of the 16th century

Pedro Texeira (Portugal) second half of the 16th century

* Father Antonio Monserrate (France) 1580–1600 (S)

Thomas Stevens (England) 1579–1619 (S)

Ralph Fitch (England) 1583–1591 (S)

William Finch (England) 1608–1611 (S)

Thomas Coryat (England) 1612–1617 (S)

Pietro Delle Valle (Italy) 1614–1626 (S)

Sir Thomas Roe (England) 1615–1619 (S)

* Rev. Ed ward Terry (England) 1615–1619 (S)

Peter Mundy (England) 1628–1634 (S)

Francisco Pelsaert (Holland) 1621–1627 (S)

Joannes de Laet (Holland) 1593–1649 (L)

Father Sebastian Manrique (France) 1628–1641 (S)

Albert de Mendelslo (Holland) 1638 (S)

Jean-Baptiste Tavernier (France) 1640–1667 (6 visits)

* Francois Bernier (France) 1656–1668 (S)

* Niccolao Manucci (Italy) 1654–1714 (S)

Jean de Thevenot (France) 1665–1667 (S)

John Fryer (England) 1672–1681 (S)

* John Ovington (England) 1689 (S)

* George Rumphius (Holland) died 1693

* Heinrich van Rheede (Holland) 1680–1700 (S)

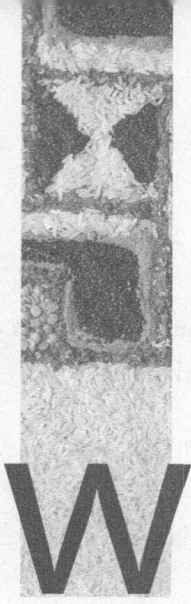

W

wadi The other names for this snack are vati and bari. The *Manasollasa* of the twelfth century AD describes them as balls of urad dhal, ground to a paste and allowed to ferment naturally for a few days, and then deep-fried to crispness. Early Gujarati literature refers to the same item as vatika, and also notes that the balls after fermentation can be dried and stored for use when needed. A century ago, wadi or bari was noted among the foods of Bihar, and indeed it is popular all over north India. The pakoda of south India is similar, but is not fermented; it is made of a thick batter of besan or mung dhal flour, and irregularly-shaped lumps are deep-fried, with rings of onion sometimes included in the batter.

walnut Though said to be indigenous to south-eastern Europe and China, the walnut (Sanskrit akshota, Hindi akrot, botanically *Juglans regia*), is a naturalized fruit all along the Himalayan range from Afghanistan to Bhutan. India and the Old World share the same delicate-tasting, oily walnut, but America has an indigenous black walnut, *Juglans nigra*, with a kernel of strong flavour tightly embedded in the shell.

water Water is required for agriculture, and domestically for bathing and cooking.

Found in vast numbers at Mohenjodaro were roughly made pottery jars with deep grooves round the middle, which are believed to have been fixed on water-wheels for raising water from rivers to the surface. In Vedic times these water-wheels were called ashmanchakra and araghatta. The true Persian wheel with a bucket chain and pin-driven gear came to India much later, in the fourth century AD according to some authorities and in the tenth century AD according to others. A solid circular stone with a hole in the centre found in Mohenjodaro and Lothal may be a stone pulley, mounted above wells for drawing up water using buckets at the end of a long rope. In later Vedic literature this is referred to as ghatayantra, and irrigation systems which used such water were in extensive use (*see* agriculture).

Water for drinking was always given careful attention. Nine sources (rainwater, well water, spring water, etc.) were recognized. Condensed atmospheric water was rated the best to drink, and in fact the best of all drinks, and the next best was water collected from porous soil. Cleanly collected rainwater was filtered and stored in a container of gold or silver or a boiled clay pot. Water meant for drinking had to be boiled exposed to sunlight and then filtered through charcoal. Either a piece of hot copper was placed in it, or the water was stored in copper vessels. Water for drinking was sometimes perfumed with the petals of the patala (*Stereospermum sauveolens*) or the lotus. The lotus was in fact frequently grown in tanks to purify the surrounding water. Buddhist texts enjoin the use of pure rainwater for drinking, but a strainer (parishravana) was an essential requirement for every monk. Jains, with their overpowering

compulsion to abstain from causing injury, are obliged to boil water every six hours, and to strain it through a cloth before; drinking.

Visitors to Vijayanagar in the sixteenth century noted that 'the king drinks water which they bring to him from a spring .... and the vessels in which they drew water come covered and sealed' (Fernao Nuniz). In Akbar's kitchen, 'for the cooking of food rainwater or water taken from the Jarnuna and Chenab is used, mixed with a little Ganges water ... His Majesty appoints experienced men as water tasters'. Indeed the use of Ganges water (q.v.) was something of a fetish with Muhammad bin Tughlak and the Mughal emperors, including Aurangzeb.

In the Hindu ethos, water has a special place. Water must never be sipped from a tumbler, but poured into the mouth from above, after tilting back the head, since one's own saliva on the rim of the glass would be polluting. Water used for rinsing the mouth cannot be swallowed, but must be cast out. Vegetables cannot enter the cooking area till they have been ritually washed to render them of sufficient rank. Prior to starting a meal, a few drops of water would be sprinkled on the leaf for purification. Water-sprinkling is indeed a part of temple ritual; it precedes a penance, and even sanctifies a corpse. A bath should never be taken in a small quantity of standing water; it had perforce to be in flowing water, or by pouring water from a bucket over oneself with a mug.

The time-honoured method of cooling water, which doubtless also achieved some microbial purification, was to stand it in new, really porous clay jars for evaporative cooling from the outer surface. According to Abul Fazl, it was Akbar who introduced the use of saltpetre for cooling water. Ice brought from the mountains was also resorted to for cooling water by Mughal rulers (*see* ice).

watercress This is *Nasturtium officinale*, in Sanskrit mandukaparni, in Hindi chanchu or chandrasur, which is first mentioned in *Sutra* literature (800–300 BC), and appears in medical literature as a material which intensifies or accelerates the body metabolism.

waterpots From the start, the shapes of natural objects like pumpkins and gourds were the inspiration for Indian waterpots. These were then adapted to functional requirements, either for balancing on the head, for carrying on the hip, or for storage in the kitchen.

The Indus Valley had a heavy copper kumbha, probably meant for fetching water, and a lota-shaped vessel with a long spout rising from the base, suggesting a pouring function. Among the vessels used for Vedic sacrifices is the ninhaya,

an earthen waterpot buried in the ground for keeping water cool. Another functional water vessel is the bhrngara with crossed straps, which every Buddhist monk is expected to carry. Old Tamil literature mentions versatile waterpots like the kallam and kundam. Pots were suspended from the roof in a rope sling (shimili) or kept in stands called pattadai, shumudu, or shum-madu.

The design of pots was governed by functionality. Thus all carrying waterpots would have narrow mouths to prevent spillage. A pot for carrying water on the head would not need to have a neck, nor would a kitchen storage vessel. But a water-pot to be carried on the curve of the hip would need a neck to be embraced by the curve of the arm, as in carrying a child. Waterpots were expected to be placed in a line on the west side of a kitchen, according to the *Shivatattvaratnakara*.

weights, measures, and lengths All later Indian systems of mensuration seem to have originated in the Indus Valley civilization. Beautifully polished and accurate stone cubical weights have been found all over the vast area. They are in two series; these were once thought to be respectively binary and decimal, but now both are believed to be connected to the weight of the rati, a small black seed with a red spot, *Abrus precatorius*, also called gunji or krsnala, which averages 109 milligrams in weight. One series of weights had a base of 12 ratis or 1.2184 grams, and the other of 8 ratis or 0.871 grams, and each had multiples of the series 1, 2, 5, 10, 20, 50, 100, 200, 500, etc.

Another series of weights in the form of truncated prisms was also found at Lothal. While still related to the basic weight of 1.2184 grams, these were in the ratios 7 by 2/7/14/28. They appear to have been related to the Assyrian shekel of the time, and were perhaps employed in sea-borne trade. The largest weight found in the Indus Valley had a mass of 10.97 kg.

Later mensuration systems for coins used weights even lower than that of the rati, like natural food-grains. The system recorded in the *Manusmriti*, which stayed in use for two millennia, read thus:

Natural weights

1 pepper seed (likya)	=	1 black mustard seed
3 black mustard seeds	=	1 white mustard seed
6 white mustard seeds	=	1 middle-sized barley corn
3 barley corns	=	1 krsnala or rati

Copper weights

80 ratis	=	1 karshapana

Silver weights

2 ratis	=	1 masha
16 mashas	=	1 dharana
10 dharanas	=	1 shatamana

Gold weights

5 ratis	=	1 masha
16 mashas	=	1 suvarna
4 suvarnas	=	1 pala or mishka
10 palas	=	1 dharana

Even today goldsmiths use rati seeds for weighing. In the Vijayanagar empire in about AD 1508, Varthema remarks that the scales and weights in use were so small and delicate that even a hair would turn them. The pala, in use till very recently, was thus the weight of 320 ratis (34.88 grams), a binary-decimal combination. In colonial times, weights in common use were the tola (gratis), the seer (80 tolas), and the maund (40 seers or 37.32 kg).

Weights

An ivory scale found at Lothal showed linear markings measuring 1.704 millimetres. The angula of the *Arthashastra* measured almost exactly ten of these, and the linear mensuration table stood as follows:

8 yava (barley corns)	=	1 angula (a finger's breadth)
12 angulas	=	1 vitasti
2 vitastis	=	1 hasta or aratni
4 hastas	=	1 danda (rod)
2000 dandas	=	1 krosa (distance of a cry)
4 krosas	=	1 yojana (a travel stage)

The *Arthashastra* gives the length of a krosa (later kos) as only 1000 dandas, which means in effect 2 yojana lengths.

The famous Indus Valley seeds carry pictographs which in one view are a numerical system, in which decimal, additive, and multiplicative combinations are all involved; even a five-figure number can be economically shown with just five symbols. There is some indication that the shunya or zero, and the decimal place value system, may have had their origins in Harappan computations.

South India adopted a numbering system based on eight. With the entry of Brahmi numerals that ushered in the unit often, the system was modified. As a relic of that period, even the current Tamil term for nine is en-patthu, or a defective ten, while patthu or ten itself is probably derived from the Sanskrit pankti.

wheat The product that we know today as wheat evolved in several steps in the Fertile Crescent area of the Middle East, where all forms in the evolutionary sequence have been recovered in sites dating from 8000 to 3000 BC. The wild ancestor, botanically *Triticum boeticum*, had only one grain to each spikelet and was called einkorn; this was cultivated by man to give a diploid wheat, *T. monococcum*. This crossed by chance with an otherwise useless grass that grew alongside, *Aegle squarrosa*, to yield a wild tetraploid, which in turn was picked up for cultivation by man as the tetraploid, *T. dicoccum*. This was a hard wheat (now called durum), which crossed, again by chance, with another wild grass (*T. tauschii*) to give hexaploids. These are the cultivated wheats of today, all of which are *Triticum aestivum*. Within this species are varieties which do not thresh easily, which can be ignored, and three threshable varieties, var. aestivum, var. compactum, and var. sphaero-coccum, which today constitute the main wheats of the world.

As long ago as 6000 BC, Mehrgarh, a pre-Indus Valley settlement in Afghanistan, yielded both cultivated diploids and tetraploids, as well as one hexaploid. Some two thousand years later, the other two hexaploids also showed up. In the Indus Valley itself, Harappa has yielded var. compactum and var sphaerococcum, and Chanhudaro in addition var. aestivum. These are the elastic roti wheats of India. The earlier evolutionary durum form has also long been, and still is, raised in India, all along the Konkan coast, under the name kaphli; it is a hard wheat, excellent for making extruded wheat products like seviyan.

From Vedic times wheat was always noted as a winter crop, sown in winter and reaped early next summer. Unlike rice, where numerous kinds are recorded down the centuries in Sanskrit literature, wheat is little noted, except for two varieties, nandimukhi and madhulika, mentioned by Sushrutha and pronounced to be an inferior food-grain. Through the ages, both hard wheats for extrusion, and bread wheats for making rotis, continued to be raised. A massive survey carried out in about 1920 showed that 11 tetraploids and 36 hexaploids were then being cultivated in India.

Archaeological evidence shows that barley and wheat were the main staples grown in most Indus Valley cities. There is literary evidence to support this; in the *Rigveda* there is frequent mention of both yava and godhuma (the old Persian term is gandum). In the later Vedas and *Brahmanas*, it is barley and rice that get top billing, and in the entire body of *Sutra* literature, from 800–300 BC, wheat finds no mention at all.

Thereafter it does get mentioned occasionally along with barley in early Buddhist literature, as well as in the *Arthashastra* and the medical *Samhitas*. In the Hindu perception, wheat was all along anna, a plough-raised food, and in ritual terms an ingredient of kaccha, family foods prepared with water in the kitchen. It was allowed to both Buddhists and Jains, and the Sikh ritual food, kavaj-prasad, used in baptism, marriage, and cremation rites, is a wheat halva (*see* wheat dishes).

wheat dishes While the Harappans were wheat eaters (*see* wheat), the Aryans initially favoured barley and later rice, so that there are few references to wheat (q.v.) in the entire range of northern Sanskrit literature, starting with the *Rigveda*. Vedic literature notes only the samyava made from wheat flour and milk, fried in ghee, and often flavoured with cardamom, pepper, and ginger; and ground wheat mixed with jaggery, which constituted abhyusa. We have to wait several hundred years for Buddhist canonical literature to mention the mandaka, a large wheat circlet stuffed with sweetened pulse paste, the present mande (*see* Karnataka, food of). Even the medical writers, for whom dietary advice is paramount, have only the samitah of wheat to offer, a wheat roti stuffed with boiled, ground, mung paste, doubtless the poli (q.v.) and holige of the present.

Thereafter it is the literature of central and southern India that reflects the most imaginative use of wheat. The *Manasollasa* of AD 1130 refers to the gulalavaniya, which appears to resemble the tiny gole-papdi of the present, perhaps made both salty and sweet. In fact most wheat-based items are sweet. The hayapunna appears to be a fried wheat preparation dusted with fine sugar. Kasara was itself a blend of wheat flour, milk, ghee, crystal sugar, cardamom, and black pepper, which, stuffed in a wheat envelope, yielded the udumbara. A mixture of wheat flour, guda, black pepper, and cardamom was termed murmura. Ghrtapura or havispura seems to have been the ghevara now common in Gujarat. The food item now called khaja was referred to as the khajjaka in the *Manasollasa* and phenaka was the strand-like extruded pheni of today. The vedhami, still called by this name in Gujarat and Maharashtra, is also mentioned. Patrika, like the leaves of a book perhaps resembled the chirotti of the present.

The *Shivatattvaratnakara*, written in western India in about AD 1700, describes the suppani as a mixture of wheat and rice grits deep-fried till brown and crisp, and fit for consumption by kings.

Literature in Kannada spans about a millennium, from AD 920, (*see* Karnataka, food of) and contains references to a large number of wheat-based items. The rotis could be roasted, baked, steamed, or fried, and included the mucchala-, kivichu-, chucchu-, savudu-, and uduru-rotis, and numerous sweet-stuffed mandiges, puriges, huriges, holiges, and obattu. Cream is blended into wheat flour to yield such delicacies as the yeriyappa, pavuda, and chilimuri. Wheat rava and wheat vermicelli are the base for many sweet confections like shalianna, ghrtapura, payasa, ladduge, pheni, chirotti, and the crescent-shaped karaji-kayi (*see* Karnataka, food of).

The wheat rotis served in the Sultanate period included the khubi (perhaps a phulka), paratas, naan-e-tunuk (light bread) and naan-e-tanuri (tandoori roti). Stuffed wheat samosas featured even as part of a meal. In the Mughal period that followed there were several items in which wheat was finely ground with spices, like harisa, hallm, and kaskh, while the samosa came to be termed qutab. When wheat flour is boiled with water and washed repeatedly, what finally remains is an elastic mass (which is now known to be the protein gluten). This was seasoned in Akbar's kitchen to a product called chikhi. The same elastic residue mixed with fruit juices and cream yielded the drink falooda (q.v.), a favourite with Jahangir. Wheat washings are also an ingredient in the chewy Sindhi halwa of today.

Wheat-based rotis of the present can be roasted on a thava or a tandoor, shallow-fried in a pan, deep-fried in a kadhai, or baked in an oven (*see* rotis). Some of these are eaten in all parts of the country, while others remain regional in nature, like the khakras of Gujarat, the batti of Rajasthan, the bhathura of Punjab, the lucchi of Bengal, the girda tschvaru and bakirkhani of Kashmir, and the khjuru relished by Muslim families. To judge from observations made by visitors in Mughal times, Muslims favoured naan with kheema at a morning meal, while Hindus preferred fried puri or bhathura with a sabzi.

whey This must have been familiar as a by-product of shrikhand (q.v.) or paneer (q.v.). It is hardly ever mentioned in literature, but is recorded by I Ching (AD 671–695) as one of the beverages served with a meal at the Buddhist monastery at Nalanda, the others being cold and warm water, buttermilk, and fermented rice gruel.

wine *See* beverages, alcoholic.

winged bean *Psophocarpus tetragonolobus*, the winged bean, is thought to have originated in Mauritius or Madagascar, but surprisingly is not cultivated in Africa. It reached India in about AD 1800, and is called chapathi-sem in Hindi and parandalavarai in Tamil, being used as both a vegetable and a flour.

winnowing basket and tray The winnowing basket is used in the field after the grain has been threshed. The Vedic sacrifices feature a winnowing basket called palava for holding the sacred grain. The winnowing tray is a domestic item, usually made of plaited bamboo strips; the back edge is raised, and slopes down to the front along either side. As it is flipped up and down with both hands, the lighter materials move forward and eventually tali off the front edge. The shurpa is described in the *Shivatattvaratnakara* as shaped like an elephant ear. The Tamil term for the winnowing tray is morram.

woodapple An ancient fruit of India, the kapittha (*Limonia acidissima*) is reputed to be a favourite with elephants, who swallow it whole. The acidic brown pulp, full of tiny hard seeds, was used as one source of the various panaka beverages described by Charaka. Curd acidified with kapittha, with pepper, and jeera added, yielded the relish khada. The *Arthashastra* describes an asava or medicated beverage which was an infusion of kapittha with phanita (molasses), and honey, which could be strong or light depending on the quantity of the ingredients used. The *Arthashastra* also lists kapittha seeds among those crushed for oil, a somewhat unusual and now forgotten source. Xuan Zang notes the kapittha as a fruit of India, and in old Tamil literature it is classed as one of the principal fruits of the palai desert areas. The woodapple is currently used in the preparation of sour ground chutneys and beverages.

words for food, in English Several food-related words have passed into the English language from Indian tongues, sometimes by way of the Greek, Portuguese, and Arabic languages. Some of these are listed below, with the English term listed first, followed by the word or words from which it was derived, with a language affiliation in brackets after each. The abbreviations used are S for Sanskrit, T for Tamil, M for Malayalam, H for Hindi, A for Arabic as used in India, G for Greek, and P for Portuguese-Indian:

areca (nut), adakka (M)

arrack, arak (A)

bazaar, bazaar (H)

betel (leaf), vettile (M)

brinjal, bringella (P), baingan (H)

camphor, karpura (S, H)

catamaran, kattai-maram (T)

chatty, chatti (T)

chutney, chatani (S, H)

cheroot, shuruttu (M)

cinnamon, karphea (G), karuva (T)

conjee, kanji (T), kanjika (S)

copra, khoppara (M), khopra (T)

curry, kari (T)

cutch, kattha (H), kvath (S)

dumpoke, dumpukht (H)

gingelly, jhuljhulan (A)

ginger, injivera (M)

gram, grao (P)

hopper, appam (T)

jack, chekka (M)

jaggery, chakkara (M)

jamoon, jamoon (H)

jungle, jangal (H)

kedgeree, khichdi (H)

mango, mangga (T)

margosa, amargosa (P, meaning bitter)

moley (moile), Malay (as used in India)

mulligatawny, milagu-thannir (T)

musk, mushka (S, via Greek and Latin)

oil, elaion and oleum (G), ellu (old T)

orange, narangi (H)

paddy, pari (Malaysia, Java)

palmyra, palmeira (P in India)

pepper, peperi (G), pippali (S)

pilau, pullao (S, T), pilav (A)

plantain, planta (P)

pomfret, pampano (P), pamphlet (P)

punch, panch (H)

rice, oryza (G), aiisi (T), varisi (S)

rolong (semolina), rolao (P)

sandal, chandan (H)

sugar, sarkara (S)

tamarind, thamar- (or tamar)-i-Hindi (A)

teak, tekka (M)

toddy, tari (H)

vindaloo, brindao (P in India)

Entries under some of these words may also be consulted.

X

Xuan Zang, and other Chinese pilgrims The indefatigable Chinese pilgrim Xuan Zang left China in AD 628, and after passing through Turfan, Samarkand and Bamiyan, visited Kashmir and Kulu, and various Buddhist pilgrimage centres like Kapilavastu, Pataliputra, Bodhgaya, Nashik, and Mathura. He resided at the great Buddhist monastery at Nalanda in Bihar on different occasions, in all for about two years. He returned to China again by an overland route, reaching there in AD 645. By his own admission he had visited '110 of the 138 kingdoms' in every part of India. The magnificent account of his journey, *Si-yu-ki*, has frequently been referred to in this dictionary. He was in close contact with Emperor Harshavardhana.

Fa Xian was in India for fifteen years, from AD 399 to AD 414. He travelled overland into the country and returned by sea from Tamralipti (Bengal) to Sri Lanka, and thence to Java and China. He noted the high prevalence of vegetarianism, and the hospitality of the people of India.

I Ching was in India for a prolonged period, from AD 671 to AD 695, not long after Xuan Zang. He wrote about the meals served in the Buddhist monasteries, and the scrupulous hygiene observed by the monks.

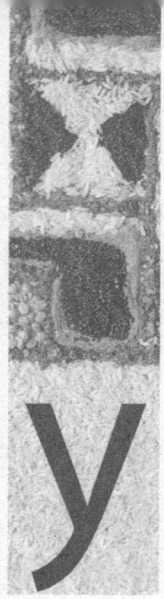

y

yams The English word yam stems from the Mande word niam, common to the west coast of Africa. It was brought to Spain by Moorish slaves who referred to *Colocasia* yams by this term. It was later applied by the Spaniards and Portuguese to the *Dioscorea* yam, and was first used by the English in such forms as iniame and yamma, before they settled on yam.

The genus *Dioscorea* has about 600 species, of which only 10 are edible. It is an exceedingly ancient plant, and the Asian and African ancestral groups may have separated as far back as 26 million years ago.

In India, *D. alata* is the greater yam, which comes in numerous variations of shape (globose, lobed, fingered, U-shaped) and colour (white, magenta, red, purple), and is called khame-alu, chupri-alu, and perumvalli-kizhangu. It may have originated in the Burma-

Thailand area. The lesser yam, kangar or valli-kizhangu, which appears in sausage-like bunches, is *D. esculenta*, which also, originated in the same area as the greater yam, with major centres of diversity for both species in Papua New Guinea. The veunti of Kerala, *D. hamiltonii*, is a hilly form with a delicious flavour, which shares a common ancestry with the greater yam, *D. alata*. The Sanskrit rat-alu, and Hindi pita-alu, is an edible but bitter form which has been used as a famine food, and is *D. bulbifera*. The vajrakanda mentioned in the *Arthashastra*, a poisonous tuber once used even to kill tigers, appears to be *D. daemona*. Aluka in Sanskrit and alu in Hindi are generic terms for underground tubers of all kinds, as are the Tamil words kizhangu and kandam.

yavana *See* Greeks, contacts with India; Rome, contacts with.

.

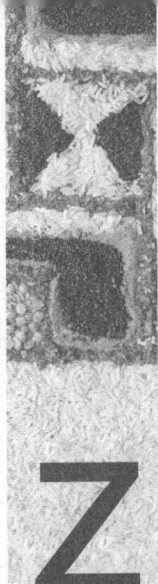

zakat A cardinal Islamic concept, that one has a duty to share food with others less fortunate, leading to such practices as eating at a common table and sharing the same plate. Zakat is particularly enjoined at Id-ul-fitr, which marks the end of the Ramzan fast.